IN THOUGHT

THE ENIGMATIC LIFE

AND ACTION

OF S. I. HAYAKAWA

Gerald W. Haslam with Janice E. Haslam

UNIVERSITY OF NEBRASKA PRESS
LINCOLN AND LONDON

Library of Congress Cataloging-in-Publication Data
Haslam, Gerald W.
In thought and action: the enigmatic life of S. I. Hayakawa / Gerald W. Haslam, Janice E. Haslam.
p. cm.   Includes bibliographical references and index.
ISBN 978-0-8032-3764-3 (pbk.: alk. paper)
1. Hayakawa, S. I. (Samuel Ichiyé), 1906–1992. 2. College teachers—United States—Biography. 3. Legislators—United States—Biography. I. Haslam, Janice E. II. Title.
LA2317.H484S37 2011
378.1'2092—dc23   [B]
2011017759

Set in Janson by Kim Essman.
Designed by Nathan Putens.

For Daisy Rosebourgh, Thurston Womack,
Jim and Jeanne Houston . . . special pals

contents

illustrations

preface

I met S. I. Hayakawa in 1963 in a hallway of the Humanities Building at San Francisco State College. I was a first-semester graduate student seeking admission to his popular seminar on general semantics, so I stammered something to the man everyone seemed to call "Don"; after asking a question or two, he signed my add slip. The course was based on a reading of Alfred Korzybski's daunting *Science and Sanity*, which we then discussed in detail, and I was impressed by the insights Hayakawa condensed from Korzybski's turgid prose.

When I returned to San Francisco State as a leave-replacement professor in 1966, Professor Hayakawa asked me to assist him with editing *ETC.: A Review of General Semantics*. I was flattered and began to spend an afternoon or two each week in the large office of his Mill Valley home. After finishing our workday, Don and I would climb the stairs and enjoy drinks at the counter in the kitchen, with his wife, Marge, and retainer and confidante Daisy Rosebourgh, while Don and Marge's younger son, Mark, was in and out of the room. Occasionally, my own wife, Jan, and our brood would also appear and we'd end up dining together.

In 1967, I began teaching at Sonoma State College, forty miles north, so my family and I left Mill Valley and relocated where I wouldn't have to commute. As a result, we saw less of the Hayakawas then, although for a time I continued working on the journal. Nevertheless, Don and Marge integrated Jan and me into their social circle, and we were frequently the youngest guests at various gatherings they hosted, usually rather large parties with a rich cast. Jazz was always the music of the day and Don's knowledge of it amazed me. He also seemed to have a personal relationship with everyone in the San Francisco scene, from Earl "Fatha" Hines to Wallace Stegner to Herb Caen.

Civil rights was the central issue of my political efforts, so I especially remember something Hayakawa observed in late 1967, shortly after H. Rap Brown had replaced Stokely Carmichael as head of the Student Nonviolent Coordinating Committee. Don read aloud one of Brown's more inflammatory pronouncements, then said, "I wonder who's paying him? It has to be someone deeply opposed to racial equality because of the damage he and Carmichael are doing to the Negro cause." Hayakawa went on to suggest that Brown and Carmichael might well be in the employ of right-wing forces that wanted to frighten the white majority into denying acceptance and opportunity to African Americans.

Early in the San Francisco State strike of 1968–69, my wife and I were present at the Hayakawa house when Don was interviewed on KQED-TV's "Newspaper of the Air." He was questioned about "Faculty Renaissance"—the group he had co-founded to urge that the campus be kept open—as well as about his view of the strike. Following his interview and departure, members of the decidedly liberal-to-radical panel of journalists continued discussing what Don had said, and he fared poorly indeed in their assessments. I was and am a moderate, and I was shocked at the sniping and cheap shots, and a little surprised at the leftist zealotry of reporters I had come to admire.

When Don returned home that evening, various other dinner guests apprised him of the events on "Newspaper of the Air," and at first he seemed bemused. As the versions of the story became more colorful, however, and perhaps as he had a drink or two, he said, "I'm getting mad. I'm getting damned mad!" It was a comical process to observe, but one that bore heated fruit when he next appeared on the program. That evening he admonished the journalists on the air for their behavior after his previous appearance, prompting one of them, George Dushek, to ask, "Don't you think you're being just a bit paranoid?" Hayakawa walked out.

During the turmoil after he became acting president of the college, "What's happened to Don?" was a question I commonly heard from mutual friends. Sadly, in the face of the public's overwhelming support of Hayakawa's efforts to keep a public college open, I never heard any striker or strike sympathizer—student, street person, or faculty—ask the corollary, "What's happened to us?" Both questions, it seemed to me, needed consideration. The Hayakawa I had known believed that the great problem of higher education wasn't dominance by the left or by the right, but intolerance of disagreement by both sides.

My relationship with him chilled a bit then, but a few years later we were together at a dinner party, and conversation made it clear that he was seriously contemplating a run for the Senate. He seemed to be talking to each guest privately in order to solicit an opinion. Marge approached me, confirmed what was up, then asked, "What do you think?"

Well, the truth is that I hadn't thought much about Hayakawa's ambitions at all, but I replied, "He needs to finish the books he's working on and not get involved in politics."

"Please tell him that," she urged. What she knew that I didn't, of course, was how unfulfilled—thus how tempted—he was.

While Don served in the Senate, I wrote him letters critical of his votes on various environmental issues. He had always been a cordial opponent when engaged, willing to listen if you were willing to do the same. For some reason, though, those critical notes of mine ended communication between us for nearly a decade. Then one afternoon in the 1980s my phone rang and it was Don Hayakawa, sounding as though we'd played poker the night before. "Gerry, would you and Jan like to join Marge and me for lunch at Dominic's next Wednesday? I have something I'd like to discuss with you."

Intrigued, I agreed, and we met at the waterfront restaurant in San Rafael the next week. Don and I had been politically compatible in the early to mid-1960s, but had drifted so far apart by the 1980s that we generally avoided the topic that day. I noted that he remained soft-spoken but persistent, and that he also never seemed to lose his

PREFACE

vision of equality and opportunity for all. He had come to believe that the GOP offered the best realistic hope for that. I disagreed.

At one point, while we waited for Hayakawa to return to the table from a bathroom visit, Marge asked me if I'd consider writing a biography of her husband. "If I do," I said, "I won't knowingly slant the story." "Good," she responded. I didn't tell her that I wanted to wait until both of them were deceased because I intended to work inductively and candidly. This book, then, is the belated fulfilling of that promise to Marge Hayakawa.

Gerald Haslam

xiv

prologue

It remains one of the most gripping images from the 1960s: bantamweight Dr. S. I. Hayakawa—plaid tam-o'-shanter ensconced on his head—scrambling onto a sound truck parked in front of the San Francisco State College campus, hoping to use it to address the assembled crowd, but ripping out speaker wires instead, and halting an illegal demonstration—or denying First Amendment rights, depending upon your perspective. Either way, he shut down the sound system. Inside the truck that day, student activist Ernie Brill was "stunned, flabbergasted."

Many commentators now point to the sound-truck incident at San Francisco State College on December 2, 1968, as the moment when the nature of campus rebellions in America changed, for photos of Hayakawa's audacious action appeared in newspapers nationally. Viewers of TV news even had the satisfaction of hearing one anonymous dissident complain that actions of the college's acting president were "Threatening! Illegal! Violent!"—a delicious reversal, given events on campuses around the country then.

While young people would continue to muster protests in the years that followed, the older generation would not fold. Unlike so many other academicians, the sixty-two-year-old Hayakawa had backed his ideas with deeds. After that day, S. I. Hayakawa, the courageous (or pugnacious) strikebreaker, was established in the public's mind. He was the facilitator of the will of the people of California, or of police riots, or of both. He certainly became a polarizing figure whose personal history was suddenly rewritten by those who loved or hated him, usually without the benefit of much information. Some

I

liberals, who had previously admired Hayakawa for his sharp attack on the luddite state superintendent of schools, Max Rafferty, or for his determined support of the co-op movement and of civil rights, claimed after the strike to have always known he was a fascist; some conservatives, who had previously considered Hayakawa an influential and dangerous leftist for those same reasons, claimed always to have admired him.

But who and what was this bold little man?

THE EARLY YEARS

one

The life of S. I. "Don" Hayakawa spanned much of the twentieth century—1906 to 1992—thus encompassing some of the most momentous events in human history. It took him from a Japanese Canadian enclave to the halls of the United States Senate, while along the way he became a scholar, an author, a college president—a man both revered and detested. Events of his later life have obscured his origins, although early experiences would foreshadow episodes that later made him famous.

Born on July 18, 1906, in Vancouver, British Columbia, Samuel Ichiye Hayakawa was the first child of Ichiro Hayakawa and Otoko Isono, both Japanese nationals. The newlyweds were en route to the United States when they were denied entry. "Mother and I were too young and inexperienced to get stranded among strangers in Vancouver," Ichiro wrote in a 1947 letter, "being unable to proceed to San Francisco where I had work and some friends waiting for me—on account of Mothers' Trachoma [an eye infection]. . . . We were entirely up against it to earn a living."

British Columbia, like California, had a long, bitter history of anti-Asian bigotry, and the Hayakawas were indeed held in Vancouver while their ship continued to San Francisco. Fortunately, the local Japanese consul, impressed particularly with the young woman's cultivation and bearing, not only worked diligently on the couple's behalf to untangle any misunderstanding but urged them to remain in British Columbia. Ichiro recalled, "I met some friends. They all said, Canada is a new country, there are many chances for success. You'd better stay. So I decided to stay."

The elder Hayakawa was an ambitious, adventurous young man from an unusual family; both his brother Saburo and his sister Satoe also migrated to Canada. Ichiro had learned English as a schoolboy in Japan, where the language had been a subject in middle school since 1876. He had attended the only boys' high school in Yamanashi Prefecture, then gone on to advanced study of English in Tokyo. He also "used to get into trouble by correcting the English pronunciation of his Japanese English teacher."

At the turn of the last century, recently graduated, Ichiro journeyed to the San Francisco Bay Area to further study English and to explore at least some of the United States. He worked for a time in Palo Alto, where he improved his conversational and reading skills while absorbing lessons about a society radically different from the one in which he had been raised. Of San Francisco at that time, in the depths of the "Yellow Peril" hysteria, Ichiro much later told a newspaper reporter, "The Japanese and Chinese were called 'Jap' and 'Chink' and discrimination was very high. You couldn't walk out alone at night; otherwise, you'd be knocked down by white people."

Ichiro eventually served as a U.S. Navy mess attendant on the uss *Pensacola*, an obsolete naval ship used as a training vessel on Goat Island, all the while perfecting his English. "When he got his monthly day off," S. I. Hayakawa later wrote, "he was paid $25 in $5 gold pieces and went to San Francisco to celebrate. He must have been 18 or 19 at that time."

Ichiro's first son further recalled, "Father, even as a high school student, was intensely interested in English literature." He, in fact, named that first son after the English author Samuel Johnson. Ichiro was also fond of Edgar Allan Poe's poetry, Samuel revealed, and "he was especially proud of his [own] Japanese version from the English of Heine's *Die Lorelei*." While living in the Bay Area, he volunteered to translate English-language literature into his native tongue for *Shin Sekai* (*New World*), a Japanese-language newspaper.

After the elder Hayakawa left the employ of the Navy, he reported, "I had to come back to Japan, giving up my dreams and ambitions when I was beginning to see light ahead, having prepared to enter

Stanford University." He did not explain what compelled him to abandon his dream. Loneliness? Love? Asian-exclusion laws? Instead he returned to his homeland, where he focused on Otoko Isono, the daughter of a prominent, progressive physician. Otoko had graduated from the only high school for girls in Yamanashi Prefecture at a time when few young women completed secondary education in Japan.

Her enlightened father, Dr. Isono, had "studied medicine out of German textbooks after he ran out of what traditional Japanese medicine taught him," according to the physician's great-grandson Alan Hayakawa. Dr. Isono read medical texts in English, as well, and was a noted author, devoting much of his time to writing texts on medical ethics. He was also credited with a famous aphorism: "A physician who gives a thought to his fee is no physician."

Although Otoko and Ichiro were both of the samurai class, Ichiro's family—rural landholders—were not the social equal of hers in the rigid Japanese social system. Nevertheless, the bold Ichiro began courting the young woman. His industry and education impressed both Otoko and her father, and so did his personality: he seems to have been a born salesman. As it turned out, he won the pretty young woman's heart before he was granted her hand; their granddaughter, Masako Gray, revealed many years later that she'd been told, "Grandmother determined to marry grandfather."

Ichiro Hayakawa's Western ways—which would have alienated a more conservative father—actually intrigued the open-minded Dr. Isono, so Ichiro and Otoko received her father's permission to wed. In traditional Japanese marriage, it was assumed that the bride joined the groom's family, thus Dr. Isono's decision was of great consequence; he would symbolically lose his daughter. "Apparently the old doctor thought this was a suitable marriage," grandson Samuel explained, "because he [Ichiro] was so ambitious—he'd been to America, he spoke English. They had a great future." And an interesting one, too, as it turned out.

The couple married in 1905, a momentous year because the Treaty of Portsmouth ended the Russo-Japanese War and established Japan as a world power. Ichiro determined that his future with Otoko would begin in the San Francisco Bay Area, so the newlyweds sailed for the Golden Gate that year, but their journey ended in Vancouver, where the young couple at first had to scramble to survive. Ichiro was offered the use of a house by a fisherman in exchange for taking care of it. With his grasp of both English and Japanese, he later explained in a letter to his sons, "I bought a desk and chair and painted on the window the sign 'Interpreter, Real Estate and Employment Office.'" By that time, "Mother was about to give birth, but I had no money, having spent all on fixing the office. I shall never forget the day that I earned the first $60.00 as a commission on [a] Real Estate deal which I put through for customer No. 1." He added, "This money has never been so badly needed and so useful in my life, as on the very next day you [Samuel] were born and I was able to pay the doctor, midwife and other expenses."

Vancouver, the city in which S. I. Hayakawa was born, was Canada's major Pacific gateway; it was also its capital of anti-Asian bigotry, so for Asian immigrants it was often a trap. In 1907 the author Rudyard Kipling embarked on a cross-Canada speaking tour. "Kipling's theme in speeches to the Canadian Clubs was 'Pump in the white men. Keep the Yellow out,'" explains Betty Kobayashi Issenman, an associate at the McCord Museum of Canadian History. Of course, Canada's west coast then as now was the natural point of entry for Asians, not for British. As a result, an "Asian problem"—really a "British problem"—predictably developed, as did a Japanese community within Vancouver, the Powell Street area, "apart as if a ghetto wall defined it."

When the Hayakawas arrived in Vancouver, the larger community still retained much of the frontier quality that had attracted many unskilled immigrants from all over the world. The Powell Street district remained far more similar to Japan than to Britain, a haven for immigrants from Nippon who felt unwelcome elsewhere in the area. A few residents there served as buffers between communities: "It seems that between 1905 and 1910, or thereabouts," Samuel Hayakawa explained to his own future wife in a 1935 letter, "my father, Mr. Nakazawa, Mr. Gotoh, and Mr. Yamamoto, and one or two others, all young men between 21 and 25, were the hope of the Japanese colony in Vancouver." Because "they could read English, carry on conversations, bicker and argue, understand contracts," the senior Hayakawa and his small group of well-educated colleagues stood out in the Japanese Canadian community. Most of the Japanese who migrated to the Vancouver area were marginally educated, so they needed help. Due to his involvement with the causes of immigrants, Ichiro's office was the scene of at least one demonstration and fire set by the booze-fueled white nationalists who forayed into the Japanese district.

By the 1901 British Columbia census, Chinese and Japanese constituted about 10 percent of British Columbia's population; they surely constituted more than 10 percent of the province's irritation, since they also held 1,958 fishing licenses of 4,722 issued in that region where fishing was a major economic activity. Moreover, at least some white citizens continued to believe it was the destiny of whites to rule what they called "wogs." Racialism—the myth that the least-accomplished white was superior to the most-accomplished member of "the yellow race"—was still common. Of course, "the yellow race" was itself an invention. Chinese, Japanese, and Okinawans, among others, were not always lumped together in British Columbia, as Canadian historian Ken Adachi reports: a December 6, 1884, article from the *Victoria Colonist* argued, "If the Chinese are free to come why not give the Japanese a chance. As a race, they are industrious, quiet and sober. . . . The proclivities of the Japanese make them peculiarly suited for helping in the development of this province." Nevertheless, in 1895, not quite two decades after the first Japanese had arrived, British Columbia officially denied the right to vote to all citizens of Asian extraction. Over the years the province more than once sought to defy Canada's national government on matters dealing with Asian immigration, issuing more oppressive edicts than the nation endorsed.

As was so often true in the United States, racism in British Columbia was cleverly manipulated by the existing power structure, and

9

economic rather than ethnic issues were often at the core of problems. In 1900, for instance, the military was called out to halt a potential battle over the price fishermen were willing to accept for salmon. As Adachi summarizes, "The intervention of the militia prevented an open race riot, for the whites were choleric, the Indians had armed themselves, and the Japanese would not have submitted meekly." When the smoke cleared, however, the beneficiaries of this dispute were the cannery owners, who could pay less per pound to fishermen of all colors.

Thanks both to Mrs. Hayakawa's social position and her husband's promise and ability, the couple eventually settled comfortably into the "Japantown" ("Little Tokyo") community. The Japanese consul and his family became their social friends. This especially suited Mrs. Hayakawa, since her English was too limited to allow her even to attempt to interact in the larger community. Her first son was born in "a small rooming house on Powell Street," in the heart of Japantown. The parents were both twenty-two years old. According to young Sammy's sister Ruth, in a letter written nearly three decades later, their mother found him to be "a rather troublesome baby."

Acutely, perhaps naively, aware of her own social position and the obligations it entailed, Otoko told young Sammy, "You are different than other Japanese," her daughter Grace later explained. Grace's own daughter, Masako, elaborated: "In Japanese society you try to give the child pride in leadership. You must be proud of yourself because you come from an educated, well-mannered family and you should behave as a leader."

Even within Vancouver's Japanese district, the Hayakawas and others could not feel entirely safe in those years. On September 7, 1907, a rally called by the Asiatic Exclusion League turned ugly after the white-supremacist speaker, Rev. H. W. Fraser, declared, "It was pure Anglo-Saxon Blood that made the Empire and it would never be made with a mixture of Asian blood. . . . Let us have a White Canada!" More than a thousand troublemakers surged into the Little Tokyo section, only to learn a startling lesson: the residents would fight back. "The Japanese met the mob at first with defensive tactics, pelting rocks down from rooftops," explains Adachi. "But then they sallied forth with sticks, clubs, iron bars, knives and bottles. Crying 'Banzai' they tore into the mob." Premier Wilfred Laurier later reported, "The Japs showed fight, a cause for rejoicing and for anxiety; rejoicing because the rowdies got a well-deserved licking; anxiety because this may make the Japs very saucy and render an adjustment of the trouble more difficult."

Two days later, the *Vancouver Daily Province* reaffirmed, "We are of the opinion that this province must be white man's country." Japanese immigration had surged in 1907, with 7,601 arriving, which in turn fueled more anti-Asian rhetoric. The next year the Hayashi-Lemieux Gentlemen's Agreement set the maximum of Japanese passports issued to male laborers and domestic servants at four hundred. The agreement "scarcely satisfied those who wanted complete exclusion and who still felt the wishes of the province were being sacrificed," points out Adachi.

two

The Hayakawas didn't remain on Powell Street; instead, they relocated with some frequency as the ambitious Ichiro sought better opportunities inland. In 1910 he moved the family to Raymond, Alberta, near Lethbridge, as a labor contractor with a party of Japanese workmen hired to harvest sugar beets. After that crop failed, the elder Hayakawa opened a small grocery store in the area, "but father was rarely there, being occupied with other business." A second Hayakawa son, Fred Jun, had been born on July 14, 1908. When he was three years old and Samuel five, the parents were doing well, so they visited their families in Japan.

Sammy's memories of that trip were slight in 1937 when he published an article in *Asia* magazine describing a more recent visit to his parents' homeland. But in that piece he did recall that little Fred had been "frightened to death" of his Grandmother Hayakawa. "To a very young Western-Canadian," he explained, "anybody with dark complexion and straight black hair was obviously an Indian. I remember very well how, when my delighted Grandmother had started to gather him in her arms, he had screamed, 'Siwash! Siwash!' and had kicked her in the stomach. I also remember how much older and more understanding I had been from the superior elevation of my five years when he had started to scream again at bedtime because there were no proper beds to sleep in."

In 1912, Ichiro relocated the family west to Cranbrook, British Columbia, where he opened another grocery store. "We lived on a farm outside town," his older son recalled, "and at the age of six I was enrolled in a country school of about 20 children of different grades and ages." More than any other factor, the decision to leave the coast likely contributed to the social acceptance enjoyed by the Hayakawa children. They endured their share of curious glances and extended stares, but were largely spared outright bigotry of the sort common in Vancouver.

The reality of the family's life as Canadians seems to have subsumed the sons, who would speak less and less Japanese and act more and more like their neighbors. They played kick the can, tossed a ball back and forth, slapped a hockey puck and complained about homework, and English was their medium of communication. Each brother was just one of the guys in the neighborhood, his Asian appearance tending to mean less and less to classmates. The Hayakawa brothers said later that they grew up assuming they were Canadians first of all, and most of their non-Japanese pals seem to have thought the same thing.

On the other hand, Otoko's situation remained relatively traditional. "There was to be no emancipation from a concept of marriage that precluded any purpose beyond the procreation of children and the continuity of family life," historian Ken Adachi has observed. Ichiro began to embark on selling trips, and Otoko was gripped by loneliness while he was gone. Only her children provided a link to the non-Japanese population around her.

By 1914, when Canada entered World War I, the Hayakawa family had moved north to Calgary, Alberta, where the front slope of the Rockies meets the western spread of the great Canadian prairie. The area was enjoying an oil boom then, and remained a major location of the cattle industry and farming, too. Ichiro, always searching for new opportunities, opened a grocery store on Centre Street there. Samuel later remembered that it was "pretty magnificent," but he also recalled that it had only two clerks. By 1913 Ichiro had opened a second operation at Eighth Avenue and Fourth Street West. A daughter, Ruth Toshiko, was born to the Hayakawas in Calgary on June 27, 1915.

Thanks to a recommendation from an old partner, Mr. Yamamoto, Ichiro hired a promising young man named Harry Kobayashi in 1913.

Kobayashi's daughter, Betty Kobayashi Issenman, recalled, "My Dad welcomed the invitation from IH to work in Calgary." Kobayashi was called to active military duty in 1918 and fought in the final, brutal push that ended the war in Europe. Ichiro, meanwhile, was forced to close his floundering grocery stores.

He then formed a partnership with an Englishman named Harry Gosling, creating Gosling & Hayakawa, Ltd. The war had halted imports from Germany, so the enterprising partners initiated the business that would make them secure: they brought from Japan everything they could find that was no longer being imported from Germany—Christmas ornaments to surgical instruments—and sold Canadian goods in Nippon, too.

In fact, the senior Hayakawa was away more than at home, and Sammy remembered that his mother spent most of her time with the children. She talked to them about the old country, read them fairy tales from there, and questioned them about their schoolwork. "I had always talked in a home-made language of our own—an absurd mixture of baby-Japanese, literary English and American slang, in which both of us expressed ourselves differently," he further recalled, "but always managed to understand each other." He never learned to speak Japanese well; his niece Masako Gray said, "He knew a few words, but he spoke a kind of baby-talk Japanese he'd learned from his mother, the kind of things you'd learn from a lullaby. Except for that, he didn't know any Japanese at all." She added, "My grandmother told me that Don was very protective of her. There was prejudice against Japanese then, and she didn't speak much English, so if someone came to the door, he'd always answer for her. He was a good son."

In Calgary that good son grew increasingly close to his mother to help lessen her sense of social isolation. His sister Grace recalls, "My mother always made sure Don had clean, neat clothes." S. I. Hayakawa much later described his own father as a dandy, but the habit of dressing well was instilled early in him as well, and he would earn that "dandy" label himself as he grew older.

Only much later did Samuel Hayakawa realize how lonely his

mother was during those years of cultural isolation. Otoko's parents had sent her from Japan a koto (a traditional, thirteen-string Japanese instrument played like a zither), and it became special to her. S. I. Hayakawa's son Alan recalls his grandmother telling him many years later that "one of her prize possessions was her koto. She told me that in one of the family's many moves, Grandfather made her leave the koto behind. 'Too big, too big,' she quoted him as saying. When she told me this story, it must have been almost 60 years later, but she still wept and wept. She couldn't put it into words, but I understood that out in the wilds of Canada, that koto was a last link to her culture and her childhood."

She had reason to feel isolated, since Calgary's entire Japanese population in 1911 was 53; ten years later it had fallen to 41. Vancouver, on the other hand, boasted 2,036 Japanese in 1911 and 4,246 in 1921. The plus of this situation for the Hayakawas, as it turned out, was that in Calgary the limited Japanese population did not pose a threat to most whites. The Hayakawa kids tended to be seen not as members of a despised or feared class—"dirty Japs"—but as individuals from an unusual background. Discrimination was the exception, or so recalled the older son.

Perhaps as a result of observing his gregarious father—by then a member of the Canadian Traveling Hardware Salesman's Association—or possibly due to his own inborn social skills, young Sammy quickly learned to succeed in the larger society. The family business had never been a "Japanese store," but a shop for the general populace, and the elder Hayakawa and his associates dealt effectively with their diverse clientele. Historian Ronald Takaki has pointed out that in America, "Japanese ethnic solidarity . . . provided an economic basis for ethnic cohesiveness." It also provided an example of a catch-22, since "their very withdrawal into their self-contained ethnic communities for survival and protection reinforced hostile claims of the unassimilability and their conditions as 'strangers.'" The situation in Canada appears to have been similar.

Sammy later recalled knowing only one other Japanese family in Calgary. As a consequence, he had to learn to deal with the larger society pretty much on his own. "The picture I get," Alan Hayakawa has revealed, "is of Don growing up with very little guidance in a world that was foreign not just to him but to his parents." Since it was the only world young Sammy knew, however, it is unlikely that it was nearly as foreign to him as it was to his Japanese-born parents, especially his mother. Otoko experienced a variation of a persistent dilemma for immigrant parents—wanting the best the new country has to offer for their children, but without them losing the best from the old one as a result. Neither Hayakawa son developed a preference for Japanese customs over the Canadian ones in which they were immersed. As S. I. Hayakawa later said of his brother and himself, "Neither one of us was brought up to be Japanese."

The elder son continued his elementary education in a neighborhood public school in Calgary, where he was the lone child of Japanese descent in his class. Asked by interviewer Julie Gordon Shearer how it felt to be the only one, Hayakawa responded, "I never even thought about it." He later recollected that in second grade "these pretty girls would compete for the privilege of carrying me. Two cute girls would pick me up and hold me between them, lug me around. They treated me like a Japanese doll."

He was an excellent student who liked school, although he described one teacher, Miss MacPherson, as "a damn racist." He seems to have early on developed a remarkable ability not to waste energy dwelling on slights, real or imagined. Of his teacher's racism, he said only, "That was in about the third grade. You get past that very quickly."

Ichiro was what his children called a secular Buddhist, while his wife was a Christian; their younger daughter, Grace, recalls that her mother had been "baptized before I was born." In any case, Samuel "went to Methodist Sunday School very early and also throughout high school." Always a music fan, the boy especially enjoyed the singing there. His family celebrated Easter and Christmas, but the future senator couldn't remember ever having observed a Japanese holiday "except New Years Day. . . . There was always special Japanese foods that are served only at New Years time, which we had every year."

16

The Hayakawa children existed on a margin: culturally Canadian, physically Japanese. Decades later, militant Asian American students at San Francisco State College would accuse Hayakawa of being "a banana, yellow on the outside but white on the inside." His response was laughter: "I may or may not be white inside, but I'm certainly a Canadian who became an American. I'm no more Japanese than Jack Kennedy was Irish. My *parents* back in Japan are Japanese. Why come here if you want to remain Japanese?" On the other hand, Alan Hayakawa has suggested that his father "was Japanese at the core," and author Jeanne Wakatsuki Houston, whose father was of the samurai class, said that "Hayakawa was a typical Japanese authority figure, tough and inflexible, not willing to accept disrespect."

How Japanese was he? S. I. Hayakawa himself rejected the notion that newcomers enter the mainstream only by abandoning their racial or ethnic roots and totally accepting "white" values, and that immigrants don't alter the mainstream when they enter it. "Who said being American—or Canadian—meant being white?" he asked. "Look at our vocabulary, look at our dining habits, our styles of dress, and increasingly our theological and philosophical concepts . . . look at our *children* and *grandchildren* . . . those are by no means exclusively Anglo-Saxon."

In 1917 the Hayakawa family relocated to Winnipeg, Manitoba— "because you had practically the rest of western Canada as your territory"—and Sammy started in a new school as he had every September since the first grade. Meanwhile, Gosling & Hayakawa, Ltd., thrived. Ichiro's younger brother Saburo became the firm's agent in Montreal, while Ichiro continued to sell on the road. He was home occasionally, since on December 29, 1919, the second Hayakawa daughter, Grace Emi, was born.

three

Sammy Hayakawa graduated from elementary school in Winnipeg in 1919, a typical boy of the Canadian prairie, but his memories of that time and place were not entirely pleasant. Many years later he told his own firstborn, Alan, about "a winter chore he shared in Saskatoon or Winnipeg, going to the outdoor pump for water and having his hands freeze to the handle. [Also] Boy Scout summer camp with canvas tents that leaked if you touched the inside of the canvas[,] and butter that was rancid." On the other hand, his daughter Wynne remembers her father "talking with real pleasure and nostalgia about his mother giving him hot potatoes, one for each pocket, so his hands would stay warm on the way to school."

The move to Winnipeg had continued the relative detachment of the Hayakawa children from Japanese culture, since that city, too, then hosted few citizens from Japan. During the 1920s, when his father began to take business trips to Japan, the older son became not merely Mrs. Hayakawa's translator but her assistant in varied situations. Fortunately, though, his mother "got some friends other than Japanese: one, because there were no Japanese in Winnipeg and, two, because she had learned some English."

Sammy, meanwhile, attended St. John's High School there—despite its name, not a religious institution. If the school's moniker was somewhat deceptive, Hayakawa's own name changed when high school pals nicknamed him "Hak," likely influenced by the fame then of professional baseball player Hack Wilson. "I think that's where that Hak came from, except his Hack Wilson was H-a-c-k, and they always spelled mine H-a-k." In any case, Hak it was throughout high school.

The Hayakawa family lived in the north end of town in a neighbor-hood dominated by Jewish residents. "They were just newly arrived immigrants," Hayakawa explained, "and the parent-generation spoke accented English if they spoke it at all. There was a whole Jewish life going on there." Many of Hayakawa's pals were from those families: "They were Yiddish-speaking at home, I'm sure," he speculated; they attended St. John's, where they constituted about a third of the student body. The gregarious Hayakawa found himself in a charmed position: "Although the Jewish and non-Jewish kids didn't associate with each other very much, the Scotch-Canadian and English-Canadian kids took me in as one of them, and the Jewish kids took me in as one of them, so I had lots of friends on both sides."

Ironically, Canada's most prominent minority had a small impact on Hayakawa. "There were no French-speaking people in my part of Calgary or my part of Winnipeg," he explained. During his high school years, French Canadians lived in a town called St. Boniface that adjoined Winnipeg. Hayakawa admitted that the situation simply wasn't important to English-speaking kids then: "We didn't even think about it." He much later theorized that the de facto segregation was voluntary, a matter of cultural reinforcement like Little Tokyo in Vancouver, although most French Canadians spoke English and worked with non-French Canadians. "They had their own high school, and they had their own college, and they were of course, Roman Catholic. So French Canadians in Winnipeg we hardly ever met."

Hayakawa also recalled, "High school was a very, very good experi-ence for me. . . . There isn't a teacher I had for whom I didn't have a high respect." Always a strong student, Hak was also active in drama (playing the First Fairy in a production of *A Midsummer Night's Dream*, for instance); he managed the ice hockey team (although he skated well, he was too small for the squad) and learned to play popular songs of the day on the mandolin (social grease for him, he later admitted). His sister Grace recalls, "Don was very popular." He had no special girlfriend during those years. Canadian secondary school students then, he said, "were younger in social behavior" than contemporary American youngsters. "So far as boy-girl relationships were concerned, when I was in high school, there was nothing going on that was of any significance whatsoever that one could detect."

"One thing we did do as a high school together, boys and girls," he recalled, "is snowshoe hikes." Students would be given a destination, then would troop together over the snow until they reached "a nice warm hall, where there would be a big fireplace and hotdogs, and we'd have a moccasin dance," the Manitoban version of a sock hop. He added that moccasins were the preferred footgear then, because "once it got to be winter in Winnipeg, it never thawed, so you didn't ever have wet feet from wearing moccasins."

Contrasting American students late in the twentieth century with young Canadians of his youth, Hayakawa observed, "They're socially so much more mature, although their algebra isn't as good." He also pointed out an important symbolic difference: boys in his generation didn't wear long pants in high school—knickers were the rule. Trousers, those tokens of manhood, weren't commonly worn until after one completed secondary school or perhaps finished an apprenticeship.

Hak held part-time jobs even before starting high school. One was as a courier, bicycling from one branch of Liggett's Drug Store to another, gathering film left to be developed, then delivering it to a photo-finishing plant. He'd pick up finished work there, then reverse his route to deliver photos to those same stores. Later, the boy's summer jobs included working for a used-tractor company. Hayakawa told Julie Gordon Shearer, "A great big hulking guy owned the tractor company, and he was almost illiterate. . . . He would say something like 'Tell 'em we ain't got none of those. . . . Tell 'em to pay up or we'll sue.' And then I'd put it into the proper language, and he'd be tickled to death."

Toward the end of their high school years, Hak and his pals enlisted in the militia—the Canadian equivalent of the National Guard—which required an evening a week of training, plus mandatory summer camp. The boys were in the thrall of one of their favorite instructors at St. John's, Sid Gardner, who not only taught Latin but was also the commanding officer of the First Squadron, Canadian Machine

Gun Corps, a reserve cavalry unit. "I suppose like many young men, I enjoyed playing soldier," Hayakawa recalled, but "we never saw one damn horse, except for one or two days when they found a few horses for us to ride. But the rest of the time we did our cavalry training on foot."

Those few horses were ridden during summer encampments at Brandon, Manitoba. There the young soldiers became proficient with the Vickers machine gun and the Webley .45-caliber pistol. "I remember my fellow members of that machine gun squadron, how terribly much they yearned to have a war! And there were some disturbances going on around Turkey or something like that, and all my friends—'Hey, maybe they're going to send us to Turkey!'"

Hayakawa also learned an important lesson: "This was one of my very early experiences in making an actual physical challenge to a guy much bigger than I." While washing at a community trough, he had removed a ring; when he finished, his ring was gone. He suspected another trooper: "He was much bigger but I was more pugnacious . . . I started threatening to hit him and, you know, he finally broke down and took me back to his tent, where he had the ring hidden in the folds of the rolled-up tent. He pulled it out and gave it to me. . . . I won on pure psychological warfare." Hayakawa knew he couldn't allow advantage to be taken of him.

Hak later came to think of his military experience as "a very, very important part of my life." In a real sense, Hayakawa would face the entire society the same way he had the thief: as a tough test he intended to pass. Much later he recalled, "I was advised in my youth . . . that there were many jobs and careers I could not hope to aspire to because of my race. Especially during the sensitive years of late adolescence, I met social rebuffs (or imagined rebuffs) which caused me at least some of the inward torture that Negroes in a mixed society must suffer." Nevertheless, he refused to assume any degree of subservience; he would not be channeled into acceptable "Asian" pursuits, nor would he be told how to live his life. As it turned out, Hak remained in the machine-gun squadron well into his college years, and eventually rose from the rank of private to lieutenant, becoming the unit's first Asian officer, just as he had been its first soldier of Japanese descent. The surprising thing was not that he was occasionally subjected to racism but that he seems to have won over so many people.

The young man graduated from secondary school—then a three-year program—at sixteen, then stayed on for a fourth year while he took shorthand, typing, and instruction in other clerical skills along with some freshman college courses at nearby University of Manitoba. He was by no means all business, and he polished his skills on the mandolin that year, too. "Since I was having a good time in high school," he used "any excuse to stay." Hayakawa would later acknowledge that, in some ways, his position as a gifted member of a minuscule minority may have aided his upward mobility.

Hak matriculated full-time to the University of Manitoba the following year, and while he was a student there his father and Harry Gosling dissolved their partnership. Meanwhile, Harry Shunsuke Kobayashi, who had been rehired to run the Gosling and Hayakawa shop in Winnipeg after World War I, joined Ichiro to form the Pacific Trading Company. Perhaps more importantly, the Kobayashi family became closer and closer friends of the Hayakawas. Mary Campbell Jamieson Kobayashi, Betty Issenman's mother, didn't speak Japanese, so she could not become intimately friendly with Otoko, but the families nevertheless socialized frequently, not only visiting one another's homes but also vacationing together at Lake Winnipeg and Lake Victoria.

"I remember going on family outings with the Hayakawas," recalls Betty Issenman. "IH was a round, jolly man, very kind and humorous." Of Mrs. Hayakawa, Betty reports, "I don't remember his wife, except she was very quiet and retiring, always deferring to Ichiro." Although she was quite young then, Betty recollected one event in particular: "One day when gathering berries we stumbled on a wasp nest. He [Ichiro] scooped us up, me and Grace, one under each arm and with great laughs and shouts ran out of the bush—no harm done."

One theme of S. I. Hayakawa's life that had emerged clearly by adolescence was his desire to please his father and mother. His own son Alan would one day suggest that "Don felt a lack of guidance from his parents alongside very high expectations from his father." Neither of Hayakawa's parents had grown up in a multiethnic community, so they could not fully understand their children's situations. They could, however, understand that excellence was an antidote for any discrimination, as was cordiality. By the time he finished secondary school, Hak had ranged far from the experiences that had produced his Japanese parents, yet his Asian features in a world fraught with racial bias forced him to be better than his white peers at whatever he did in order to be treated as an equal. As it turned out, S. I. Hayakawa frequently accomplished that.

two

YOUNG MANHOOD

four

In 1924, Ichiro Hayakawa decided to relocate his firm's main operation to Japan so that he could more conveniently handle purchasing. Traveling there alone, he found a residence and opened an office in Osaka. He also established a relationship with a mistress. Somehow, Otoko learned of her husband's infidelity and immediately bundled up her two daughters and returned to Japan. The Hayakawas' two sons remained in Canada, not only because it was their choice but because both parents recognized that Samuel and Fred weren't culturally Japanese. In Japan they would have been inducted into an increasingly jingoistic military, where their unusual backgrounds and poor grasp of the language would have marked them as targets for abuse.

The young men saw their mother and sisters off at Vancouver. Grace Emi, then six, remembers waving at her brothers ("I had to stand on a stool because I was so small") from the ship that would take her to her new home and end family life as she and her siblings had known it. To her, the young men she called Sammy and Fred seemed grown up, but to their mother they were still boys—one was nineteen, the other seventeen—and Grace also remembers it as a sad, sad moment for her mother, who had remained especially close to her firstborn. That son seemed to deal well with his family's departure, but his younger brother, still in high school, was upset. Alan Hayakawa later said that he thought his uncle never got over that separation.

For Samuel and Fred Hayakawa, the Canadian environment had transcended the Japanese home, because there had been in their lives no surrounding community to reinforce the old culture. Historian Ken Adachi's generalization about Canadian Nisei (second-generation Japanese immigrants) seems to describe Hak and Fred: "Since they were unable to handle the Japanese language properly, the children came to look upon themselves as Canadians of Japanese origin, persons who did not know how to speak, act or think like Japanese." In terms of his obvious behavior and preferences, Hak was indeed Canadian—ice hockey was his favorite sport, e. e. cummings his favorite author, jazz his favorite music. He majored in English at college, not only excelling at the study of literature in that language but also coming to write it well indeed. Ironically, his son Alan much later recalled, "Don was discouraged from majoring in English on the grounds that it was inconceivable that a Japanese could ever teach English."

The Hayakawa family had been unusual from the start in that the father was so fluent in English and so gregarious; he had penetrated the western Canadian business community. It became more unusual when Otoko left for Japan, where she refused to live with her adulterous husband, so he had to maintain two households, plus provide in part at least for his Canadian sons. As a result, those sons were freed from the dependence on parents that was "fostered and even institutionalized into its [Japan's] social structure." Hak Hayakawa moved easily among non-Japanese Canadians, and old friend Betty Kobayashi Issenman speculated that her brother and Sam "felt like non-Asian Canadians. Perhaps this is because, being male, they were less easily victimized, but mainly because they were surrounded [at the university] by people who had an education beyond public school and were secure in having a good home and income, at least before the Depression. Also having so few Japanese or other Asians in the city meant we didn't constitute a perceived threat to anyone."

In 1925, Fred Hayakawa moved to Montreal to live with Uncle Saburo and his wife, Aunt Nora, who was English. Their house was in Outremont, "a middle to upper class district in Montreal where one encountered educated people." Hak, meanwhile, moved in with the family of one of his professors at the University of Manitoba, William Talbot Allison, a poet (*Amber Army*, 1909; *Blazing a New Trail*, 1920) and a "kindly critic," as well as a popular teacher. Allison's sons, Gerard (later a physician who served as president of the university's alumni association) and Carlyle (who became a newspaperman and author), had been two of Hak's closest high school friends, and soon their younger sister Mary Jo would become a pal, too. Another of his chums was the neighborhood paperboy, a youngster named Marshall McLuhan, whose path would cross Hayakawa's several times in the decades to follow. Such connections led Hayakawa to report, "I had enough Canadian friends so that I wasn't going to miss my parents."

Hak had taught himself to play the piano, and his interest in music blossomed with the Allisons. "Gerard and I became very good friends. At his house, with his encouragement and Mary Jo's, and the whole family's encouragement, I used to play ragtime and popular songs like 'Yes, We Have No Bananas.' Things like that." He also continued to pick the mandolin and seemed to have a knack for quickly learning tunes. According to Alan Hayakawa, his father's first paying gig was "playing the mandolin at a Polish wedding."

Professor Allison was not only Hayakawa's favorite teacher, but he also wrote a newspaper book-review column. Don told Shearer: "When I was nineteen years old—I remember this very vividly— Professor Allison was way behind in his weekly column. . . . He said, 'Would you sketch one out for me?' . . . I wrote the column—the draft of a column—the right length. He read it over and said, 'That's just fine; I'm going to send it out just the way it is.' He sent it out over his name. . . . And then the next time, he sent it out over my name." Hak "was already determined to be a writer anyway . . . I was ambitious to write, it didn't matter what, so long as it could get published." Allison's inspiration, and maybe the fact that he'd complimented Hayakawa by pirating one of his efforts, was most encouraging. "I was thrilled. I was tickled to death."

A few years later Professor Allison would write a letter of recommendation to Mount Holyoke College, where Hayakawa had applied for an instructorship. In it Allison referred to the young man as "one of the most brilliant students that I have ever had." He summarized this way: "Mr. Hayakawa was in the same class with one of my sons and lived in our home for over a year, so I feel I can speak of him from intimate knowledge. He has a beautiful character, much more sunny and frank than that of the average Japanese student. I feel that I am not exaggerating when I say he is a perfect gentleman."

Because the University of Manitoba was nearby, Hak chose to go there after high school. "He was probably the only J-C [Japanese Canadian] student at UM then," Betty Issenman speculates. He worked part-time for his father's company, which still imported varied products from Japan, everything from toys to syringes and bulbs for automobile lights. The university, meanwhile, housed classes all over town, even in "quonset huts or something of that kind . . . temporary shelters." Nevertheless, Hayakawa added, "I felt we had a very good university, except for the buildings."

When he graduated, Hak joined the family enterprise full-time. About then, Harry Kobayashi "found Montreal business was slipping." He placed the young man he called Sam in charge of the Winnipeg branch while he traveled to Montreal at Ichiro's request to investigate why Hayakawa Bros. & Company was not doing well there. Ichiro eventually had to return from Japan and reorganized the business under the name Mikado Company. The main Canadian office was relocated to Montreal with Kobayashi in charge, while the Winnipeg branch was closed. Harry moved his family to Montreal and "took care of Fred and Sam after closing the company in Winnipeg." Eventually, the new firm would open branches in Quebec City and Toronto. It thrived until World War II destroyed its source of products as well as the good will it had previously enjoyed. That was a dilemma no amount of business acumen could transcend.

After the senior Hayakawas had left Canada, the Kobayashi family also assumed some responsibility for Hak and Fred, doing its best to provide support. "My father was a kind of surrogate parent," recalls Harry's daughter Betty, "and helped [Sam] with pocket money, school fees, and health care." This support would continue when Hak pursued advanced degrees at McGill University and later at the University of Wisconsin.

The older son, meanwhile, was ripe for youthful adventure. A holiday journey with Winnipeg pals to International Falls, Minnesota, taught him a bitter lesson: "When we got to the U.S. border, immigration officials refused my entry, despite the protestations of my friends that I would be back in Canada in three days. 'But I am a Canadian citizen, born and brought up in Canada,' I said. 'It doesn't matter,' said the immigration officer. 'You are Japanese by race—and that makes you inadmissible to the United States.'"

His next trip was more satisfying. With Gerard Allison, he rode a cattle train to Toronto. As he explained to Julie Gordon Shearer, they got a free ride because "in the event of a train derailment or wreck the cattle would start running away and the railroad wanted a few extra men on the train to help recapture them." No such catastrophe occurred, and eventually the young men made their way to Montreal, where they stayed with Uncle Saburo and Aunt Nora.

Since he was in Montreal, "it naturally occurred to me to go to McGill University," Hak recalled, adding, "Canada's most famous university." To his delight, his application was accepted and soon he, a western bumpkin "determined to be a writer," became part of "The McGill Group," future authors and critics who would significantly alter and enhance their nation's literature. Literary historian Ken Norris notes that the gang of bright youngsters that coalesced at "the Harvard of Canada" became the "enlighteners and propagators of Modernism" in Canadian letters.

In his history of that gathering of young literati, Peter Stevens elaborates: "Their poetry was in the nature of a critical rejection of overblown romanticism in Canadian verse taken over from late-Victorian and Edwardian sources." In fact, the young radicals at McGill found their nation's poor imitations of all British culture an easy target. A. J. M. Smith, Frank R. Scott, Leo Kennedy, Leon Edel, and A. M. Klein, among others, "working with a new sense of form and an extended range of subject matter, . . . began to carve out a new poetry adapted to the age."

Hayakawa's own taste in poets ranged from such American modernists as Ezra Pound and William Carlos Williams to British versifiers such as A. E. Housman and Siegfried Sassoon. Sassoon, in particular, seems to have grabbed the young, would-be poet from Manitoba, for whom World War I remained a turning point in modern history. Years later, Hayakawa's daughter Wynne remembers that her father would recite from memory Sassoon's haunting works, such as "Survivors": "Of course they're 'longing to go out again,'— / These boys with old, scared faces, learning to walk." It's difficult to overestimate the impact hard-edged language like that had on Hak and his chums, just as it is difficult today to imagine how much the Great War shaped their values. Here was verse without hearts, flowers, and fluttered eyelids; if Brits and Yanks could write that honestly, so could Canadians. In a 1936 commentary on a high school girl's patriotic essay, Hayakawa would offer his view of the state of Canadian verse: "Who will say that she is not Canadian to the last spurt of her untidy Wordsworthianism, which is practically identical with that of some leading bards of the Canadian Authors' Association?"

While interest in poets and poetry—and in young ladies, of course—dominated at the time, Hayakawa would later observe of his McGill pals that "the person most distinguished in that lot so far as accomplishments in literature were concerned was Leon Edel, who became the great authority on Henry James." Edel's name would become well known indeed among literary scholars, and whole generations of graduate students would read his incisive studies.

Hayakawa became increasingly interested in writing both poetry and criticism. His own verse at the time, while not up to the standards of his most accomplished pals such as Kennedy and Smith, seems to indicate that he was working somewhere between modern and traditional schools of verse. A handwritten 1928 effort, for example, is entitled simply "pome to lady":

how soulfully you seek above
a cosmic import in our love!
you persuade me we imply
a universe in harmony
that stars would lurch the planets veer
the moon would leap from there to here

and comets drop their tails aghast
o'erwhelmed by interstellar blast
if i should cease to love you more!
not really well may i implore
your kind attention i *have* ceased
and lo the stars move not the least

No record remains of who inspired that verse.

Another effort, entitled simply "Pome," was also written in Montreal in 1928:

Perhaps I have not depth enough
to know that such as these —
wondrous deeds. ecstasies,
the puppet-show of chivalries,
and heroes grim and gruff,

are only shadows in a night
of hollow harlequins.
The puppet-master grins:
do martyrdom and grimy sins
present a comic sight?

But yet I know that since I be
such a thing as this,
I fight, I kiss,
enjoy unintrospective bliss, —
a glad nonentity.

In fact, he wasn't a glad nonentity at all, but an ambitious, gifted student carving out his own niche in defiance of racial stereotypes. He was also living on campus in a basement room at the Student Union, so the university became for him an island within the larger city, a community where he had many friends and was highly regarded.

five

Throughout his McGill years, Hak remained close to his Uncle Saburo and Aunt Nora, as well as to Harry Kobayashi and his family. The latter's daughter Betty recollects that the Hayakawa boys "were at our home frequently, and came on their summer holidays with us since my father would rent a cottage on Lake Champlain or in the mountains north of Montreal." As to Sam and Fred's tastes then, Betty says, "Both liked to swim, but it seemed to me that Sam loved to read and Fred liked to go fishing with us," adding, "Sam was a gentle teaser." Her most impressive memory, she reports, "is of them bringing a portable, wind-up Victrola plus a stack of records. Thus I was introduced to the world of jazz and pop music. Whenever I hear 'Ramona,' 'Tip-toe Through the Tulips,['] or 'Am I Blue?' I think back to those sunny days of fun. Later they passed on to me an old ukelele that I taught myself to play with their help. They brought us wonderful books that we would read over and over: *Winnie the Pooh*, *A Child's Garden of Verses*, and Edward Lear's *Nonsense Rhymes*."

But all wasn't sweetness for Japanese Canadians in Montreal then, and Betty's recollections by no means paint the picture of a color-blind society. She recalls, for example, that she and her older sister, Mary, were "tormented on the street, called names, even threatened by French boys [who said] they would wipe us out." In high school she continued to be "called names on the street or being stared at wherever I went." Her family was "very active in the United Church, . . . [but] when we transferred from Zion United to Wesley United . . . the church board had a special meeting to see if they would admit a Japanese family. . . . My father had to have special references for my

34

sister to be admitted to the Nursing School of the Montreal General Hospital. The list [of indignities] could be longer."

Of the older Hayakawa brother, Betty remembers, "To me, Sam was quite elegant in the way he dressed, and I loved to hear him speak." She adds, "He had a motorcycle for awhile and gave my sister rides." Betty also recalls that "my sister and I were involved in the movement to boycott Japanese goods (alas, my poor father!), and to help Spain and China. So he [Sam] chided us about being radical reds although we could see he was fooling . . . [although] I believe that he himself had written an article or two for liberal or left-leaning journals, but I've lost the magazines."

Hak, meanwhile, received his MA in 1928, but he remained at McGill University an extra year, an interlude that allowed him to work intensively on his writing and also to take up fencing. During that time, he associated increasingly with Leo Kennedy and Abe Klein, both of whom would become memorable figures in their nation's literary history, but both of whom, like Hayakawa, also found at that stage of their careers they needed day jobs to support their writing habits.

Kennedy had been born in 1907 in Liverpool of Irish immigrant parents, and arrived in Canada when he was five years old. His family's impecuniousness did not allow him to attend school beyond the sixth grade. Although he is considered a major figure in the McGill Group, he was not a student there when he became a force among them. In fact, he published only one volume of verse, *The Shrouding* (1933). Nonetheless, his brilliance was recognized not only in his verse but also in his essays. In one of the latter, "The Future of Canadian Literature," he quoted his chum Hayakawa as having observed: "The bulk of poems written in Canada may be briefly classified under four heads. They are, Victorian, Neo-Victorian, Quasi-Victorian, and pseudo-Victorian. . . . Our poets carol (regrettably) in Victorian English."

Abraham Moses Klein, who was born in the Ukraine in 1909 and arrived with his family in Canada the next year, became, arguably, as renowned as Kennedy. During World War II and beyond, his poems became especially intense. He was also a major figure in Canada's Jewish community, organizing Zionists and editing the *Canadian Jewish Chronicle*. Of the three young men only Hayakawa was a native Canadian, but he was also the one most apt to be considered a foreigner.

The three and their circle of pals enjoyed youthful good times, a few drinks, a love of music, and, of course, the company of young women. Recalls Betty Issenman, who was a preteen during these years, "I could certainly see he [Hayakawa] would be most attractive to girls, for his elegance, his way of speaking, his overall style." They were just Leo and Abe and Hak to one another, buddies who met regularly near campus, often at a favorite tavern called the Pig and Whistle, for a drink and to "talk poetry and read our poems to each other." Those were heady days indeed for Hayakawa. He and his "small coterie of poets and would-be poets" were certain of the past's errors and equally certain and somewhat contentious about how to remedy them. He was rubbing elbows with those soon-to-be-major figures in his nation's literary heritage, although at the time "We didn't have a following. If we didn't meet together, we had no audience at all."

The McGill Group was deadly serious about changing not only literature but also perceptions generally, in their native land. In "The Future of Canadian Literature," Kennedy suggests that a new generation of authors would "approach the task of expression fortified by new ideas and original conception; they will learn the lesson of all precursors, discovering in a western grain field, a Quebec *maison*, or in a Montreal nightclub, a spirit and a consciousness distinctly Canadian." A few years later, Hayakawa would have reason to write, "Wouldn't it be ironic if the real poetic stuff of Canada came from this small group of enthusiastic youngsters who first found their poetic voices by damning each other's verses over glasses of beer in the Prince of Wales Hotel Taproom, on McGill College Avenue, Montreal." It did indeed turn out to be ironic.

Hayakawa worked hard to improve his poetry, and throughout his life he would demonstrate the ability to write reasonably good verse. He also published a bit in the *McGill Daily*, and his circle of students produced the *McGill Fortnightly Review* as well as the *Canadian Mercury*, an experience that was the likely precursor to his later founding *The Rocking Horse* at the University of Wisconsin. The mature Hayakawa would acknowledge that the years he spent among the literary group at McGill were "a very important part of my life." In all likelihood, the group was more important to him than he was to it, since in the long run he neither practiced poetry as a primary endeavor nor remained in Canada, but the impress of literary theories and notions about language he shared with those gifted colleagues endured.

Hak didn't extol any particular classes at McGill, but he did praise Professor G. W. Latham, who taught Chaucer, Spenser, and Milton—and whose avocational interest in slang may be credited with stimulating his student's lifelong study of it. He also recalled Professor Harold G. Files, who taught modern literature and creative writing. Hayakawa much enjoyed his Montreal years and, moreover, "All in our group were determined to become writers—and I believe we all did."

The Montreal in which Hak and his brother then lived was "a city divided along language lines." During the summer of 1929 Hayakawa drove a taxi, but he was rarely asked to venture into the Quebecois section, where a different company featuring French-speaking drivers held sway. Clerks in major stores had to be bilingual then—Fred Hayakawa, a salesman, had become fluent in French and English—but most citizens were not. Hak later recollected that the two language communities seemed largely to ignore one another. Hayakawa observed, "You can't be a Canadian and not be concerned about the effect of having two official languages."

Hak was ready to move on after his extra year at McGill. He had decided to pursue a PhD, "because I wanted to have full professional accreditation in case I wanted to become an English professor"; he laughed as he added, "in case I couldn't make a living as a poet." Hayakawa could find no suitable PhD program in Canada, and he sensed that it was time to expand his experience, so in 1929 he applied to graduate programs at several universities in the United States, sticking to those that had been recommended by friends. Did he intend to emigrate then? "I don't think I ever thought about that. I just wanted to attend a good university and get to know the 'States' a bit, too." He told Julie Gordon Shearer, "I didn't know one American university from another—one state from another in the United States." He was soon to learn about one, at least, since he was accepted to the University of Wisconsin in Madison and awarded the Mary Adams Fellowship and a teaching assistantship in English.

Armed with a student visa, the young Canadian crossed the border by train in 1929, the first time he had ever visited the United States. He spent his first American night in Chicago, where, he recalled, "I went for a walk that evening before getting my train to Madison and got beaten up and robbed by two black men." When interviewer Shearer asked "What part of Chicago?" Hayakawa replied, "I have no idea. Whatever it was, it was the wrong part."

The following day Hak journeyed 142 miles northwest into and across Wisconsin and arrived at one of the prettiest towns he would ever see, Madison, with its four glacial lakes, its statehouse, its university, and of course its reputation as the umbilicus of progressive politics.

A character in *Crossing to Safety* (1987), the final novel published by Hayakawa's University of Wisconsin colleague Wallace Stegner, observed of Madison in the 1930s, "I think a little city like this, with a good university in it, is the real flowering of the American Dream. ... It might have felt like this in Florence early in the fifteenth century, just before the big explosion of art and science and discovery." One of Hayakawa's students at the university, the writer Maurice Zolotow, later recalled that "the flavor of freedom was very powerful ... the willingness to think about and discuss any idea."

The university turned out to be an agreeable place to Hayakawa, who quickly fell in with a group of student writers and artists that in some measure constituted a community within the community, just as the McGill Group had. One of the first things that happened to the newcomer, though, was that he acquired a new name.

Hak had over the years gradually developed a clipped British accent, something that hadn't especially distinguished him among the student literati at McGill. To Yankee ears, however, he sounded pompous enough to be dubbed "Don" by an English professor who said Hayakawa spoke "like an Oxford don." Since he was also a dandy who, for a time, even sported a fashionable walking stick, the name took hold and he would be called Don by most of his friends during his mature years, although many of them didn't know why. Professionally, this man of many names at that time became known as S. Ichiye Hayakawa, a version that began to appear on his bylines. As for his British accent, "I fell among barbarians and lost it."

[three]

ROMANCE

six

It's not known how many other students of Japanese ancestry attended the University of Wisconsin at Madison at that time, but Don Hayakawa wasn't the only one. Stewart Johnson, then an undergraduate working his way through school, recalls, "I washed floors, windows, rubbish, etc., for Hayakawa and 3 other Japanese graduate assistants in their apartment. . . . I think the 4 came from an area near Vancouver, Canada." He adds, "Hayakawa paid me 40 cents per hour. As a 'go-fer.'"

In any case, Don was certainly visible on campus. Maurice Zolotow described him then as "a slender, immaculately dressed chap. He wore glasses. He spoke in a soft, cultured voice, like Clive Wood or Ronald Coleman." Hayakawa became, in fact, a university character: the Japanese Canadian speeding among the nearly all-white student body on a motorcycle, "a crimson bike he rode with great panache," according to Zolotow. Professor Greg Robinson adds, "One roommate, Robert Frase, later recalled how he sold Hayakawa, who loved motorcycles, his bike upon graduation." Robinson adds, "Hayakawa then gave him a lift to commencement, with the two of them scooting through campus in cap and gown."

Moreover, Hayakawa, who still retained a flair for verse, had quickly become one of the campus's literary personages. He also enjoyed fencing and played pick-up softball games with students, and was an aspiring lady's man. At UWM he formed at least one affectionate relationship with an unnamed woman of whom he wrote this 1931 poem, titled "Rondeau" after the French verse pattern it employed:

My lady love is somewhat svelte;
(Lucky cards has destiny dealt!)
   She's clean of hand and clear of eye
   Her Nordic cheekbones modify
A facial line distinctly Celt.

Her puzzled puzzling eyes have spelt
My doom. Yet vainly have I knelt
   With sugared words to mollify
     My lady love.

I gaze on her, and round my belt
An emptiness is sharply felt;
   High-handed means I dare not try
   For no Neanderthal am I
Where can I find a prayer to melt
     My lady love?

Whether or not he ever melted her was not recorded. Such intimate yet whimsical writing was a far cry from the scholarship he was then publishing, and it illustrated that the poetic lessons he had learned at McGill were far from forgotten.

Poetry such as that also made him noteworthy among fellow students and teaching assistants, but his academic writing seemed even more promising from a professional perspective. In 1932, for instance, he published a piece in the prestigious PMLA—something only a few tenured faculty at UWM had managed. His "A Note on the Mad Scene in Webster's *The Duchess of Malfi*" led a senior professor to send him a memo of praise, an unusual kudo for a graduate student. Hayakawa's obvious gifts as a scholar also opened the door for him to offer lectures at Arden House, a residence for women English majors, where other aspiring writers and critics—Maurice Zolotow referred to them as "literary bohemians"—gathered; Don shared his poetry there, too.

One night an attractive blonde freshman attended a lecture by Hayakawa at Arden House. He would eventually marry her.

Margedant Peters was born in Evansville, Indiana, in 1915 to Clara Adelaide Margedant and Frederick Romer Peters. She was the younger of two children, her brother, William Wesley, having been born at Terre Haute in 1912. The Peters kids enjoyed childhoods that were far from stereotypically midwestern because their parents were far from stereotypical. Margedant—called Marge by most—would later observe that the greatest thing she had inherited from her mother and father was a sense that "you don't have to be like everybody else." As it turned out, her brother—then called Bill, later Wes—would one day become the head of Frank Lloyd Wright's Taliesin West in Arizona, while Marge would become an editor and activist. He would marry first Frank Lloyd Wright's stepdaughter, then Josef Stalin's daughter, while she would marry S. I. Hayakawa.

Their father, editor of the *Evansville Press*, the town's evening newspaper, was an Ohio native, a graduate of the University of Cincinnati, and the son of a Methodist minister. He was also a crusading journalist "who would not allow himself or his newspaper to compromise what was right and what was fair," according to his citation in the Indiana Journalism Hall of Fame, into which he was inducted in 1982. He was especially noted for his "long-standing and unrelenting campaign against graft and oppression in public office."

Various of young Margedant's aunts, as well as her father, had traveled abroad—which in itself set them apart from most of their neighbors. The fact that Frederick Peters was the founding editor of not only the *Press* but also of the *Terre Haute Post*, both Scripps newspapers, likely accounted for the considerable clout he wielded in the community, as well as the many shares of Scripps' stock he would one day leave his children. Despite being courted by the local elite, he felt that "newspapers should not be closely tied to the local financial and political powers," Marge later revealed. "The newspaper was a watchdog and an outsider."

Marge and her brother played in a ten-acre park next to the family residence in Evansville, visited the library across the street, and attended a grade school kitty-corner from their house. "My brother

and I could start after the first bell rang and get to school by running."
It was, she later said, a happy childhood in a close-knit family. They
visited their mother's kin in Hamilton, Ohio, each summer and again
at Christmas. Aunts Carrie and Augusta lived there in "the House
on the Hill," built after their flatland residence had been inundated
by a Miami River flood in 1913. "Sitting outside at the House on
the Hill on summer evenings, we children heard all sorts of accounts
of wonderful places and adventures," Marge reminisced.

The Peters family could also afford a country home, which they
called "The Farm"—a hundred acres of woods and apple orchards
with a house—some sixty miles east of Evansville on the Ohio River.
"We loved the place," Marge recalled. "My father liked to drive up
there for weekends, work hard for two days cutting weeds or painting the house or whatever. He'd get terribly sunburned and would
have to drive home with his shirt off."

Like the man she would one day marry, Margedant Peters enjoyed
school. S. I. Hayakawa had studied the mandolin as a youth; she, on
the other hand, took dance lessons. Unlike little Sammy Hayakawa,
no one carried her around, but she did sense that she was suspended
between the community's rich and non-rich due to her father's position and independence, which precluded much interaction with
Evansville's gentry. Marge said she "never felt I was part of the local
elite. . . . Not that I was sensitive or timid in my inferior position; I
was kind of proud of it."

Not timid, perhaps, but her daughter, Wynne, recalls, "She told
me she was extremely shy. . . . She hated her dance lessons and had
almost nothing to do with boys." Tall, dark blonde, and somewhat
coltish, Marge was a top student at Benjamin Bosse High School
(named, she noted, for an ex-mayor her father said was a crook)
and was noted as creative and conscientious. She was editor of the
school's weekly newspaper, and planned on a career in journalism.
That goal veered her toward the University of Wisconsin's Madison campus, despite the fact that her father "didn't think highly of
journalism schools." Her choice was also influenced by the school's
political reputation; "Wisconsin seemed quite a bit more interest-

ing with La Follette liberalism and so forth." Swayed less by her father's opinion of journalism than by her own experiences in classes at Madison—as well as the influence of Professor Charlotte Wood and a young instructor named Samuel Ichiye Hayakawa—Marge Peters would finally take her degree in English and become a noted literary figure on campus.

During the fall of 1932, only seventeen and a first-semester freshman, she resided at a dormitory called Langdon Hall. She had visited seven sororities, but none had asked her to pledge. "While I should have been upset, I was strangely unmoved," she wrote in her diary. "In fact it took the load of decision off my mind." When a sorority she had not visited later invited her to pledge, she declined the invitation.

Dorm life was of necessity communal. On September 30 of that year her diary note reported, "Oh lord! I have just been listening to a recital of thrills and heart throbs by a bunch of crazy kids. But I guess it isn't crazy, just natural, but I am so out of it all. I am the spectator." What she heard that night led her to speculate, "I wonder how I will react to my first sexual thrill. I can't believe I will be the same [as they]. . . . But then no one thinks he will be the same."

Marge became a special favorite of Professor Wood, who invited her to gatherings sponsored by the campus literary society, the Arden Club, at Arden House. That organization—named for a reference by Touchstone in *As You Like It*—attracted English majors and even some faculty to lectures and discussions at its large cottage on campus. Marge became a regular. "Now this is more like it," she thought. "Now this is really interesting."

On Sunday, January 15, 1933, just prior to her first semester's final exams, Marge and a friend named Julie Rosenblum "went to the Arden Club for supper to hear a Japanese with a name like a sneeze give a talk on T. S. Eliot's 'Waste-land.'" Little could she then guess that she would share that name like a sneeze for more than fifty years. Her diary entry goes on to say, "God, that poem is a regular riddle. He who figures it out is a better man than I am, Gunga Din. Followed an interesting discussion which finally led into theology and philosophy—and I was in my element—listening, I mean." Not coincidentally, she also remembered the Arden Club's gatherings as "a place where men and women could meet and get to know each other on the basis of common interest without the artificiality of dating."

Hayakawa's topic on January 15, Eliot, was then considered notoriously conservative by some students and faculty on that self-consciously liberal campus, yet also judged quite avant-garde by many older professors. In any case, Marge much later remembered the speaker's slightly British accent as well as the way he "refused to be badgered, and held his own" when other instructors in attendance attacked not only his views but him for holding them. Marge recalls, "There was division between those with strong social consciousness and motivations. . . . people who believed that the important thing was to become involved in political activity. . . . They were very scornful of the people . . . who were more interested in literature or in the personal development or some other aspect. Don was flexible and open to ideas, and he was impossible to categorize."

She would later describe that lively evening as "momentous." After the presentation, her diary records, she and Julie walked home with "Herman Kerst (Herman the Vermin)," whom Marge, without much enthusiasm, was then dating. In fact, events of that fateful spring are best followed in Marge's diary, since Hayakawa kept neither diary nor journal. Two weeks later, for example, Marge wrote, "I gave Herman my declaration of independence tonite, tho I don't know if he knows it." Apparently he didn't, because on February 15 she wrote that she'd received a valentine "from Herman the Vermin, actually the first valentine I have ever received from a boy." On April 28 she noted that the Arden Club's "new president," Don Hayakawa, "seemed to be trying to influence me to be an English major."

On May Day of 1933 she wrote that on campus "they have communist demonstrations and those with Red leanings cut classes all day." Her own concern that day was that "phys. eds. dominate Arden House, but there is good stuff in the club and I think something could be made of it. Don Hayakawa is the Hope of the club." Nine days later she referred to Don as "the dating bureau" who "is going to get a date for Margaret Meyer for the party Saturday." As it turned out, he also got a date for Marge, an unsatisfactory encounter with "dear old Milton," whose "hands began to wander. It was the first time I had ever been pawed by a boy." That memorable encounter took place, ironically enough, in Hayakawa's apartment.

On May 15 she wrote, "Though still, as always, open to disillusionment, I am getting to like the Arden Club more and more and am filled with all sorts of plans for its rejuvenation. . . . Don H., acting in his new office of president, appointed me to the House Committee tonite—a body with many and very elastic duties."

On June 3 the tone of her description of her relationship with the young instructor gradually changed. "Last night's free and glorious adventure" was "nothing more than talking with Don Hayakawa. But it seems the most important thing that has happened in my uneventful and uninspiring freshman year." After expressing some wonder that "he had a very high opinion of me," she further notes, "God, Hayakawa is so damn unpretentious & interested I can't help feeling at ease. (This sounds too much like the good old wheeze about 'someone that understands you'.)"

From that point on, Don became a central character in Marge's diary. On the next night, for instance, she wrote, "Went to Don's apartment and we lay on the bed & read T. S. Eliot, Ezra Pound, and E. E. Cummings, (pardon e.e.)[.] Then we went out and had some beers at a couple of different places and talked and talked."

The following night, Marge was still trying to describe the turn in their relationship: "It feels so good to have a friend with whom I can share in my interests." After expressing satisfaction at having found "people very much brighter than I," Marge continued: "Don is no great intellectual genius or anything like that. If he were I should not feel half so comfortable with him." Only a night later, Don again dominated the entry: "It is really fun. Just as school is over and everybody pulls into his shell to study for exams, I begin to go out for the first time. . . . [T]onite Don and I went swimming and canoeing. This is really a new and very swell experience for me.

The nicest thing yet is that he understood perfectly when I insisted that we go Dutch treat on the beer we had tonite. For the fellowship of it one is to pay for the drinks after this, but sometimes it'll be I and sometimes he. I admire him. That takes courage."

Two nights later, Marge reported that Don brought pipes and that she and her friend June smoked them ("I confess, it felt rather silly," she noted). On Friday, June 9, she wrote, "This day I added several experiences to my collection. . . . I know now it is counterclockwise that the world revolves when one is slightly tight. I have been swimming completely au natural. . . . I have been to a speakeasy and have omitted to go home to Langdon Hall. I am no longer sweet eighteen and never been kissed."

Five days later still, she would write in her diary, "Damn you, Hayakawa, why couldn't you have come home today, I had thought we might go up to Taliesin."

seven

Throughout the summer of 1933, "Peters" sent a steady stream of letters to the intriguing Canadian instructor. Since few of his notes to her from this period have turned up, the picture of the developing intimacy is provided by the teenager's letters to him. Their tone ranged from breathless to self-consciously intellectual and embarrassingly superior, full of allusion to books and writers, as well as criticism of middle-class values. They also made clear her continuing infatuation with Hayakawa.

On June 22, for instance, she announced that she was acquiring material for "a couple of extra chapters for the great work on American bourgeoisie." She was referring to a vacation with her family at "the summer cottage of the Hoffmann's [*sic*]. . . . Oh these ghastly communities of cottages to which the bourgeoisie treks annually! Papa Hoffmann I found a particularly obnoxious character — the self-important *haus vater* type I could gladly strangle."

Further illustrating the vapidity of middle-class standards in the same note, she wrote about buying a pair of shorts:

> Absolutely the funniest comment they aroused came from Louise, our fat, simple-hearted German maid whose ideas are about as primitive as any that could be found for miles around. One day while we were gone, one of my friends came around to borrow something or other. In talking to Louise, he happened to mention the fact that I had bought a pair of shorts one night before. "Oh, is Marge going to wear shorts?" she said. "How short are they, about up to here?" indicating somewhere in the neighborhood of

her knee. "Oh no," he said, and approximated their length, quite a good deal less modest. Louise turned a deep red and looked away. She was really pained. "No wonder," she said, "that God is angry and doesn't send us any rain." Wow! Can you believe it? She actually meant it.

The next month Marge complained that "a Langdon Hallite" attending summer school in nearby Evansville had visited, thus requiring that Marge reciprocate. "Damn these social conventions," she wrote to Don. "Good practice, however, for the art of being hypocritical," she added, "which, I suppose, stands one in good stead in later life, if one wants to live amicably with his neighbors." In a letter dated only "Friday the ?" Marge mentioned attending a revival service and, with the certitude of the young, unleashed a harsh judgment: "The dull, empty faces of those work-worn peasants—the most unanimously stupid looking group I have ever seen—the emptiness of their lives that forces them to turn to something so cold and unhealthy as the religion they were professing—it was rather awful." She also discussed trying to convince her roommate at Langdon Hall into joining her in the Arden Club's residence, enthusing over "books, music, beer, and comradeship—the best things in life."

Like so many undergraduates before and since, she had embarked on a minor crusade to enlighten her parents. "I have been trying to convert my family and friends to my literary prejudices. Neither Mother nor Dad, however, shares my passion for seeing humanity pictured ruthlessly, so Huxley and Maugham (I made them both read 'Of Human Bondage') haven't gone over terribly big. With others I have been more successful."

Lists of books she had read could be found in many of her notes. The June 22 letter, for instance, commented on no less than ten, everything from D. H. Lawrence's *Last Poems* ("a very nice book") to James Branch Cabell's *Cream of Jest* ("don't know yet what to think of Cabell"). In July she extolled *Mrs. Dalloway* and *To the Lighthouse* and announced, "I have been exceedingly taken by the [Virginia] Woolf style on my first encounter with it. . . . I never read prose that so demands the constant strained attention of all one's faculties."

Later that summer she learned that Don had accepted her essay "Thirteen Easy Rules for Beginners In Literary Conversations" for publication in the literary journal, *The Rocking Horse*, that he would launch at UWM the next fall. Since she was a new English major and full of literary conversation herself, it was a natural topic. In response to his card informing her of the essay's acceptance, Marge wrote, "I am glad you can use the article. . . . I feel sure that you are more concerned about the quality of the Rocking horse [*sic*] than about my feelings or those of any contributor. At least you should be."

Amid such juvenile affectations, though, flashes of Marge's lifelong deadpan humor surfaced. In response to his mention of "adventures of the soul," for instance, she wrote to Don, "I don't know what these adventures of the soul are that you talk about, never having had one, but that must be what I lack. The only adventure of any sort I have had, soul or otherwise, was getting run into by a truck when I was in Cincinnati."

Infatuated with the instructor who was nine years her senior, and missing him, Marge asked her mother and father if she could invite him to meet the family at the 1933 "Century of Progress" World's Fair in Chicago; they assented. "Don arrived this morning after a bus trip from Boston and we 'did' the fair," she noted in her diary. More telling, she also wrote, "I had been awfully afraid that when I saw Don again I would be disappointed for I realized that it was the idea of Don that I liked more than Don himself, but I still think he's a nice egg. Everyone stares at us as we walk along. Let them."

Marge had, of course, told her mother and father in advance that the young instructor was a Japanese Canadian, so she was stunned at the reaction of her otherwise liberal parents, especially her father. "I was completely unprepared for the explosion that happened after Don appeared," she recalled. Her father "said that he had felt humiliated by the way people apparently looked at Don, the reaction of other people. I was really quite astonished and dismayed because he, as well as others in my family, had always implicitly taught me not to care that much about what other people felt." This from a man who in 1921 had become "the first editor in the state to condemn the Ku

53

Klux Klan as insidious and cowardly." Marge added that her family feared the worst; they "just saw a wrecked life for me. They brought up . . . stories about tragedies that had happened with people they knew. I knew they were genuinely concerned for me and I didn't want to hurt them. When I told my aunts and uncle about Don, they were supportive though apprehensive."

That was a considerable fuss over a couple that was barely dating, but perhaps the Peterses knew their daughter well enough to perceive where this would likely lead. During the period that followed, Ed Mayer, who was Jewish and considered Marge's parents "liberal and tolerant," understood "they were upset at the x-racial proposed union and in family circles I was 'the Great White Hope.'" Hayakawa, the focus of the problem, pointed out, "A Jew at least is white," then laughed. In any case, Mayer was often invited to Evansville. As for his own relationship with Marge, he later recalled that "for all of her gifted intelligence, she had an elfin quality," but "there was never anything between us other than a discreet, chaste kiss now & again."

Even in the face of family objections, Marge continued to write to Don. Since Hayakawa's own kin already included at least one inter-racial couple—his father's brother had married an English woman (as would Don's younger brother, Fred)—Marge's ethnicity wasn't a problem. Besides, at that early stage in the relationship matrimony didn't seem a likely, let alone an inevitable, outcome.

In fall of 1933 Marge returned to school, taking up residence in Arden House. Don Hayakawa was by then a major interest. Her final message that summer, for instance, concluded, "There will be important business to transact with you before school starts. For you are going to be my advisor from now on. You didn't know did you? We'll let Miss Wood do all the signing on the dotted line. This is no easy job I'm conferring upon you—helping me choose among the 1323 courses I want to take." Don did not object, and he found ample reason to visit her new residence or to invite her out for walks or for meals at his apartment.

Arden House served as home for eight female English majors at that time, and Marge later spoke fondly of housemates such as

Marjorie Heebink and Elinor Price. She also wondered at her own energy, which allowed her to carry a full academic program (including honors courses), attend plays and concerts, and, increasingly, date Don Hayakawa. The housemother at Arden House was Charlotte Wood, whom Ed Mayer described as "the demon who had life & death control over awarding of TAs [teaching assistantships] in English." He recalls that "one aspiring graduate student paid heavy court to this woman, angling of course for a TA job the next semester & once obtaining it, dropped her."

Winifred Haynes, who would eventually marry Mayer, was another resident of Arden House, and she, too, became a close friend of Marge and Don. At Arden House during those Depression years, "Males came around at meal time—not all connected to the Eng. Dept.," Mayer remembered. He further acknowledged that more than English literature interested the aspiring literati: intimate pairings, though discreet, were "no great secret, hetero or homo," at Arden House. Moreover, "there were informal parties, song-fests . . . walks over the effigy mounds, beer drinking . . . Dago red wine at Peretori's." Other bistros on Regent Street during the early 1930s also did a thriving business, as did hangouts such as the Paul Bunyan Room and the Rathskeller.

Don and a roommate cooked dinners in their apartment, and Marge sometimes dined with them. "Life had become very full and rich," she remembered, "full of friends and learning and lots of pleasures—fencing on the front porch. . . . Don was teaching us to fence." Marge also recalled, "There were walks [with Don] along the lake . . . rides in a canoe a departing friend had willed him." In fact, they had become a notable couple on campus—the tall, Nordic woman and the shorter, Asian man—both attractive, both bright, both accomplished. The 1933–34 yearbook featured a full-page photograph of Marge, named one of the university's outstanding undergraduate students.

Win Haynes and Marge would eventually work together with Don on *The Rocking Horse*. Zolotow remembers Hayakawa as the magazine's "guiding spirit." Once more Hayakawa showed his contrary nature: "When Don started *The Rocking Horse* in September of 1933, he opposed the prevailing idea that literature should be a weapon in the class struggle," writing in his first editorial: "The Arden Club . . . presents *The Rocking Horse* to remind this campus that charts, statistics to three places of decimals, political disagreements . . . all boil down ultimately to events in individual human lives . . . events, that is to say, that are adventures in that inner life that literature endeavors to record."

Still very much a poet as well as a scholar and editor, Don dedicated the initial issue to William Ellery Leonard, and in it he published one of Leonard's poems as well as two of his own, "Sestina Written in Dejection" and "Alba." Both of his were so self-consciously literary that they parodied the kind of writing he had attacked as a student at McGill. The former, for instance, contains the following stanza:

> Fie on my mad soul who would have none of peace!
> O give me peace: I wish a tranquil life
> In which I may with steady, calm devotion
> Adore thee ever with untrammeled art,
> And cease to fret my absence. How my love
> Frets for the sight of thy dear, graceful lines!

Fie on that kind of writing, Hayakawa had earlier suggested, so it is reasonable to assume this "Sestina" was intended as a parody, as were several other of his contributions.

That assumption is reinforced by the fact that he was at about the same time publishing hard-edged verse elsewhere. The December 1934 number of the University of Manitoba's *Alumni Journal*, for instance, featured "Calgary," a poem by S. Ichiye Hayakawa:

> Night is a clatter of angular shadows
> unskillfully pieced together.
>
> How scramble over these leaning ridges? How surmount
> their infinite perplexities? Who will hold down
> the scrawny arms of tenements? Who will abate
> the writhings of these tortured streets?

Night being, God knows, a dismemberment
of roofs and chimneys, a scattering
of tank-cars on a broken prairie.

Marge contributed the aforementioned witty essay "Thirteen Easy Rules for Beginners In Literary Conversation." With tongue firmly planted in cheek, she offered such advice as "When discussing an author of whom you have never heard, be careful with your tenses until somebody says something that tells you whether he is living or dead," or "If you pull a boner, stick by it. Pretend it's a well considered literary credo. Cite Gertrude Stein in support of your position. You can prove anything by her."

In the next issue of the magazine, Don's continued growth as a literary scholar and writer was evidenced by his essay "Harriet Monroe as Critic." An admirer of the singular Miss Monroe, founder of *Poetry* magazine, he pointed out that "it is practically impossible to figure out what important poet, major or minor, of the last twenty years, is not to be found in Harriet Monroe's files." As to how she managed to ferret out greatness from among unknowns, Hayakawa suggests, "She has elasticity of taste, broad sympathies, and is given to generous enthusiasms. All are, perhaps, as essential as her courage and intuitive recognition of sincerity."

The publication also contained a smattering of the high jinks often associated with student publications. One author's biography, for instance—quite possibly describing one of Hayakawa's nomes de plume—read simply, "Horatio Hapgood III is the son of Horatio Hapgood II." Don also developed a column, "Whiffs from Other Stable Doors," in which he assessed other literary magazines. These were often whiffs of the sense of humor for which he would later be noted.

The Rocking Horse had originally been endorsed by Dean George C. Sellery, a historian who also happened to be Marge's favorite teacher. It had received a subsidy from the university's president, Glenn Frank, but that was cut off when "the magazine's English Department advisers resigned in a huff over its publication of [Win] Haynes' article criticizing what she saw as the department's dull

57

courses and outdated curriculum." In fact, Haynes spared few egos in her piece, titled "The Gulf Stream," concluding that "the English Department will continue to be the last stand of the play-boy, the recruiting ground of prom-queens, and the earnest student of litera- ture will continue to be embarrassed to admit that he is an English major." That essay cost the journal most of its faculty support.

Hayakawa, as a faculty adviser and de facto editor of *The Rocking Horse*—as well as something of a campus rabble-rouser—presumably agreed to some degree with Haynes's opinion, or he likely wouldn't have published her essay. As it turned out, events would soon vali- date Haynes's assessment of a once-distinguished department gone hidebound and unimaginative, looking toward the past as it elevated scholarly triviality to high rank, while disdaining communication, creativity, and nearly anything modern.

The Rocking Horse lasted for seven issues, folding in the fall of 1935 along with Arden House itself, "both of them victims of the depression," according to *The University of Wisconsin: A History*. "We had high hopes and high standards," Marge later reflected. "I don't think we did so badly." No indeed. Wallace Stevens, William Carlos Williams, Horace Gregory, William Ellery Leonard, and Ezra Pound, as well as two of Don's distinguished Canadian buddies, A. J. M. Smith and Leo Kennedy, contributed pieces to the final issue, as did Hayakawa's students Ken Purdy and Zolotow.

One of the more successful poets on the campus then was none other than S. Ichiye Hayakawa, who received strong endorsement when his poem "To One Elect" appeared in the September 1934 issue of the prestigious *Poetry* magazine.

They come not within the tall woods,
neither they nor their enemies;
their commerce is but chaffering in
futilities.

We are the proud, the light-hearted—
we are they who have felt
the shattering of the farther stars; but we
are also they who have knelt.

58

Into the tall woods then,
where the fretful come not!
Unleash your hounds and shout! We are they
whom the gods harm not.

Publication of that poem vaulted Don's already high stock among
fellow graduate students and at least some faculty. He was a poet
with whom to reckon—in Madison, at least.

Some students considered Hayakawa more enlightened and up-
to-date than many senior professors, according to Zolotow. In fact,
most students were "way ahead of the faculty, reading W. H. Auden,
C. Day Lewis, and Stephen Spender." Zolotow found most of his
professors to be "all bogged down in pre–World War I writers." He
even recalls one "asking to have the work of T. S. Eliot explained to
him," this more than a decade after the publication of "The Love
Song of J. Alfred Prufrock" and only slightly more than a decade
before the "obscure" Eliot would win the Nobel Prize for Literature.

Despite agreeing that some professors were not knowledgeable on
renowned modern authors, Zolotow—like Hayakawa—nevertheless
loved the University of Wisconsin at Madison. He later recalled that
the campus had "a great atmosphere of freedom and a willingness
to discuss any idea. . . . Wisconsin was a place where you could do
anything you wanted, no matter how outlandish, as long as you
didn't interfere with other people's rights." A notable student radical, Zolotow recalled that he and his chums were "rather proud of
unconventional clothing, . . . of unconventional attitudes, proud of
getting drunk . . . everybody got drunk. Getting drunk was a form
of rebellion." Zolotow also pointed out that students then weren't
much different from students now. At Arden House gatherings,
"Men and women met as people who loved poetry. They also loved
sex, of course," he added. "The Lake Road was a popular trysting
place."

When student writers such as Zolotow or Purdy or Delmore
Schwartz read their work aloud at Arden House, they faced an audience that listened without hooting them down but that was nevertheless strongly opinionated. Biographer James Atlas reports that

when Schwartz, soon to be acknowledged as a major poet, presented his early verse to the Arden group, it "was apparently not impressed either with Delmore or with the poems he read to an audience of demure girls and earnest young men. . . . an ominous silence followed his performance."

Schwartz and Zolotow were actually part of a remarkable cadre of student writers who clustered around the English Department and Arden House; the group also included future authors Ken Purdy, Miriam Ottenberg, Howard Teichman, Charlotte Shapiro, and Leslie Fiedler. As adviser to the Arden Club, Don Hayakawa knew them all well.

Zolotow, who would become famous for his books about Hollywood, added, "The esthetes at Arden House—Don Hayakawa, Delmore Schwartz—looked down on movies. . . . I remember having an awfully difficult time finding people who would go with me to the movies." Plays, on the other hand, were respected by the "esthetes," and Zolotow later came to believe that Hayakawa's "most significant contribution to the campus was his staging of the first American production of T. S. Eliot's *Murder in the Cathedral* in the spring of 1936." The play, with its cast including Hayakawa as the Fourth Tempter, was performed at the Episcopal Cathedral in Madison; so successful was it that it went on tour and played Episcopal churches all over the state. In those days prior to World War II and the forced scattering of populations, many in the audiences had never before seen a man of Japanese ancestry, so Don was often the center of attention.

eight

The growth of romance over those past few months were summarized in a diary entry by Marge Peters dated January 7, 1934; she noted, "How amazed I should have been to have been able to foresee the march of events which would have me Wisconsin bound with one of the faculty—and a Japanese to boot—and calling him 'Tootsy' and making calf-eyes & acting crazy in order to forestall confessions of love!"

By the end of that month, she was "necking in dark corners with an English instructor . . . I wouldn't neck indiscriminately, but I like Don tremendously & I am quite sure he loves me." In fact, her diary entries of 1934 record their march toward deeper involvement. She also noted that "Don loses his inhibitions about telling me he loves me when under the influence of alcohol."

As if to confirm that, Hayakawa wrote her a poem, "Timorous Lovesong," for Valentine's Day.

> I would sing my love, my love
> my love I would sing, my love.
>
> Ask me:
>
>> Would I shove this song
>> down the frozen throat
>> of February? would I weave
>> the crisp winds and cold sleet
>> into cunning designs?
>> would I gather exultation
>> off the icy streets?

I would my love,
and do my love;
but, at your approach,
my love, my love, becomes shy stars.

Say boo to me, my love,
    and they (it) scatter(s).

She was grateful but ever the English major: "This is sort of a nice poem, but suffers as do all of Don's from an excess of cleverness and too little emotion."

A bit more than a month later, after again spending an evening at Hayakawa's apartment, she wrote, "Gee, Don gets more insistent that he loves me." She was both flattered and uncertain: "I am touched at Don, whether it is silly to be or not, & I believe he is sincere, tho I may be taken in—But there's no reason he should be bluffing."

Don had immediately hit it off with Marge's older brother, William Wesley Peters. Wes (as he was beginning to be called) was nearly a foot taller than Don, and the two young men soon developed a jocular relationship that allowed Marge's brother to address a 1934 letter to "The Late Admirable Toga. Department of Hari Kiri. Quarterdeck of the Rockinji Horsii Maru. Arden Club. Irving Place. Madison, Wisconsin." The letter was delivered to Hayakawa.

Peters was on his way to a distinguished career as an architectural engineer. At the time he was Frank Lloyd Wright's first apprentice at Taliesin Foundation in Spring Green, Wisconsin, and eventually, according to Richard Carney, the foundation's CEO, he "provided the engineering that made many of Mr. Wright's buildings possible, and Mr. Wright inspired Wes to reach beyond anything he could have achieved alone." That year, though, Wes was still bubbling with the mischievousness of youth when he wrote to his future brother-in-law, "I received your recent communication and the clipping indicative of the conditions at Spring Green. I was aware that they were bad but I had no conception of the true nature of their descent—of the extent of their descent, I mean. My idea of it all—strictly for your ears, Mr. Togo—is that the place is at last drained down to a remainder of boot lapping satellites who sort of hover around waiting for the death of the Master—nursing a sort of 'faithful to the End' philosophy." As it turned out, many years later Wes himself would be faithful to the end, his own life entangled with Wright's and with Taliesin.

Marge's letters to Don during the summer of 1934, written while she was home and he was back in Canada and then in Boston, working on his dissertation about the writing of Oliver Wendell Holmes, lost the self-conscious, adolescent tone of her 1933 notes. No more was she sending long lists of books or tumbling into sweeping generalizations to impress him. She had apparently grown up considerably, and gained confidence in her relationship with the young instructor. In June she wrote "Dear Don" and concluded with "Yours, Peters." By August, her notes began "Dearest Don," and concluded "Love, Peters."

The final passage of a letter written by Marge on June 21 revealed the growing intimacy of their relationship: "It's a strange feeling, this being two personalities, one separated from the other by a railroad journey. Please write soon to help me bring the two together." A little over a month later, on July 26, Marge wrote, "Oh, Don, I am decaying & collapsing. It's my eyes now. . . . I am afraid to get my reading glasses changed because I know the dr. [sic] will tell me I must wear glasses constantly. And you wouldn't love me any more."

Marge later recalled that their romance was a gradual process that lasted throughout her undergraduate years. But the attraction was great and had been almost immediate in both directions. They were young and in love, but they were not naive; both understood a mixed-race union, especially one involving a Japanese in those years, could be a major problem.

Nevertheless, by that fall their relationship was "firmly established," according to their friend Ed Mayer, who added that they "were both fun to be around." Marge was "quiet & reserved; her activities on campus were, as I recall, focused on *The Rocking Horse*." Don Hayakawa, like other teaching assistants, instructed freshman composition and, as Mayer further recollects, he "would take glee in reading parts of freshman English themes . . . a description of a drowning in the Wisconsin River and the subsequent recovery of the body: 'with an ugly sucking noise Henry Martin's (?) leg parted from his body at the hip.'"

In October, Marge and Don had enjoyed a motorcycle outing on what she called "one of the most perfect autumn afternoons I have ever seen," an afternoon during which she marveled at "the wonder of this man sitting before me, and the wonder of the bright flow of spirit between us." When she returned to Arden House, however, the bright flow was clouded when she was called into the room of her housemother, Miss Roberts: "I knew what was coming. She had been told 'officially,' she said, and therefore could no longer ignore it, that I was breaking certain rules about women students entering males' apartments. . . . She wanted to know if we were willing to meet the English dep't. on its terms." When Marge protested, Miss Roberts responded, "It hadn't occurred to me that it would seem as important to you as that. A few minor concessions to what are after all the social amenities, certain small sacrifices on the part of all of you." Marge's diary entry concluded melodramatically, "Small sacrifices! Minor concessions! I shall sacrifice the bigger part of my present happiness and concede the independence of my soul!" Her soul may have lost its independence, but she continued dating S. I. Hayakawa, albeit more discreetly.

Student life proceeded apace at the University of Wisconsin, with hooch smuggled into dorms and smooching at the lakeside, and even a book or two to read. Zolotow recalls that he and Purdy were "slouching on the steps of the Moorish-pillared Student Memorial Union on Langdon late one afternoon in 1935 when Hayakawa came hurtling along on his motorcycle with Marge Peters sitting on the pillion. He was wearing a tam-o'-shanter on his head!"

Zolotow further remembers that Purdy "started going on about our friend, whom we thought of more as another student than as a faculty member": "He pointed out that this Japanese assistant instructor was painstakingly creating a work of fiction in which he was the protagonist. He was, for instance, teaching English instead of Shintoism. He was writing his Ph.D. thesis on Oliver Wendell Holmes instead of the Meiji dynasty. Instead of a rickshaw, he rode this motorcycle. . . . We were, Purdy opined, witnessing the self-made creation of an American." Apparently, the youthful Purdy never wondered why his Jewish pals such as Zolotow and Leslie Fiedler studied English instead of Yiddish, Mark Twain rather than Sholem Aleichem, and coveted automobiles, not oxcarts.

Hayakawa's tam-o'-shanter, which would become so famous later in his life, was one of the symbols of his Canadian past that he never relinquished. Given his background, it would have been remarkable if he *had* emerged more Japanese than Canadian; he'd had to assimilate or perish. He didn't perish, so his demeanor and interests baffled those who insisted on judging him on the basis of their subjective ideas of what he should be: *He looks Japanese but he doesn't act Japanese.*

The year 1935 was a pivotal one for the Peters family and for Hayakawa as well. The twenty-two-year-old Wes, meanwhile, almost lost his position at Taliesin when he eloped with Frank Lloyd Wright's fifteen-year old stepdaughter, Svetlana. Wright was enraged and a tough time followed for the young couple, but Svetlana was resolute and Wes was smitten. Once all had finally settled down, though, that relationship would facilitate a friendship between Wright and Hayakawa.

Then Frederick Peters, Marge and Wes's father, died suddenly on June 16, 1935, suffering a stroke while working at his desk, and his demise stunned his daughter, who had been his little girl, his pet. Her grief was considerable, but she followed her mother's lead by not falling apart. If Mr. Peters's passing also eased—but by no means eliminated—tensions about the daughter's romance with a man of Japanese descent, it also had the effect of postponing the marriage Don and Marge were already discussing. She felt she had to help her mother adjust to the new situation, so she devoted much of the next year to doing that.

Marge had, of course, discussed her parents' negative feelings with Don, and later admitted, "I didn't know how things were going to

65

turn out myself. Everybody predicted dire things, and I couldn't let them be right. Don fortunately understood very well. He was very wonderful about it. But we just had to bring people around slowly."

Don completed his PhD that year when his 311-page dissertation, "Oliver Wendell Holmes: Physician, Poet, Essayist," was accepted and defended. The rather lengthy thesis had been earlier summarized in "The Boston Poet Laureate: Oliver Wendell Holmes," published by the young professor—signing himself S. Ichiye Hayakawa—in the October 1934 issue of *Studies in English Literature*. It began this way: "Holmes spoke of writing a poem as a process something like having a fit: 'you can't have one when you wish you could . . . and you can't help having it when it comes itself.' It would seem that Holmes had only one authentic 'fit' in his life." Hayakawa's deft use of language, his employment of humor and irony in this mild parody of what passed for conventional scholarly writing, marked him as an exception among his academic peers—and likely raised a few faculty eyebrows.

Nevertheless, the very fact that he would not only write his dissertation on so conservative a literary figure but also continued to give attention to T. S. Eliot—artistically innovative but personally moderate and an orthodox Christian—seemed a bit out of character for the young poet, editor, and instructor. When people read closely what he had written and discovered the critic's unique approach, though, they tended to appreciate his efforts. Hayakawa well understood the realities of academia, so he published literary analysis that academics had to respect, while at the same time he continued to write poetry that was, if not cutting edge, at least modern.

Victoria Beach
Innumerable and sweet the soft rains pipe
against the fluted trunks of the bare trees,
drip from the blackened leaves, drip from the ripe
brown berries, drip with infinite melodies,
sibilant, liquid, sharp, into the brown
cold tangled grasses underneath the feet.

Down leap the small disparate waters, down
covering the stones with tiny even beat,
down, till at last, in conclave underground,
they meet like Christian saints, who secretly
filled the dark earth with the murmurous sound
of praise to their forbidden deity.
    No bird, no motion, and no life sustains
    the sounds of the vast comminglement of rains.

By the time he completed his PhD, Don had—as a teaching assistant—for all practical purposes been functioning as a faculty member for several years. The scholarly pieces he published during those years were both sharply reasoned and written with an edge of humor and parody that made them somewhat distinct. For instance, "Mr. Eliot's Auto Da Fe" in the July 1934 number of the prestigious *Sewanee Review* had credited Eliot with having "restored theology to us as a living subject." Hayakawa concluded the piece: "One looks forward therefore, to his next book with keenest interest; the general expectation is, of course, that he will grow narrower and more disapproving in tone as he grows older. But Christ has worked miracles before." Such irreverence and originality marked the Canadian as a "comer."

A year after her husband's death, Clara Margedant Peters moved to Hamilton, Ohio, to live with her two sisters, but her gentle lobbying against a mixed marriage didn't stop. The Great White Hope, Ed Mayer, was still invited to visit, and he remembers that he found Marge's "wild mother" very funny: "At breakfast she might say, 'Have another slice of Canadian bacon; it's 57 cents a pound!'" That spring, too, Don sent Clara a copy of *The Farm* by the acclaimed Ohio novelist and distant kin of hers, Louis Bromfield. Mrs. Peters was not much impressed: "Don't think that I am looking a gift horse in the mouth when I express the opinion that 'Cousin' Louis Bromfield is a bore," she wrote to her future son-in-law. "Even tho we do criticize *The Farm* we've all enjoyed reading it. It was good of you to send it. Many thanks." The letter also contains a suggestive paragraph: "Probably the writing germ that seems to live in the

Peters family will develope [*sic*] into full beauty in the works of the young daughter." In that context, the "young daughter" could refer to either Bromfield's progeny or her own.

Responding to another present from Don, Mrs. Peters wrote to him in August, "Didn't your mother teach you to be wary of gift shops? Surely she told you that no one entering such a place, especially a Shoppe, ever escapes without paying a high ransom." He had also sent a sample of his verse, so Mrs. Peters concluded the note, "For that one beautiful poem as well as the gifts, in the name of the entire family I thank you."

nine

Despite their unease over international problems, romance intensified for Don and Marge in 1935. While Germany threatened all
of Europe, events in Japan in particular would have an impact on
Hayakawa, as they would every other Canadian and American of
Japanese descent. The ancestral homeland had fallen upon hard
economic times early in the 1920s, and those became worse still
in 1929. As a result, the Japanese military began to assert control
of a failing government and, in a 1931 quest for resources, invaded
and occupied Manchuria, then turned that Chinese province into a
Japanese territory called Manchuko.

The old country, increasingly driven by a perversion of the samurai
code of Bushido,[1] continued to extend its influence in Asia throughout
the decade: in 1933, Japan withdrew from the League of Nations; in
1937, it would attack China and inflict the "Rape of Nanking"; in
1940, it would occupy French Indochina, leading to an oil boycott
by Great Britain and the United States. A new level of "yellow-
peril" threat was perceived in both Canada and the United States
as newspapers and magazines began to feature photos of men who
looked like Don Hayakawa bayoneting and beheading prisoners of
war and civilians alike. It was not a good time to be Japanese in the
United States or Canada.

---

1. "*Bushido*, literally translated 'Way of the Warrior,' developed in Japan between the
Heian and Tokugawa Ages (9th–12th century). It was a code and way of life for Samurai,
a class of warriors similar to the medieval knights in Europe" ("Bushido," at http://
mcel.pacificu.edu). By the 1930s, however, it had been perverted into a jingoistic and
nationalistic political movement that bordered on fanaticism.

69

Throughout the period of the Hayakawas' courtship (and the early years of their marriage, for that matter), the nation where Don's parents and sisters lived was on a collision course with the two Western countries that had shaped him. Worse still, Japanese residents in the United States and Canada were portrayed as untrustworthy by such as Miller Freeman, president of the Anti-Japanese League and head of the Washington State VFW: "The Japanese of our country look upon the Pacific coast really as nothing more than a colony of Japan, and whites as a subject race." A dangerous cycle was at work: exclusion and threat led to a siege mentality and self-segregation among Japanese, which in turn was used to justify more exclusion and threat.

Historian Ken Adachi points out another problem: by the mid-1930s, "86% of Nisei in British Columbia were dual citizens although most had never so much as visited Japan." A similar situation existed in the United States, as historian Ronald Takaki explains: "By 1940 over 50 percent of the Nisei had Japanese citizenship. . . . American by birth, Japanese by registration." There was a countervailing sentiment in the community, and many Issei leaders sought to end the practice of automatically bestowing dual citizenship. The Japanese Parliament passed an act allowing the parents of younger children to renounce double citizenship and, in 1924, an amendment to the act abolished involuntary citizenship based on paternal descent. (As it turned out, many European-immigrant parents also had American-born children who were dual citizens.) To help address their problem of cultural isolation, in 1936 the Japanese American Citizens League denounced dual citizenship and recommended what president and co-founder James Sakamoto called the "Second Generation Development Program," which urged Nisei to join the mainstream.

In middle America, S. I. Hayakawa had already done that, and those who judged him as a man rather than as a Japanese were considerably impressed. He had been tempered by a Canadian past that taught him not to hide his distinctiveness. Instead of being "that Nip student," he'd been "that brilliant student" who had become "that popular instructor." Instead of being unobtrusive, he was a notable figure on the University of Wisconsin's campus—the somewhat foppish, somewhat dashing, and highly sociable Japanese Canadian who rode a crimson motorcycle. Never shy, on the day he turned in his PhD dissertation "He had come roaring down State Street on his motorbike waving his thesis."

He was also a well-liked instructor; Stewart Johnson recalls that "about a dozen freshmen took English with Hayakawa as graduate teacher of them. All liked him, a lot." That he was escorting one of the campus's top undergraduates, who happened to be a fair-skinned lady, did nothing to diminish his local celebrity.

Shortly after completing his PhD in 1935, "I had to return to Canada to be readmitted with new documentation," Hayakawa explained. "It gave me permanent residence, so long as I continued to be employed in the work for which I was admitted. But I could not be naturalized." He could also not know how permanent his residence in the United States was apt to be.

Because he felt "a vague sense of moral obligation to acquaint myself with the culture of my forefathers," Don had traveled to Japan after completing his degree. He seems to have come to terms with the Japanese side of his heritage during that memorable summer. He first traveled by rail to Vancouver in late June, then later proceeded on an ocean liner, the *Hiye Maru* (at his father's expense), for a reunion in Nippon.

An article in the Japanese-language *Continental Daily News* of Vancouver noted his visit. It read in part, "Dr. Ichiye Hayakawa, the eldest son of Mr. Ichiro Hayakawa . . . was born in Vancouver (Powell St.) twenty-eight years ago and is a man of culture and high academic interests. He does not know at present whether he will accept a post at some University or enter into a political career in the province of Alberta, on his return from Japan, but one thing is obvious, and that is that he is a young man with a brilliant future ahead of him."

In fact, Vancouver itself turned out to be an education for the newly minted PhD, who had rarely visited there since boyhood. His increasingly savvy eyes noted, "Powell St. has gone strangely dingy since I saw it last. . . . the innovation that surprised me most about Powell St. . . . was the Sino-Japanese alliance that is implied in the Asahi ('rising sun') *Chop Suey* House."

He was also surprised by how many people had remembered his father, who had "only been among the Vancouver Japanese for three or four years at most." Don had been met at the railroad depot by an old colleague of his father, Mr. Nakazawa, whose home and hospitality charmed the young man. Even more impressive was the conviviality with which Mr. Nakazawa ran his store; Hayakawa wrote to Marge that it "is not a business. It is a home, a school, an orphanage, a society."

> The clerks who have been working there for a long time have been with the firm almost since childhood, and Mr. and Mrs. Nakazawa watch with parental eyes over their courtships, marriages, and children, and provide for them handsomely if by chance they go away to be married, or wish to seek better fortune elsewhere. . . . [S]econd-generation Japanese who speak only English are brought into his store to learn to speak Japanese. Orphans are taken care of[,] for it is a hostile Anglo-Saxon world they are living in.

Like many inland Canadians, Hayakawa had been unaware of many of the barriers faced by Asians in British Columbia. "I think the greatest surprise I had in Vancouver was to discover that there is a law in British Columbia which denies the franchise to all Orientals, even when born in Canada, or naturalized." The right to vote would seem to be a federal matter; not so in Canada. The original prohibition in British Columbia had been aimed at the Chinese, but in 1895 the provincial legislature had extended it to include the Japanese.

Don believed that when second-generation Japanese Canadians came to the fore, the issue of the franchise would be resolved. "Most of them are thoroughly Canadian in attitude, and many of them are graduates of the universities. There is, therefore, a great deal of discussion of the franchise. . . . [T]he older generation is determined to work and organize and fight for a franchise for their children."

He noted one more irony: "People in British Columbia, in many cases, do not know that the Japanese do not have a vote, and at every election time, send canvassers into their district."

The example of his own family and of his personal experiences led him to conclude that "what the second-generation Japanese must do is to get away from the Pacific Coast." In that 1935 note to his wife-to-be, he offered an opinion he would hold and refine throughout his life, one that would later sharply influence his own reputation among Canadian and American Japanese:

> They must go where there are no other Japanese, or else they associate with people of their own race and never become Canadians. Anywhere but in British Columbia, the Japanese [are] not sufficiently well-known to have generalizations made about them. Away from other Japanese, he can make his own reputation and be judged solely on his merits as an individual. I am not thinking now in terms of the higher good of Canada, nor of the higher good of Japan . . . I am simply concerned with the individuals. They want, as a rule, to be Canadians, or in America, Americans. To do so, they must live Canadian or American lives, that is, lives among white people in white communities. And unless they become at home in such lives, they will never be anything but foreigners.

Two days after writing that letter, Hayakawa composed a note from aboard the liner bound for Yokohama explaining that he was traveling third class but had a room to himself. Since all the other third-class passengers were Japanese, however, so was the food: "Even for breakfast, there is no change—rice, soup, fish, tea, pickles." Saying he liked Japanese food, but not all the time (and on a swaying ship), he added, "I would give an awful lot for a glass of milk and an apple this minute." The next day he wrote, "I finally gave up and have asked to have, at the cost of a few dollars . . . dinners in English for the rest of the trip." In what was surely an unintended irony, Hayakawa added that he had encountered "a couple of architecture students in tourist class, graduates of Yale. . . . [W]ith them, I am among my own people. I don't know what I should do without them to talk to, and to have a drink with in the evenings." He had indeed been among his own people.

Don Hayakawa's journey to Japan became an exploration of a part of himself he had long ignored, and it led to two of the most relaxed and personally revealing essays he would produce in the 1930s: "A Japanese-American Goes to Japan," published in the April 1937 issue of *Asia*, and "My Japanese Father and I," which appeared a month later in the same magazine. In 1935 that Japanese father, Ichiro Hayakawa, "was prospering. Besides his head office in Osaka, he had branches in Kobe and Nagoya. He had customers in many parts of the world."

By the time Don had departed for his parents' homeland, he understood that "I was a pretty thorough American, because I had never had the chance to be anything else." Unable to speak Japanese in anything but the most rudimentary fashion, and ignorant of Japanese social customs, he memorized a few set responses and followed the advice of his mother: "If I became tongue-tied or ran out of speeches, I was to continue bowing over and over again." As it turned out, he would many times observe the social utility of bowing.

When he had visited his grandmother Isono, widow of the renowned physician, he'd found her "very tiny, very charming. . . . She seemed on the verge of tears any minute, she was so tremendously happy." After a stop at his grandfather's grave, Don and his mother had to hurry to catch a bus. As they began to run, Don's grandmother started crying—"sure she would never see me again"—and tried to run along. "So I grabbed her by the hand and we ran together . . . I also starting to weep." When they reached the bus, "Mother and I got in and managed to bow several times, while everybody bowed outside." He was left with the image of his tiny, kimono-clad grandmother, "standing there, frantically waving her handkerchief, weeping and bowing again and again."

Don and his mother had then traveled to his paternal grandmother's residence, where, after many bows and tears, the old lady

took me to one side of the room, to the family god-shelf, a little niche in the wall where, in a lacquered shrine were a number of little tablets with names written on them, the photographs of my grandfather and other deceased members of my family and, in front of them, little dishes of cakes and fruits such as Grandfather had liked—offerings to his departed spirit. Here I was to pay respects to my grandfather whom I had come too late to see again; so I lit some sticks of incense, placed them in a bowl before the shrine, clapped my hands twice and made profound obeisance. I had been coached for this . . . by Mother, but, by the time I was performing it, it had ceased to be the rigamarole I had thought it to be, and I was glad that my grandfather was there in the spirit to receive my respects. Meanwhile Grandmother was sobbing with joy.

That connection with his family had profoundly moved the young man. In fact, the entire trip was an exercise in both cultural enrichment and personal fulfillment.

"My Japanese Father and I," written in some of Hayakawa's most sensitive prose, surveyed culture and cultural differences, speaking particularly of the awareness of heritage and of the relationship to the land of one's ancestors.

To any one coming from the Middle West, where everything was built yesterday or the day before, it is perhaps always a matter of tears and joy to see beautiful and ancient structures, the Shinto shrines, austere and fragrant of clean wood surfaces, . . . the ferocious but lovable demons guarding the entrances against evil spirits and brandishing strong winds and thunderclaps against the wicked and scowling at all except the pure in heart, the graceful lift of terrace after terrace of dragon-wound cornices—all so old it fills the heart with pride that artists have been so great, and that devotion has been so deep, and that human beings have been so splendidly human for so long a time.

His wryness also was evident in the article. After noting that "men in Japan seem to get all the advantages," he went on to explain, "My grandmother and my uncles and aunts in Japan are all very sorry for an uncle of mine in Canada who is married to an Englishwoman. They are not concerned about intermarriage; they simply believe that he has to wait on his wife hand and foot, and patiently suffer the innumerable indignities that western women always inflict upon their husbands." Very much in love with a "western woman" himself, Don was willing to chance it with her.

For all his admiration of many things Japanese, though, the writer finally concluded, "I am, like most Americans . . . too much the skeptic, too much the congenital heretic . . . to be happy with the closely-knit feudal and family ties that bind Japanese lives. . . . I could not, therefore, ever be completely at home in Japan, because, for better or for worse, I was brought up with the wrong cast of mind to be a Japanese."

Perhaps as a result of his relaxed acceptance of, and occasional wonder at, the multiculturalism of his surroundings in Canada and the United States, Hayakawa was generally a flexible man, able to fit into varied social situations without sacrificing his own sense of self. "By evening," he wrote of his visit with Grandmother Hayakawa and the extended family, "I was so much at home, so surrounded by geniality and affection, that I accepted the situation without much concern." While previously he considered himself "Japanese practically in nothing but my features," he returned from the trip more certain than he had ever been of his heritage, and more grateful for it. Most of all, he was thankful for the knowledge of a family's love that the circumstances of his life had previously denied him. "I could hardly believe that I had grandmothers who could weep for joy at seeing me."

Much later, Hayakawa recalled that one of the first things his mother had asked him when he arrived in 1935 "was whether she should look for a bride for me. Apparently she had some eligible young ladies lined up. . . . I said, 'Don't trouble yourself. Your job is to protect me.'" He added, "When I told my parents about Marge and her family, they immediately gave their blessing."

On August 23, 1935, a letter from Don's future brother-in-law, Wes Peters, had been addressed to "Mr. Don Ichiye Hayakawa." In his typical bantering tone, Peters responded to an earlier note from Hayakawa, "greatly pleased to hear of your feelings about the Tokio [*sic*] Hotel," the Imperial, which his mentor, Frank Lloyd Wright, had designed. The balance of the letter deals with architectural criticism, except for an intriguing, if wordy and flip, question: "How is the Great Japanadian Novel coming or have you perhaps changed your intentions toward the production of some such piece as 'Through Fugiyama with Gun & Camera' or 'The Land of Cherry Blossoms as I know it'?" If Don had indeed begun writing a novel on or about that trip, no evidence of it has been found.

ten

On Valentine's Day of 1936, Don Hayakawa's mind wasn't entirely on academic or political matters. He sent Marge a new verse he had written, both playful and seductive, entitled "pome for peters":

> o wise and perfect lady-friend
> o sizzling babe o love divine
> o thou whom cupid's doves attend
> o thou whom fragrant winds entwine
> o phoenix in the phoenix' nest
> o nonpareil o apogee
> o swell with every beauty blest
> wilt thou my palsy-walsy be
> and share with me the rapture sweet
> of hearts in harmony complete
> beat soft retreat from Time's defeat
> and meet at the drugstore down the street?

Only the writer and the recipient know if they met that February 14.

Despite his residence in and fascination with the United States, Don Hayakawa never forgot his Canadian roots or the plight of fellow Japanese Canadians, especially in British Columbia. He published a controversial essay stimulated by his travel the previous year, "The Japanese-Canadian: An Experiment in Citizenship," in the April 1936 issue of the *Dalhousie Review*. "It is not known to the majority of Canadians outside British Columbia," he pointed out, "that Japanese, Chinese and Hindus, even if they are British subjects by naturalization or by birth are not permitted to vote in that province."

Displaying the double-edged humor that would characterize much
of his mature writing, Hayakawa suggested that perhaps the Japanese
aren't really interested in democratic citizenship, "but are turning
Canadian catch-words upon the Canadian in sly, oriental fashion for
the attainment of wicked, inscrutable, oriental design." He quickly
turned that stereotype around, pointing out that the Japanese is "a
curiously loyal Canadian . . . [who] occasionally feels cynical about
the people who glory in democratic institution at the same time as
they withhold from him those common privileges which enable a
society to call itself democratic."

While praising the "inestimable gift of a dual culture," he also
urged that dual nationality be abandoned along with "Japanese habits and ways of life as might seem strange or offensive to delicate
British Columbian sensibilities," his language merging pragmatism
with sarcasm. Finally, pointing out what white citizens refused to
see, he concluded: "If the child is in any way the father of the man,
it looks as if British Columbia is depriving herself unnecessarily of
some quite promising political intelligence."

The wry, pointed commentary of "The Japanese-Canadian: An
Experiment in Citizenship" in a Canadian periodical revealed, too,
a maturing of Hayakawa's writing style as well as his concern with
politics. He was opposed by such as the "Native Sons of B.C.," who
proclaimed: "The Canadian-born Japanese never has and never will
think of himself as Canadian (100 percent or 1 percent)." Such silly
racist assertions made Hayakawa appear clear-eyed indeed.

Perhaps the high point—but bitterest pill, too—of Hayakawa's
Canadian citizenship came in May 1936 when he appeared as leader
of a delegation before the Special Committee on Elections and Franchise Acts of the House of Commons in Ottawa. The recently formed
Japanese Canadian Citizens League (JCCL) had filed a brief requesting for Nisei the right to vote in British Columbia during federal
elections. Don was asked to head the group, which also included
dentist Edward Banno, teacher Hideko Hyodo, and businessman
Minoru Kobayashi. As if to exemplify how ill-informed most of
their countrymen were, one committee member asked, "Do they

need interpreters?" Another commented, "You all speak English so fluently that if we did not see you face to face we would take you to be Englishmen."

In any case, the JCCL presented persuasive, in some cases elegant, arguments that it was time to grant the franchise to Canadians of Japanese descent, as well as to open professions such as pharmacy, law, and public office to them. No presentation was more telling than Hayakawa's in countering the argument that the delegation was somehow unrepresentative: "Hundreds of young boys and girls have been sacrificing ice-cream sodas and movies, and contributing their quarters and fifty-cent pieces, in order that we might appear before you to secure the rights for which they are hopefully preparing themselves," he said. "We can only point out that like yourselves, we are perhaps a little better endowed with the gift of gab than those whom we represent, and we are therefore as representative of the Canadian citizens who have sent us, as you are of the less articulate Canadian citizens who have sent you to Ottawa."

According to poet Roy Miki, "Hayakawa brought a decidedly intellectual, even academic, air to the delegation." Don's eloquence and gentle humor triggered an outburst from one of the House's arch Anglophiles, A. W. Neill, who alleged that the delegation "may represent a few people for whom they are seeking votes, but they do not represent the condition of Orientals." Neill chose to believe the stereotype in his head rather than the real people testifying before him. Thomas Reid, another noted anti-Asian British Columbia politician, "insisted that the agitation was all part of Japan's plan for conquest, along with illegal entry, the high birth rate, the planting of spies in the fishing industry." Neill then closed by warning that the Japanese would be on their way to controlling "half of Canada tomorrow" if granted the franchise. Although many members expressed admiration for the delegation's presentation, Parliament by law could not overrule British Columbia's provincial government, so the JCCL dug in for a long fight.

Don's 1936 letters to Marge indicate that he was searching diligently for a full-time tenure-track job somewhere, anywhere—South Dakota

State College, Colorado College, Bowling Green State College, Colby College, the University of Michigan, as well as the University of Wisconsin Extension. "As soon as I have a job, and at the moment I feel quite confident about it," he wrote to his love, "I am going to write to your mother, a long, long letter, asking for your (!) hand."

In a more revealing section of the same letter, he urged Marge, referred to as "my love," to "permit yourself the luxury of kidding yourself":

> Get rid of the subconscious horrors, and trot out your will-to-believe, exercising it on such articles of faith as these: A. one of these (and not far distant) days, we shall be living together again, probably in sin. B. we shall always, even if only intermittently, continue to do so till death us do part, unless, of course, you trick me into marriage, in which case we shall live together without sinning [!]. C. If we don't go before that time, we shall at least count on going to Japan together in 1940 to see the Olympic games in Tokyo.

Despite his activities, Don was desperately lonely for Marge—whom he called his "precious worm"—and growing frustrated. He even considered giving up on finding an academic position and returning to Canada to enter politics. Mostly, he missed his girl: "It's a bit dreary Saturday nights and Sundays, being so much alone. I know quite a few people casually now, but have no friends to speak of." Marge was then on a trailer trip with her mother. He added, "You mustn't stop clawing the pillow, because my only satisfaction when I am doing that is the assurance that you are doing the same thing!"

It's not certain when Don and Marge had become lovers, but the ardor of their correspondence, as well as some of his poetry, makes it clear that they had. For instance, he wrote in "First Anniversary," an undated poem from that period,

Now that a whole year has passed
  And it's time for retrospect,—
How, may I ask, have you managed
  Without your self-respect?

81

Your honor had no stain then,
    Your name was above reproach—
How skillfully you avoided
    My carefully-planned approach!

Until that fatal evening,
    Just twelve mad months ago,
You were a stubborn maiden,
    And I a designing beau.

But ha! with my wiles I trapped you
    In my den on Conklin Court,
(Served you right for entering
    Such a questionable resort!)

As you look back, proud fair one,
    On your subsequent life of sin,
Don't you ask, was it worth the candle?
    Does your conscience stir within?

I'll bet it doesn't, depraved one!
    For now you are hardened to crime:
A slave to unbridled lusts,
    Even now you are biding your time

To resume your lascivious career
    And riot in passions unfettered—
Whoops, my dear! I just can't see
    How your plans could be bettered!

But though I approve your depravity,
    I pray, be considerate and kind,
For you only lost your virtue,
    But I—I've lost my mind.

Less than a month later he was in New York City, trying to place an extended article he had written based on his trip to Japan the previous year, and his mood had changed dramatically. "Loads of news, my love, and a most interesting time I am having of it in NY. First of all, Harpers [*sic*] has decided (practically) to accept 3500 words of the Japan article." On top of that, Lee F. Hartman, the editor of *Harper's*, had given him an introduction to Richard J. Walsh, the editor of *Asia* magazine (and the husband of Nobel Prize–winning author Pearl S. Buck). Don was able to place in *Asia* a longer piece (which was eventually broken into the two aforementioned separate essays and published in the April and May 1937 issues of the magazine) about the previous year's visit to Japan, and since that magazine shared offices with the *New Republic*, Don also met Malcolm Cowley, who said he would consider him as a possible reviewer.

It was a remarkable turn of events for a young man who had lately been discouraged and ready to pursue local politics in Canada, and he certainly understood its importance: "I now have introductions to Herald-Tribune Books, Sat. Rev. of Lit., and to the New York Times Book Review, and hope to call on them all this week. It's wonderful what it does for one to say 'Harper's has just accepted an article of mine.'"

That New York City odyssey would remain one of the great adventures of his life, and a turning point. Although his quest for a teaching job at Columbia, NYU, or Hunter College came to nothing, he remained buoyed by his good fortune at *Harper's* and *Asia*. He also learned a harsh reality since, ironically, he didn't particularly want to write more about Japan, but Walsh had advised that "when I went to the other reviews, I tell them right off that I *want* to review books about Japan—in that way I shall be sure of getting in even if I am hardly competent to write on the subject. Ouch, what a blow to my scholarly conscience!"

Despite his rounds at offices, he squeezed in some tourism, and especially enjoyed the chorus line at Radio City Music Hall—"I had never seen a perfectly trained chorus in my life before . . . but tonight I saw them kick together." He was becoming infatuated with the city. "It's astonishing how easily one gets accustomed to New York," he wrote to his betrothed. "And the place is not so preposterously expensive to live in as I thought, and if we are to starve together, this might be quite as good a place to do it as we can find."

Thanks to his brother—"Fred seems to be reconciling himself to contributing to my support"—Don was staying in the city with a University of Wisconsin friend, Ed Austin, and as was often true of him, he struck up a friendship with an attractive lady. Hayakawa seems rarely to have been without female companionship. How intimate these relationships were depends upon who tells the tale, but this one—frankly revealed to Marge—seems innocent enough. "Last night we suddenly decided that Grace Long & I should go into the theatre, because there must be some way non-naturalizable aliens get into the country when they happen to be jugglers or acrobats. Grace and I both had never considered theatre, of course, but we decided at once that going around B'way looking for a part in a play would be a good way to do some systematic sightseeing." Those references to "Grace and I" may have been troubling to Marge, but Don likely eased that when he closed his handwritten letter this way: "I've changed my mind about living with you in N.Y. . . . [A]s long as we are dreaming about it, we might as well dream of more practical places to do our sinning in."

Hayakawa's politics were revealed from his letters that summer, such as a report of "a terrible fight" he had with a University of Wisconsin friend named Peg Meyer; she, "like so many other political conservatives, feels that she has a sort of monopoly on Americanism, so that not only Jews and Communists, but Socialists, Townsendites, Longites, Roosevelt, Father Divine, and Mayor Laguardia are 'un-American.'"

Peg's friend Johnny Hite, "a republican worker," then joined the fray: "From him I learned that [Alf] Landon is 'no true republican,' apparently because he has had two or three progressive ideas. . . . [A]nd 'we should have done like the Communists—sabotaged everything he [Roosevelt] was trying to do so that he couldn't have accomplished [even] one of the good things he was trying to do.' If that isn't revolutionary violence for you!"

Don felt he had a good chance at a teaching position with Hamlin

College in Saint Paul, Minnesota, since his friend Lynn Beyer, a Rhodes scholar, whose father was a professor there, had lobbied hard for him, but in the end he lost to a candidate from the University of Minnesota who had not even earned a doctorate. Many years later, Don would admit, "After I had decided to be trained as a writer and a teacher of English, I saw what I thought were dozens of people with smaller abilities than my own getting jobs while I cooled my heels in graduate school waiting for an opening, and wondering if I was being discriminated against." As fall semester neared and no job materialized, he grew more discouraged and all but gave up, writing to Marge: "I have practically made up my mind that if I don't get a job, I shall stay in NY and write, and register for a course or two in Columbia University so as to fulfill the immigration requirements. I shall write Fred, and try to get an allowance of $50 a month, and I think I can earn the rest."

eleven

Despite Hayakawa's increasingly prestigious list of publications, along with his PhD, he did not receive a job offer until virtually the last minute in fall of 1936 when the University of Wisconsin Extension hired him. He faced the realization that he was indeed being discriminated against, but he also understood that to complain in the atmosphere of the time would not only be futile but probably counterproductive. He was, after all, seeking to enter what was then still seen as a white man's world.

The position he did accept was better than nothing. Wisconsin boasted no widespread junior college system at the time, so, in a forward-looking and practical program, the university sent courses—usually freshman composition in Hayakawa's case—to people who couldn't come to Madison, holding classes in local public buildings all over the state. The new instructor was conspicuous in the hinterland, especially after a piece in the *Waupaca County Post* on November 11, 1937, announced: "JAPANESE IS ENGLISH PROF FOR U.W. HERE." The first paragraph read, "Young Scandinavian-American and German-American youths of this and nearby communities who are attending the University of Wisconsin freshman extension course here, are being taught this school year by a full-blooded Japanese, a Canadian and British subject, who is making a notable success of teaching the English Language."

The new teacher's candid opinions quoted in the article surely startled readers, since as had already become his style, Don did not hesitate to challenge popular assumptions. "Rather belittling to our western boastfulness is his statement that Japan has a higher degree of literacy than America. . . . As a liberal thinker, Mr. Hayakawa sees a surcease of world conflicts only through greater education, tolerance, an end of chauvinistic and narrow nationalism."

Once instruction began, the young professor logged many road miles in a newly purchased used car. "I remember with the first year of extension I lived in Wausau and taught there, but I [also] had to teach in Antigo, Merrill, and Rhinelander. Later I taught in Manitowoc and Waupaca." Eva Revie, whose husband, Gerald "Jerry" Revie, was a mechanic at a Conoco service station in Wausau, remembered, "One day Doc Hayakawa (he was then known as 'Doc' to his friends) stopped in to have his car repaired. Jerry repaired his car, and they became good friends. . . . Doc came to our house many times after that," Mrs. Revie revealed, "and usually ended staying for a home-cooked meal."

His classes at the extension were full, and Margaret McDonald O'Melia, a student of his in Wausau, later told her daughter that "she loved him as a teacher and felt that he was a very perceptive man because he was speaking out about the danger of Hitler even before the World recognized the evils that he was capable of." She also "had a high regard for his command of the English language."

Mrs. O'Melia's admiration for Hayakawa's grasp of English may reflect an assumption that he was Japanese rather than Canadian, thus not a native English speaker. Helen Williams, the wife of fellow professor T. Harry Williams, who traveled regularly with Don from town to town offering classes, seemed to respond to a stereotype when she recalled Hayakawa as "an old country Japanese male whose wife stepped two paces behind his shadow." Of course, Don wasn't yet married, and Marge Peters wasn't a woman to walk behind anyone's shadow. Mrs. Williams also noted that her own husband and Don "were amateur musicians and would entertain, or attempt to, on the violin and piano as long as the audience could tolerate their sour notes."

Certainly, Don didn't pass unnoticed by his white neighbors. University of Wisconsin library director, James Gollata, recalls an anecdote told by his high school English instructor, Eugene Cramer, who had taken a course from Don at the now-defunct teachers' college in Manitowoc. Cramer said he asked an old-timer there if he remembered Hayakawa, and the man replied, "He was a good guy. He was a Jap, but he was a good guy."

During that school year, while Don resided in Wausau teaching in a classroom at the normal school, as well as in those outlying communities, he remained professionally and socially active. He had by then taken up the violin, and he practiced it as frequently as he could. Like so many of his Depression generation, he smoked cigarettes and, like many others, had learned to cut them in half and to puff each down to its nub, often while enjoying a drink with colleagues or new friends.

At the Central Wisconsin Teachers' Convention, he skipped lectures by well-known Korean Chinese author Dr. No-Yong Park and the aviatrix Amelia Earhart, but he didn't miss the dance that followed. "I'm going to that," he wrote to his future wife, who by then knew he seldom missed a dance.

Hayakawa was a recognizable figure in rural Wisconsin, and he had become familiar with the Cloverbelt Cooperative, organized as a credit union by local farmers in order to create their own source of financial support. The young instructor at first became socially involved with Cloverbelt, explaining, "It was a congenial thing. We went to their potluck suppers and met a lot of people there." In 1939 the credit union would go into the fuel-oil business and considerably increase membership because urban customers then joined. One of them was Don, who had long been interested in the co-op concept.

He soon became especially friendly with Louis Doede, the co-op's general manager, and his wife, Ruth. Despite the slowly intensifying anti-Japanese sentiment nationally, the young professor felt accepted in the communities where he taught, traveling from town to town in all seasons. Nevertheless, he could not help being troubled by international events, and he published one of his strongest works, "Poem for Courage," in the September 1936 issue of the leftist Canadian journal *New Frontier*:

Gentleness is no easy virtue; it is wrung
only from hard materials, hammered out
with the accompaniment of fierce heat.

How splendid are the names of those who in times
    past
clutched to hot hearts the message of gentleness
and fought for love, for mercy, for brotherhood,
with the dogged courage of mutineers;

Who, while the world for bread of preferment jostled,
while cut-throat princes flung at each other their
    squadrons,
alone and inviolate with their stern soul wrestled,
prayed, taught, exhorted, upheld
in sinewy hands their badge of holiness.

O shieldless champions! O fighters who fought with
    prayer!
O you who endured straight-lipped rope, faggot, and
    engine!
Stand by us now whom terror freezes facing
the savage stammering of Lewis-guns.

Much of the poem—which was credited to "S. I. Hayakawa," not yet a common way for Don to identify himself—reveals the continuing influence of one of his favorite poets, Siegfried Sassoon. After slipping into the breathless sentences that begin with "O" and end with exclamation marks, his powerful final two lines render the work memorable. He remained, despite his increasing immersion in scholarship, a promising poet.

He could write prose too. His essay "Japanese Sensibility" was printed in *Harper's Monthly* in December 1936. Its publication was a triumph for the still unknown writer, whom it revealed to be an observer, a reporter, a scholar—and perhaps a man not entirely facing political reality. He seemed genuinely intrigued by "the distinctive native [Japanese] aesthetic sense, which is unlike that of any other nation or race I know."

This analysis was tempered by a disclaimer: "Perhaps my amazement and joy were but the natural response of any North American visiting an older civilization for the first time." His amazement and joy also seem to be the products of a thoughtful man coming to grips with and taking pride in his own ancestral heritage, but his account completely ignored international political events, the rise of militarism, and the continuing perversion of Bushido that was already dishonoring Japan's reputation in the world.

Riding the wave of congratulations about his essay in *Harper's*, Don attended an academic conference over the New Year's holiday and was interviewed by several potential academic employers. Returning to Madison on January 3, 1937, he was confident that he'd be offered a job at schools such as Colorado State, Rensselaer Polytech, Wayne State, Kent State, or his two favorites, Ohio State and Louisville. He wrote enthusiastically to Marge: "I wish I could tell you of all the nice people I met—especially from the U. of Louisville English Dept. with whom I spent most of my time, and all sorts of others,—people who had read my things (there were a number who spoke of my Harper's article)—people who know interesting things to talk about—people who hold their liquor well and get more brilliant the more they drink." Don added, "I also made a big hit apparently with a chap from the U. of Calif., (of all places!) who seems to be interested in looking up my record." Given what would follow in his life, Hayakawa's next sentence is ironic indeed. "I'm sure I shouldn't like to go to Calif., but I'd love to get an offer."

The heart of this revealing note, however, was personal, not professional: "You must brace yourself for it now, Peters, but we have got to do something about ourselves. . . . I can't bear to think of love filming over into helpless regret & longing—because by that time too much will have happened to separate us. And this your mother knows, at least unconsciously, and it is this fact that gives her opposition so much of an advantage in the long run. O my love, we must stop now & dig our heels into the ground, & not be dragged along by circumstance." Whether this appeal finally convinced Marge isn't certain, but something strengthened her resolve and she, with or without family approval, determined to marry this man she loved.

On March 23, Don closed a letter, "miss you mightily, mostly at bedtime. not that i feel ambitious. i don't. but you are sort of good company anyway." Two days later he would write, "I love you madly, you worm"; he closed the note with "ARF!"

During the following semester, while Marge completed her degree, the couple continued seeing one another as frequently as possible, often with the old gang from the now defunct Arden Club. "At school there was always the activity," Ed Mayer said, "yet the interludes of walking with her [Marge] & Don to Harold's, favorite speakeasy[,] for a 25 cent whole half of a frier [sic] dinner. Conversation—between them—on D. H. Lawrence. And a trip to Chicago to see Lysistrata . . . how many of us? 5 I think, Don, Marge, Win, Alan Drummond & me." Despite such good times, Mayer believes "Marge pined for 2 years because even her enlightened family opposed her & Don's marriage."

Meanwhile, Hayakawa's academic stock seemed to be rising apace. That April and May his articles "A Japanese-American Goes to Japan" and "My Japanese Father and I" appeared in *Asia* and gave his name more recognition. Although other editors contacted Hayakawa after those pieces were published, "One awful thing I am finding . . . is that whether I like it or not, I shall have to do a great deal of writing about Japan."

After Marge graduated with honors from the University of Wisconsin in 1937, she at last felt free to marry Don, but first she took her mother on a motor trip with what Ed Mayer described as a "wee trailer." Marge herself recalled, "We had a wonderful time," because her mother "was a very engaging, intelligent, witty person." The pair traveled to New England, where Hayakawa on his motorcycle joined them. While Mrs. Peters wasn't overjoyed, "she was getting fond of Don." Along the way the two women toured a Vanderbilt estate, and Marge sent a card to Mayer that read in part, "One of the best arguments for communism I've found is that the rich have such bad taste."

The journey completed, Marge told her aunt Augusta, with whom her mother then lived, that she would marry Don imminently and, to her surprise, her aunt offered to host the wedding. Clara Peters "took it very well." In fact, Marge later recalled that "everything that happened to her, she took very well indeed." As bad luck would have it, though, Mrs. Peters fell and broke her leg shortly before the wedding, and Ed Mayer accused Marge, "I didn't think you'd have to break her leg!"

With the unconditional blessing of Hayakawa's parents, who were of course in Japan at the time, the wedding took place in the Peters family's House on the Hill in Hamilton on May 29, 1937. Marge's mother was in bed with a cast on her leg while the young couple exchanged vows in front of a fireplace. It was, Marge recalls, "a really very nice wedding."

The *Hamilton Journal* described the Peters-Hayakawa wedding in the almost comic style of society reporting then in vogue:

> Marked by exquisite simplicity and great dignity, the wedding of Miss Margedant Peters, only daughter of Mrs. Clara Margedant Peters of Evansville, Ind., and the late F. Romer Peters[,] and Samuel I. Hayakawa, professor of English at the University of Madison, took place Saturday evening at 6 o'clock at the home of the bride's uncle, C. E. Margedant, 605 Crescent road.
>
> The bride, a cultured and charming young woman, very attractive in a smart travel ensemble of gray and carrying an armful of lavender larkspur.

On May 29 Don wrote to his bride perhaps his most delightful poem, "Epithalamion"—a wedding song:

> I guess we couldn't live in sin forever,
>   (The arrangement really had its charming side.)
> It's just as well we'll now be parted never
>   In bond by social usage sanctified:

No more we'll tremble 'neath your mother's glance,
    Nor quiver when she calls you from upstairs;
No longer stand in fear of those mischances
    That make us leap in haste to separate chairs.

We'll never now, when visiting, be compelled
    To sleep in separate rooms and toss all night;
Nor startled by a footstep, be impelled,
    To jump about a foot or two in fright.
(Do you suppose the time will come, my love,
    When you and I are married years and years,
When romping rats in corridors above
    Will cease to rouse involuntary fears?

When garbage-men nor icemen will not shake me,
    Nor grocery boys, nor other circumstance?
When rattlings of the door-knob will not make me
    Leap out of bed and quickly grab my pants?)
No longer need we borrow friends' apartments,
    Nor fear the dropping of a careless word;
We may unblushing ride in train compartments,
    By nervousness or Mann Act undeterred.

Farewell, ye narrow studio-couch caresses,
    Farewell ye blisses of the folding bed;
Farewell ye rapid jumping into dresses,
    Farewell, ye clutching, momentary dread.
Farewell the use of phony noms d'hotel,
    Farewell th' ensuing months of sex starvation,
Farewell the nights of wanting you like hell,
    And gnawing at the pillows in frustration.

And welcome, union holy, pure and true,
    O welcome, sanctions legal and divine,
O welcome, beds quite wide enough for two,
    Whose central ridges do not crack the spine.

Ring, bells, in great relief and jubilation,—
  Laugh, gods—with lust insatiate us endow!
By lawful, droll, peculiar transformation,
  Our immorality is moral now.

Following the marriage, Ed Mayer's congratulations were effusive, if a tad wistful: "O dear Peters, how can I say how much of my blessing you have! It sounds so simple to say 'I wish you joy,' but that doesn't touch what I want to start saying. . . . And don't think that our friendship will be affected by it; I don't see why it should." Marge had decided not to change her name, and Mayer chided her in the same note: "Tell me, tho, staying M.P., what title goes with? I ain't had traffic with any Lucy Stoners heretofore Miss."

After the wedding, the newlyweds headed for New York, making at least one stop in Wisconsin along the way. Eva Revie recalled, "One day he showed up at our door, and said he had gotten married, and he and his new bride were on their way up north for the honeymoon. So I made them a nice meal, we visited for awhile, and then they left for their honeymoon. That was the last time we saw him. Then one day our daughter, Dawn, received a postcard from [the Hayakawas in] England (it was a picture of the 'Changing of the Guard')." Mrs. Revie summarized, "We always remembered him as a friendly, somewhat homesick, hungry (ha!) young man whom we had the pleasure of knowing for a time."

The Hayakawas' honeymoon began with a steamer trip across the Atlantic to Glasgow. From there they bicycled all the way to London, "traveling through Robert Burns' country and Sir Walter Scott's country and Shakespeare, Thomas Hardy country. We were such terrific English majors at the time," Don laughed years later as he recalled that trip.

In marrying, as in many other activities, Nisei Don functioned more like a member of the thoroughly assimilated third-generation Japanese, the Sansei. Ken Adachi points out that while only 1 percent of Issei and Nisei in 1941 married people of non-Japanese lineage, 59 percent of postwar Canadian Sansei married non-Japanese. The historian further suggests, "Their education is job-oriented, they speak little or no Japanese, they enter secure professions, and their upward mobility leads them into an almost exclusive level of social interaction with non-Japanese groups." His generalizations sound like a description of S. I. Hayakawa.

twelve

With news of Japan's 1937 attack on China, Don couldn't help but become even more aware of political, economic, and social pressures on his family in Nippon. An informal boycott of goods imported from there, as well as calls for a formal boycott of virtually all things Japanese, spread across Canada. Resentment against Japan destroyed Ichiro Hayakawa's business, white patronage drying up. When Don returned to his appointment with the University of Wisconsin Extension in the fall of 1937, he could feel the increased tension.

He was scheduled to teach in Wausau, Antigo, Wisconsin Rapids, and Waupaca in 1937, so he and Marge rented an apartment in a house owned by a furniture store owner, Abe Krom, in Antigo. While searching for a rental there, the couple responded to a newspaper ad for lodging. Marge laughed when she recalled ringing the front doorbell of the house: "It wasn't too prepossessing, and a fat, and not too prepossessing woman came to the door. We said, 'We came to see about the room you advertised.' . . . [S]he looked, and she said, 'It's too unusual.' She closed the door in our faces. . . . [O]therwise, we had no trouble at all."

Don reportedly considered northern Wisconsin "a vast educational wasteland" ripe for cultivation, so he cultivated it by helping students understand and value their home regions. "I put a lot of emphasis . . . on their telling me in their papers about their own communities. . . . It was very strange how many people feel their dumb little town is not worth writing about. I asked them to observe what actually was in it, and write about the things that gave the town an economic *raison d'etre*." Employing the work of midwestern writers such as Willa

Cather, O. E. Rølvaag, and Sinclair Lewis, Don illustrated the power of the local, urging students to tap the power of places and people they knew. For many students, this was a revolutionary approach.

In a revealing exchange many years later, he would recall, "I was never discontent with that extension job." Then he added, "It was a very great adventure, really. We got to know an awful lot of people." He remembered with special fondness the Petersons of Rhinelander, whose son was in one of his classes, and who "were so hospitable that they insisted on our coming every week, so we always had a big, hot dinner at noon" in the "freezing, below-zero weather." In a 1938 letter, he reported to Marge, "Spent afternoon & evening at Chez Peterson." In fact, he spent many afternoons and evenings with those convivial friends.

He was on the road more than he liked, though, teaching in far-away towns, while Marge often remained in Antigo or occasionally Madison or Hamilton. In Wausau that year Hayakawa also met and found himself taken with Helen Van Vechten, the founder of Philosopher Press, which had produced hand-printed "fine" books on intellectual topics. She was then semi-retired and "terribly lonely for someone with whom to talk about her literary interests" when Don called on her. As he explained in a letter to his wife, who was away visiting her family, Helen Van Vechten "has an amazing collection of wonderful bindings, and book-collectors' items that are simply astounding." Convinced that "a tremendously important piece of research-work . . . in american [sic] literary history can be done with her assistance," he also noted that "it's terribly hard to stay objective about facts, dates, editions, etc.—because . . . she keeps grabbing for your soul." She never quite grabbed his, although the young professor did make an effort to visit the aging intellectual as often as he could.

In the same letter to his wife, he mentioned having received a magazine, *The Phoenix*, devoted to the work of D. H. Lawrence: "It's perfectly terrible, although interesting." The editor, J. P. Cooney, Don complained, "is a terribly sloppy laurentian [sic]. . . . [I] think he wants to start a colony somewhere and receive the strength of

97

the sun, trees, etc." He closed the note by telling Marge, "I look forward to your opinions on it when you get back," then he added, "(there are other things i [sic] look forward to even more when you get back.)"

He also humorously celebrated the kind of minor triumph that might considerably buoy the ego of a struggling young instructor. On March 28 he wrote to his wife, "SUCCESS SUCCESS. messrs. barnes & noble have got out a circular advertising one of their textbooks (college outline of english lit.) and they quote Chas. Osgood of Princeton, Karl Young of Yale, Lewis Mumford, Lewis F. Mott, and many others including ME in the summaries of critical opinion. boy, that ought to sell their book for them!"

During that spring, Hayakawa, by then a member of the American Dialect Society, found a book on language that especially gripped him: Stuart Chase's *The Tyranny of Words*, a volume based in large measure on the ideas espoused by Count Alfred Korzybski in his 1933 volume *Science and Sanity: An Introduction to Non-Aristotelian Systems and General Semantics*. The Chase book helped Hayakawa focus a number of related ideas, and he would later explain, "My interest in semantics developed as a result of my excitement about the rise of Hitler in the 1930s." That may have been true of many at the time, because Joe Axelrod, a student then, remembered, "There was lots of talk on the University of Chicago campus about Korzybski."

Chase recognized that the merit of the Count's book was not its tortured style, so he summarized what he called its "cardinal point" this way: "If we wish to understand the world and ourselves, it follows that we should use a language whose structure corresponds to physical structure. . . . [M]ost languages (English, French, German, what you will) with their equating verb 'to be,' their false identifications, spurious substantives, confused levels of abstraction, and one-valued judgments, are structurally dissimilar to our nervous system and our environment. The effect is like a bone crosswise in the throat. We get orders and levels tangled up; we misunderstand and misinterpret relations."

Although Korzybski didn't appreciate others gaining attention at his expense, he was astute enough to understand that Chase's book spread the word and perhaps led readers to tackle his own daunting text or at least to recognize his name. Certainly Hayakawa's life was changed by reading *The Tyranny of Words*. Don was so impressed with the concepts Chase explored that he decided to tackle *Science and Sanity* right away. On March 23 he wrote to Marge (capitalizing randomly), "Korzybski's science and sanity [*sic*] came today. . . . [It's] the toughest-looking book in all the books I own. . . . [T]here are some 800 pages of it." Two days later, he again wrote to her, "Korzybski's *Science and Sanity* is a perfectly amazing book."

Curiosity drove him to finish this "amazing mish-mash of ideas. . . . Its synthesis seemed original to me, though, configurations conventional scholars wouldn't think of because their training taught them to make other assumptions and to see other patterns." The young scholar was interested enough to develop on his own a few practical applications of Korzybski's ideas—as he then understood them, anyway.

During that academic year, Don had applied to Professor Thomas Knott for a summer scholarship at the University of Michigan. On June 9 he announced to Marge that he had indeed been awarded one, and that he hoped to study not only with the lexicographer Knott but with the linguist Leonard Bloomfield ("both Bloomfield and Knott are very big shots"). He also informed his wife that students at the University of Wisconsin in Madison "are thinking of starting a new *Rocking Horse*. . . . You would be delighted to know in what high esteem the R-H is held among the young."

Before Don enrolled in the summer seminars with Knott and Bloomfield, he and Marge moved to "a tent on a platform on the western edge of the U/W campus," then off he went for the summer session at Michigan. In a strange turn of events, though, he misread a schedule of classes and turned up on campus at 8 a.m. for an 8 p.m. course. With twelve hours to kill, Hayakawa found a class offered by James Marshall Plumer, a noted authority on Chinese ceramics. Hayakawa recalled: "The first thing this professor did was to go around the class and ask, 'Are you taking this course for credit?' If you said, 'No, I'd like to audit,' he threw you out. So it got down to me and I said, 'I'm taking it for credit.'" Plumer awakened a love of art in Don, who "got to be very good friends with him."

But Chinese art was only a sidelight that summer. The young man's ear for language—as well as his commonsense approach to building an academic résumé—led him into his first major foray in lexicography, *The Middle English Dictionary*, a vast volume being assembled at the university in Ann Arbor. Begun in 1930, the ongoing manuscript had since 1935 been edited by Knott. In those days before computers, lexicography was a laborious process.[1] Hayakawa described it this way: "In writing a dictionary, what you do is get a three-by-five card . . . and you put the word and the exact quotation in which that word appears, writing it down then indicating its source. You collect simply thousands of those cards, and then ultimately you sort them all out and find how all the words are used." It wasn't entirely drudgery to a young man fascinated by words and livened by a sense of humor. Hayakawa chuckled as he told Julie Gordon Shearer, "We had to read very carefully an enormous number of books written in Middle English, and one book I remember having to read and understand is *The Treatise on the Fistula in Ano.* . . . [T]hat's one great piece of literature that stands out in my memory."

Perhaps more important, when students told Professor Knott that they were interested in general semantics, he

asked the class, "Has anyone here read Korzybski?" I was rash enough to raise my hand. Said Professor Knott, "Hayakawa, why don't you give us a lecture or two on Korzybski's *Science and Sanity*—perhaps early next week?" I was aghast. I had come to Michigan

---

1. Many editors and researchers later, *The Middle English Dictionary* was completed, and on May 9, 2001, its publication was celebrated at the campus in Ann Arbor. In his remarks to the assemblage, Fawwaz Ulaby, University of Michigan's vice-president for research, said, "Only rarely do we witness anything that might be called 'Big Humanities'—a large-scale, long-term project involving so many individual scholars working together toward a common goal." The sheer magnitude of the project was staggering—seven decades of scholarly labor, documented by some three million citations, culminating in a thirteen-volume dictionary of nearly fifteen thousand pages. By the time this early contribution to scholarship was published, Don Hayakawa had been dead for nine years.

to learn about Korzybski, not to explain him. But I was stuck with the job, and the following week I did the best I could.

In the course of preparing my lectures on Korzybski, I wrote to him in Chicago asking about further instruction in general semantics. That is how it happened that he invited me to a seminar.

Hayakawa also informally introduced elements of general semantics to Bloomfield's linguistics seminar, where he met and discussed the possibilities of Korzybski's work with the noted anthrolinguist Morris Swadesh. As a result, Hayakawa began to discover wider applications for the ideas in *Science and Sanity*.

That same year, two early proponents of "GS" (as many devotees called Korzybski's work), Charles B. Congdon and Douglas Gordon Campbell, psychiatrists at the University of Chicago, convinced manufacturer Cornelius Crane to underwrite an Institute of General Semantics, basically just a storefront a few blocks from the university's campus. Korzybski's seminars, which had previously been held at various sites, had managed to attract some luminaries. Finding an ostensibly permanent setting, Korzybski hoped, would increase enrollments and bring more luminaries who would help spread the word, and gain wide acceptance of his ideas.

After completing his session at Michigan, Don traveled to Chicago to enroll in one of Korzybski's seminars and to at last meet the theoretician. "He greeted me very cordially, and said, 'You have been giving lectures on general semantics at the University of Michigan, and you don't know a God-damn thing about it!' And he smiled. I just laughed. . . . Anyway, we became pretty good friends after that."

In November, Marge was visiting her family and a note from her ardent young husband told her that he was thinking of more than general semantics: "In spite of all the hard work I've done today, my mind has been obsessed with lust. . . . Wait till i [*sic*] get you. Pant. Pant." Betty Kobayashi Issenman recalls that the newlyweds visited her family in Montreal during that period: "What does stand out in my mind of that meeting is how thrilled Margedant and he were with each other and how much in love they were."

four

GENERAL SEMANTICS

thirteen

Count Alfred Habdank Scarbak Korzybski was born into a family of Polish aristocrats on July 3, 1879. He studied chemical engineering at the Polytechnic Institute in Warsaw, and later served with distinction in World War I, where he was injured three times before being sent first to the United States and then to Canada as an artillery expert (he joked that his prior experience with artillery had been as a target for enemy guns). Already conversant in German, French, Russian, and Polish, he studied English upon arrival in North America and added it—albeit heavily accented—to his repertoire.

Korzybski pondered his war experiences and the causes of such bloodbaths. He decided that humanity's most unique behavior was what he called "time-binding," the ability to learn from experience and to pass on those lessons from one generation to the next by the use of symbols. Most animals, he asserted, were "space-binders" in that they could move in response to environmental forces but not pass on cultural lessons, while less intellectually complex organisms such as plants were what he called "chemical-binders" with, for instance, the capacity to become dormant.

Thanks to assistance from the distinguished mathematician Cassius J. Keyser, Korzybski's ideas were published in 1921 as *Manhood of Humanity: The Science and Art of Human Engineering*. That volume established the Count as an original thinker, if not a clear stylist in English. The book had been written with the high hope that the lessons of the Great War would render any more such conflicts unlikely. During the years that followed the publication of *Manhood of Humanity*, Korzybski studied omnivorously, everything from mathematics to art to psychiatry, refining and enriching the ideas he had earlier presented.

By 1928 he had begun writing a second volume that gathered his accumulated insights. Five years later, *Science and Sanity*—an 806-page intellectual bouillabaisse with 657 references—was self-published. It managed to catch the attention of a number of significant scholars and writers, many of whom in the final analysis weren't impressed, but some who were. Reviewing it in the *Saturday Review of Literature*, Sidney Hook of NYU wrote, "I believe that Mr. Korzybski's fundamental position is sound and that his obiter dicta contain some seminal ideas which undoubtedly will bear the fruit in the minds of others. But if he had deliberately set about to obscure his primary insight he could not have proceeded any differently from the way he had—or succeeded so well."

Science and Sanity's murkiness eventually offered a great opportunity to skilled writers like Stuart Chase and Hayakawa, whose efforts would spread interest in general semantics. The Count was not burdened by much modesty or gratitude, so he didn't always appreciate the suggestion that his ideas were less than clearly presented. Chase, like many other observers, wondered why a book on the clarification of meaning should be so difficult to understand, but he also said that reading *Science and Sanity* had been for him a pivotal experience: "As I read it, slowly, painfully, but with growing eagerness, I looked for the first time into the awful depths of language itself—depths into which the grammarian and the lexicographer have seldom peered, for theirs is a different business. Grammar, syntax, dictionary derivations, are to semantics as a history of the coinage is to the operations going on in a large modern bank."

In his initial seminar at the Institute of General Semantics (IGS), Don Hayakawa found that he was part of a mixed bag of students, some bright and sincere, others simply "joiners." Among those he met was psychiatrist Douglas Kelley, who later served as a consultant at the Nuremberg War Crimes trial, and also an amateur magician whose tricks Korzybski used in class to demonstrate deception; a University of Wisconsin dance teacher, Margaret H'doubler; Bertha Ochsner, another well-known danseuse; noted painter Charles Biederman; educational theorist Porter Sargent; Professor Wendell Johnson; a "delightful Canadian" named Douglas Campbell, to whom Don took an immediate liking; and Charlotte Schuchardt ("a mysterious somewhat pretty young women [*sic*]"), who would one day become director of the IGS.

Ex-vaudevillian Vocha Fiske, a GS devotee, described the theatricality of a Korzybskian performance this way, "Slowly moving to as near the front of the platform as he could, he seriously surveyed the varying faces, leaning heavily on his cane in dramatic silence. Then, lifting his cane a la a signal to charge, he plunged with action and words into a torrential fanfare on the science of man." The Count's performance on the first day of the class, employing H'doubler as a foil, was described in a serendipitously capitalized letter from Don to Marge:

> the lecture was a riot. k. has a way of saying frequently, after asking a question and a person starts to answer, SHUT UP. . . . h'doubler kept piping up, and she was constantly being told to shut up. he insisted on using her for experiments, such as bumping her head against the wall to verify the difference between two and three dimensional surfaces. she was alternatively distressed and pleased. k. is nothing if not tactful, in a curious, brutal way. after he had mistreated her for some time, he changed the subject, and later came back to her (apparently incidentally) with a compliment. "I haf heard of your work ass a teacher, h'doubler, for some time. I haf heard the finest compliment a teacher can ever get under present educational circumstances applied to your work. I am told that you do less harm to your students than any other teachers my informant knows of," gosh, she was pleased. of course, k. had spent considerable time prior to this saying what criminal damage parents and teachers were doing to their students in every phase of education.

Korzybski's physical bearing also impressed Hayakawa, who described the theoretician as a very astonishing man. big. weighs prob. 200 lbs. but not tall. huge shoulders. walks with a decided limp, and uses a stick. wears khaki trousers and shirt, and no tie. very bald. a funny protuberance on the right side of his stomach, plainly visible by the bulge in his shirt. speaks with a marked foreign accent. he is extremely cordial, has a very engaging peculiar smile, in which the lips (which are full) are set somewhat grimly, but the corners thereof turn up delightfully, while his eyes laugh.

Four decades later, Hayakawa would remember that first encounter: "Korzybski's 'seminars' were certainly not seminars in any accepted academic meaning of the term. They were unabashed indoctrination sessions." He recalled the master's style this way: "I found it breathtaking to listen to Korzybski take all knowledge as his province, leaping freely from psychiatry and neurology to symbolic logic to quantum mechanics to the rise of fascism to the chemistry colloids to cultural anthropology to non-Euclidian geometry to biology and back to the human nervous system. Why the human nervous system? Because that's where everything happens."

Hayakawa was hooked, although he didn't yet know it. He had been observing the rise of international forces he was coming to abhor. As Canadian writer Greg Robinson summarizes, "In the shadow of fascism, [Hayakawa] grew increasingly conscious of the dangers of propaganda and racial hatred, and how people substituted facile stereotyping for thought. He concluded that ethnic particularism and ghettoization invited social division, while assimilation and participation in democratic society promoted communication and equality." Here, it seemed to Hayakawa, was a system he might use to expose the falseness of totalitarianism.

Charles Stade, one of the Count's admirers, described sessions at the IGS somewhat differently than Hayakawa or Fiske: Korzybski "knew that the subject that his students were primarily, if not solely, interested in was themselves," explained Stade. He would "start by asking someone to make a decision about some apparently innocuous object. . . . He would then point out some of the consequences of the decision. . . . Only after he had convinced the group that many of their decisions/assumptions carried unacceptable consequences would he proceed to explain why such things happen." Stade added, "Some students had nervous breakdowns in the classes."

Hayakawa wasn't one of them. He found the Count to be a less-than-scintillating lecturer. "Korzybski had a terrible way of feeling that what he had to say was so important you've got to listen to it a second time," he reported, "and a third time, and a fourth time, and every time I found myself in a situation where I had to listen to the same stuff again, I would go to sleep on him. He would get mad as hell!"

Don also considered one of the Count's activities, a method of manipulation to help achieve "neuro-semantic relaxation," particularly amusing. Charlotte Schuchardt tried to explain it objectively in her booklet *The Technique of Semantic Relaxation*, but Don recalled that the Count, who liked ladies, offered private and rather intimate "semantic massages" to some women he found especially attractive. When Hayakawa further revealed, "He really wanted to get together with Marge," his wife laughed and said, "Fat chance." W. Benton Harrison asserts that Korzybski's "bearing and force of personality seemed to have a special appeal to the ladies." Apparently, Marge was an exception.

That November, Don delivered a paper, "General Semantics and Propaganda," before the National Council of Teachers of English in St. Louis, the first major presentation on Korzybski's thought to so large and diverse an assembly of educators. Later that month, Hayakawa wrote to his wife, "My dearest love: It's amazing the number of new ideas & new presentations of old ideas I have been getting the last two days. I have had private conferences from 2 to 3 hrs daily with K, & in addition have met many other interesting people."

He went on to mention an evening with, among others, the Count's principal disciple, Marjorie Mercer Kendig (whose professional name was simply M. Kendig), and Korzybski's "Confidential Secretary," Pearl Johnecheck, as well as the Count himself, Douglas

Campbell and Charles Congdon, sociologist W. Lloyd Warner, businessman Cornelius Crane Jr., and "a Mr. Peevey, young English apparently-sociologist." After the formal gathering broke up, "We went to Kendig's—a beautiful office-apartment—where I made sukiaki [*sic*]—Douglas, Pearl, Kendig, K. & I. Douglas & Pearl made terrific pigs of themselves, much to my delight."

That party actually celebrated the appearance that week in *Time* magazine of an article on Korzybski's work that read, in part, "Whether General Semantics will become a cult such as technocracy, or will rank in historic importance with the work of Aristotle and Einstein, as not a few scientists believe, it is spreading rapidly in the U.S." This was attention on a popular level far beyond any previously attained by the non-Aristotelian system. General semantics, it seemed, was on its way, and so was Alfred Korzybski.

Despite the distraction of semantic massages, boring lectures, and a prolix book, Hayakawa saw considerable value in the system, but he added, "I think Korzybski himself was his own worst enemy, as far as spreading the word." For some, Korzybski's overbearing personality became too much. Anatol Rapoport, considered a major figure in the GS community, once employed the term "crackpot" when describing him. In his book *Semantics*, Rapoport wrote: "In view of Korzybski's fundamental theses, his misuse of scientific terminology is ironic, and many scholars and scientists were quick to dismiss Korzybski as a dilettante, at times a crank. This impression was reinforced by Korzybski himself."

Don Hayakawa looked past Korzybski's personal flaws at his ideas, paying attention to those making sense to him. Soon he incorporated into his classes principles and pedagogic devices such as non-identity (which became "The map is not the territory"), non-allness (which became "The map does not show all the territory"), and self-reflexiveness (which became "An accurate map must contain a map of itself"); he also developed his own version of Korzybski's "Structural Differential" (which he called the "Ladder of Abstraction": "Bessie" is not the same as "cow"; "cow" is not the same as "mammal"; "mammal" is not the same as "animal"; moreover, "cow"$_1$ is not "cow"$_2$

is not "cow"$_3$, etc.), and he examined intensional (subjective) and extensional (objective) orientations. As a result, Hayakawa came to better understand real-life events, such as the way British Columbia's representatives to Parliament had in 1936 responded to their own internal maps of Orientals rather than the external territory (the actual Japanese Canadian delegation).

However, when Don applied his own creative approaches and insights, he made enemies among GS devotees; Stade, for instance, asserted, "Hayakawa never understood anything Korzybski said." Allen Walker Read alleged, "From reading Hayakawa one would never get the impression of richness and depth that Korzybski actually provides." In a thinly veiled slap at Hayakawa and other popularizers, F. S. C. Northrup, Sterling Professor of Law and Philosophy at Yale, wrote, "The problem . . . of understanding Korzybski's semantics is much more complex than many of his simple-minded expositors have supposed."

The Count and his system had many critics, the most persistent of whom was Martin Gardner, something of a professional naysayer who attended a GS seminar and described it this way, "The Count—a stocky, bald, deep-voiced man who always wore Army-type khaki pants and shirt—conducted his classes in a manner similar to Kay Kyser's TV program. . . . Frequently he would remark in his thick Polish accent, 'I speak facts. . . . Bah—I speak baby stuff.' He enjoyed immensely his role of orator and cult leader."

"In a sense we *were* 'cultists,'" W. Benton Harrison responded, "if by 'cult' one means a group who accepts certain ideas and attempts to get others to consider them. However, 'cult'$_1$ is not 'cult'$_2$ and this particular 'cult' appealed to many graduate students and taught its 'followers' to 'distrust generalizations including this one.'" Charlotte Schuchardt Read reported that Korzybski himself rejected cultism.

Gardner also somehow managed to confuse GS with scientology, then called Dianetics. As Allen Walker Read explained, Gardner "was unduly influenced by a published report from Los Angeles that a group of Korzybski's followers were founding a 'General Semantics Church' and were about to go underground to preserve the purity of the faith. . . . It turned out that within a few weeks this group lost its interest in general semantics and embraced scientology."

As for the charge that GS was not original, Korzybski himself would explain in 1941, "The separate issues involved [in general semantics] are not entirely new; their methodological formulation as a system which is workable, teachable and so elementary that it can be applied by children, is entirely new." This maverick intellectual believed he fit well in Chicago, since the reputation of the scene there had elevated in the mid-1930s, and original ideas were welcome. The apogee of Chicago's ascendancy likely occurred when surviving members of "The Vienna Circle" (Rudolf Carnap, Otto Neurath, Hans Hahn, et al.) relocated in the Windy City, making the University of Chicago their base of operations. Publishing the *Journal of Unified Science*, that group stimulated the local scene but ignored Korzybski and his acolytes, considering them amateurs in semantics.

fourteen

Although intrigued, Hayakawa was by no means committed to general semantics as an academic specialty. In 1939 he agreed to coedit with Howard Mumford Jones a collection titled *Oliver Wendell Holmes: Representative Selections.* His work on the introduction and notes indicated that Don retained his flair for the literary, but—save for a few later articles in *Poetry* magazine—this would prove to be one of his final forays into traditional literary scholarship.

He attended a general semantics meeting in Cincinnati that year, where he met William Pemberton, a psychologist who specialized in Rorschach testing. Pemberton remembered that Hayakawa in those days was "a de facto socialist" and "a good guy." By 1939 Pemberton was beginning to seriously study Korzybski's work; he recalled that the consensus among students then was that the great man was "a paranoid genius but more paranoid than genius." He added, "Korzybski didn't like Don. He was too independent." Many years later, Marge Hayakawa said to her husband, "You brought in other ideas and applied his theory in your own way, and that was kind of heresy."

Once Don began to write in earnest about general semantics, his independent thinking showed, and he brought a level of communication skill well beyond Korzybski's, as well as a better understanding of how to practically implement GS—or his own version of it, anyway. He was, however, always careful to credit Korzybski, whom he knew was not one to be neglected. Hayakawa began working on a series of articles, and underlying all he would write was the practical assumption that general semantics offered a formula for rationality.

Soon that prescription would change Don's teaching and far more. For example, he applied Korzybski's "rules" to help individuals assess their own evaluative processes, and he promoted his version of them in his college classes:

1. *Indexing*: "Words lump together unique individuals under a common name." Hence the practice of adding index numbers to all general terms: Republican$_1$ (Lincoln) is not Republican$_2$ (Hoover) is not Republican$_3$ (Nixon), etc.

2. *Dates*: The world and everything in it is in the process of change, but many behavior patterns, opinions, beliefs, tend to remain fixed. As a result, all terms, statements, opinions, beliefs, tend to remain static in spite of changing circumstances: Supreme Court$_{1954}$ is not Supreme Court$_{2006}$. This also takes into account that the same object or person may differ from day to day: violin (dry day) is not violin (wet day), etc.

3. *Et cetera*: All statements should be accompanied by an implicit "etc." to remind one that no statement about objects or events in the real world is apt to be final or complete; "That's all there is to it" is more often a statement of attitude than a description of dynamic reality. One must remain open to new insights and experiences, etc.

4. *The "is" of identity*: The common injunction to call a spade a spade has the profoundly misleading implication that we call it a spade because that's what it *is*; in fact, that's one arbitrary name of an implement. To be cautious of the "is" of identity is to guard against confusing verbal descriptions with actual entities or events, etc.

5. *Quotation marks*: Much beloved by intellectuals who use hand signals to indicate them, the use of quotation marks grew from the awareness that many terms in everyday use have pre-scientific metaphysical or profoundly abstract implications. Words like "race," "mind," "objective," "subjective," "love," and even "sane" should be used in at least implicit quotation marks as a reminder that, if a context is not defined, they are not to be trusted, etc.

6. *Hyphens*: Traditional language has separated structurally things
not separated in nature. A revolution in physics was accomplished
by Einstein's demonstration that "space-time" is one. The use
of hyphenated terms such as "socio-economic," "bio-physics,"
"geo-political," "socio-cultural," even "hip-hop" and "boogie-
woogie," sharpens the awareness of the interrelatedness (or
"inter-relatedness") of events which traditional language can
treat as unrelated, etc.

The admonition of some critics of GS that using language to discuss
itself was an inherently flawed process—especially in the hands of a
non-academic like Korzybski—led the latter to point toward Ber-
trand Russell's theory of types. That is, a class cannot be a member
of itself, so you can have language$_1$ about objects and events, and
language$_2$ about language$_1$ and objects and events, and language$_3$
about language$_1$ and language$_2$ as well as objects and events, etc. This
extrapolation from Russell's groundbreaking mathematical work led
to Korzybski's Structural Differential and Hayakawa's Ladder of
Abstraction.

All those techniques and insights were swirling in the young scholar's mind when he wrote "The Meaning of Semantics," published
in the August 2, 1939, issue of the *New Republic*. The essay, perhaps
Hayakawa's finest early publication, was composed to counter a negative reference to general semantics ("the opium of Stuart Chase") in
the pages of the *Partisan Review*. Don's presentation demonstrated
how accomplished a writer he had by then become. For instance,
scorning the "right name" superstition and the "defining-your-terms"
superstition, which have their roots in word magic, he suggested that
readers be aware of the aforementioned "*is* of identity" ("Bossie is a
cow"), which "conveys no structural implications which might show
the symbolic relationship that exists between Bossie [the animal] and
the word 'cow.'"

He then extrapolated to some loaded terms in common usage:
someone is a "Jew, Stalinist, Trotskyite, banker, workingman, nigger," or any of thousands of other powerful words that often stop

our active evaluations when used because we think we know what the things they stand for really *are*. That kind of "knowledge," when accepted, is so inflexible that it renders the accumulation of new, possibly conflicting information unlikely indeed. As for defining terms, he pointed out that meaning is derived from a context not dictionary definitions, and "the verbal context itself derives its meaning from a larger social context. *The 'meaning' of a term is a statement of its relationship to its context, or possible contexts.*"

Finally, the young professor took on the omnipresent "two-valued orientation," which means thinking of things only in terms of "good and bad, hot and cold, God and Satan, rich and poor, etc." Pointing out that such judgments may be true to language but not to nature, he wrote, "This two-valued orientation underlies most of our thinking except in technological matters. . . . How far could modern engineering have got if we had thermometers which could give only two readings, 'hot' and 'cold'?" He further pointed out that "authoritarian regimes such as those of fascism hold their power and silence criticism by the strictest adherence to two-valued orientation: Aryanism *vs.* Non-Aryanism. . . . [O]ur two-valued orientation is not an adequate instrument for evaluation in an increasingly complex world."

Hayakawa concluded this powerful rebuttal of the criticism by noting that the works of such varied scholars as I. A. Richards and Rudolf Carnap, Leonard Bloomfield and Bronislaw Malinowski, like Korzybski's, "reveal a determination to increase the efficiency of thought through an improved understanding of how language works."

He applied such insights in yet another stimulating early publication about Korzybski's work, "General Semantics and Propaganda," in the April 1939 issue of *Public Opinion Quarterly*; it was an expanded version of a speech he had given to the National Council of Teachers of English the previous year. The essay urged the employment of Korzybski's insights for "epistemological re-education" to counter the effects of propaganda: "The propagandist will have lost his most powerful weapon, his ability to create automatic, associational responses [U.S. flag = patriotism]. . . . Without epistemological re-education, each such identification has to be separately refuted—and the ad-writer and propagandist can manufacture them much faster than a legion of teachers can refute them; whereas with epistemological re-education, refutation becomes unnecessary." Never an uncritical true believer, Hayakawa also pointed out that "difficulties or defects in Korzybski's theories may reveal themselves as they are put into practice by more people in more places."

Despite his growing prominence, Don, like most young instructors in the Extension Division, the next year taught mostly freshman composition, a course that senior professors avoided. Hayakawa introduced principals of general semantics into the mix and found that students responded positively. Wright Thomas, who was then a leader in the freshman English program at the university, later wrote, "I remember vividly the excitement of discovery in Hayakawa's reports to me on his experimental class taught without a text-book." Thomas further recalled, "When I proposed teaching his material in my division of Freshman English at Madison, he wrote a first version of the book." During the 1938–39 academic year Don began composition in earnest, planning and drafting what he thought would be a freshman English textbook: "Essentially it was also a political act, asserting my belief in a rational society as opposed to a Nazi society where people go crazy over slogans, incantation, and torch-light marches. It was written so that young people could learn to be wary of propaganda." He tried out various exercises and insights on his classes that year without the endorsement of the Count. Marge Hayakawa added, "He never showed his work to Korzybski, because Korzybski never looked at anybody else's work."

That employment of ideas for and elements of the text in freshman classes was successful, and the book-in-progress was altered to reflect what worked and to reject what didn't. Fortunately, much of it worked well indeed. As a result, in 1939 under Thomas's aegis, the class of about two thousand entering students was divided into three groups: one would be taught a program based on the Great Books approach promoted by Robert Hutchins at the University of

Chicago; another, led by activist professor Bill Card, would focus on current events; the third was assigned Hayakawa's semantic approach and would use mimeographed and spiral-bound copies of what he called *Language in Action*. That self-published version of Don's book was used on the Madison campus as well as in his own hinterland classes. Recalled Thomas, "It kept students awake all night reading it."

Jackson Benson, biographer of Wallace Stegner among others, offers a perspective on the adoption: "Not only were the young instructors [at UWM] closely supervised, they were all required to teach the same text and give the same assignments. This was extremely difficult for young people who were experimental by nature and bursting with creative ideas and energy. S. I. Hayakawa's *Language in Thought and Action* [a later title], begun as a freshman composition text, was written in part as a protest to this enforced conformity." The university had assembled a rather remarkable cadre of young instructors then, including not only Stegner and Hayakawa but Curtis Bradford, Claude Simpson, and Stuart Brown; the latter remembered Stegner "challenging his classes with parts of Hayakawa's work-in-progress, a somewhat revolutionary view of language and communication at that time."

Such a gang was the more extraordinary since, as Stegner later wrote, "deep in Depression, universities had given up promoting and all but given up hiring." Of that group of untenured professors, Stegner, a novelist who had previously studied at the University of Utah, reflected, "We were all interested in the same things, and the quality of conversation at parties and so on, as between Salt Lake City and Madison, was—whew!—up like that. It was like the first year in graduate school. You had the feeling you were learning at four times the normal pace." Those young faculty and their families frequently socialized, and Stegner's widow, Mary, remembers the Hayakawas as social friends.

Meanwhile, Don's review-essay "Is Indeed 5" appeared in the August 1938 number of *Poetry*, arguably the most prestigious of all journals of verse. "No modern poet to my knowledge," he wrote, "has such a clear, child-like perception as e. e. cummings—a way of coming smack against things with unaffected delight and candor. . . . [This is] a quality he shares with William Carlos Williams, just about equally, although, to be sure, Williams is not child-like." Poetry remained Don's first—but no longer his only—love, and his own verse would sporadically appear not only in *Poetry* but in other journals.

More important to him, though, was that students and colleagues alike discovered that his book-in-progress on language offered an innovative, interesting approach to freshman composition. Word spread of Hayakawa's highly original text, and "somewhere between twelve and fifteen publishers' representatives bought copies of the book and sent them back to their head offices."

However, Don's success didn't endear him to senior faculty at UWM, because, writes Benson, English departments at that time "often had a positive antipathy for those who were considered 'mere journalists,' faculty members who published in general-audience magazines or wrote nonacademic books. Wisconsin, which considered itself something of an elite school, had a good measure of that kind of snobbery, as well as a protectiveness that set the older generation of faculty against the younger." Stegner, for example, had embarked on his acclaimed literary career earlier by winning the Little, Brown Prize for his novelette *Remembering Laughter*. Remarkably, this placed his career there in jeopardy. Hayakawa was scorned in large measure because his own book was so readable.

As it turned out, UWM would eventually have to flourish without either Stegner or Hayakawa, and the university's reputation wasn't enhanced by that. Why the school would not retain young men as promising as those two is perhaps best explained in Stegner's final novel, *Crossing to Safety*, when English professor Sid Lang explains to the protagonist, Larry Morgan, who has not been retained by the department, "You threaten the weak sisters. They don't want distinction around, it would show them up. Energy and talent like yours are bombs under their beds. . . . They're ingrown, inbred, lazy, and

scared. They don't dare let people like you into the department."
The character of Morgan was based closely on Stegner himself.

Don continued to use *Language in Action* with his own students,
and he consulted with other teachers to find out what in the text
worked and what didn't in their classes. Then he rethought, revised,
and polished the text. At the same time he continued seeking a
tenure-track position elsewhere, but during those tight economic
times jobs were scarce indeed. Ultimately he found an instructorship
at the Armour Institute of Technology in Chicago for $1,900 a year,
though the process that led to the job was far from straightforward.
He later recalled, "The idea of hiring a Japanese to be an English
instructor was too far out. They had to have a full faculty meeting,
despite the fact that I already had my Ph.D. and a book out by then.
I don't mean *Language in Action*, but my scholarly work on Oliver
Wendell Holmes. But imagine! A full faculty meeting. To decide on
one lousy instructor!" Instructor was a low rank for a teacher with
a PhD, but it was better than no rank at all. In the fall of 1939, he
and Marge moved into a two-bedroom apartment in Chicago on
Sixty-seventh Street facing Jackson Park, and he began teaching.

Armour Tech was a solid but not an especially prestigious school,
much overshadowed by Northwestern and the University of Chicago.
Founded in 1893, Armour Tech offered courses in engineering,
chemistry, architecture, and library science, and it soon developed
strong ties to major local industries like electricity and insurance,
making the school a positive force in the Midwest. The city had been
in a state of transformation in 1893, as Robert Kargon and Scott
Knowels explain in *Annals of Science*: "Chicago also transformed itself
into the incandescent 'White City,' hosting the World's Colombian
Exposition. This event, above all others, established Chicago in the
American public consciousness as the symbolic home of cutting edge
technology." By the time the Hayakawas arrived, the Windy City
was an exciting place indeed, with many cultures, much innovation,
and a sense of the possible, despite the lingering shadow of the Great
Depression.

But for the young instructor, the city's first appeal was simple: it offered a job. The institute had no English majors and not much of an English Department; it offered no literature courses that would allow its new professor to explore the work of Eliot or Holmes, let alone extol the wonders of Middle English. Rather, Don taught freshman composition and some technical writing to future engineers, chemists, architects, and librarians, nearly all males, many of whom were not particularly interested in English when they began his class. The young instructor pointed out that writing well is an advantage in virtually every profession and a disadvantage in none. "It's not just for English majors." One student, Morgan Fitch, noted that he and his classmates were Hayakawa's "guinea pigs for *Language in Action*. I remember him trying to explain language by saying, 'Do you call a piece of beef filet mignon or say it is a piece of a dead cow?'"

In 1940 Armour Tech merged with Lewis Institute to become Illinois Institute of Technology, but Don's classes didn't change much: "We were teaching people grammar, spelling, etc., so they learned how to write instead of just babbling on. . . . That was good experience for me in organizing my own ideas, how prose ought to be organized." He added, "I got to be very good friends with a lot of my students at that time. . . . I appealed to some very, very nice students, who were tired of talking about engineering all the damn time and wanted to talk about something else, about the rest of the world, about politics, about poetry—anything. I got along well with them."

With international events continuing to spiral out of control, fascism and Nazism swarming Europe while Japan continued to dominate Asia, Don stripped the glory and romance from war with one of his most powerful, original poems, "A Matter of Linguistics," which appeared in the *New Republic* on January 8, 1940. "The syntax of Force is simple," the work began, and it closed with this line: "Its lexicon, the simple semantics of destruction." Like every thinking person of his time, the poet could not help but be both moved and worried by international events.

Moreover, as a man of Japanese extraction, one who believed in a broadly American identity, since both Canada and the United States were his home, Hayakawa was especially concerned about events in Asia because, symbolically at least, he was caught in the middle, while his parents were there in fact. Concurrently in the United States, Curtis B. Munson, a special representative of the State Department, at the behest of President Franklin Roosevelt, wrote a report about the danger posed by Japanese on the West Coast and in Hawaii. "There is no Japanese problem on the Coast," he concluded. "There will be no armed uprising of Japanese in the United States." Historian Ken Adachi might have spoken for all when he observed, "To the Nisei, it was not a question of what *they* would do—as they were so often asked by curious friends—but of what Canada and white Canadians would do." Even in the midlands of both the United States and Canada, people of Japanese extraction couldn't be certain what war would bring them, but they tended to hope for the best. Reports Adachi, "The desperate naivete of their belief in 'democracy'—in retrospect almost childlike—was touching and pathetic."

Marge was visiting family in March 1940, and her husband wrote her a newsy letter, telling her about a meeting at the Hyde Park Co-op that led him to join, about a movie "date" with M. Kendig ("Saw the 'Earl of Chicago,' with Robert Montgomery."), and about his excess energy ("It's terrific the number of themes I have got through. I'm really all caught up. And the car is washed—I washed it yesterday, and over half of it is waxed"). Then he cut to the chase: "Everything is going well. Am eating regularly and am extremely sex-starved. If you don't get back soon, I shall have to join the YMCA and work it off in the gym."

Meanwhile, Don continued tweaking "the book"—still only mimeographed and spiral-bound. It had begun to take on a life of its own; word of its novel approach spread, and some other colleges adopted the book that hadn't really been published yet, most notably Syracuse University, which assigned it to the entire freshman class—two thousand copies. As the author summarized, "They invited me to speak at a convocation with a huge audience. I had never addressed such a large group. I was scared to death." Many publishers were by then aware of the interesting and available little text, so offers to issue it began to pour in from major publishers, including Houghton Mifflin, Harper Brothers, Harcourt Brace, and Little, Brown. Don chose Harcourt Brace because it published e. e. cummings, one of his favorite poets.

fifteen

Harcourt Brace released *Language in Action* in late 1941. Ironically, between March and August of that year, while the book was in production, all Japanese men and women in British Columbia were registered and fingerprinted by the government. Neither aliens nor citizens of Italian or German descent were required to be similarly enrolled.

Upon publication, Hayakawa's book received widespread and enthusiastic reviews—an amazing response to what had been intended as a textbook. One opinion without byline in the *New Yorker*, for instance, described it as "a beautifully simple and illuminating introduction to semantics." Albert Guerard in *Books* wrote that *Language in Action* "is written with delightful simplicity and unobstructed humor. I note this 'general principle': 'the prevention of silence is itself an important function of speech': a remark so ingenious that it borders on the profound."

More impressive, perhaps, was W. E. Garrison noting in *Christian Century* that "when a literary editor reads a book twice before reviewing it, that's news. But this one was worth it." Alvin Adey, in *Current History*, topped even that kudo when he described the work as "a masterpiece of exposition, so simple and incisively written as to be nothing less than brilliant, and it's moreover enlivened by a constantly flashing humor and pithy common sense."

NYU professor Sidney Hook, a witty curmudgeon, begged to differ. Something of an elitist, he was not impressed by this popularization. "Presented as a textbook in rhetoric on the high-school level," he wrote in the *Nation*, "its naive and crude approach to the problems of language might be held excusable on pedagogical grounds. But it is offered to all and sundry as the wisdom 'of the twentieth century's newest science, semantics,' as an indispensable safeguard against superstition, propaganda, and inaccurate thinking."

So trenchant a view of *Language in Action* was countered by Henry Hazlitt's equally influential opinion in the *New York Times*: "It is precisely what a popularization should be. It is very smoothly and lucidly written; it is compact; it is lively; it is logical and informative, and it reveals unusual intellectual acuteness. It makes no claims to basic originality."

The cover of the November 22, 1941, issue of the *Saturday Review of Literature* featured a rather glamorous portrait of S. I. Hayakawa. Within its pages, the featured article—more essay than review—was "Do Words Scare Us?" by Fred C. Kelly, well known as the biographer of the Wright brothers. Kelly's piece summarized many major precepts from *Language in Action* and illustrated their value and usefulness. "Most of us are incapable at times of looking at facts, because our thinking is obstructed by mere words," he observed. "Many of us seem to think words are actually the same as the objects they are supposed to 'stand for.' If this were not true, why would thousands of radio listeners write fan letters to imaginary characters in radio dramas and even send gifts to nonexistent babies?" Kelly recognized the practical value of Hayakawa's book, and his evaluation of it in arguably the nation's most influential literary magazine helped vault the young professor to something bordering on celebrity.

Beyond flattering reviews and cover photos, events behind the scenes were conspiring to make Hayakawa's book even better known and to heighten the author's public profile. The distinguished botanist David Fairchild, a close friend of Korzybski's, had lectured at the Institute of General Semantics on August 28, 1940. While there he met Hayakawa, who gave him one or more prepublication proofs of *Language in Action*. Fairchild, in turn, gave a copy to a friend of his, the novelist Dorothy Canfield Fisher, who was one of the selectors for the Book-of-the-Month Club. She read the bound page proofs, was taken with Hayakawa's work, and actually asked the publisher to delay its release until a final decision on adoption could be made by the club. This was in early 1941 while Don was finishing the index for the Harcourt Brace edition. Korzybski, who closely followed these developments, reportedly wrote to Fairchild, "We are also elated with the appreciation of the book by Hayakawa. It will mean a great deal to us."

Marge, meanwhile, found herself in Ohio dealing with the death of an aunt and the tangle of family business that ensued. Don, more than a little stunned at his good fortune, sent her notes he had received from Fairchild and Fisher. Very much his partner in the enterprise, she wrote back on February 18, "I *will* be home to help you with the index, anyway. How is the rest getting on? . . . I miss you constantly, but things are so awfully sad and mixed up here that I've had to be what help I can."

That summer, prior to his book's release, Don had been just another young professor when he attended the Second American Congress on General Semantics at the University of Denver. A few months later he was a fledgling star when *Language in Action* became the first textbook ever offered by the Book-of-the-Month Club, a double selection (with George R. Stewart's novel, *Storm*) for December 1941. Korzybski wrote to Don: "Dear Heathen: We are most excited about the Book-of-the-Month Club news. Certainly Fairchild through Fisher made good. Please accept my warmest congratulations. With warmest wishes, yours Cordially."

Club members were sent information about the selections and had to decide to purchase or reject by December 1, six days before the bombing of Pearl Harbor. A great many responded affirmatively, and the book became a minor best-seller. The stars had certainly been aligned in Don's favor for, as his wife pointed out, "The book came out and was distributed at Pearl Harbor time, . . . a book by an author with a Japanese name would have been dead in the water if the announcement had come out two weeks later."

Another kind of attack would rumble into Don's life as a result of *Language in Action*. "It must have been a stunning blow to all kinds of professors who wrote books, to have a book hit this kind of jackpot," Marge speculated. Among a certain segment of the academic community, Hayakawa would henceforth be dismissed as a popularizer, as if all his academic achievements and publications prior to *Language in Action* meant nothing. Had he continued publishing thoughtful, clever essays on writers and literary topics, there is reason to believe that a career which had already found his work appearing in important journals such as *PMLA*, *Sewanee Review*, *Studies in English Literature*, and *American Speech* might one day have led to a post at a major university.

That seemed unimportant at the time, because Japan's December 7 attack on America's Pacific Fleet changed the world. Japanese Canadians and Japanese Americans, in particular, were profoundly affected. For instance, Ken Adachi reports that in British Columbia "the bombing of Pearl Harbor provided anti-Japanese interests in the province with a savoury propaganda item which far exceeded their most optimistic hopes." The same, sadly, was true in the United States, and a dark period indeed ensued. Political scientist Daniel I. Okimoto explained, "No matter how vehemently sympathy for the enemy cause was disclaimed or instances of subversion disproved, the Japanese in America simply could not escape the stigma of nearly a century of racist paranoia abruptly rekindled by Pearl Harbor."

Ken Eidnes, who would eventually serve in the Army Air Corps unit that dropped the atomic bombs on Hiroshima and Nagasaki, remembered the war's first dark days this way: "In December 1941 I was a student at Armour Inst. of Tech [by then it had become Illinois Tech]. Mr. Hayakawa was my English teacher. On Dec. 8th he did not come to school, being Japanese we thought he went into hiding. He did come in on the 9th and continued for the rest of the semester. He was a great man and it took a lot of courage to do that." Hayakawa himself recalled that on December 7, one of his students had telephoned and asked, "Hey, Doc, are dey boddering ya?" As it turned out, the Hayakawas were not harassed, but "eight or ten students from the ethnic part of Chicago, the children of Slovak and Italian immigrants, . . . offered to come over and gang up and protect me from anti-Japanese demonstrations or anything that might occur."

Don revealed his most candid feelings about the conflict in an undated essay titled "Why I Hope America Will Win." Seeking to deflect the negative sentiments and the growing threat of government action against Japanese Americans, he pointed out that most of them were more American than Japanese, perhaps far more: "All of them have been imbued with the ideals of democracy, which they have understood and appreciated in spite of the discrimination which they have often suffered. Most . . . , like myself, have never been seriously exposed to any other kind of ideals than those which America offers." He pointed out, too, that "the 'nouveau American' is often twice as patriotic as one who has long taken his Americanism for granted" as well as "committed to the American way of life. It is the only one we know, and the only one we would care to fight for."

Hayakawa, the Canadian, wasn't through. He argued further that "all his present rights as an American and all his hopes for the future are bound up in the triumph and extension of democracy.

> The Japanese Americans are willing and eager to do their part. And from what I know of them, they will do it willingly and well. But there is one thing I earnestly implore the reader to remember: lay off that stuff about "yellow rats." There are thousands of "yellow" men fighting for us. . . . If, through careless talk and misdirected anger, we make a "race" war out of this fight, we shall be doing the very thing which outrages us most about Hitlerism. This is not, let me repeat, a war of peoples, but a war of ideals: the open, free, equalitarian [sic] ideals of the democracies against the closed, barbaric tribalism of the totalitarian mob-states. Let's not forget what the shooting is about.

Despite such reasoned appeals, the anti-Asian sentiment that had long been simmering just below the surface on the West Coast erupted. Census figures showed that 112,353 Japanese Americans resided in California, Oregon, and Washington, so those states seemed to some to be threatened from within. On January 29, 1942, the

U.S. Justice Department began removing Japanese and Japanese Americans from areas selected by the Western Defense Command of the Army, but that wasn't nearly enough for extremists. Even famed columnist Walter Lippman joined the anti-Japanese cacophony when he wrote, "The Pacific Coast is in imminent danger of a combined attack from within and without. . . . Since the outbreak of the . . . war there has been no important sabotage on the Pacific Coast. . . . This is not, as some have liked to think, a sign there is nothing to be feared. It is a sign that the blow is well organized and it is held back until it can be struck with maximum effect."

Canadians weren't much wiser. The redoubtable anti-Asian Thomas Reid "grumbled in the House of Commons that there had been no sabotage committed in Canada because the time was 'not yet ripe.'" As if to prove the need for a book such as *Language in Action*, both Lippman and Reid used the fact that there had been no attacks to prove the danger of future attacks.

Don had his own run-ins with misdirected anger. That same year, for instance, while waiting for a train in a small Wisconsin town, he entered a crowded bar:

> There were two men over here, and there was me, and there were two women over there.
>
> Somehow the conversation involved the two women and the two men and me. . . . But some drunk came in and said, pointing at me, "I want that Goddamn Jap out of here." Being my particular size, I wasn't going to go after him with my fists, but I could pretend I was going to, which I did. . . . The two girls grabbed me and said, "Don't do it! He's twice your size, for God's sake!"
>
> And this great big guy sitting next to me said to the assailant, "Why don't you pick on somebody your own size?" They had some words. . . .
>
> And you know, those two guys went outside and had a fight right there.

Only Don's advocate returned to the bar, but he did so minus a tooth. "We all sat down and had more drinks."

Don Hayakawa readily acknowledged it had been his good fortune to be residing in the Midwest when Pearl Harbor was bombed and war was declared. On the day after the attack, Representative John M. Coffee from Washington's Sixth District pleaded in Congress, "It is my fervent hope and prayer that residents of the United States of Japanese extraction will not be made the victim of pogroms directed by self-proclaimed and by hysterical self-anointed heroes. . . . Let us not make a mockery of our Bill of Rights by mistreating these folks." Unfortunately, voices like his were drowned out by the bigots, the opportunists, and the fearful, calling—usually in the guise of patriotism—for concentration camps or relocation or worse, making a mockery of the Bill of Rights.

Occasionally, "patriotic" groups or individuals were so emboldened by the anti-Japanese climate that they told the truth. A spokesperson for the Grower-Shipper Vegetable Association, for instance, reportedly said: "We've been charged with wanting to get rid of the Japs for selfish reasons. We might as well be honest. We do. It's a question of whether the white man lives on the Pacific Coast or the brown man. They came into this valley to work, and they stayed to take over. . . . If all the Japs were removed tomorrow, we'd never miss them in two weeks, because the white farmers can take over and produce everything the Jap can grow."

Undisguised racism and more than a little lingering "yellow-peril" thinking were also revealed when Lieutenant General John L. DeWitt, leader of the military's Western Defense Command, wrote in a recommendation for relocation of Japanese and Japanese Americans, "In the war in which we are now engaged racial affinities are not severed by migration. The Japanese race is an enemy race and while many second and third generation Japanese born on United States soil, possessed of United States citizenship, have become 'Americanized,' the racial strains are undiluted. . . . It, therefore, follows that along the vital Pacific Coast over 112,000 potential enemies . . . are at large today."

Japanese Americans (and Japanese Canadians) made considerable efforts to disprove such allegations as well as to demonstrate their loyalty. Shunzo Sakamaki of the Oahu Citizens Committee for Home Defense, for instance, declared, "Japan has chosen to fight us and we'll fight." Still, the political forces assembled against West Coast Japanese prevailed, and on April 30, 1942, Exclusion Order no. 27 was posted, leading to the evacuation of Japanese and Japanese Americans there; Ronald Takaki reports that one of the Sone brothers asked, "Doesn't my citizenship mean a blessed single thing to anyone?"

In Canada, nearly everyone of Japanese extraction became an "enemy alien," even World War I veterans, so all those living west of the Cascades were uprooted and relocated inland under the mandate of the War Measures Act. Their properties were confiscated and sold without their consent. At the same time, Adachi reports, "Those Nisei who took pride in being steeped in the tradition of 'British justice' and 'fair play' . . . felt an acute sense of betrayal."

During that same period, life flowered for the Hayakawas in Chicago. He was a professor and a nationally recognized author: "By that time I was known. I was writing book reviews for *The Chicago Sun*, and I had just become part of the community." Marge was also busy reviewing books for the *Sun*, while becoming an increasingly important cog in Chicago's co-op movement, the first female president of the Hyde Park Co-op. The Hayakawas were financially secure due to not only Don's job and royalties but also to Marge's inheritance from her father's estate and other family legacies. When the poet Leo Kennedy, Don's McGill University pal, moved to the Windy City in 1942, he and his wife "began life in Chicago as guests of the Hayakawas, then moved to a small, walk-up second-story flat that their hosts had helped them find" in the Hyde Park district. Leo had by then become an adept advertising man, a career Don had encouraged him to pursue. The Hayakawas could afford to share their digs, time, and talents generously, and they did.

When Don was offered the opportunity to become a columnist for the *Chicago Defender*, one of America's most important African American newspapers, an administrator at Illinois Tech "thought it was very damaging and dangerous for any of us to be mixed up with a Negro newspaper, especially for a Japanese," Hayakawa later explained. "This was during the first nervous months of the war. There was even a rumor published in the Hearst newspapers that Japanese naval officers had been working in the Negro community to create disloyalty for the United States." Don replied, "Thank you for your advice. I'll think it over. . . . I never went back to see him, and just kept on writing [for the *Defender*] right through 1947."

He would produce columns about many topics, and he found in the black community subjects that challenged his assumptions. His interest in music would also lead him into the local jazz scene, another largely black domain, where he would become an acknowledged authority, and he would begin the study of African art that eventually led him to become something of an expert as well. Increasingly, his intellectual eclecticism became evident in his writing, and he seemed to manage reasonably deep understanding of most subjects.

As the decade progressed, the Hayakawas were a conspicuously successful couple about town, though not members of high society. "We never had any real organized social life," recalled Marge. "We saw all the people that we could get into our crowded lives through his teaching work and other interests we had." As something akin to fame propelled the young professor onto the national lecture circuit, he was afforded a taste of celebrity as well as enhanced income. Don's Japanese name and face made him exotic to many in his audiences, and while there was no question that he enjoyed the attention, he rode the wave in typical low-key fashion. "What I remember so much about the Book-of-the-Month Club selection, which was really hitting the jackpot, is that we bought that Nash convertible, the snappy-looking number."

The couple drove to California, where Don had a speaking engagement. Despite the gasoline shortage, Marge remembered, "We had a marvelous trip West, and there's nothing like traveling through the West in a convertible." That Hayakawa was able to make such a journey and enjoy his newfound prominence at the very time Japanese Californians—including his aunt, uncle, and cousins—were languishing in internment camps bespeaks the absurdity of the time.

Among followers of general semantics, Hayakawa was indeed a celebrity, and in Los Angeles they were met by Vocha Fiske, whom they had earlier encountered at one of Korzybski's seminars. Fiske was one of the genuine characters of the semantics movement, an ex-vaudevillian and a flamboyant redhead who required no assertiveness training. "We stayed at the Hollywood Roosevelt," Don remembered. "Vocha Fiske came into our room and said 'This won't do, this won't do.' And she called the main office at once and said, 'Don't you realize we have Dr. Hayakawa here?'" She "got us a more magnificent room right away."

"She was an interesting person," he explained, "because she was halfway between being an interesting and serious student of general semantics, and the other half of her was the kind of nut that gets mixed up in any damn movement." Late in her life, Fiske wrote a highly opinionated manuscript, "Sanity Fair," about her experiences with the general semantics group, but it was never published.

Back from the trip to the West Coast, Hayakawa worked his way up the professorial ranks like every other young teacher at Illinois Tech. "Easily recognized by his trademark tam-o-shanter," writes Elizabeth Kaye, "Hayakawa cut a vivid figure on IIT's campus." It was common for young PhDs to be hired as assistant professors, a step above Don's initial rank, but he never bothered to publicly discuss the why of his lower initial status; he simply set about proving himself worthy of a higher rank, and he did that.

His colleagues all recognized that the success of Hayakawa's first book had been unusual indeed, and some reacted negatively. Don would later recall especially the response of literary critic Elder Olson, who was Illinois Tech's other well-known English professor. Olson was a proponent of the literary school of thought called "Chicago Criticism," and his work was actually similar to Don's—a language-based approach to literature that involved "semantic orientation," "propositional structures," "truth value," and "principles of validation," among other elements that could have come from Hayakawa's own writing. But Olson's approach was more literary and abstract: "The words must be explained in terms of something else, not the poem in terms of the words," he wrote, "and further, a principle must be a principle of something other than itself; hence the words cannot be a principle of their own arrangements." As Hayakawa, a student of the theory of types, might have summarized, a class cannot be a member of itself. Whether it was the perceived threat posed by the similarity of their interests or merely jealously at the younger prof's sudden and quite remarkable prominence, Olson was, Hayakawa recalled, "always competing. Instead of respecting each other's work, being friends on that account . . . he always regarded me as a kind of threat." It would not be the last time colleagues made assumptions about S. I. Hayakawa based on their own insecurities.

Meantime, from his perch in Chicago, Hayakawa observed language being misused and misunderstood on all sides as international tension seemed to strip rationality. André Gide, for example, would later write about his experience with the Communist Party this way: "They explained to me that a word like 'destiny' must always be preceded by the epithet 'glorious' when it referred to the destiny of the Soviet Union; on the other hand they requested me to delete the adjective 'great' when it qualified a king since a monarch can never be 'great'!" The word was indeed becoming the thing—in international politics at least—and Hayakawa's book exposing that problem continued to sell.

As his own name became more and more identified with general semantics, Hayakawa began to overshadow Alfred Korzybski in the public's perception. The latter, who spoke of himself in the same breath as Aristotle and Newton, resented his disciple's prominence, while at the same time he appreciated the new acceptance it brought to his work. Onetime GS acolyte Anatol Rapoport said that *Language in Action* "clarified the basic ideas of Korzybski's magnum opus, *Science and Sanity*, retaining their full strength but trimming away the author's narcissistic posturing and obscure verbiage. I read *Science and Sanity* in Alaska in 1943 and at the time dismissed it as pompous nonsense. But soon afterward I stumbled on Hayakawa's miniature masterpiece and changed my mind."

Certainly even Korzybski acknowledged that interest in the subject had been much heightened by the success of Hayakawa's *Language in Action* and Chase's *The Tyranny of Words*, drawing many prominent and soon-to-be-prominent figures to GS. At the 1940 seminar, for instance, Hayakawa had met and become friendly with the science-fiction writer Robert Heinlein, who then lived in Chicago, as well as with the philosopher Gaston Bachelard.

five

WORLD WAR II

sixteen

Don's Canadian citizenship placed him in an uncommon bracket for someone of Japanese descent in the United States. "It really peeved the authorities that the categories didn't work out very well," recalled Marge. Her husband had been summoned for several interviews, but as a Canadian national who didn't live on the West Coast, he didn't fit categories that would have resulted in internment. At a time when the intention was to move Japanese Americans and Canadians inland, he was already there.

Meanwhile, on the west coasts of both nations, "Japs" or "Nips," as they were called, were forced to "endure social ostracism and financial losses, as well as the harsh and largely primitive living conditions in the [relocation] camps. Families were turned upside down as Japanese-speaking fathers relinquished their positions of authority in the household to their English-speaking children. Worse yet, some fathers were removed from the family altogether and placed in separate camps," explain Deborah Mieko Burns and Karen Kanemoto. As an anonymous haiku from that time puts it:

Birds,
> Living in a cage,
> The human spirit.

The camps were the worst of it, but the war also prompted simmering racism to bubble to the surface nearly everywhere. William Hohri, who later founded the National Council for Japanese American Redress, recalls: "I hated being Japanese in wartime America. The use of the J-word was blatant. We were 'Japs' all over the place—in newspaper headlines, political speeches, radio comedy routines, popular songs ('You're a Sap, Mr. Jap'). We were 'sneaky,' 'treacherous,' even 'lecherous.'"

Although spared internment and relocation, Don Hayakawa could not avoid racism; fortunately, midwesterners were far less vehement in their practice of it. In 1984 he told the Commission on Wartime Internment and Relocation of Citizens that "as a Japanese-American, I find myself both awed and humbled by Japanese-American behavior during World War II." He further explained, "My wife and I . . . followed with intense interest what was happening to the Japanese in California. We read accounts in newspapers and . . . particularly pictorial weeklies like *Life Magazine*. We saw newsreels. What impressed us again and again was the dignity, the grace and realism of Japanese behavior under these difficult and humiliating circumstances. They kept their dignity."

After observing that the internment "was not necessary for the defense of America, but there was no way of telling in January, 1942," Hayakawa especially praised the "stoicism and dignity" of the Issei as they accepted "the discomforts and the agonies of relocation," as well as the courage and sacrifices of Nisei who fought for the United States not only in Europe but in the Pacific theater. "Since they had been suspected of disloyalty, they had to prove themselves loyal beyond all questions, beyond all doubt." They certainly did that. As General Joseph Stillwell summarized, "They bought an awful hunk of America with their blood. . . . [T]hose Nisei boys have a place in the American heart, now and forever."

During the war, some interned Japanese Americans found the prospects of relocation in Chicago far more desirable than life in isolated camps in the West. "In 1942, Hayakawa was contacted by his old Wisconsin roommate Robert Frase, who had been recruited to join the War Relocation Authority (WRA) by director Dillon Myer," Canadian writer Greg Robinson explains. "In part through knowing Hayakawa, Frase was convinced that Japanese Americans were loyal, and he and his supervisor Tom Holland opposed confinement and lobbied Myer to authorize immediate resettlement. When Frase visited Chicago to establish a resettlement office there, Hayakawa hosted him at his house and advised him on securing jobs and housing for resettlers."

Part of the dormitory at Bethel Theological Seminary in the city was designated as a resettlement hostel for displaced Japanese Americans, and programs were developed to help people adjust to their new surroundings, to find a place to live and to work. Rev. Daisuke Kitagawa, who visited the Chicago hostel, warned against "what one might call self-imposed segregation. There was, or should have been, nothing wrong with this under normal circumstances, but in 1943, when American sentiment was running high against anything Japanese, it was not a very wise choice, to say the least."

The resettlement hostel in Chicago became so successful that versions were opened in Minneapolis, Brooklyn, Cleveland, Philadelphia, and Des Moines, and the War Relocation Authority paid travel costs of internees to their inland destination of choice, as well as two weeks of living expenses; after that they were on their own. Many chose to remain in Chicago. Burns and Kanemoto explain: "In the months and years that followed, these Japanese American evacuees faced continued challenges as they were allowed to leave the camps, move eastward, and resettle in areas away from their original homes. During the resettlement years, roughly 1942–50, nearly 30,000 Japanese Americans, attracted by the availability of jobs, sought to make new lives for themselves in Chicago."

Don's aunt Satoe (then called Mary), her husband, George Furuyama, and their children—William, Charles, and Helen—had been shipped to a camp in Rohwer, Arkansas. The family, which had been running a small hotel in Stockton, California, before the war, lost that property, and took advantage of the opportunity to move to Chicago, where they, somewhat serendipitously, connected with their nephew.

Helen Furuyama Yoshida recalls seeing the name S. I. Hayakawa in the literary section of the *Chicago Tribune*. "I told Momma, who immediately called her brother, Saburo, living in Montreal. 'Yes,' he replied. 'Our older brother, Ichiro, has a son, your nephew, living in Chicago.' Excitedly, she asked me to make contact." Helen hesitated, wondering, "What could a young, naive inexperienced girl from the country have in common with such a personage as Dr. Hayakawa—except for the same set of grandparents."

Finally overcoming her reluctance, Helen telephoned her famous relative. "My first call elicited the reply that he, Don, was also overjoyed to discover a relative and that we should meet as soon as possible. . . . Soon Don and Marge enveloped my parents and me with their genuine warmth and care and love at a time we needed it most." Don explained that before Helen's call, "I had not even known of their existence, since my father and Mary, although brother and sister, were far apart in age, had emigrated at different times, and had lost touch with each other."

Helen's older brother, William "Bill" Furuyama, had been drafted in 1942 and was "given basic training several times over, while the army tried to figure out what to do with its Japanese-American recruits." Bill eventually served first in Italy, then in Germany, and was twice wounded. He returned home "covered with medals," according to his proud cousin. The younger Furuyama son, called "Chuck," would serve with the American Occupation Forces in Germany. Helen married George Yoshida in the Hayakawas' Chicago apartment, and George would serve with occupation forces in Japan.

Of the Furuyamas, Marge noted that they came to Chicago in the first place without knowing how they'd be received, and that it "took a lot of courage. But Chicago was very open." Pragmatism seems to have been a characteristic of the extended Hayakawa family; when she was asked about the relocation at the time, Don's aunt replied, "What do you expect, there's a war on!"

During those tough years, the Hayakawas did what they could to help others relocated from the West Coast, and welcomed into their home a young scientist, Dr. Mikeo Murayama, from San Francisco. Removed from his residence and college position, Dr. Murayama lived with the Hayakawas for most of 1943 while doing research at the University of Chicago. He eventually departed for a career that would see him become one of the world's authorities on sickle-cell anemia, coauthor of a book considered definitive on the disease, and winner of the first Martin Luther King Award. Although they lost contact with Dr. Murayama after the war, the fact that the young couple had opened their door to a stranger in distress was typical of the time.

Don also met a Mr. Toguri, like himself a Canadian expatriate, who nearly four decades earlier had hired young Ichiro Hayakawa when Don's parents had been stranded in Vancouver. In a later letter, the elder Hayakawa recalled with considerable gratitude, "Mr. Toguri was kind enough to offer me a job to work in his store, not because he needed an assistant, but just to help me." The resourceful Mr. Toguri would later open a store in Chicago.

Not since his infanthood in Vancouver had Don Hayakawa lived in a city with a large Japanese presence, so his experience of ethnicity and culture was significantly different from that of most Nisei raised on the West Coast. Although proud of his heritage, he had throughout his memory been part of the larger, heterogeneous society, and he was an unabashed assimilationist. Later, when the renowned sociologist Setsuko Matsunaga Nishi invited him to join the board of the Chicago Resettlement Committee, he reportedly replied, "Why do you want to pull me back? Can't I just be a model of what a person of Japanese ancestry can achieve by assimilating?" Despite that, he did serve.

Chicago had no Japanese section, but it was a somewhat balkanized community with this group or that dominating neighborhoods—blacks here, Italians there, Ukrainians across the way. The most important bridge Don and Marge would find to those enclaves was the consumer co-op movement. The Hayakawas were powerfully committed to the co-op concept. Being liberals, they "thought at the time . . . that the capitalist system was essentially exploitative, and we liked the idea of cooperatives in which there was no exploitation, in which business is organized to actually serve the people, rather than to make a profit." Marge was no "joiner"—she refused to become part of Korzybski's circle, for example—but she was a prodigious and gifted worker when a cause seemed right, so she soon found herself not only on the board of directors for the Hyde Park Co-op but also volunteering for the staff of Central States Co-op, a wholesale company jointly owned by midwestern cooperatives to which it provided goods. As assistant education director there, as well as editor of *Co-op News*, she met members of many affiliated organizations. She would later recall the various strains of European cooperators in the Chicago area, noting Finns and Lithuanians in particular.

Don remained popular with students at Illinois Tech. "He was one of the swinging-type professors," Paul Flood recalled, "a great teacher able to keep students awake and interested first thing in the morning." Another IIT alum, Mary Manella, described Don as a "showman with an almost theatrical presence in class." Mitchell Goluska, who graduated in 1943, said, "I took the class taught by Professor Hayakawa, and I still have a copy of the book he published, *Language in Action*. I loved that class!"

Hayakawa continued to be busy at Tech—even serving as volunteer coach of the fencing team—and equally occupied by his increasingly rewarding role as an author and speaker. Moreover, he endorsed his wife's activities, especially her co-op service. "I think we were both interested in reforming the capitalist system," he would later explain, "that is, the distribution of the profits."

Their interest in cooperatives led them into the heart of the city's dynamic African American community. "We joined and patronized the People's Cooperative in the black neighborhood near Illinois Institute of Technology," Marge recalled. Without at first realizing it, they found themselves on the edge of one of twentieth-century America's great cultural phenomena. Between 1910 and 1930, Chicago's black population had exploded from 44,000 to 230,000, and it kept growing as the 1940s dawned. One result of that diaspora was the Chicago Renaissance; during the 1930s and 1940s, the Windy City's African American population enjoyed a creative explosion in everything from journalism to literature, social sciences to art, but especially in music.

Chicago's south side hosted considerable talent, both homegrown and migrant. Chicago Renaissance artist Eldzier Corter recalled in

1979 that among those whose accomplishments contributed to that flowering were the dancers Katherine Dunham and Talley Beatty; writers Richard Wright, Frank Yerby, Margaret Walker, Willard Motley, and John H. Johnson; sociologists St. Clair Drake and Horace R. Cayton; entertainers Nat King Cole, Ray Nance, and Oscar Brown Jr.; photographer Gordon Parks; poet Gwendolyn Brooks; and the graphic artists Elizabeth Catlett and Hugh Lee Smith. Add to that formidable list the likes of musicians such as Louis Armstrong, Earl "Fatha" Hines, Dizzy Gillespie, and Charlie Parker, as well as perhaps the most famous name of all, author Langston Hughes.

Writing for the *Defender* was then no insubstantial accomplishment. Journalist Jerry Large would observe in 2006, "You know how significant the *New York Times* is. Well, the *Defender* was once more important to black folks, and its influence touched the whole nation." How so much was accomplished is explained by Drake and Cayton: "With the outbreak of the Second World War, the Negro press emerged as one of the most powerful forces among Negroes in America." The *Defender*'s circulation increased dramatically during the war, and it became the self-proclaimed "World's Greatest Weekly." Over the years it had featured columnists as significant as Mary McLeod Bethune, Wendell Smith, and Dan Burley, the latter famous as the author of *The Original Handbook of Harlem Jive*. He was a special favorite of Don's, who wrote in a 1962 letter, "One of [Burley's] amusing accomplishments was to sit at the piano and illustrate dozens of Chicago South Side piano styles, all the varieties of the blues, boogie woogie, and skiffle, while giving a running account of the origins of each."

Back in 1942, the paper's editor in chief, Dr. Metz Lochard, had announced a new team of five distinguished columnists; Walter White, John Robert Badger, Dr. U. G. Dailey, Hughes, and Hayakawa. Don was the first non–African American to fill such a position on the *Defender* (the paper had earlier employed non-blacks but not as writers). Lochard himself was a considerable luminary in the African American community at the time. "A Frenchman educated at Oxford University as well as at the University of Paris, he had been an interpreter for Marshall Foch and then a language teacher at two noted black universities, Fisk and Howard," explains Ronald Edgar Wolseley. Hayakawa much later said of the editor, "He sort of fancied himself an intellectual. I was glad to join in with him and treat him as one." Perhaps that's why the editor hired Hayakawa, since Don "discovered that nobody else on the *Defender* staff had any particular enthusiasm for me." He added, "I never got to know them particularly well. Dr. Lochard took all my time on the occasion when I visited the *Chicago Defender* office."

Don's strong opinions quickly manifested themselves in his columns. He did not avoid what had been taboo topics for a non-black, and he did not mince words. On December 12, 1942, for instance, he wrote of discrimination: "When minorities . . . are discriminated against, they are the victims of the two-year-old mentalities in the majority culture. Haven't we, who are members of minorities, got trouble enough without making even more trouble for ourselves by acting like two-year-olds towards each other?"

In April 1943 he wrote a piece for the *Defender* on the racial beliefs of Nazis: "Aryans" on top, allies of the Nazis next, and so on; blacks were on the bottom, just as they still tended to be in the United States. The superficiality of "racial" judgments galled him, and so did the sloganistic patriotism of the kind that led to the mistakes that followed World War I. Don wrote in his January 16, 1943, column that this war was an opportunity to go "forward to decency on a world-wide scale, with a dynamic ideal of the United Nations looked upon not as a clique of nations united in a conspiracy to hang on to everything, but as an alliance for universal betterment open to every nation and every people who want to play the game with improved rules and in a civilized way."

More pointed and far more controversial was his column published the next month on anti-Semitism among blacks. He recalled a "Negro I was talking to the other day who . . . told me that Jews 'had all the money,' that they 'grabbed everything,' etc. . . . I asked him right back if it wasn't true that all Negroes were thieves, they were all lazy, they all loved watermelons, and they all had a tendency toward rape. Naturally he was angry and said it wasn't true." Don summarized that fiery piece by advising, "Next time you meet an anti-semitic Negro, tell him to get wise to himself. He is Hitler's little pal."

Those blunt words offended many readers, and on April 3 of that year Hayakawa wrote a column about a letter he'd received from someone who asserted that Jews were "responsible for the evils of the world." Don responded that hatred "poisons the heart, as both psychiatry and the Christian religion tell us. Hatred of the Jews has poisoned this letter-writer's heart just as . . . hated of Negroes has poisoned the heart of many whites." Concluding his rebuttal, Don cited the letter's author: "He pointed out as evidence of Jewish wickedness that 'the Jew, Judas Iscariot, betrayed Christ.'" After pointing out that Jesus was himself a Jew whose teaching was based on Jewish principles, Don asked, "Why is it that the anti-Semites always remember Judas, but forget the 11 faithful disciples and the four gospel-writers, all Jews, without whose devotion and effort and missionary work Christianity would never have been heard of?" He concluded, "I'm not a preacher, but now that we are on the subject of Christianity, I should like to remind my angry correspondent that Jesus said 'Love one another.' He did not say 'Love one another—Jews excepted.' He did not say 'Love one another—Negroes excepted.' He said 'Love one another.'"

seventeen

Like so many men at that time, Don was of two minds about his role in the conflict: "I didn't want to be left out. At the same time, I just felt I didn't want to go into any goddamn war." Finally, though, he decided to volunteer, only to learn that a Canadian of Japanese descent wasn't welcomed by the American military, despite the fact that an officer with his expertise in language and communication might have been a considerable asset. Spurned by the U.S. military, he inquired at the office of the Canadian Consul General in Chicago, but despite his earlier experience in that nation's reserve, his native land wasn't interested in him either. Finally, in order to stabilize his position, he filed an Application for Relief from Military Service (DDS Form 301) and an Alien's Personal History and Statement (DDS Form 304), which in combination formally exempted him from the draft.

Feeling guilty, as did so many other deferred men, but also grateful, Don carried on. Many of his students at IIT were in a Navy V-12 program designed to earn them both a degree in engineering and an officer's commission. Bill Sirvatka recalls that Hayakawa "made his course and classes something to look forward to, and he gained the favor and respect of all who knew him at that time." One particular incident stood out in the future Ensign Sirvatka's memory:

> Being Navy students we all wore sailor uniforms constantly, even to class. Hayakawa quite often wore a Japanese kimono over his shirt and pants, usually to his early morning classes. No one thought much about it until one day one of the guys got the idea we should all come to class wearing kimonos too. So we all showed

with kimonos or what passed as such, and all of us got to class before H. did.

He realized immediately he was being put on and said absolutely nothing about the kimonos we were wearing. Never gave an indication he was aware of it. After his lecture was over, his last words were "I hope your commanding officer won't deem you to be out-of-uniform. I'd hate to have an empty class tomorrow. But you do look cute." With that he just left the class room totally unoffended, and laughing all the way down the hall. Our Commanding officer heard of the incident and posted an order "not to wear kimonos without Prof. Hayakawa's approval."

When he wasn't a fashion maven, Don had become a regular contributor to *Poetry* magazine. His May 1942 review-essay "A Linguistic Approach to Poetry," for instance, caused a stir when it sought to reconcile the ideas of Allen Tate, Thomas Clark Pollock, and Kenneth Burke. Don's reviews and articles—as well as *Language in Action*—had made him something of a local luminary, so he was a welcomed guest at the prestigious magazine's office in Chicago. George Dillon had replaced the deceased Harriet Monroe as *Poetry's* editor, and on one visit Don took Marge to the office to meet Dillon and his longtime assistant Geraldine Udell.

The four dined at a Japanese restaurant, and before the evening was over, Marge was invited to join the magazine's staff. Already the editor of *Co-op News*, she accepted and would eventually become the journal's prose editor. That connection would, in turn, become another powerful base of the Hayakawas' social life, since it linked them even more solidly to the city's rich artistic circle, which then included Nelson Algren, Saul Bellow, Studs Terkel, Langston Hughes, Gordon Parks, and a remarkable young poet named Gwendolyn Brooks.

In the meantime, Don continued to write the widest-ranging columns being carried by the *Defender*; he explored topics as varied as zoot suits, co-ops, African objets d'art, general semantics, the ongoing war, sexual attitudes, and, of course, racial discrimination in

America. Don's unusual perspectives created a large circle of fans, one of whom was Langston Hughes, then publishing in the *Defender* his often biting tales about the fictional commentator Jesse B. Semple. Ironically, as C. K. Doreski has argued, Hughes seems to have written more critically about the plight of interned Japanese Americans than did Hayakawa at that time.

In any case, Hughes and Hayakawa became good friends. "He was a very gentle, quiet man. Never saw him drunk or angry," Don said of Langston. "Very gentlemanly. Just a nice fellow." When in Chicago, the poet—who, like many black writers of the time, lived on the edge of poverty—often socialized with Don and Marge, and was a welcomed houseguest. Longtime Hayakawa housekeeper Daisy Rosebourgh remembers one visit that lasted two weeks: "One night Mr. and Mrs. Hayakawa had a big party and Mr. Hughes was staying with us. Well, for some reason Mr. Hughes didn't have him a tie, so I took him into Mr. Hayakawa's wardrobe and had him to pick out a tie there. He chose Mr. Hayakawa's best one. Well, when he came out, and Mr. Hayakawa saw that tie, his eyes just bugged out and he had to give it a second look," she chuckled, "but he never said a word about it to Mr. Hughes. Afterwards he said to me, 'Isn't that my best tie?'"

By no means did Don limit his associations to the uptown elite and literary giants. Long a music buff as well as an amateur musician, he took advantage of Chicago's rich jazz scene to enhance his understanding of those three remarkable African American musical contributions to the nation's culture: jazz, blues, and gospel. Attending nightclubs, he became friendly with artists such as jazz piano wizards Earl "Fatha" Hines, Meade "Lux" Lewis, and Jimmy Yancey, as well as Jimmy's wife, the esteemed blues singer Estelle "Mama" Yancey. Hot pianist and singer Eurreal "Little Brother" Montgomery was another acquaintance, as were the fabled bandleader and vocalist Memphis Slim and the bassist Ernest "Big" Crawford, who accompanied many of Muddy Waters's great performances. Don was also friendly with gospel singers Mahalia Jackson and Brother Joe May, considered by many to be the greatest female and male voices in the history of that music.

Living in Chicago then seemed to Hayakawa to be a great blessing. Inherently curious, he talked to musicians and critics and became friends with many of the aforementioned artists. He also studied publications on the various forms of jazz and blues and began writing about them for both the *Sun* and the *Defender*. (The latter, in particular, seemed an oddity to some: a Canadian Japanese analyzing African American music—and not coincidentally, analyzing racism—for a largely black readership.)

Jimmy and Mama Yancey resided on Chicago's south side near Comiskey Park, home field of the American League White Sox, and just across the street from Illinois Tech. Don visited them often, and soon they became his close friends. Life was frequently not kind to black musicians in those years and, despite his renown as a pianist, Jimmy worked as a groundskeeper for the White Sox. Don dropped by the Yanceys' house for after-work drinks with them and other groundsmen who were also unwinding. "They'd sit around after work in Mr. Yancy's [*sic*] living room, having a beer," Don recalled. "They didn't talk to each other very much. Someone would say something like, How about Bill Boston? The next guy would say, Fuck him. The others would say, Yeah, Fuck him. . . . There would be a long silence, then someone would say, How about Ray John Stone? The next guy would say, Fuck him, etc., etc."

Fortunately, Jimmy Yancey was a far better musician than conversationalist, and he performed when the Hayakawas organized a jazz concert to benefit the Hyde Park Co-op's nursery school. Jimmy and Mama also livened an illustrated lecture, "Reflections on the History of Jazz," that Don presented at the fashionable Arts Club of Chicago. A benefit for *Poetry* magazine, it attracted an upper-crust audience, many of whom had likely never before heard—or even heard of—the Yanceys.

Later, Marge and Don organized another benefit for *Poetry*, this one staged at the Saddle and Cycle Club facing Lake Michigan.

Calling on his associations in the music world, Don assembled a cast of boogie-woogie pianists the likes of which had never before been seen in Chicago: the dynamic Roosevelt Sykes, classically trained Robert Crum, Art Tatum protégée Dorothy Donegan, "tonky boogie" man Forrest Sykes, and the masterful Meade "Lux" Lewis. This was a "mixed" concert, and Hayakawa later noted in his *Defender* column that the musicians had not only helped *Poetry* magazine but had "performed a service for race relations as well, by appearing together, white and Negro, in the camaraderie of their common musicianship. Serious artists and serious connoisseurs of the arts, whether of boogie-woogie or of Beethoven, know no color line."

As seems to have often occurred in S. I. Hayakawa's life, during the early 1940s he once more found himself associating with an illustrious person when he studied with the artist László Moholy-Nagy. The eclectic Hungarian has been described in a Getty Museum biography as "ever the innovator," someone who "counted among his artistic hats those of photographer, filmmaker, typographer, painter, sculptor, writer, graphic designer, stage designer, and teacher." Moholy-Nagy, who had fled his country in 1919, became a leader in the German Bauhaus school during the next decade. He relocated to Chicago in 1937 to become director of the New Bauhaus. When it closed after a year, he joined others from the faculty to found the School of Design, which was renamed the Institute of Design in 1944.

Don spent "summer session after summer session . . . making art and having fun" at the School of Design. He thought Moholy-Nagy was a wonderful teacher, and as a semanticist Don fully understood that "we have tended to believe that the traditional and familiar art styles of art of the West are the direct representations (or imitations) of reality," when in fact they are abstractions, as are the artistic traditions of other cultures. He added, "In a sense, the camera has liberated the artist to do all sorts of things that you can't do with a camera." Of course, Moholy-Nagy was in the process of—among other things—demonstrating how much one *could* do with a camera.

According to Hayakawa, the two men became "very good friends," each stimulated by the other. Don especially recalled an exercise Moholy-Nagy had directed. It began by gluing together six small boards of varied thicknesses: "Here you have essentially, a rectangle. Made out of other rectangles," the semanticist explained. "Then you try to sculpt something out of it to break out of rectangularity. So everything seems to flow. The fact that they were flat boards once upon a time disappears." Performing such exercises helped Don to think like an artist. That, in turn, led the maestro to invite Don to offer some courses at the Institute of Design.

Hayakawa had a mind that could extrapolate and create new possibilities. He began to look ever closer at visual representations, pointing out that modern artists "are convinced that traditional ways of seeing are not adequate to express the visual experience of twentieth century man and are searching for better ways of symbolizing our new kind of visual experience." Hayakawa came to believe that "when we look at a traditional painting, we are made to think as little as possible of the canvas . . . we are made to think of the object painted." In contrast, modern artists required that observers participate in the art, helping assemble its reality by considering not only the subject but the medium and the context. "Every way of abstracting produces its own kind of truth, which, in the hands of one who orders his abstractions well, results in its own kind of beauty."

Concluding that he lived in "an age of inward exploration more exciting, possibly, than the exploration of new continents," Hayakawa saw a larger meaning for the artistic innovation of his time: "Modern artists are then contributing profoundly to the break-up of cultural provincialism. . . . The cultural anthropologist and the sociologist, studying different and exotic cultures, try to understand each culture on its own terms. The effect of that attempt, as we all know, is the diminution of that provincialism that stands as a wall between one class and another, between one people and another."

At that time, Hayakawa's continuing intellectual growth was also revealed in his ongoing revision of *Language in Action*, expanding his perceptions as he challenged and enriched earlier insights. For instance, applying the Ladder of Abstraction to innovation in art, he wrote:

> When the materials of a story do not fit into the conventional pattern of a novel, the novelist may create a new organization altogether, more suited to the presentation of his experience than the conventional pattern. . . . In such cases . . . the order may seem like disorder at first—one thinks of Laurence Sterne's *Tristam Shandy* and James Joyce's *Ulysses*. . . . Literary greatness requires, therefore, great extensional awareness of the range of human experience, as well as great powers of ordering that experience meaningfully.

Don's sense of the value of—perhaps of the necessity of—general semantic insights was constantly intensified by events of the ongoing war, a reality that was never far from his mind. He pointed out, for instance, the two-valued orientation inherent in Hitler's use of the term "Aryan." Chickens that didn't lay enough eggs were non-Aryan; rabbits were non-Aryan but lions were Aryan; Hitler's allies the Japanese were Aryan, as were Mexicans when Germany sought an alliance with Mexico, but Jews could never be. As Don summarized, "The official National Socialists orientation never permitted a relaxation of the two-valued conviction that nothing is too good for the 'good,' and nothing is too bad for the 'bad,' and *that there is no middle ground*. . . . 'Whoever is not for us is against us!' This is the cry of intolerance armed with certainty."

Hayakawa's increasingly eclectic quest for knowledge and his growing reputation led to an invitation from the Menninger Clinic in Topeka, Kansas, during the summer of 1943, where he not only lectured staff on general semantics but also taught a class to patients. That marked the beginning of a long association with the renowned hospital. He was spending more and more time on the road, and a plaintive note crept into his wife's letters that summer: "I wonder what you do on weekends down there," she wrote on July 11. A week later, she wrote in a special-delivery letter: "We never seem to get to celebrate your birthday properly together," then added in a handwritten postscript, "I have given up the idea of trying to send you anything like an appropriate birthday message. I love you too much."

In another special-delivery birthday greeting, Clara Peters wrote to Don, "If you keep on being as super successful as you've been in the last years, you'll be getting on such a high rung of the ladder that I'll get a stiff neck watching you climb. But I'll glory in my neck pains as long as you'll have Marge climb with you." He had by then become a beloved son-in-law.

eighteen

In early 1942, Irving Lee, Wendell Johnson, and Don Hayakawa decided general semantics needed a scholarly publication that "didn't have the nutty flavor emanating from Korzybski's own pronouncements" in order for it to be taken seriously by academics. Financial backing for the journal would require a membership association of some kind, so those three, among others, in April founded the Society for General Semantics.[1] Korzybski's Institute of General Semantics lacked a stable economic base; it did not sell memberships, and neither its occasional publications nor its seminars were hot items, so Korzybski welcomed a new group that might to a degree subsidize the IGS.

Earlier publications such as Chase's *The Tyranny of Words*, Lee's *Language Habits in Human Affairs*, and Don's own *Language in Action* had by then stimulated wider interest in Korzybski's work, so the time for a popular organization seemed right. Hayakawa further explained: "I wanted to treat general semantics as a subject, in the same sense that there's a scientific concept known as gravitation, which is independent of Isaac Newton. . . . So after a while, you don't talk about Newton anymore, you talk about gravitation. You talk about semantics and not Korzybskian semantics." The journal *ETC.: A Review of General Semantics* was to be primarily financed by membership dues. Don would serve as its editor, with his Illinois Tech colleague Henry J. Webb as assistant editor. Korzybski, Lee, Johnson, and a noted professor of surgery, Raymond W. McNealy,

1. In 1948 the organization was renamed the International Society for General Semantics.

were consulting editors. Despite that talented cast, Hayakawa pretty well ran the magazine as he saw fit, although he especially credited Johnson, Lee, and later Anatol Rapoport with offering valuable advice and concrete help.

While Don endeavored to get the first issue of *ETC.* off the ground—a slow process—the Hayakawas continued to be prominent in Chicago's co-op scene, with Don dedicating several more of his *Defender* columns to that subject. In his February 6, 1943, piece he wrote, "Every co-operative society welcomes everybody regardless of religion or race. They promote their employees regardless of religion or race." He pointed out that "their very structure is such that the more democratic they are, the more efficient and prosperous they become. . . . Think how silly a color-line or a religious or class prejudice would be under such circumstances."

In his column a month later, he warned readers that they were voting with their dollars, usually unknowingly, for Jim Crow employment policies and inferior merchandise. The answer: "One kind of business organization that is striving the hardest to improve the quality of goods, to abolish discrimination in employment, to establish the highest standards of dealing with consumers is of course the consumer co-operative."

Don wasn't through with the topic even then. His column on August 10 of that year dealt with the steadily rising cost of living. "So long as other people own the distributive channels that supply your food and clothing, you will have to pay the prices they ask," he pointed out. "And, as we all know from recent shopping experience, they are asking almost any price they please—price ceilings or no price ceilings." On the other hand, "Co-ops can't profiteer. Their profits . . . go back to purchasers in direct proportion to their purchases." He also pointed out that labor leaders in Britain and the Scandinavian countries considered co-ops "an indispensable weapon in organized labor's fight for decent standards of living." Predictably, rumors that the Hayakawas were leftists—"fellow travelers"—circulated. They were certainly unabashed liberals.

In spite of being only an assistant professor at a minor university, in 1943 Dr. S. I. Hayakawa had become one of the best-known persons of Japanese extraction in the United States. His image had graced the covers of national magazines and major newspapers, his articles were increasingly being not only published but republished, and *Language in Action* continued selling. Moreover, Don's popularity on the lecture circuit, his newspaper writing and periodical pieces, his journal editing, and his unintimidated but rarely harsh (and frequently quotable) views on all manner of subjects contributed to his growing celebrity. He had along the way become manifestly independent, writing unexpected words and holding unexpected views. Even his allegiance to so suspect a field as general semantics was typical: he would personally make it academically respectable, or so his work seemed to suggest.

That Hayakawa was going his own way should not have been surprising given his background. He had to develop a personal social strategy that often took him in unexpected directions. His behavior made clear early on that he had no intention of being unobtrusive or of accepting dismissive treatment. He would simply be good at everything he tried, as well as open, innovative, and socially gracious, and gain acceptance that way rather than by performing according to stereotypical expectations.

By 1943 Don had largely achieved a balance, but two matters in particular troubled his wife and him. One was that his grandparents, parents, and sisters were still trapped in embattled Japan and he could not even communicate with them; the other was the question of having children. The former problem was unsolvable; Don would have to endure isolation from his family until the war finally ended. As for children, "We'd thought about it during the early years of the war, when we didn't know what was going to happen to Don," Marge recalled. "He was a non-naturalizable alien and could have been sent away to a relocation camp somewhere. So until that possibility was eliminated, we didn't want to think of having any children."

Throughout 1943 the Hayakawas remained prominent in Chicago. On April 4, for instance, the *Chicago Sun Book Week* featured a six-photo spread about the couple, including a shot of Don at the piano; the caption reads, "Not long ago Hayakawa discovered boogie-woogie and has learned to play eight-to-the-bar. . . . In serious moods, he turns to Bach. . . . In music as in painting, he does not take his talents very seriously. His enjoyment of it, he says, is purely recreational." Nevertheless, he continued to take Chicago's music scene seriously indeed. The city was a center of what some called the bebop revolution, and the band of Hayakawa's friend Earl "Fatha" Hines featured none other than Dizzy Gillespie and Charlie Parker. Don recognized that something special was under way, as his columns reflected.

He continued to be perhaps the best link between general semantics and popular audiences, too. In August 1943 Don dedicated one of his *Defender* columns to the subject, and to his new journal, concluding in his usual straightforward manner, "General Semantics is in large part instruction in how not to act like an idiot or a savage."

The first issue of *ETC.* saw print that month. As word of the creation of the new periodical got out, there had been rumblings among the GS faithful who feared that Hayakawa would turn the journal into a forum strictly for his own views. These were unfounded, since the initial volume of the journal contained diverse and intriguing material, much of it reprinted. At most, it reflected Don Hayakawa's multidisciplinary approach to general semantics and to life itself. Nonetheless, some of Korzybski's disciples thought it was not narrowly enough concerned with the great man's ideas.

The lead article, "Science and Values" by Edward L. Thorndike, was actually Thorndike's retirement speech from the presidency of the American Association for the Advancement of Science, and had in fact been recommended by none other than Alfred Korzybski. "General Semantics and Modern Art" by Oliver Bloodstein was endorsed by Wendell Johnson. Charles Glickberg contributed "General Semantics and Psychoanalysis," while "Chemical Semantics" by S. Weiner was a reprint from the *Journal of Chemical Education.* Also reprinted was Margaret Mead's "The Problem of Changing Food Habits: With Suggestions for Psychoanalytic Contributions" from the *Bulletin of the Menninger Clinic.* Perhaps the most significant of the articles, at least in terms of endurance (it is still in print and being used by composition teachers), was Wendell Johnson's provocative "You Can't Write Writing."

Also reprinted was the poem for which the publication was named, "etcetera" by e. e. cummings. In a letter to the editor, Korzybski somewhat turgidly endorsed the journal's name, about which some GS purists had complained. "Personally I feel the publication of the Society could not have a better title," he wrote. "In a non-aristotelian infinite valued orientation we do not assume that whatever we may say covers 'all' the characteristics of a situation, and so we remain conscious of a permanent 'etcetera' instead of having the dogmatic 'period and stop' attitude."

Beyond editing the issue, Hayakawa contributed a review of Gregory Zilboorg's book *Mind, Medicine and Man.* One other intriguing item was reported in the first issue: "In recognition of their work promoting GS through their writings, three fellows of the Institute of General Semantics were appointed last fall. They are: Wendell Johnson, associate professor of psychology and speech pathology at the University of Iowa, S. I. Hayakawa (IGS '38) assistant professor of English at the Illinois Institute of Technology, Irving J. Lee (IGS '39) chairman of the speech division at University College, Northwestern University."

General semantics purists were correct to fear that Don's more eclectic view rather than a narrow emphasis on Korzybskian doctrines would dominate *ETC.*, making it a readable and provocative journal — and a relatively successful one throughout Hayakawa's twenty-seven-year tenure as editor. Nevertheless, GS buff Charles Stade asserted that Hayakawa "never believed that there was anything in Korzybski's work to be understood. . . . I will maintain that neither *ETC.* nor the *GSB* [*General Semantics Bulletin*] ever printed a single sentence about g.s. that makes any sense." But, Stade conceded, "They have printed a lot of interesting and useful material that could be confused with g.s." One way or another, the new journal would both elevate and expand Don's reputation.

During the 1943–44 academic year, life continued largely unchanged for the Hayakawas, with Don again teaching at Illinois Tech, traveling to lecture here and there, while both he and Marge continued editing and writing. When he was at last promoted to associate professor at Illinois Tech that academic year, Don wrote a letter of thanks to college president Henry Heald that read, in part, "The present is far from being the best possible time for the IIT to be harboring in its faculty a person like myself who, because of an accident of birth, is an object of suspicion among jittery and/or unenlightened people. . . . The fate of Japanese-Americans on the Pacific coast has made me doubly grateful for the fact that I am here among understanding and sympathetic colleagues."

About then—he didn't remember the exact date—young Louis Forsdale, along with several pals, visited the University of Wisconsin's Madison campus on a day when Hayakawa also happened to be there. The men met and their conversation turned to the work of Frank Lloyd Wright. Don asked Forsdale and company if they'd like to meet the famous architect, with whom he had become friendly thanks to Marge's brother, by then an important cog at the Taliesin Fellowship. Forsdale, who would go on to become a distinguished Columbia University professor, eagerly agreed. As he remembered it, "When the car pulled up to Taliesin East, Wright was outside. Hayakawa said: 'How are you, you damned artist. You know your buildings wouldn't stand up without engineers.' Wright responded, 'Yeah, you damned scientist . . . , you couldn't design anything to put on an engineer's base.' Then they shook hands." Wright, a man of no small ego, would not likely have exchanged such friendly barbs with anyone but a close pal.

In fact, that exchange revealed a bit of Hayakawa's sense of humor, a characteristic that his chums much enjoyed. Although he abjured the scatological and the negatively racial, he also loved jokes. One of his favorites—and this was about as close to "dirty" as he ever got—was about the husband and wife who were making love, and the man wasn't performing well. "What's wrong, honey," his wife asked, "are you tired?" "No," he replied, "I just can't think of anyone." Don rarely failed to laugh when telling that one.

Perhaps because of his own various names, he also got a great kick retelling Myron Cohen's story of the older Jewish lady whose son invited her to visit him at his new penthouse in Miami. When she didn't arrive on time, he grew worried and telephoned the front desk and was told that an older woman had been sitting in the lobby for some time, so he hurried down and there sat his mother. "Mama," he cried, "I was worried sick. Why are you sitting here?" She looked up at him and said, "I couldn't remember your room number." He shook his head and said, "But why didn't you just go to the desk and ask my suite's number?" She again looked up at him and replied, "I couldn't remember your new name."

nineteen

Don tried to keep abreast of events in Canada, and news from his native land disappointed him in 1944. The Soldiers' Vote Bill passed in the House of Commons enfranchised many voters who were or had been in the Canadian military, but it disqualified citizens from countries at war with Canada. Although the bill originally barred Italian and German Canadians, it was finally narrowed to apply only to Japanese, and basically it reaffirmed the policy in British Columbia. It also confirmed Hayakawa's perception that racism remained a cancer there as in the States. He continued to hope that general semantics might one day correct that.

Thanks to Professor Elwood Murray, the University of Denver had become a leader in integrating Korzybski's work into academic curricula, and in 1944 Murray invited Don to teach a summer session there. Hayakawa readily accepted and traveled to Colorado alone, since Marge had professional responsibilities in Chicago. Upon arrival in Denver, he responded to a call from a onetime Broadway showgirl, Mercedes Taliaferro, and visited her. At Taliaferro's apartment he met a Mrs. Luginbuhl, "a kind of picker up of strange and interesting characters, apparently well-heeled and connected with many liberal and radical circles in California. Under her maiden name of Virginia Allan she used to work for Upton Sinclair and EPIC. She knows something about cooperatives, communism, and lots of other crackpot doctrines."

As the war dragged on, with not just manpower but men scarce on the home front, lonely women were the rule, not the exception, and Don seems to have encountered his share. During the visit, he explained, Taliaferro "made, I am sorry to say, quite a play for me; and she was mad as hell because I refused to notice, let alone respond. . . . [S]he was trying to show off for Virginia Allan and the show didn't come off." As it turned out, Mrs. Luginbuhl was leaving the next day for California, so she rented her house to Don. "I came over to see Taliaferro and got a house," he concluded.

Don had arrived in Denver in time to also attend a major folklore conference at the university and to meet B. A. Botkin, who had just published *A Treasury of American Folklore*. As usual, Hayakawa got on well with his new acquaintance, and on July 23 he wrote to Marge that Botkin "is going to send me some Jelly Roll Morton records." The following day he wrote to his wife about meeting yet another prominent figure, the celebrated Rocky Mountain poet Thomas Hornsby Ferril. Don enjoyed Ferril's verse, but said of him, "There is a curious compulsiveness and a demanding for attention when he talks, but on the whole he tends to remain very silent in company."

At the conference, Don lectured on African American music, emphasizing boogie-woogie. "The whole thing went over, as usual, terribly well, because, damnit, people simply started getting excited when they hear[d] that stuff." After hooking his audience, though, Hayakawa moved them to a more daunting topic: "The lecture was ended on a very solemn note. I switched abruptly to the race question, and ended by playing them . . . Billie Holiday singing 'Strange Fruit,'" a powerful lyric about lynching. "So immediately everybody afterwards gathered around, very learned profs of music, of folklore. etc., and a batch of undergraduates who are very groovey [*sic*]."

Hayakawa began teaching the summer session at the university with two early-morning classes. He also team-taught an afternoon "Communications Workshop" with Murray and the distinguished folklorist Levette J. Davidson. Don described the former, tongue-in-cheek, to Marge as "the same kind of dope as ever," adding, "he keeps surprising me with some very good ideas he has about using g.s. in a minorities problems project here in Denver. It sounds like a terrific job he is undertaking, but extremely well thought-out. I was impressed."

As he worked more and more with general semantics, Don's version continued veering from Korzybski's approach in that he sought practical insights and applications and was open to information from virtually any field. Hayakawa would later summarize his own variation this way: "General semantics deals with the way in which our understanding of the world is influenced and shaped by how we talk about it. . . . [E]valuations (value judgments) are built into many of the words we use and . . . those evaluations govern, and sometimes distort our thinking." Korzybski and many of his most devoted disciples continued to consider Hayakawa's approach a trivialization of the theoretician's work. They felt that way, in part at least, because a certain playfulness and a considerable glibness enlivened Hayakawa's writing.

Some playfulness amid unhidden pining marked the correspondence between Don and Marge throughout that summer, too. On July 26, for instance, on a *Poetry* magazine postcard, she sent him a formal request that he review *News of the Phoenix* by A. J. M. Smith. She concluded the note with a postscript: "Haven't we met somewhere?" On August 6, Don closed a letter to her, "Can't you please come out? Am awakening in the middle of the night with steam up. Love, & lust." Later that month she would write, "I miss you like anything. And I'm really now getting a taste of staying alone, and I don't like it much."

Earlier, Don had written to tell his wife that he had spoken to a meeting of the Japanese American Citizens League (JACL), admitting, "My talk rambled around, but I suppose it was okay." In the same letter he criticized a presentation by Saburo Kido, national president of the JACL: "He talked on and on about fighting for our rights, etc., when it seems to me that nisei [sic] in most respects don't have to fight for rights—all they need to do is to exercise them." Nevertheless, Hayakawa joined the group, impressed by "its platform of assimilation and multiracial civil rights." Ironically, in the very next paragraph of the letter he told his wife that the university's chancellor, Ben M. Cherrington, "wants to introduce me around to some Denver bigshots who are interested in preventing two serious anti-Japanese bills from going through the next session of the Colorado legislature."

In early August, Korzybski and his primary assistant, M. Kendig, arrived in Denver. Interest in general semantics nationally was still on the upswing, thanks to the efforts of writers such as Chase, Johnson, and Hayakawa. Don wrote to his wife, "Today AK & Kendig are in town, ready to take over tomorrow, giving me a much needed rest for vocal chords." He was by then growing tired of the affectations of the great man and his assistant, whose styles so differed from his own easy manner. "A.K. lectured at big military hosp. at Fitzsimmons," Hayakawa wrote to his wife. "Big social affair afterward—cocktail party with officer medics. Was acutely embarrassed by Kendig only part of the time."

Marge knew the situation. Despite being a woman of sweet demeanor, she replied, "Why don't you choke Kendig? Seriously shouldn't somebody inform her and AK of the effect of cigarette holders and other affectations on an audience?" Korzybski and company were enjoying what turned out to be the high-water mark for GS, and their over-the-top mannerisms showed it.

"A.K.," as he was often referred to by followers, brought a certain style of repetition to his seminars, or so reported Vocha Fiske, who attended six of them. She described a lecture on the hazard of separating verbally what cannot be disunited in nature.

> He would thunder: "Let's see about the structure of language," and take a few steps. Raising his cane he would ask: "Can you divide matter, space and time in this, an object?" His hearers would reply "no." Sometimes "Of course not."
>
> A satisfied grin would start curling up the corners of the spacious mouth. Then holding the cane high above his head on a horizontal line, Alfred would detonate: "Take away matter, you have no stick; take away space, you have only a point; take away time, you have just a flash" . . . . . . [sic] "Those are facts; they are the structure of nature—processes, not words. A[s] life-facts they are non-elementalistic; they don't split; you can see them.["]

The cane would come down and he'd continue; "The work of Einstein is revolutionary for physics because the language fits the facts. the [*sic*] language fits the structure, the process. In the living organism body-mind, emotion-intellect, etc. are interconnected. But do we separate them verbally? Do we split matter, space and time verbally? You know we do. Life is non-el,[1] the proper structure of language has to be non-el. We have to learn to adjust the structure of language to be nearer life facts.

While in Denver, Don became intrigued by the titillating story of the three Shitara sisters from the internment camp at Amache who were being tried for treason—which could have resulted in the death penalty. He sent clippings about them from the *Rocky Mountain News* and the *Denver Post* to Marge. The young women—Flo Otani, Billie Tanigoshi, and Toots Wallace—were accused of aiding two German POWs to escape from the POW camp at Trinidad, Colorado. More than the possibility of capital punishment made the proceedings significant. The *Rocky Mountain News* speculated, "It is possible that the challenge as to whether the government has authority to evacuate American citizens from any area by compulsion will be injected into the proceedings." It was also clear that treason would not have been charged if the three American citizens had not been perceived as Japanese, although all had been born in California and, according to the *Denver Post*, "had associated almost exclusively with Caucasians."

The prosecution presented photographs taken at a farm where German prisoners and Japanese American internees were working; the images revealed the sisters smooching with the Germans. The prosecution then paraded the two POWs, wearing full Afrika Corps uniforms, into the courtroom to testify against the women. The defense, however, argued persuasively that the affair was more about

---

1. Dualisms like "spirit" and "body," "time" and "space," etc., which separate verbally what aren't necessarily separate in nature, were called elementalistic ("el") by Korzybski; compounds such as "space-time" and "psycho-somatic," etc., which restored unity, he called non-elementalistic ("non-el").

libido than treason; it was a case of wanting to aid their boyfriends, not the Third Reich. The women were acquitted of treason but found guilty of conspiracy to help the men escape. Following the verdict, Don wrote to Marge, "Everybody seems to feel J-A's came out very well—proves the gals were human just like other Americans. Much private comment on dreariness of region near Trinidad, Col., as explanation of girls' fooling around with any men they could get hold of."

At the time, Hayakawa's attitude toward the relocation and internment seems to have remained unsettled. On August 18 he wrote to Marge, "Today finally got in touch by long distance with Granada Relocation Center and am going out there by train this afternoon." Rarely short of female companions during those war years, he also added what to her may have been a disquieting note: "Barbara [Samuelson] (whose name is revoltingly shortened to Babbie, and who is doing a Ph.D. at Harvard on minorities) wanted to come along if it could be arranged, so it has been arranged. . . . She is quite a good egg."

Don and "Babbie" were actually driven to the camp at Amache, Colorado, by one of its residents, Mr. Kodama, an old acquaintance of Ichiro Hayakawa's. Don had met Mr. Kodama socially in 1941 but hadn't seen him since. As he would later learn, Ichiro had met Kodama only once, too, more than forty years before World War II broke out, when the two were young men with literary aspirations. Kodama and Ichiro had at that time enjoyed a meal, discussed English literature, and even shared a hotel room. "I cannot recollect his face now," Ichiro would later write to his son. "Dimly, I remember he was a plump and round-faced youth."

At the relocation camp, "Mr. Kodama told me how proud he was that I had become a professor and had written a couple of books. He said, glowing with pride, that I had achieved every ambition he and my father had had back in San Francisco before I was born." Ichiro Hayakawa, in an uncharacteristic moment of self-revelation, would later write to his son in a 1947 letter: "I had to work, to earn money from necessity of bringing up the family. I feel that I have given myself to you and you have achieved that which I longed for. So your friendship with Mr. Kodama is also mine. . . . Mr. Kodama is a born poet, so he may see it in that light, too."

Unfortunately, Don Hayakawa wrote no detailed account of his trip to the relocation center. An August 23 note to Marge said only, "My trip to Amache, about which I shall tell you in detail as soon as I return, interrupted things so much that I'm far behind in my work. . . . [A]ll this week students in the semantics workshop are delivering themselves of their term papers, and we are listening to them with sometimes delight and sometimes horror."

The condition of his own family in Japan kept Don constantly concerned. The elder Hayakawas, meanwhile, did their best to stay out of harm's way as American bombings intensified. Don's son Alan recalls that his father later learned that Ichiro had "moved his company's major capital asset, 21 typewriters, to a farmhouse in the countryside well out of Osaka, to keep them safe from Allied bombs. A bomber crippled by anti-aircraft fire strayed over the countryside and dropped its load of bombs (apparently in an effort to make a safe return to base), and the typewriters were destroyed." Alan added, "Don told this story as a sad irony, without rancor."

As usual, Don had little trouble finding friends to fill his free time. In Denver that summer he became especially close to musician Woody Martin and his wife, Jeanne, and borrowed records from them to illustrate his lectures on boogie-woogie and jazz. They also provided transportation "in their delivery truck (in which we all ride on the floor)." The Martins took a gang to see Benny Carter perform ("colored dance—whites as spectators," he wrote), then later that evening to Elitch Gardens to see *Tomorrow the World*, a new movie starring Agnes Moorehead and Frederic March. He continued, "Theater tickets give one a discount on the dance hall. We, i.e. Martins plus me plus one Edith Thornton, librarian, who insisted she hadn't danced in 10 years & who soon proved it, went dancing" to the music of Hal MacIntyre's band.

He also reported, "Gave lecture on co-ops . . . at Chapel assembly this a.m. & MOWED 'EM DOWN. I did an unusually good job—with possible important outcomes." The specific outcome was not discussed, but he reported being offered a visiting professorship at Bennington by none other than the noted poet Theodore Roethke. He did not accept, and why is not recorded.

He had, as well, joined a "boogie" radio program on KMYR where he shared the mic with announcer Dick Schmidt, Gene Reid ("local hepcat and collector"), and Jeanne Martin. "The 3 of us constitute a board of experts commenting on the records during a 50-minute program, interspersed by some awful commercials," he wrote. "Dick tells me that the fact of a college professor being on the jazz board . . . has elicited much excitement among the high school followers of the program."

Hayakawa's significant knowledge of jazz and his connection with the *Chicago Defender* opened many doors for him in Denver. In one letter he wrote to his wife, "Negro students came up in cafeteria this morning to ask me if I was he who wrote for Defender." He added, "Thanks for sending in my story. I still am." On August 18, he noted, "By a miracle I keep getting my Defender articles mailed off in time." He was casting about for subjects on which to write while in Colorado.

Marge, his not-so-silent partner, had written to him on August 12 that residents of Altgeld Gardens, a new housing complex in extreme southern Chicago and a segregated black ghetto, were trying to establish a co-op. Volunteers were canvassing door-to-door in the unprosperous neighborhood, selling shares of membership at fifteen dollars each. "This doesn't give you much for a column," she noted, "except the idea occurs to me that you could do one on the difficulty of getting democratic and constructive things under way, overcoming lethargy, etc. How hard it is to get up steam to do things for ourselves, how easy to relax and let others do it. Dire consequences for the latter, etc. . . . This is all trite as hell, but done in your inimitable style, it might be something."

Mid-August, Don reported to his wife, "Last night I went with the Martins and Barbara Samuelson to Negro district and talked with leading hotel proprietor (in his bar) and local city councilman

about minorities in Denver. Very interesting details about the city."
As usual there were others present and he had good reason for the
outing, but his "dates" (with Samuelson in this case) couldn't have
comforted his lonely spouse. She would write later that summer, "I
miss you increasingly as the time gets shorter."

In Chicago, Marge had added apartment hunting to her busy
schedule. Finding a large flat at 1356 Hyde Park Boulevard near
Madison Park, she telephoned her husband and asked, "How would
you like to have a ten-room apartment?" With its maid's quarters and
abundant space, it would accommodate the larger family the Hayakawas hoped to have. In fact, finding the Hyde Park unit seemed too
good to be true: "There must be something wrong with the place,"
Marge wrote to him. "It's also too big & too much work for most
people to want. The furnishing situation is going to be fantastically
difficult. We may be insane. But it is a wonderful apartment and I do
want to try it." Besides, she added, "this one at $170 is dirt cheap."
The accommodations would work out so well that the Hayakawas
eventually bought the entire building because "We didn't want anyone
putting us out," Marge explained.

six

THE POSTWAR YEARS

twenty

For Don and Marge, as for most Americans, the major event of 1945 was the end of World War II. Long before August 15 of that year—V-J Day—while the destruction of Japan was progressing, Hayakawa increasingly worried over the fate of his family there. He had been trying to contact them for some time, and on April 25 of that year he again wrote a letter to his father and asked the Red Cross to try to deliver it.

Then he waited . . . and waited . . . while news of saturation bombing by B-29s, of firestorms in Japanese cities, of the forthcoming suicidal "Nip" defense of the home islands, then of the A-bomb destruction of Hiroshima and Nagasaki all tortured him. He had no way of knowing if his family had survived; as usual, he kept himself busy, but thoughts of them were never far from his mind.

On September 1, aboard the battleship *Missouri*, the Empire of Japan's representatives at last signed the articles of surrender. In December a letter addressed to Don arrived from overseas, this one with an unfamiliar return address:

Pfc. Philip Litwer, 12151244
Co. H—303 Inf.
APO 445
c/o Postmaster
San Francisco, California

Within the envelope Hayakawa found a note from Private First Class Litwer: "I thought it would be wise if I wrote a few lines explaining the enclosed letter from your father." Don read no farther, but

175

instead turned to the two typed pages also enclosed in that cover. They began, "Dear Sam Hayakawa . . ."[1]

He learned that his own letter of April 25 had finally been delivered thanks to "the kindness of Mr. Philip Litwer of the U.S. Occupation Army." He learned a great deal more from Ichiro, whose writing skill in English had slipped but was still easily understood: "Our home at Fukae is damaged by nearby bomb explosion, almost unfit to live. I am still staying here, hoping repair will be made before Winter sets in. Fortunately none of our family or relatives was killed or wounded although victims of U.S. bombing were quite heavy. Property damages are unimaginable. . . . Worst of all, the Nation is almost starving." Don was also informed that his sister Ruth was now a widow, while his sister Grace was divorced and living with their mother in Kusakabe, a farm village where they had established a residence, and were "well-fed" and were "better off than city folks where extreme shortage of all food-stuff exists."

The elder Hayakawa, who had been roughed up by Japanese jingoists because of his connection with Canada and the United States, was not an entirely accurate reporter when he informed his son, "100 per cent of Japanese nation are glad that we lost the war to be able to be free from the bond of militarism and are looking forward to better and prosperous time." Many years later, in response to an interviewer's question, Ichiro Hayakawa said, "I think, in a way, those atomic bombs saved Japan. Because without that, everyone in Japan would have fought until everyone was slaughtered."

In that first note to his son, Ichiro also admitted, "Your parents are becoming old and not likely to live until such days [of national recovery]." The father's letter concluded with three requests, the first a parent's plea: "Is it not possible for you to obtain a position in Japan to work for the Occupation Army. . . . The work may be

1. Over the years that followed, Ichiro would employ several salutations when writing to his son and daughter-in-law, the changes perhaps revealing his sense of comfort with the couple: "Dear Peters & Sam" (December 11, 1946); "Dear Sam & Marge" (November 28, 1953); "Dear Marge and Don" (October 1, 1954).

a short one, but we shall then have an opportunity to be together for a while at least." The second, much understated, was for "food-stuff." The third read, "Please write, if possible, all about you and tell Fred about us." The letter concluded, "Yours affectionately, I. Hayakawa."

It was indeed possible, and Don immediately responded with a long letter. After expressing sorrow about the death of Ruth's husband as well as Grace's divorce, he launched an explanation of the relocation of Japanese Americans.

> As you probably know, during the war the Japanese-Americans on the Pacific Coast were moved inland to Relocation Centers, where they were cared for by the U.S. government. As soon as their loyalty was established they were free to leave those camps and come further East—anywhere outside the Pacific Coast defense area. Those of us who lived elsewhere than the Pacific Coast were at no time molested by the government. . . .
>
> Among the first to leave the Relocation Camps were your sister and her husband, Mr. and Mrs. Furuyama.

Why this topic merited such a prominent place in an otherwise personal letter was known only to Don.

In any case, Hayakawa followed with a report on his and Marge's activities: "Peters and I have been busy throughout the War. I was not called into military service, but was engaged in many volunteer activities." A paragraph later he presented his father with the biggest news of all: "Your letter came just in time for us to be able to give you an interesting announcement—Peters is expecting a baby, due probably around June—No one had been told about this here yet. Naturally, we are looking forward to the event with great excitement."

The tone of his communication changed as he wrote, "In view of all the sufferings that other people have had all over the world, we almost feel guilty about how little we have been affected beyond having to work harder than usual. A year ago we moved into a very handsome new apartment, and all our life has been very pleasant indeed."

177

The note then surveyed the situations of family, friends, and events in Canada and added that he was trying to find a job—perhaps as a newspaper correspondent—that would allow him "to come to see you as soon as I can." Then he added, "The feeling in America towards Japan these days is one of profound curiosity, mixed with considerable genuine friendliness . . . [I]t would not surprise me to find that this may be the beginning of genuinely friendly relationships between Japan and the U.S." Finally, he promised to send merchandise to Japan as soon as it was permitted, and asked his father to "please canvass the entire family to find out what more they want."

It had been a remarkable month in which Don Hayakawa had not only reconnected with his family after nearly five years of silence but had also learned that, on the threshold of middle age, he was to become a father. Marge recalled, "It was just after the war and everyone was coming home and having children and having them close together. Getting on with having a family quickly. We felt the same way." Don and Marge had no particular concerns about mixed-race children; on the other hand, Marge admitted, "We'd been married so long, we liked our lifestyle very much. We realized there would be a change. But we thought it was high time we faced the question."

The Hayakawas had by then settled comfortably into their posh Hyde Park apartment, which proved to be everything they'd hoped. They hired a young African American woman, Mary Walker, to clean and otherwise help the busy couple keep their digs comfortable. Don had, as well, become acting chair of the Department of Language and Literature at Illinois Tech and was in demand on the speakers' circuit, so his hours were unpredictable, especially with *ETC.* increasingly a one-man operation.

Except among the curia of general semantics, in fact, Don was increasingly the public voice and public face of the movement, troubling indeed to Korzybski, Kendig, and company. Hayakawa's unpretentious, often humorous, yet penetrating presentations contrasted with Korzybski's more inflated manner and endeared Don to audiences. On St. Patrick's Day, 1945, he had delivered the *Poetry*

Magazine Modern Arts Series lecture at the Arts Club of Chicago, "Reflections on the History of Jazz." He was accompanied by musicians Elizabeth Jeffries, Oro "Tut" Soper, Richard M. Jones, Darnell Howard, and Jimmy and Mama Yancey. The talk raised money for the sponsoring magazine and prompted a less likely periodical, *Illinois Tech Engineer*, to print the text of the speech alongside articles like "The A-C Network Calculator" and "New Developments in Wire Recording." Hayakawa's piece argued that "Jazz is not merely a Negro expression. It is an expression of America, or at least of something very precious to Americans." *Illinois Tech Engineer* followed the text of Don's speech by reprinting as addenda several of his columns from the *Defender*, including essays on such musical stalwarts as Louis Armstrong, Edmond Hall, and James P. Johnson.

Marge, meanwhile, prepared for motherhood while busy with her many co-op activities as well as editorial duties at *Poetry*. Her mother continued to have some fear about how a mixed-race child would be accepted, but was finally a pragmatist and as delighted as any potential grandmother might be. Besides, she also understood that any problem would be society's, not her family's.

At the end of the year, Don appeared on *The Reviewing Stand*, a radio program on WGN Mutual Radio, Northwestern University's campus station. He joined a formidable panel that included Harrison Smith of the *Saturday Review of Literature*, Fannie Butcher of the *Chicago Tribune*, Bergen Evans of Northwestern, and moderator Irving Lee, also of Northwestern. The topic was "What Is America Reading?" The transcript of various remarks makes Hayakawa appear to be the most concrete of the group, naming specific books rather than casting opinions without definite evidence. He also comes off as considerably less elitist than some. For instance, Mr. Evans asserted, "I think popular fiction is always sentimental." Miss Butcher responded, "Not necessarily. Take *Of Human Bondage* by Somerset Maugham."

Mr. Evans: I think it is very sentimental.
Mr. Hayakawa: Mr. Smith mentioned *A Walk in the Sun* by Harry Brown. That is popular and it is not sentimental. It is reasonably

realistic, in fact, impressively realistic, and gives us insight as to how people had to live as infantry combat men.

Mr. Evans: It has a limited popularity.

Mr. Hayakawa: It is a best seller. Nevertheless, in literary terms it is fiction and in your sense of the word it is reality. It seems to me we are just debating terms here.

Miss Butcher: There is your semantics again.

Mr. Evans: I would not regard *A Walk in the Sun* as *popular* fiction.

Mr. Evans did not say what he *would* consider popular fiction after declaring that a best-seller wasn't it.

In January 1946 a card and a letter contained in a single envelope from Ichiro Hayakawa arrived. The card was addressed to his older son, while the letter was intended for Fred as well as Don. On the card, the elder Hayakawa congratulated his son and daughter-in-law on their forthcoming baby. "We pray that you will take good care of yourself for coming event," he wrote to Marge. "If Mother was near you she would run to help you." The brief note on the card also requested that, after reading it, "Sam" forward the enclosed, longer missive to Fred, adding, "I believe he will share the burden of rescue goods to us. We hope to live long enough to meet you again."

The enclosed four-page letter began, "Dear Sam and Fred Hayakawa . . ." The tone of this was far less restrained than the first one had been, and it revealed some of the father's emotions: "This time last year, we never dreamed to be able to exchange letters with you, lost all hopes of meeting our Sons [*sic*] alive. What a change and what a joy!" The word picture he painted of Japan was also less restrained.

Conditions became worse and worse day by day and our life of 5 months since was nothing but fear and desparation [*sic*] trying to escape from perpetual hell fire, Death and destruction. American aerial attacks were so complete that 90 percent of all cities in Japan with population over 30,000 are burned and destroyed. You can imagine the condition, 10 million homeless, clothless [*sic*] hungry mass! . . . Truth was covered by Military government and even at the worst conditions, the nation was told that we will win the war. We did not grumble if our homes burned, rations became less and less to the point of near starvation. But when Japan surrendered and real situation became clear before us for the first time, the whole nation stunned.

After revealing how little food was available, Ichiro explained to his sons that the "majority of city population are near starvation. Social order is broken, law disregarded, virtue refinements non-existent, all are hungry beasts. . . . The desire and aspiration for democracy must begin after their belly is filled up."

The letter concluded with an admonition to Fred: "You will kindly co-operate with Sam in sending things we need, looking for an opportunity or an occasion for forwarding parcels to Japan. With Love, I. Hayakawa." Both sons immediately began to search for a means to send food and clothing to their parents and sisters, no easy matter at that time.

Don stayed busy at his work, too. "Poetry and Advertising," a talk he had delivered at the Sixth Conference of Science, Philosophy and Religion at Columbia University, appeared in the January 1946 issue of *Poetry*. His controversial thesis that "poetry and advertising have much in common," since "both attempt to make the objects of experience symbolic of something beyond themselves," led *Advertising Age* to reprint it only a month later, perhaps because the editors liked his suggestion that "almost all advertising directed to the general public is the *poeticizing of consumer goods*."

His interest in jazz had, if anything, deepened and broadened by then, and he several times urged that the music be recognized as the cultural treasure it was. In a 1946 book review for the *Chicago Sun Book Week*, for instance, he wrote that "hundreds of Illinois Tech students daily walk unseeing past the place where Louis Armstrong stopped the streetcars with the crowds that thronged to hear his music, it is just and proper that historians clarify the record while a few landmarks can still be pointed out."

Meanwhile, Don received a note from an acquaintance, Wil Austin, who after discharge from the U.S. Army had remained in Japan as a writer for the General Headquarters' news weekly, *Maptalk*. Wil, who was bilingual and so managed a more intimate understanding of currents in the country, reported, "Japan is an important experience for the GI's. They've all become less violently anti-Japanese than the folks back home. In fact a good many soldiers express downright enthusiasm for the people."

Like so many other Americans of Japanese descent, Don took special pride in the 442nd Regimental Combat Team in which his cousin Chuck had served with distinction. When that unit composed of Japanese Americans finally came home in 1946, Hayakawa found himself especially moved by President Harry Truman's acknowledgment, "You have fought not only the enemy, but you fought prejudice—and you have won." Unlike most others, though, he saw a larger lesson in the 442nd's triumph. In the draft of a column written for the *Chicago Defender*, he observed, "The accomplishments of the 442nd were no accident. . . . Much of the credit for the Nisei victory over prejudice goes to the Nisei themselves, but a significant part of it also goes to the officials in government who saw to it that the Nisei got a chance." Then he dropped a contrarious bomb that took some of the glow off the illusion of American inclusiveness. Hayakawa wrote, "But the Negroes got no such breaks. . . . With many times the number of Negro troops as there were of Nisei troops, Negroes could have made many times as brilliant a record as the Nisei. But they were not given the chance."

Despite Don and Marge's always busy professional schedules, this was a season dominated by family, and on July 16, 1946, Samuel Ichiye Hayakawa and Margedant Peters Hayakawa became the parents of Alan Romer Hayakawa, a robust, alert baby, who weighed over eight pounds at birth. The new parents were high-energy achievers capable of juggling several tasks at once, and they did just that. "When we decided to have children, I accepted that they would have priority, but I always hoped I would continue to be able to do other things as well," Marge recalled. As a result, she remained on the staff of *Poetry* and retained as many of her duties for the co-op as she could, working at home, only visiting the office occasionally. Their relative affluence made life easier for Don and Marge, who could afford to hire domestic help and had free time for personal pursuits.

Marge's mother, Clara, "came to live with us," Marge recalled, "and she was a permanent part of our family then." Whatever her early misgivings might have been, the grandmother became a prime mentor for Alan. "She was very, very good with children," agreed Marge. "Every contact with her was a possibility for education. She had a marvelous sense of what level on which the child could learn."

Don Hayakawa, the Moholy-Nagy trained amateur artist, was involved with his son's development, too. He would later recall, "When our little boy was about 17 weeks old, I suddenly got an idea and I made a mobile with colored cardboard and thread and hung it over his crib, where it revolved for minutes if you wound it up by twisting the string. To my great delight it not only attracted his attention, but he would watch it revolve for ten and twenty minutes at a time, kicking and waving his arms and gurgling with pleasure. He was undergoing what I imagine must be one of the most tremendous of an infant's adventures—he was learning to see." Alan would be ahead of the developmental curve at every stage, but that came as no great shock, given his pedigree and the doting attention of three bright adults. Despite dark hair and eyes, the child looked much like his mother.

A postcard dated October 19 came from Grandfather Hayakawa in Japan, "greeting you all for a very Happy Christmas, especially to Dear Baby for his first Christmas from Grand-pa and Grand-ma. Altho we can not send any presents you will accept our Sincere [sic] love & greetings."

Before 1946 ended, however, tragedy would strike the clan when Svetlana Wright Peters, the live-wire wife of Marge's brother, Wes, and their two-year-old son, Daniel, were killed in an automobile accident near Spring Green, Wisconsin. Only four-year-old Brandoch Peters survived, and the extended family was devastated. Caring for her new grandson, Alan, proved therapeutic for the grieving

Clara, as well as for Marge. Wes buried himself in work, traveling a great deal, so Brandoch would grow up at Taliesin with his adoptive grandfather, Frank Lloyd Wright, bringing a measure of joy to the aging architect's final years. Artist Peg Miller, a friend of Brandoch's, later observed, "He's the only one who walked at Mr. Wright's knee his whole life—even his [Wright's] own children didn't do that."

1. Samuel Ichiye Hayakawa was the first child of Ichiro Hayakawa and Otoko Isono, both Japanese nationals. Here he is at one year old, in 1907.

2. The Hayakawa family in Canada, 1908. Sammy is in the front, and Otoko is holding Fred.

3. "Sammy" Hayakawa is about two and a half years old
(1908) and living in Raymond, Alberta, Canada, where his
father had opened a small grocery store.

4. "Hak" (*far right*), the First Fairy in a production of
A Midsummer Night's Dream at St. John's High School,
Winnipeg, Canada, 1921.

5. The Hayakawa family in 1923. *Back row, left to right:* Grace Emi, Samuel Ichiye, Ichiro, and Fred Jun; *front row, left to right:* Ruth Toshiko and Otoko.

6. An early high point—but bitter pill, too—for Hayakawa
came in May 1936 when he appeared as leader of the Japanese
Canadian Citizens League delegation before the Special
Committee on Elections and Franchise Acts of the House of
Commons in Ottawa. *Left to right:* Minoru Kobayashi, Dr.
Edward Banno, Hideko Hyodo, Samuel Ichiye Hayakawa.

7. According to Maurice Zolotow, Hayakawa's "most significant contribution to the University of Wisconsin at Madison campus was his staging of the first American production of T. S. Eliot's *Murder in the Cathedral*" (1936). Hayakawa appears on the left.

8. (*Above*) Don Hayakawa and Marge Peters on their wedding day. They were married at Marge's aunt Augusta's home in Hamilton, Ohio, on May 29, 1937.

9. (*Right*) Alfred Korzybski, the father of general semantics.

To S. I. Hayakawa, the dear old faithful
'master' with warm best wishes and appreciation
December 1941.   Korzybski

10. (*Above*) Helen Furuyama and George Yoshida were married in the Hayakawas' Hyde Park Boulevard apartment in Chicago, 1945. *Left to right:* Samuel Ichiye Hayakawa, Mrs. Satoe Furuyama, George Yoshida, Helen Furuyama Yoshida, Mr. and Mrs. Yoshida, Marge Peters Hayakawa.

11. (*Right*) Samuel Ichiye Hayakawa in 1946. Portrait by Ken Uyehara.

12. Hayakawa and his son Alan (1949), who recalls his dad
"puttering around the apartment in Chicago, fixing things or
assembling gadgets out of a collection of nuts, bolts, saved
string or wire, and pieces of wood."

13. Marge and Alan visit with Don's family in Kusakabe, in Yamanashi City, Japan, 1953. *Left to right:* Otoko Hayakawa, Marge, Alan, Great-Grandmother Misa Hayakawa, and Don.

14. The Hayakawas and Daisy Rosebourgh in their Mill
Valley, California, home remodeled by Wesley Peters, chief
architect of Taliesin Associated Architects of the Frank Lloyd
Wright Foundation, 1960. *Left to right:* Alan Romer, Marge,
Don, Wynne, Daisy, and Mark.

15. Don and his son Alan in their Mill Valley home, 1960.
Don had a natural talent and taught himself how to play the
mandolin.

16. (*Above*) Marge and Don in their Mill Valley living room in 1961. Photo by John M. Brenneis. Used by permission.

17. (*Right*) "Chef Hayakawa" filets a striped bass, 1964. Don often pitched in to help prepare meals. "He was a good cook," Daisy stated.

18. (*Above*) Otoko, Don, and Ichiro Hayakawa in Japan in
1970.

19. (*Right*) Don started fencing in 1928 at McGill University.
Here he is exercising and practicing at the Pannonia Athletic
Club in San Francisco on March 18, 1970.

S. I. Hayakawa
June 1973

20. (*Left*) By 1973 Hayakawa was an ex-president of San Francisco State College contemplating a political run.

21. (*Above*) Margedant Peters Hayakawa, 1975. Photo by Wynne Hayakawa.

22. Hayakawa—aka "Hayakama" and "Hiawatha"—took
advantage of his popularity in the Republican Party to meet
with President Gerald Ford to discuss the "Tokyo Rose" case
in 1976.

23. U.S. Senate Inauguration Day, January 1977. *Left to right:*
Lilith Hayakawa (Alan's daughter), Ruth Hayakawa Braley,
Marge Hayakawa, Samuel Ichiye Hayakawa, Vice-President
Nelson Rockefeller, and Wynne Hayakawa.

24. The year's most satisfying event for the senator was his ninety-six-year-old mother's visit to the White House (1977). *Left to right:* Senator Samuel Ichiye Hayakawa, Otoko Hayakawa, President Jimmy Carter, and Ruth Hayakawa Braley.

25. The Hayakawa family in Japan, 1979. *Left to right:* Grace
Emi Hayakawa, Gene Prat, Samuel Ichiye Hayakawa, Marge
Hayakawa, Otoko Hayakawa.

26. Don (shown here in 1979) tap-danced as a form of
exercise and a way to calm himself when under tension —
even in the middle of meetings.

27. By the late 1980s, the former senator was the spokesman
for U.S. English, a group that advocated declaring English
the official national language.

28. Senator Hayakawa with Cambodian refugee children at
the holding center for Kampucheans in Bankang, Sakaew,
Thailand, 1980.

29. Senator Hayakawa and President Ronald Reagan at the
White House, 1981.

30. Daisy Rosebourgh, pictured here with Alan Hayakawa's
wife, Barbara, in 2009, was an integral element of the
Hayakawa family: nanny and housekeeper, but mostly friend
and confidante.

twenty-one

The fate of Japan was much on Don's mind during the immediate postwar period. He wrote two apparently unpublished "Second Thoughts" columns for the *Defender* on the subject. In "What to Do with Japan?" he suggested, "With the destruction of the Emperor, who is the major symbol around which Japanese culture in recent decades had been structualized [*sic*], the Japanese will have to reorganize their lives around whatever other symbol they have left." Hayakawa proposed Buddhism as a possible alternative to the nationalistic excesses of Shintoism. In the other column he asked and answered the question "Democracy in Japan?" His response: "The principal difference between Japanese and Americans is the fact that Japanese are so accustomed to authority. . . . A profound need in educating Japanese towards democracy is to cultivate a sense of narrower limits beyond which they will not permit authority to go."

In August 1946, as professional activities increasingly occupied them, Don and Marge hired a young couple, Vladimir and Ibby Dupre, as live-in help to aid Mary with household chores and help care for Alan. Marge became their immediate (and easy-to-work-for, according to Vladimir) supervisor. The Dupres were students at the University of Chicago, with Vladimir completing a PhD. Their situation was somewhat unusual, since they were occasionally invited to join one of the Hayakawas' many parties after they had prepared and served the meal. As a result, they got to know people from Moholy-Nagy's Institute for Design, from Frank Lloyd Wright's Taliesin, from the worlds of general semantics and co-ops, music and liberal politics. "We were fortunate to have that experience," said Vladimir in 2006.

Vlad and Don shared a passion for music, especially jazz and the blues. "We would, late at night, sometimes head to clubs on the south side" where Don was known. "He'd be the only Nisei and I'd be the only white person, and we sure had some good times," Vladimir reminisced. One outcome of those visits was that Vlad and Ibby became friendly with singer Billie Holiday.

Don and Fred Hayakawa finally managed to ship packages of foodstuffs and clothes to their family in Japan late in 1946. The thank-you letter Ichiro wrote to his sons on December 11 opened: "That instant coffee was simply wonderful." He continued, "I shudder to think over many millions of homeless and clothless [sic] people. Fortunately by our Boys and Peters' sympathy, our women and children here are clad warmly. My eyes become cloudy with tears whenever I think of it. How lucky we are to have left Sam and Fred there when we returned to Japan 20 years ago."

It's unlikely the Hayakawa boys had agreed with that sentiment at the time the family departed, but "Sam" surely did by 1946, since he was not only a North American, but a successful one. His father didn't grasp the latter, and he wrote, "I have just read a book called 'The Folded Leaf.' The plot is concerned with University students in Chicago in about the period Sam was studying in Madison." Then, in a touching, if inaccurate, vein, he continued: "It refers to a professors' life occasionally and I note, without variation, professors are all poor, although highly respected and honored. So I came to the conclusion that Sam is one of the poor ones, or less endowed with money. We must refrain therefore to crowd him for things we want, as he will be needing all the money for his family. . . . I believe Fred can better afford to send us money and relief stuff as he is a single and won't know what to do with all the money he earns, barrels of it perhaps." Of course, between the money and stocks Marge had inherited, the royalties and speaker's fees Don was earning, and his salary at the university, the couple was comfortably fixed, and had in fact loaned or given money to various relatives, especially Wes.

Don had once jocularly said to his friend Bill Pemberton, "I see no reason why I shouldn't marry a rich girl."

They could certainly afford a family. Having begun theirs relatively late in life, the Hayakawas were delighted to learn that Marge was again pregnant a year after Alan's birth. That joy turned to sadness when she miscarried the full-term baby, a daughter they planned to name Carolyn, causing the couple to wonder if more children *could* be added to their family. They determined to at least try to conceive again.

News from Japan continued to be grim. "I am still unable to go into any business or to find an occupation," Ichiro wrote on January 15, 1947. "Altho I am still in good health there seems to be little chance for a fellow like me with no experience except in import and export which is banned at present." Despite his rusty English skills, Ichiro's letter, which was composed of three pages, presented clearly a bleak picture of postwar Japan: "Not only acute shortage of all commodities causing such alarming inflation, but it is also social revolution, upsetting old orders, modes and refinement. It is the ruination of middle class, overthrow of intellectual layer of community, pushing them to starvation." He also had two requests: "I need a typewriter very badly, even a portable. . . . Don't hesitate to send anything, even worn out clothes, used articles are useful and handy. We have unashamed cravings for everything and all things."

Don initiated the process of obtaining and sending a typewriter, which his father did not receive until mid-June. (When it finally reached Ichiro, Don's sister Ruth wrote that their father "was frisking about with joy as a Kid [*sic*] who got first Bike [*sic*] and then sat to pound his first typed letter to you.") Before that, however, the elder Hayakawa dropped a note to his elder son on February 8, and his tone was much more positive: "Confidence is coming back to me and I am now planning the future, to work the remaining years of my life, however short it may be. I foresee a great influx of American goods into this country as soon as trade is opened." Preparing to take advantage of improving conditions, Ichiro wrote that he intended to import and export foodstuffs: "I should like to be the first line of action when trade commences. Therefore I would like you and Fred to spare some of your unsparable [*sic*] time in looking around the possibility of my enterprise and if you think it is a good way to spend a few dollars for 'want add' [*sic*] in some papers of large cities call attention of your manufacturers and exporters offering my services as their agent." Don complied with his father's wishes and prepared an ad that ran for a week in the *Chicago Journal of Commerce* before being sent to other outlets.

In June, Ruth wrote to him from Japan to tell him that the notices had resulted in a number of contacts—"Continental Trading Corporation," "B. Schlosberg Associate," "Kanley & Genoverse," "Badger Glove and Slipper Company," and finally "Robert S. Wild," a banker interested in foreign trade. The letters "served . . . to give psychological effect on Dad's mind to lift his low spirit, showing him a streak of light ahead and I am sure that you have done good to our dear Father, who is getting impatient and irritable for not doing anything these many years while aging year by year mercilessly."

Meanwhile, Don's writing in ETC. continued to illustrate the breadth of his interests, his felicity of expression, and his sense of humor. In reviewing the latest edition of *Roget's International Thesaurus*, for example, he questioned whether learning vocabulary for its own sake would improve communication: "The trouble with most people—and I suspect that it was so in his [Peter Mark Roget's] day too—is not that their vocabularies are too small; it is that they are too large relative to the actual amount of knowledge and experience they possess." To exemplify this, he added, "We all talk about things we know little about. (You ought to hear me sometime on the subject of atomic energy.)"

The easing of restrictions on fuel and travel in the United States after World War II allowed Don to accept more guest lectureships and visiting professorships. He decided to resign his full-time position at Illinois Tech, telling colleague Roy Wilcox that he wanted "to take time off from academia to develop my interest in co-ops, jazz, and writing." Just as likely he also wanted to try to catch on elsewhere, perhaps at one of the more prestigious institutions inviting him as a guest speaker.

One of his talks aroused attention that year, especially after it was published. "The Revision of Vision" was presented several times that year to various learned societies before being printed in the summer 1947 issue of ETC. Influenced not only by studying with László Moholy-Nagy but by his increasingly detailed reading of the work of theorists such as Gyorgy Kepes (*The Language of Vision*, 1945) and Alexander Dorner (*The Way beyond Art*, 1947), Hayakawa responded to the popular criticism that modern art failed to be representational ("It doesn't even look like anything!"). He summarized: "(1) The entire modern movement in art is a revolt against the semantics of identification, and an attempt to establish the semantics of non-identification. (2) The modern movement in art attempts to establish a dynamic semantics of time-and-relation-mindedness, and to abolish the static and rigid semantics of object-mindedness." Thus the primary subject of Marcel Duchamp's controversial *Nude Descending the Stairs*, for instance, is not the nude but the descent itself; or, "Looking at a mobile is like watching the waves of the sea or the flames in a fireplace."

Letters critical of Hayakawa's speech-turned-essay suggested that he not only knew little about art but that he wasn't much of a general semanticist either. Guila F. Beattie, MD, wrote, "When '*Etc.: A Review of General Semantics*' publishes papers in which the term 'semantics' is NOT used as Korzybski and his students use it, I would suggest that the editors make this clear to readers." R. S. Shuman was even more outraged: "I find its direction so misleading and its disregard of general semantics methodology so startling that I cannot refrain from comment," he fumed. "Has he [Hayakawa] ever heard of what people describe as 'charlatanism' and 'insincerity'? (Mr. Hayakawa's acknowledged contributions to the discipline of general semantics require that a curtain of silence be interposed at this point)."

Due perhaps to its condescending tone, the latter missive merited a response, and Don's tongue-in-cheek reply was not likely to have pleased the critic. "Concerning Mr. Shuman's communication, which I have read several times with increasing bewilderment, I can say only that I wish he would read my article before replying to it."

"The Revision of Vision" illustrated why *ETC.* under Hayakawa's editorship gradually gained more readers; he chose for its pages well-written, diverse, sometimes controversial pieces often reflecting his own myriad interests rather than strict Korzybskian theory, a fact that remained galling to purists, many of whom did not consider *ETC.* a general semantics journal at all. Korzybski and his inner circle reportedly continued to resent Don's popularity and to denigrate his "simplified" version of the Count's ideas, although Don remained one of only two people other than the Count permitted to offer seminars at the Institute of General Semantics while Korzybski was alive. In 1946 the IGS had left Chicago and relocated in the countryside near Lakeville, Connecticut, an event that eased tensions between the institute and the Society for General Semantics; their proximity had gradually been becoming a problem.

Marge continued her editorial activities at *Poetry* magazine and the co-op newspaper, while her husband was by then serving on the co-op's board of directors. He wanted a more significant academic position than he'd previously enjoyed, but the couple was so well established in Chicago that an aggressive job search played a distant second fiddle to having more children and providing them with a stable life. Hayakawa had unintentionally made a bargain with the devil, though, becoming famous in a field not held in high esteem in the academic mainstream. His success with *Language in Action* continued to overshadow his promising start as a literary scholar. Searching for options, he taught a course at the University of Kansas City and did research at Menninger Clinic while he was revising and updating *Language in Action.*

In Kansas City he encountered a famous painter, Thomas Hart Benton, but wasn't impressed. He wrote to Marge, "Benton is a crashing bore. He's good natured enough about it, but he shouts and interrupts and has violent prejudices and talks as if he knew everything. I was quite irritated." While in Kansas City he received a letter from Rudolph Carnap, to whom he had offered a membership in the International Society for General Semantics (ISGS). "It was kind of you to think of me in this way," the distinguished philosopher wrote, "but I do not wish to appear as a supporter of Korzybski—I hope you will understand." Don's final word to his wife when he informed her of the rejection was "Ouch!"

Meanwhile, correspondence from his family in Japan revealed that conditions were gradually improving, yet their situation remained a constant worry for Don. Ichiro revealed in a letter dated February 10, 1948, "We are the happiest of families being well cared for by both you and Fred and relatives as well in food and clothings [sic] which are sum total of our existence these days. No aim, ambition or aspiration of life except problem of living." But matters weren't entirely gloomy, since "Gradually, I am gaining weight." The elder Hayakawa closed the letter referring to his wife: "Ma is always regretting that she cannot write english [sic] and that you do not read Japanese. Otherwise, she would have written oftener than I. She wishes me to convey her deepest love to you, Peters and Alan. Fortunately we are *all* in good health and God granted we shall see each other some day."

Don's father also revealed that he was seeking "reinstatement of my canadian [sic] Nationality by naturalization, according to news item seen in Japanese canadian New paper [sic] which you mailed to Ruth." He continued: "Citizenship of Nisei or naturalized canadian is automatically revoked after staying away from Canada for more than 6 years, but may be cleared and reinstated on application explaining circumstances of staying out and swearing that one did not take any part in war or in official capacity while here. I made necessary statement and applied to Can. Government through Tokyo office. I told them that you and Fred will be responsible for my expenditure and living expenses when I go back to Canada." Despite his sons' efforts, Ichiro would never return to Canada as a citizen; however, his widowed daughter Ruth, who had been born there, but whose citizenship had been revoked when she married a Japanese national, would eventually recover her Canadian passport.

A little over a month later, Ichiro again wrote and this time divulged that he had not emerged from the war unscathed. "Exactly 3 years ago this month, my left ear stopped hearing. It was caused by severe shock and nervous strain during day-and-night bombing period when I was running in and out of city under imminent danger of life and riding trains overcrowded and shrieking." By then, Don had arranged for the Hostess Pantry Shop at Mandel Brothers department store in Chicago to ship food packages to his parents every month and to an aunt every other month.[1] Establishing a standing order freed him from assembling monthly packages, something for which he had scant time.

Ibby Dupre also began to have scant time, because she enrolled in graduate courses at the University of Chicago. She and her husband, with Don and Marge's blessing, "sub-contracted" some of their duties, particularly caring for Alan, by then nearly two years old and a live wire. Mary Walker suggested that they consider her sister-in-law, Daisy Rosebourgh, who wasn't happy with her position at the time. "Somethin' went wrong there," Daisy explained. "I didn't even get a day off." As it turned out, Daisy would become part of the Hayakawa family's core and would remained connected to them for the rest of her life.

A native of Batesville, Mississippi, Daisy was born in 1913, one of thirteen children of a lay Baptist minister. A dedicated angler, she later remembered with special fondness fishing with her family back home, as well as their church activities there. She also remembered segregation and racism. To help his family escape those scourges, her oldest brother, James Jr.—called Jimmy—had established himself in Illinois in 1922. He then returned to Mississippi each year to bring a sibling back with him when he returned; his family's venture north was part of the great diaspora of southern blacks. In 1932 he brought Daisy north after she finished high school, and he didn't stop transporting relatives until the mid-1930s, when he at last convinced his mother and father to also migrate.

---

1. Two samples of the packages the Hayakawas had Mandel Brothers send to Japan: *Package No. 171 ($16.95)*, 3 lbs. steak, 2 lbs. butter, 2 lbs. bacon, 2 lbs. coffee or 1/2 lb. tea, 1 tin thick cream, 10 oz., 3 lbs. flour, 2 lbs. sugar, 2 pkgs. noodle soup, 5 oz., 4 bars soap, 1 lb. *Package No. 168 ($7.75)*, 4 lbs. finest quality candy, 2 lbs. fruit cake "rich and fruity," 1 lb. dried fruit, 1 lb. nuts, sugared and toasted, 1 lb. fruit jam, 1 tin.

Daisy learned immediately after being hired that the Hayakawas were different from her previous employers. "When I first started, Mrs. Hayakawa and I sat down and talked and she told me that I had Thursdays and Sundays off. It came down to holidays. She said, 'Now there are two major holidays—Thanksgiving and Christmas.' She said, 'Now, I would like to have Christmas and you can have Thanksgiving.' So I never had to work on Thanksgiving, but always on Christmas. That's fine with me."

Daisy was hired just as Alan turned two, and she soon found she was involved in a family that entertained frequently. She met celebrities such as Cab Calloway, Mahalia Jackson, Larry Adler, Duke Ellington, and Langston Hughes at the Hayakawas' parties, and she was especially impressed by a visit from the movie actor Frederic March. Of the great gospel singer Mahalia Jackson, Daisy said, "She was nice, very nice, and she could really sing." Despite encountering such well-known friends of the Hayakawas, Daisy found herself enfolded in a family without elitism, where good humor was the order of the day. Members of her own family were welcomed guests in the home: "It could be Mr. Hughes or my brother Jimmy, they'd treat folks just the same." Don often pitched in to help prepare meals. "He was a good cook," she said. Many years later she recalled that "Mr. Hayakawa"—as she always referred to him"—made wonderful crab salads. One day I said to him, 'I'd love to have that recipe.' He told me, 'You can have it but you have to pay me five dollars.'" Retelling the story, Daisy waved a pale palm as she recalled saying, "Never you mind. You keep it," and reported that they'd both laughed.

She also recalled that "Mr. Hayakawa didn't put on the dog. If he was going to have someone to dinner, you just take what's here and that's it." What most impressed her was the egalitarianism of the Hayakawa family: everyone did chores, including the paterfamilias, who could also lose arguments with his housekeeper and laugh at himself. "He was just that type of a person," she remembered. "Humorous. He never made a fuss out of anything. Everything went along smooth."

One dinner in particular was memorable to Daisy. On a night when his wife wouldn't be home, Don called and told the housekeeper that he'd be bringing two couples to dine. "One of the ladies . . . nobody had told her that Mrs. Hayakawa wasn't home," Daisy explained. "I guess the lady decided she was just going to ask, so she said, 'Well, where is Mrs. Hayakawa?' Mr. Hayakawa was sitting right there at the table and said, 'Well, she left me.' There was a minute of silence. I looked at him and said, 'What?' Then he said, 'No, she's on a field trip.'"

Don and Marge—especially the former—had also become regulars at Mama Yancey's chitlin' parties, where they became friendly with more and more black musicians, including many luminaries, who were interested in meeting the Japanese Canadian who wrote so intelligently about African American music. Don ate soul food and jammed at the piano with them. Daisy chuckled when she recalled, "That man would eat *anything*, chitlins, even some nasty fish guts he brought back from Japan."

Don's love of and involvement in the jazz scene was a wonder to Daisy. "I didn't care too much for the jazz business," she admitted, "but he loved it . . . all of them old jazz singers and players. Some of them were very poor. Especially Big Crawford, who played the bass fiddle, because he was kind of like an alcoholic, but Mr. Hayakawa hung in there with him and got him a job at Warners bookstore in downtown Chicago, and Crawford came out to be somebody. He turned his life around, because there wasn't anyone would hire him before." She added, "Big Crawford turned out to be one of the nicest, friendly, honest, workin'est persons you ever met." Hayakawa's philosophy was, Daisy reported, "When somebody's down, don't try to hold 'em there. Help 'em."

There was one more aspect of Hayakawa's involvement in the jazz scene. Novelist Ernest Callenbach, who was a student at the University of Chicago then, remembers the city as largely segregated. "But not the jazz clubs," he said. "Blacks and whites mingled there." And not just blacks and whites; an Asian Canadian professor who was deeply committed to integration was also a frequent presence. Another University of Chicago student, Joe Axelrod, recalled of Hayakawa, "He was, of course, very well known because of jazz."

194

twenty-two

Early in the summer of 1948, the year the Dominion Elections Act finally allowed Canadians of Japanese ancestry to vote in federal elections, the Hayakawas were delighted to learn that Marge was again pregnant. Alan was by then keeping Daisy and his parents busy, but the household continued running smoothly. Still, Daisy recalled a moment of dissonance that she found amusing: In August, Don announced that he had purchased coveted tickets to a night baseball game in which future Hall of Fame pitcher Satchel Paige, a recent acquisition of the Cleveland Indians, would start against the Chicago White Sox. Hayakawa's friends who worked for the Sox had urged him not to miss Paige, a legend in the Negro leagues long before being admitted to the majors when he was in his forties (becoming the oldest rookie in league history). Many authorities still consider him the greatest pitcher of all time; he was also a folk philosopher ("Don't look back, something might be gaining on you") and a genuine character to boot, so Don—like much of Chicago, it seemed—was looking forward to seeing him in action.

Unfortunately, Hayakawa had chosen tickets for a night when one of his aunts, Mrs. Satoe Furuyama, who spoke poor English, was scheduled to visit the family. Daisy recalled, "You know I never did see the Hayakawas to have an argument. They was never mean to each other. But that day, Mrs. Hayakawa she said, 'You need to stay home to talk to your aunt. We can't even talk to her.' Well, he just stood there for a minute, then he stuck his tongue out at her," she chuckled at the memory. "Stuck it right out! But he stayed home." The geriatric rookie, Paige, pitched a 1–0 shutout over the White

Sox and attracted a crowd of 78,382, setting a new major-league attendance record for a night game. Despite that minor dispute, the Hayakawas began preparing a room for their new baby.

Don, meanwhile, delivered a paper at the 1948 meeting of the National Council of Teachers of English in Chicago. Entitled "Recognizing Stereotypes as Substitutes for Thought," this classic Hayakawa combination of scholarly insight and common sense was reprinted the following March in the organization's periodical, *English Journal*. The peril of stereotypes, he wrote, "lies not in their existence but in the fact that they become for all people some of the time and for some people all of the time *substitutes for observation*." He recommended that an extensional orientation be cultivated to avoid problems with stereotypes: "This means training one's self not to guide one's self by verbal association patterns inside one's head but by observation of the non-verbal realities of fact or of sensation before one acts or verbalizes."

That speech also contained one of those insights that so often livened Hayakawa's work. "We are so enamored of words," he suggested, "that we forget that the magic of words in the great writers comes from the fact that they thought earnestly, felt deeply, and observed accurately the world of not-words. We, however, often give our students the impression that literature has less to do with representing human life and experience truly than with dressing it up for show."

As the 1948 presidential election approached, the Hayakawas—even nonvoter Don—were dedicated liberals who supported Harry Truman in his uphill reelection bid against not only the favored Republican, Thomas E. Dewey, but also Dixiecrat Strom Thurmond and Progressive Henry Wallace. Predictions of doom surrounded Truman's candidacy, but Don expected the incumbent to triumph, and triumph he did. Don, the successful prognosticator, began a note to Marge on November 3 celebrating: "My love: Isn't it simply terrific about Truman and Douglas and Stevenson and Helen Gahagan Douglas and everybody else who got in?" He had earlier told friends—including fellow University of Wisconsin grad Morris Rubin, coeditor of *The*

Progressive—that he couldn't see why Truman didn't have a chance and, as his wife recalled, "everybody was trying to show you why he should be counted out."

A bit of gloat crept into Marge's letter to him following the election: "I knew you would be excited at the election, and hoped you were at a Democratic campaign headquarters. I too listened in growing amazement until around 3 a.m. and awoke to tune in at 8:30 the next morning. Did you hear [H. V.] Kaltenborn around 10:30 or so spouting [?] 'Republican trends' in the figures that were coming in? He sounded more and more sheepish as time went on. The Tribune had several 'Dewey Leads' and 'Dewey Wins' headlines, which the Sun-Times has cruelly reproduced." Marge, who had feared the Dixiecrats and Progressives would siphon too many votes from the incumbent, had placed a small bet with Mary Walker. "With the greatest of pleasure I lost $1 election bet with Mary, who was the only person in the U.S. besides Mr. Truman who was absolutely certain Truman would win. . . . You certainly had things sized up, too," she wrote.

Mark Hayakawa was born on February 6, and an unexpected challenge and opportunity was presented to the entire clan, including Daisy and Mary, when Mark came home from the hospital nearly three weeks before his mother, who had developed a blood clot. Mary was still keeping house for the Hayakawas, while Daisy assumed responsibility for Alan and "Markmarkmark," as the baby was called by his older brother. She and the new arrival quickly bonded. "That's my boy!" she said throughout his life. "He was a sweet baby—very easy—not at all demanding." Mark's father agreed, "He was an 'easy' baby, quiet, friendly, and passive; but he needed a baby's care for a long time."

When Don observed Irving Lee's infant son, David, he was "astounded" by the relative maturity and strength of the baby. "Not at all the vegetative type that Markmarkmark is." He sensed that something might be wrong: "We had known that he was slower than the average child in smiling, in sitting up, in responding to others around him," he wrote in a memoir entitled "Our Son Mark" for

197

McCall's magazine. "Having had one child who was extraordinarily ahead of such schedules, we simply thought that Mark was at the other end of the average range."

Not until Mark was eight months old were his parents informed that he suffered from Down's syndrome. Don was out of town, so Marge had little support when a social worker informed her, adding in no uncertain terms, "You can't keep a child like this at home." When Marge asked, "What can I read to find out more about his condition and how to take care of him?" she was told, "You can't get help from a book. . . . You must put him away." Her husband noted in that 1969 remembrance, "Today this sounds like a dialogue from the dark ages. . . . Today professional advice runs generally in the opposite direction: 'Keep your retarded child at home if it's at all possible.'"

The Hayakawas at first "had a hard time coming to terms with Mark's Down's syndrome," recalls Vladimir Dupre, but finally they determined to keep the boy at home and help him become as much as he could be. As the parents said later, "There is no minimum I.Q. required for membership in this family." Mark Hayakawa was a lucky little boy.

To compound the burden of that day when Marge learned that her younger son was retarded, she had also been told "that it was too risky for us to have any more children, that there was a fifty percent chance of us having another mongoloid child." That news and their baby's condition added other layers of complexity to the already complicated lives of the Hayakawas, but they seem not to have flinched. They would make Mark as much a part of their lives as parents could, never hiding him or apologizing for him, and they would indeed have another baby. "We did not go on dwelling on what might have been," the father reflected, "and we have been rewarded by finding much good in things the way they are." In fact, Don's concern for and love of Mark revealed a softer side of the father's often competitive nature.

Don and Marge never sought credit or attention for what the entire family was doing for Mark. Said Daisy, "When we found

Mark had Down's syndrome, all the love I had went to him." Of her employers, she recalled, "Oh, they were wonderful with Mark." Mark would actually strengthen the family's bond, because both Don and Marge were determined to do everything possible for the boy, and so was Daisy. In discussing the physicians and social workers who had advised that the baby be "put away," Don pointed out, "Their reaction to Mark was to a generalization, while to us he was an individual."

The Hayakawas were not sanguine. "It has not all been easy," the father wrote in "Our Son Mark," "but when has easiness been the test of the value of anything?" Besides, "From the beginning, we have enjoyed Mark for his delightful self. He has never seemed like a burden." Don also observed that Mark's "mental limitation has given him a capacity for contentment, a focus on the present moment, which is often enviable. His world may be circumscribed, but it is a happy and bright one." Don concluded that emotional 1969 account by admitting, "It's a strange thing to say, and I am a little startled to find myself saying it, but I often feel that I wouldn't have had Mark any different."

Don's professional life proceeded apace while everyone adjusted to the new son's needs. His wife recalled Don working at home revising the book or writing his newspaper columns as well as caring for Mark: "When Mark was small, we had one of these baby carriers that was called an Australian sling. You could put the baby around on your hip and carry it. He used to walk around, carrying Mark and sit at his desk and Mark sitting here. . . . [Mark] was passive and loved to be carried. So Don carried him that way." Alan was by no means neglected. He remembers "playing on the black marble-pattern linoleum floor of [Don's] study while he and my mother and other grown-ups read galley proofs for ETC. I must have soaked up some of their conversations," he adds, "because for years afterward he proudly quoted me as saying, 'All crows are black, at least all those I've seen.'"

Later that same spring, Don was in New York to teach a seminar at Hofstra College. He had become well enough known by then that both *Time* and the *New Yorker* sent writers to cover his appearance. He would enjoy even more exposure when a lecture he gave at Cooper Union drew 850. "I've never had such a terrific sense of having put something big across in a convincing way as I did after this time," he noted in an undated letter from the Parkside Hotel.

Something big was in the works at Harcourt, Brace and Company, too, where editors were excited over the prospect of a new edition of Don's book. With his colleague Basil H. Pillard, Hayakawa had expanded *Language in Action*, and it was tentatively agreed, after consulting with editors in New York, to retitle the book *Language, Thought and Action* and to "have a foreword explaining relationship to the older book. There is far too much new stuff in it—they [the editors] both feel—to use the old title with only the explanation '(Revised).'" The finished project was published late that year with the title *Language in Thought and Action*.

No less a figure than rhetorician James M. McCrimmon (*Writing with a Purpose, Teaching with a Purpose*, et al.) reviewed the new edition in *ETC.*, and he found it to be a significant improvement over the first edition, which, he asserted, had been "too easy to read and too hard to teach." McCrimmon added, "Apart from its [improved] use as a teaching instrument, *Language in Thought & Action* is a more mature book than its predecessor. . . . [A]t least in academic circles, the study of semantics has changed from a cult to a movement since the first edition was published."

Despite the new round of fine reviews his book garnered, Don was again unsuccessful in his search for a better teaching position; his application to Northwestern led to no job offer, so he continued offering courses part-time at the University of Chicago. Rumblings about a merger of the Institute of General Semantics and the International Society for General Semantics led Hayakawa to become politically active within the latter.

"The year 1949 proved to be a pivotal year in the history of the two organizations," Steve Stockdale later reported. While Count Korzybski continued attracting pupils to his institute, its salad days were over. Hayakawa reached far more potential students—and, of course, potential donors—with his essays and lectures, as well as with the magazine he edited, so Korzybski and Kendig decided to assert their primacy and take over the other organization, with its much larger membership roll. By then, Don's relationship with Korzybski and the institute had deteriorated, in no small measure due to a 1946 change in the society's bylaws that limited financial obligations to the institute. The two organizations in effect had begun to vie for the same dollars. Irving Lee, who remained a bridge between Hayakawa and Korzybski, told the former that he didn't "want to split the movement" and said he'd "do what he can to prevent AK from taking it out in the open." Of course, the movement already *was* split.

"Francis P. Chisholm, President of the society since 1947, ran for reelection . . . on a platform based on 'unifying' or 'merging' the two organizations," Stockdale explains. "This plan, [was] supported in principle by the Institute and four of six members of the ISGS Governing Board." Only Don Hayakawa and Anatol Rapoport were opposed; Don was astute—and perhaps ambitious—enough a politician to know that he'd win a popularity contest against anyone Korzybski might endorse, so he placed his own name in nomination against Chisholm. He wrote to Marge saying that Lee "thinks if I'm elected President, AK will *really* start to fight against me." Lee supported Don's successful bid for the presidency, and the merger was avoided.[1] Possibly in response, Korzybski and company soon began plans for a journal of their own, to be called *General Semantics Bulletin*.

Meanwhile, Don and Marge in their capacities as members of the board of trustees of the Modern Poetry Association—the parent group of *Poetry* magazine—early in 1950 found themselves embroiled in another controversy. In January the board named the noted poet Karl Shapiro editor of the journal, and he soon fired longtime business manager Geraldine Udell. Gerry Udell had been on the staff

---

1. Ironically, the two groups—both suffering from diminishing membership and clout—finally did merge on January 1, 2004, as the Institute of General Semantics. Fort Worth, Texas, is presently the combined organization's base.

for twenty-five years and was a special friend of Marge, who was then chair of the board. Fireworks followed. Peters, as she was still being called by pals, sent a five-page, single-spaced letter to editor emeritus Peter DeVries and sent a copy to Shapiro. It read, in part, "I am sure Karl had no idea how many people would be furious and outraged by what he has done—a lot of them influential in various groups around town, whom he presumably wants to cultivate. It has certainly spoiled what was a most auspicious beginning of his editorship."

Shapiro responded in a conciliatory tone less than a week later: "There is nothing I can say about my decision to drop Geraldine except that it was an immediate necessity. . . . Could you come to dinner?" Marge and Don declined and Karl offered an explanation to DeVries, who in turn wrote to Marge and Don. They were not moved, and she replied: "There are such things as self-fulfilling prophecies. There was no anti-Shapiro feeling. There is now. It's just too damn bad."

That was followed by a letter in which she and Don resigned from the association, its board, and its executive committee. Karl's wife, Evalyn, who had replaced Gerry Udell, accepted their resignations, and her husband—not blinking in the midst of the battle—followed with a letter to Don and Marge. "It is just short of amazing to me that you refused to take the trouble to find out what was going on," he wrote. "It is too late now, of course, but I can only interpret your strange attitude as deliberate blindness." That sad business ended the Hayakawas' long association with *Poetry* magazine, which thrived under Shapiro's editorship.

Beyond the politics of general semantics and *Poetry*, Don's professional life remained busy. In September he traveled to California to speak at the Modern Language Association's annual conclave. From the Southern Pacific Overlander as he traveled west, he wrote to Marge, "Tell Alan and Mark that they are both much nicer than the many children on this train. Of course one of the great reasons, obvious at first glance, is that their personalities are respected more by their parents. I've seen a good deal of slapping, scolding, and whining." He added that he and Kenneth Cameron, the scholar and editor with whom he attended the MLA meeting, would be staying in San Francisco rather than Palo Alto because, Ken had told him, the latter "is bone dry."

When Don returned from that conclave, Marge and the kids were visiting Grandma Peters. "The house is nice to be in," he wrote to his spouse, "altho not as nice as when it isn't empty. Love to Markmark-mark, Romer Hayakawa Alan, Clara, & you, my love." The children's nicknames—both reflections of Alan's immature speech—especially tickled their father.

Mark remained frail, and while Don was lecturing at Amherst in November, the baby suffered a heavy cold that led to choking. To treat the fragile boy, the Hayakawa family's doctor recommended "nose drops and a cough tent." In a note to her husband, Marge explained, "Dr. Spock's book emphasizes the good effects of warm moist air, and an even temperature, so we draped the radiator with wet towels and ran the showers, not knowing how to rig up a cough tent or how to keep him in it." Dr. Spock's advice was good indeed: "Its effect on Mark's choking was miraculous—as long as it was over 75 [degrees] and very moist."

Don lectured at the University of Massachusetts in November, and while he was received enthusiastically, a hoped-for job offer didn't materialize. Meanwhile, the family news from Japan was positive: "My business is now showing signs of activity," Ichiro wrote to his son three days before Christmas of 1950. "My hard work of many a month seems to be rewarded by orders coming in gradually from various parts of the world. . . . Export procedures are becoming easier and factories are restoring quickly. I am convinced that this country will again become a great industrial area of the Far East supplying goods to all asiatic [sic] nations as well as other markets of the world."

twenty-three

Alfred Korzybski died of a heart attack on March 1, 1950. "AK had worked in his office as usual the previous day and well into the evening," reported Vocha Fiske. "For nearly two years he had been confined most of the time to a wheel chair." Despite that, his death was unexpected and it stunned the GS community. In reflecting on her own emotions, Fiske wrote: "There was no regret that Alfred had coagulated. This was his term, a colloidal one, for death. He didn't use the latter term due to its emotional overloads."

The Count's accomplishments elicited a generous eulogy from the *American Journal of Psychiatry*, which said in part, "The death of this great teacher . . . deepens appreciation of his essential contribution to human understanding, on an individual, widely social, or international scale." The *New York Times'* obituary called Korzybski "a pioneer in semantics": "Widely credited with having expanded semantics from its ordinary concern with only the meaning of words in a new system of understanding, Mr. Korzybski held the conviction that 'in the old construction of language, you cannot talk sense.'" The Count's loyalists were even more effusive about his life and accomplishments; for instance, the Canadian ex-Jesuit J. Samuel Bois, who would become in many ways Korzybski's spiritual successor, wrote on May 8 of that year: "K is a saint, I tell you. He belongs to that group of men whom we French call *'les grands coeurs.'*"

The Count's personality had dominated the Institute of General Semantics, so that organization was thrown into disarray following his death. Soon, however, his erstwhile assistant, M. Kendig, assumed the directorship and began to schedule seminars and to move ahead with plans for the publication of the institute's *General Semantics Bulletin*. Hayakawa wrote to Kendig following Korzybski's passing, "It was with deepest regret that I learned last night of the death of Alfred Korzybski. There is no need for any of us in the International Society to tell you how profoundly we feel his loss."

The obituary tribute to Korzybski in *ETC.* consisted of a two-and-a-half-page biographical summary by Anatol Rapoport, plus a four-page "Bibliography of the Writings of Alfred Korzybski." It seemed a strangely perfunctory send-off for the man who had been, after all, the developer and the soul of general semantics, but in fact the spring 1950 issue was already being typeset when Korzybski died, so Hayakawa and company scrambled mightily to make a quick adjustment.

In his biographical summary, Rapoport suggests that "Korzybski's main contribution to thought centers around the linking of the fundamental problems which arise in connection with these central facts of human existence: first, the fact that man, upon being born, finds a ready-made orientation to the world, accumulated in centuries of time binding; second, the fact that man functions in a variety of ways, which can be graded on a scale ranging from 'insane' to 'sane.' Korzybski posed a crucial question: Are there any criteria for sanity other than those which relate sanity to conformity of behavior with that of the prevailing group?" Rapoport also quoted the mathematician Cassius Jackson Keyser, long an admirer of Korzybski's system, who said *Science and Sanity* was "beyond all comparison the most momentous single contribution that had ever been made to our knowledge and understanding of what is essential and distinctive in the nature of man."

That same March, Hayakawa and the ISGS found itself the target of attacks by the Hearst-owned *Chicago Herald-American* and the WGN News Bureau of the *Chicago Tribune*, both of which demanded that Don, as president of the organization, cancel a lecture by Larry Adler, the man credited with taking harmonica music to concert halls. Adler was also a student of general semantics, as well as a pal and occasional houseguest of the Hayakawas. He had been branded a Communist and blacklisted in 1949 when he refused to testify before the House Un-American Activities Committee. Hayakawa was telephoned at home by a representative of the *Herald-American*, who threatened to cause a disturbance if the harmonica virtuoso appeared. Don told him to go fish, and Adler appeared at Thorne Hall of the downtown Northwestern University campus, bringing down the house when, accompanied by Anatol Rapoport on piano, he concluded his performance by playing Vivaldi's Violin Concerto in A Minor.

The forces of the know-nothing right, as exemplified by the Hearst newspaper in Chicago, suspected that Don was, if not a Communist, possibly what was being called a "com-symp" or a "fellow traveler," and not only because of his association with Adler. His friendship with several "suspicious" black artists and intellectuals like Langston Hughes and Metz Lochard, as well as his and Marge's "anti-capitalist" co-op connection, were also considered questionable.[1]

Hayakawa continued offering only a night course as adjunct faculty at the University of Chicago; he also offered a general semantics course in the university's prestigious correspondence program. One of the students was William R. Vizzard, who recalls: "While in Korea, during the Korean 'Police Action,' I completed the course. He had (surprisingly!) asked my permission to use one or two of my lesson submissions as exemplars in his resident classes—of course I said OK, and he also asked me to meet him in western Japan where he was planning to visit relatives and [the] old family site, to interpret for him since he didn't speak Japanese (and I did)." Vizzard concludes, "The correspondence course . . . I deemed the most important college course I had ever undertaken (I hold a PhD)."

Don hosted a weekly radio show, *Hayakawa's Jazz Seminar*, on Chicago's fine-arts station, WFMT-FM. "Among station personnel who might have been acquainted with him," suggests Art Weber, "were writer Studs Terkel, announcer/now film director Mike Nich-

1. The Department of Justice has refused to make its files on the Hayakawas available, despite a Freedom of Information Act request.

ols, announcer Robert Conrad, and program director/announcer Norman Pellegrini." Hayakawa also continued to be popular on the national lecture circuit, sought by colleges and universities that would not offer him a tenure-track position. "The people at Ohio State called me up again this morning to say that they wanted me to come on May 20, which is the day after my speech at Lincoln Univ., Jefferson City, Mo.," he wrote to Marge, who with Alan was visiting her mother. "When I said I couldn't make it, the guy insisted that I had to, that there was a plane from St. Louis to Columbus. . . . Also, Valparaiso Univ . . . called me this morning about another lecture in the next three weeks or four. It's getting to be terrific!"

Two days later he wrote her a note that contained this household vignette: "This morning Daisy bathed Mark in the big bathtub with the new gadget you bought by mail order. Mark had a terrific good time splashing and kicking like mad, and resisting altogether the idea of getting out again. Finally we were all in the bathroom, Daisy and Mary and I, watching him enjoy himself."

The other big news that day, however, was professional, not personal:

> Big excitement this morning. Dean of Arts and Letters at Colgate University, Hamilton, N.Y., called to invite me to speak there at a series involving 3 speakers, Gardner Cowles of the Cowles publications, George Denny, and me. Fee: $500!!! Unfortunately the evening they chose was impossible, so I gave them my schedule and they said they'd try to arrange another date. I told Daisy and Mary about it—I was pretty excited by the offer—and they were horrified at the notion of my having to pass up $500. . . . [F]or the moment I was dreadfully sorry I had taken the job at U. of C. Ten weeks and 16 lectures at U. of C., $400; 1 evening, 1 lecture at Colgate, $500. Ouch! Anyway, my conclusion is that I'd have to go buy a suit or two, to go with my new self-concept as a $500 lecturer.

Marge's responding letter opened this way: "My, how you impress me! I guess I can't be disrespectful of you anymore now that you're a $500 lecturer. What a disappointment not to be able to take it."

In Chicago, Hayakawa was considered something of a character, in a positive sense of the word. A newspaper feature story with the intriguing title "Beat Me, Professor, Eight to the Bar" described him as "a former taxicab driver known to his customers as Sammy," now a professor and a director of the Central States Co-op as well as "one of the country's leading semanticists" who "has become, and darned if he knows how, a historian of jazz and an amateur boogie woogie player." According to writer Emery Hutchison, location as much as anything had exposed S. I. Hayakawa to jazz greats and jazz history; Illinois Tech was situated only a few blocks from the heart of Chicago's jazz and blues scene. Not only had a number of great black musicians emerged from the neighborhood around the college, Hayakawa noted, but "all the early white musicians like Benny Goodman, Mugsy Spanier, Gene Krupa and Bud Freeman used to come for their education in jazz." As for his own abilities, "There are a lot of things I'd like to do if my fingers moved fast enough."

His mind apparently moved fast enough, though, and he hosted a series of thirteen half-hour shows about general semantics for National Education Television, while still appearing with some frequency on local radio as a jazz commentator. In fact, life was full for all the Hayakawas. Alan recalls his dad "puttering around the apartment in Chicago, fixing things or assembling gadgets out of a collection of nuts, bolts, saved string or wire, and pieces of wood. I remember him playing catch with me and pitching while my friends and I took turns hitting."

When the paterfamilias was not writing his columns for the *Defender* or playing with his son, he might be associating with a pal like jazzman Big Crawford one day and a fellow semanticist like Hugh Walpole the next, or perhaps writing a bit for Metz Lochard's new publication, the *Chicago Globe*, then flying to New York for a lecture. When Don traveled, as he did so often, he conversed with porters or bellhops or maids, learning what he could from their experiences. He seems to have assumed that there really was a wisdom of the folk, different from but as valuable as any he could learn from the elite. He conversed comfortably at most levels of usage, and he never gave evidence of considering himself a member of the elite. This became one source of the energy and originality of his writing. As Alan Hayakawa would later report, his father's basic belief was that "to cooperate and survive, we have to be able to talk to each other, that having a common language—or languages—can join us together."

Don was also as shocked as most Americans were when hostilities broke out on the Korean Peninsula. For the third time in his generation, war threatened to engulf the world, and Hayakawa, like so many other intellectuals, was convinced that failure to communicate was perhaps the core problem.

Before Christmas, Marge learned that she was once again pregnant. She and Don couldn't avoid some trepidation, given the warnings they'd received from doctors after Mark was born, but that did little to temper their joy. Taking every precaution, Marge managed an unremarkable pregnancy until late May 1951, when she began experiencing premature labor pains. Don rushed her to the hospital, where a tiny baby girl weighing slightly less than two pounds was delivered. She was about as small as an infant could be at that time and survive, so her parents had to wonder if they'd lose their second daughter. The baby was rushed to a hospital that specialized in treatment of premature infants, where she responded to care. Marge, meanwhile, endured postpartum depression fueled by the fear that she'd also lose this baby, but she pumped breast milk and delivered it to her daughter at the hospital, while everyone in the family joined the vigil.

Marge had delivered four babies in less than five years—one with Down's syndrome, another stillborn, and a third premature. Many years later, Alan suggested that his mother increasingly did not express her deep feelings. This could lead to unsettling situations: "When I was a kid, my dog died and my mother cried as we buried him," her older son revealed. "That scared me because I'd never seen her weep before."

The parents had planned to name this baby Carolyn, but Alan suggested Carol Wynne. Winifred Haynes had been one of Don and Marge's closest friends when they were at the University of Wisconsin, so the name appealed to them. In fact, the new baby was immediately called Wynne rather than Carol, and that never changed.[2] Daisy recalled that when the baby finally came home she was so small that her head fit in one hand while her feet just reached the crook of her nurse's elbow. "That was one tiny child," the woman said, "but could she make a racket!" Wynne herself was told that "I looked like a little rat when I came home after six weeks in the hospital. I probably looked like a baby possum when I was born."

Don was an involved father, one who made time for his children. Daisy recalled that "Mr. Hayakawa never said the kids couldn't come down [to the study] while he was working. . . . When he was writing *Language and Thought in Action* [sic] and he was doing something away from the desk he would carry Wynne in a pouch hanging in front and when he would sit down to the typewriter he would have her on his back." She also remembered that "Mr. Hayakawa would be at his typewriter with her hanging on his back and I would come and look and see if she was sleeping. As soon as I would just ease her out of this thing on his back, 'Waaa!'"

Hayakawa had since 1947 conducted a friendly correspondence with Joseph Henry Jackson, the literary editor of the *San Francisco Chronicle*, who invited him to visit when possible. In May 1951 Hayakawa became an occasional reviewer of books for that newspaper and, more importantly, a name on the Bay Area scene. During that year the Korean conflict continued to dominate the news nationally, especially after the Chinese had become involved. Ironically, the states of war against Germany and Japan had not been formally declared closed until that year; in San Francisco on September 8, forty-eight nations signed a peace treaty with Japan.

When his stint as president of the International Society for General Semantics ended, Don submitted a presidential report to members, noting not only the death of Korzybski but also the strengthening of relationships between the ISGS and foreign learned societies with

2. When she was seven, Wynne's name was legally changed, dropping "Carol."

similar aims, such as the Asociacion de Epistemologia in Buenos Aires and the Institute of the Science of Thought in Tokyo. By mid-1950 there were 1861 members of ISGS plus 572 subscribers and subscribing libraries. The organization seemed to be thriving.

So was Don's popularity on the lecture circuit. In July he spoke on "The Aims and Tasks of General Semantics," a talk sponsored by the Committee on Mathematical Biology of the University of Chicago, focusing on what Korzybski called "time binding," defined by Don as "the unique survival mechanism among human beings . . . the ability to organize social cooperation *at a distance* and to accumulate knowledge *over generations of time* though the use of symbols." In October he presented a variation of the same topic at Columbia University. That month, Hayakawa was also a guest lecturer at a three-day Conference on General Semantics at Ohio University in Athens. Hope that GS might one day enter the academic mainstream continued to buoy him.

Then forty-five years old, S. I. Hayakawa was often referred to in the press as the "famed semanticist" or, less accurately, as the "noted linguist." He was invited to address everything from conventions of businessmen to gatherings of consumers to academic meetings. Despite the continued success of *Language in Thought and Action*, his academic career hovered on the margin, just as general semantics did. The family discussed the possibility of relocating if a suitable position was offered Don, but no one was in a hurry to leave Chicago. Still, Marge recognized how unfulfilled her husband was. She also knew that a move away from the Midwest would be more difficult for her, since she remained close to her family there.

While Don cast about for an academic appointment, his published work continued to be stimulating. He wrote a long review essay of L. Ron Hubbard's *Dianetics: The Modern Science of Mental Health* for the summer 1951 issue of *ETC.*; it was a tour de force. Titled "From Science-Fiction to Fiction-Science," it was a thoughtful consideration and effective skewering of Hubbard's book. "The lure of the pseudoscientific vocabulary and promise of dianetics," he observed, "cannot but condemn thousands who are beginning to emerge from scientific illiteracy to a continuation of their susceptibility to word-magic and semantic hash." Add to opinions like that a tone that was far from respectful ("one fell swoop" became "one swell foop"), and it's little wonder that Hayakawa became for decades a target of scientologists, or that he didn't much care about their ire.

The fact that something like scientology made the pages of ETC. at all demonstrated to true believers in GS that, under Hayakawa's editorship, the journal continued to take Korzybski's work ever farther afield, separating Don from purists but endearing him to generalists. His own mind tended toward eclecticism and extrapolation.

[seven]

SAN FRANCISCO STATE

twenty-four

The summer of 1952 began with an event in Washington that had a deep impact on the Hayakawas. On June 25, President Harry Truman vetoed the McCarran-Walter Immigration Act. The following day, the House of Representatives overrode his veto, and the day after that the Senate did the same thing. The act, a product of cold war mentality, imposed limits on Americans abroad, tightened laws controlling the admission and the deportation of aliens, limited immigration from eastern and southeastern Europe, somewhat altered other immigration quotas, and removed bans on Asian and Pacific immigration. When the Japanese American Citizens League supported it, Don announced that he would no longer contribute to the JACL's Anti-Discrimination Committee, although he was one of those for whom the act brought the possibility of citizenship.

In July he was lecturing at Louisiana State University and fishing nearby, "observing the fact that those funny little artificial bass bugs actually do catch a bass now and then." The fishing may have been fine, but the heat and humidity of Baton Rouge bothered him and he wrote to Marge, "Hot as hell. One escapes from inferno of blazing sun to the damp mausoleum of air-conditioned office and restaurants. O Canada!"

Also, and not for the first time, he found himself nearly devoured by chiggers, critters that seemed especially attracted to him. On July 9, he wrote to his wife: "My nemisis (sp?) has overtaken me again. Maybe it was somewhere yesterday in Mississippi, perhaps in a roadside park where I ate a sandwich, but this morning and this afternoon have been developing chigger swellings—38 on my left leg alone. . . . But feeling itchy all over (or ichiye, if you insist) makes the heat much more intense."

The climate would be different indeed at his next stop. In early spring Don had received an unexpected proposal: "I was invited to teach a summer session at San Francisco State College. I must say that I was surprised at this invitation from a California institution, because I had known since high-school days in Winnipeg that California had been, throughout its history, the principal source in the U.S. of anti-Chinese and anti-Japanese agitation and politics." Marge and Don's conversations about this offer were, of course, not recorded, but he later wrote, "I accepted the invitation and enjoyed the experience very much."

San Francisco was then in flux. According to journalist Carl Noltek, it "tore down half of its Victorian Houses, tied up the last of its old ferryboats, [and] nearly junked its cable cars." It was then "crowded, noisy and vibrant. It had a booming port, a strong economy based on manufacturing, and it congratulated itself that it did not have the problems of Los Angeles. . . . [T]he city was a self-contained community, where everybody knew everybody—the West's biggest small town." It seemed to have fallen in love with the famous visiting professor. The *San Francisco Call*, *San Francisco News*, and *San Francisco Chronicle* printed stories announcing that Hayakawa would be offering courses at State.

There was considerable cultural ferment in the Bay Area, too. The North Beach neighborhood, nominally an Italian stronghold in San Francisco, was also attracting a new group of literary Bohemians, the Beats. Bongos echoed through the streets, and the aroma of espresso became common. In a small apartment there, Jack Kerouac lived with Neal and Carolyn Cassady; Lawrence Ferlinghetti published Allen Ginsberg's "obscene" poem, "Howl," there too; across the Golden Gate, an Oregon poet named Gary Snyder camped in a cabin nearby on the slopes of Mount Tamalpias.

While Don taught that summer session in San Francisco, the weather was often overcast, windy, billows of fog slowly rolling in from the Pacific. Mark Twain's reputed remark, "The coldest winter

I ever spent was a summer in San Francisco," rang true. "The City," as residents liked to call it, was then as smug as it was attractive. Don was even more taken with the setting than he'd anticipated: "This is a very beautiful city and I'm having a wonderful time"; but, he added, "It is cold evenings." He also found himself in an area very much in the midst of Korean War churning. A seaport with a direct link to the Far East, it was thus a port of departure for troops on their way to the ongoing conflict in Korea. San Francisco, the community that had once housed Hayakawa's father, retained its Pacific link as well as its Gold Rush past and cosmopolitan present—and a less publicized de facto segregation: Asians here, blacks there, Latinos nearby. Still, it was a fine place for a man like Don Hayakawa who preferred to wear suits and ties, just as it was for women who favored dresses and hats, or so went the rumor.

The visiting professor reported in a note to his wife that "the College and the Dept. and the Administration are tremendously excited and pleased." San Francisco State College (SFSC) was at the dawn of an upswing in prestige then, in no small measure due to an informal link with the University of Chicago. A dozen faculty and administrators from that institution had moved to State, and a more innovative, less-traditional approach came too, one that would characterize the English Department chaired by Caroline Shrodes. She, according to Don, "took me in to meet the president of the college [J. Paul Leonard], whose extreme affability indicated the degree of appreciation of the favorable publicity my visit is attracting."

That publicity likely contributed to the number of students drawn to Hayakawa's course offerings. "The class enrollment is terrific—150 or so in my lecture course, 48 or so in the seminar," he wrote. "The result is that I have been given three assistants." The seminar included students such as noted entomologist Peter Tamony and Frank Carmondy, the "retired head of a big California employers' association, famous to all liberals hereabouts as an enemy of the unions." It was a response that could turn the head of most academics, especially one not pleased with his teaching situation at home.

Don stayed first in Mill Valley with an old friend, psychologist Bill

Pemberton, before moving to an apartment in the house of English professor Justine Van Gundy, whom he described as "50ish, I guess, sort of tart and angular in manner, but very friendly and pleasant." He also found "in many of my colleagues (especially Justine) more than a trace of what we now regard as extremely outdated anti-anti-communism." Nevertheless, his apartment pleased him: "There is a TREMENDOUS view from the front window," he reported to Marge. "You will like it very much." He added, "Driving in SF is an exciting experience—hills and valleys incredible to behold, up which our Gnash [*sic*] races magnificently. You can't possibly use the overdrive in this town. It's been put out of operation for the duration."

As for the people he was encountering, aside from new colleagues, he joined old pals Wally and Mary Stegner, plus novelist George Stewart, for dinner with Joseph Henry Jackson. He also met general semantics fans such as Bill Leary, Jim Smith, John Caffrey, and Fred Wheeler, and noted, "I get a lot of suggestions with GS people around here of pro-ISGS, anti-IGS feeling, which I haven't dug into, not wanting to appear overanxious." He found time to visit local jazz clubs, too, and struck up a friendship with Dixieland bandleaders Turk Murphy and Bob Scobey. Eventually, he was able to use his new contacts to help book old Chicago friends like Jimmy and Mama Yancey in California clubs.

With the bands of Murphy and Vernon Alley, Hayakawa drew a crowd of "about 1000" to his presentation of "Reflections on the History of Jazz" at Everett Junior High School, a crowd that noted jazz critic Ralph J. Gleason found "quite remarkable." The critic continued: "Perhaps jazz is coming out of the doghouse a little bit these days; most of the audience seemed seriously interested in hearing what Dr. Hayakawa had to offer and in listening to music. But one cynical jazz fan was heard to mutter on leaving, 'How many people would come out to hear Duke Ellington talk on semantics?'"

Despite Don's notoriety, SFSC had until recently been no more prestigious than Illinois Tech, although it at least had English majors. It was, moreover, well established in the business of salvaging the good minds of students, especially those from working-class and immigrant families. Originally a teachers school, San Francisco State Normal College's history can be traced to the mid-nineteenth century. It was part of the state's "second-tier" higher education system, the collection of onetime teachers colleges that would come to be known in 1960 as the California state colleges; there were eleven such institutions in 1952.

In the state's Master Plan for Higher Education, the state colleges were seen primarily as institutions for undergraduate education and teacher training. Many students and faculty affectionately referred to them as "blue-collar colleges," and historian Arthur Chandler wrote in 1986 that "the story of San Francisco State University is the biography of an especially American dream: the belief in self-betterment through education." Explains Chandler, "The school has never been a place where the scions of the wealthy and the powerful come to receive their final polish before taking the places prepared for them in the world. From the first teacher training classes in 1855 down to the advanced graduate seminars today, San Francisco State has been a place for working people." In fact, Chandler further points out, "at every stage of its growth, San Francisco State has had to fight for its existence and integrity against public indifference, political interference and external pressures of every kind."

Hayakawa was called a professor of language arts at SFSC, and when asked about that he explained, "Language arts is a kind of School of Education term . . . looked down upon by the English Department people. San Francisco State was not organized originally to turn out literary scholars but to turn out English teachers for public schools." In practice, however, and over the objections of officials at the University of California, SFSC by the 1960s offered master's degrees in several fields.

From the point of view of faculty, the principal difference between the two systems of higher education was that state college professors taught twice as many classes each semester—usually four—and received less pay than their sometimes haughty peers at the University of California. Because SFSC and its sister state colleges were not research institutions, teaching was (ostensibly at least) their primary mission, and publish-or-perish was not supposed to be a factor. In practice, though, it was often a consideration, despite those relatively heavy teaching loads.

"In some ways then we were closer to being junior college teachers than university professors, even though the Ph.D. was required," recalled Caroline Shrodes. Another English professor at State, Dan Knapp, chuckled when he recalled, "I was warned not to work for one of the state colleges when I finished my Ph.D. at Berkeley. Senior professors advised me to find a job at a university, any university—Nevada or Oregon—but not at a state college. I was told it would finish me, and I guess it did, because I loved San Francisco State, the diversity of it, so I stayed there for my entire career."

Due to people like Shrodes, Van Gundy, and Knapp, sfsc had also developed an English Department whose offerings were somewhat unusual because it had interpreted "Language Arts" broadly and moved beyond traditional requirements, developing, along with courses such as "Shakespeare" and "Chaucer," others such as "Literature and Psychology," "Communications and the American Cultural Community," "Literature and Society," "Theory of Communications," and a full range of creative writing offerings often taught by distinguished authors. If there was an open curriculum in which general semantics might fit, this seemed to be it.

Hayakawa liked the college immediately, although in 1952 it was still housed on a small downtown site similar to the one he had known at the University of Manitoba three decades earlier—hardly a campus at all, in any traditional sense. Chandler wrote that "the campus itself was a dismal joke." The original setting, obtained in 1906, included an old orphanage chapel and a series of ratty wooden buildings that had provided all classrooms until a somewhat more modern building, Anderson Hall, was squeezed onto the property in 1928.

After World War II, the state college system was becoming a more important player in the state's newly democratized higher education scheme, offering opportunities to a wider range of students than previously. "Many of them were married and working full-time, many military veterans, many were junior college transfers, and many were the first members of their families to ever attend a college, working-class kids," Don later remarked. "They were good students as a group, very ambitious, and there were real gems in every class." Marge added, "Don has always shown an ability to stimulate students who have never been stimulated before, by his approach and his personality. . . . He assumed they were all potentially eager young learners and would respond to new points of view. They did in large part. He was a very good teacher."

He was by no means the only good one at San Francisco State. Benefiting from its location in one of the world's favorite cities, an international literary hub, the college during the 1950s and 1960s would add distinguished faculty such as writers Walter Van Tilburg Clark and Mark Harris, Leo Litwak and Kay Boyle, Herbert Wilner and Mark Linenthal, as well as scholars such as Robert Thornton, Kai-Yu Hsu, John Beecher, and Ray B. West Jr. The music department that decade enrolled such stellar students as Johnny Mathis, Vince Guaraldi, Paul Desmond, and John Handy. As Wilner recalled, "The S.F. State prof was almost insolent in his smugness of place. He certainly believed he was living in the best community in California. He might have believed it was the preferred place in the country. Identification with the college took on the same pride of place that went with San Francisco itself," which, he added, "contributed a feisty quality to the faculty."

Soon SFSC would be ensconced on an attractive new ninety-seven-acre campus near Lake Merced, where it became—suddenly, it seemed—much better known, due in part to its association with the "San Francisco Renaissance" then being publicized nationally. In fact, more than a few locals then began to suggest that it, not its better-known neighbors in Berkeley and Palo Alto, was the region's most stimulating college, especially in the arts and humanities.

As a result, it became an "in" school among California students, one of whom, Ronald Schiff, an ex-Marine who was an art major there while also supporting a family, says, "My God, it was the most exciting place. There were all kinds of innovative programs. You had the sense anything could happen and that virtually any experiment could be tried. People were dancing in front of movie screens and reading poetry to jazz and writing non-linear novels and painting with whole new perspectives. It was rigorous and never . . . what? . . . never staid or dull." It was also open enough to welcome a controversial writer and teacher of general semantics. Asked about what kind of department he found when he arrived at San Francisco State, Hayakawa said simply, "Genial. Innovative."

Marge responded to Don's extolling of the Bay Area: "It all sounds very wonderful including the city and the people and I'm eager to get out there to share it with you." On June 21 she wrote to inform him that he had received a note on behalf of "the Friends of American Writers" from a Miss Sander. As Marge typed the note, she told her husband, "Wynne is sitting on my lap and practicing her typing in the interstices. . . . She keeps saying Dewey, Dewey, Dewey. I think this must indicate she will be a librarian or a teacher, for I do not take it as a political remark." Marge also noted that Mark—"Whether it's Mother's constant teaching or Wynne's example, . . . is learning to imitate more sounds and says Bap for Bama [the children's nickname for Marge],[1] and Bupm for Button, and Pat for Pat." She added: "Mother is a wonderful teacher for Mark and I think he is making progress through her constant reading and encouraging him to speak. He rocks the doll and says Bye (or rather Ba) Ba-Ba-Bobby (baby) and he carried out a surprising numbers of directions, distinguishing between forks and spoons verbally, taking things to people, and this morning he followed Daisy's instructions to empty one waste basket into another. He is an indefatigable table clearer and does a most careful and earnest job." Wynne, she added, "is not walking yet . . . but she does stand for long periods alone, and will be striking out for herself within the month I feel sure." Since "Bama" planned to soon join her husband in San Francisco, leaving her mother—called

---

1. "Bama was used only in the immediate family. . . . My mother was called Marge by anyone who knew her. . . . Gang Gang, by the way, was pronounced Gung Gung." Wynne Hayakawa to author, e-mail, December 15, 2006.

"Gang Gang" by the kids—and Daisy to look after the youngsters, she added, "It grieves me to think I won't be around for it."

"Alan has been very nice," she also wrote. "He has a new version of the story about the Buses. Now when it comes to the part about his waking up in the morning I had to tell him that it's the day that Don is coming home, and how we get the house cleaned up and decide on a menu for you to eat . . . and how you drive up in the Nash, etc., etc. Your spelling of Gnash amuses him mightily, by the way." Alan himself included a brief note in which he revealed, "I have a Loose TOOTH—No, four Loose teeth."

The older son also caused a degree of humorous consternation in his staunchly Democratic family. "You'd be horrified to see your son wearing a [Robert] Taft button, which he found," Marge wrote. "I gave him a [Adlai] Stevenson lapel tag, which he wears too, but it is awfully inconspicuous in comparison. He also stands on the back porch and shouts to [neighbor] George Sang: 'I'm for Taft. Who are you for?'"

Her letter closed on what she called "a bit of unpleasantness."

Some man with a nice enough sounding voice called up and said his name was Christianson and asked to speak to you. I said you were out of town, And he proceeded to tell me that he was calling for a friend (he actually said "a husband's husband"—he was a little rattled) to tell me that you were—now I'm trying to remember his words "carrying on" or maybe it was "running around" with this husband's wife, who was in one of "these groups" and you were conducting this "affair"—I'm not sure if he used that word, but that was the idea, I believe—in person and by correspondence and "now if he's out of town he's probably carrying it on by letter."

She followed that revelation with something of an understatement:

I was naturally taken aback and couldn't decide if I should cut him off abruptly or try to find out for you some clues to what he was talking about—some unbalanced student of yours. Or it might be some gal with an unbalanced husband who has written to you about her problems. But I couldn't get anything more out of the bastard—he just kept going around in the same circles, saying the husband was getting very upset and angry about this. I don't think this was the husband, though I don't *think* his name was Christianson either. He called me Mrs. Christianson once . . . He did say it was somebody from Chicago. . . . Is there anybody who fits this picture?

Whether or not Hayakawa was carrying on with a woman then was not established, but certainly Marge's letter disturbed him. He responded immediately, writing:

I know how horrible the anonymous phone call must have made you feel. There is just a possibility that it might be from the husband (or a friend of the husband) of Marie Balfanz. . . . she, after attending my Highland Park conference (at which she and I had quite a bit of talking), was among those who felt . . . a great increase of self-acceptance and internal strength through having listened to me.

Since that date she has written to me to tell me that she has left her husband, and that she was grateful to the course for having given her the strength to do so.

That was their final correspondence on the subject.

Shortly, another letter from Marge revealed how important Daisy had become to the family. "Today's most spectacular incident was when Mark, sitting naked at the piano, had a very loose BM and proceeded quietly to decorate the piano keys and smear himself from head to foot. Daisy, tired as she was, cleaned him up (I was bathing Wynne) without a word of reproach or disgust. She is marvelous." Marge would have many occasions to make such an observation about the woman who had become an essential part of the family.

While he awaited his wife's arrival in the Bay Area, Don continued to be courted by high rollers. On July 13 he wrote, "Tomorrow I am to see the Attorney General of the State of California and some of his friends, including a couple of judges (of these people all will be

Democrats). He wants me to have a bull session with them about introducing more sense into political campaigns."

A few days later, Don and Marge were together in California, and Clara Peters—along with Daisy, of course—was babysitting in Chicago. The grandmother sent a snapshot to the parents which she described this way: "The greatest tradgedy [*sic*] is pictured on Mark's face on the group on the bench after Wynne had hit him with a cantaloupe." Gang Gang seemed willing to allow kids to be kids.

A California Conference on General Semantics was scheduled by the ISGS in San Francisco for early August 1952. It would feature psychiatrist Douglas Kelley, psychologists J. Samuel Bois and William Pemberton, as well as Hayakawa. While individual supporters of the IGS were welcome, the institute itself wasn't invited, and M. Kendig was understandably miffed. She announced that her organization would be hosting "an evening of questions and answers about GS at the Mark Hopkins Hotel on July 8 for 'friends of IGS.'"

Bois, an IGS and Korzybski loyalist who was, according to Pemberton, not too fond of Don, made presentations at both gatherings. Nevertheless, Hayakawa and his group dominated, gaining far more publicity and coverage for general semantics and apparently gripping San Francisco's imagination as well. In a city and a state with a large Asian and Asian American population, a terrible history of anti-Asian discrimination, considerable pride in its intellectual tone, and more than a little social snobbery, the guest professor continued to be noticed. He was invited to lecture at many nearby colleges. At San Francisco State, his host institution, Hayakawa felt that he was accepted by the faculty and that his ethnicity was not a factor. When queried later, none of his ex-colleagues, supporters, or opponents so much as mentioned Hayakawa's race or nationality.

twenty-five

When the 1952 summer session at San Francisco State closed, Caroline Shrodes, who "liked glamorous academics who appeared to fashion something new from stuffy old disciplines," according to English professor Manfred Wolf, asked the decidedly unstuffy Don if he was interested in a full-time, tenured position at the college. "'Nothing doing,' I said at once. 'I've enjoyed myself here, but I don't want to bring up my children in the anti-oriental climate for which California is famous.' Dr. Shrodes replied, 'Come again for summer school next year and bring the whole family.' So we came the summer of 1953 and the summer after that."

His decision to return seems to have pleased the college as much as it did him. He liked the school and remained intrigued by the Bay Area's cultural scene, especially the increasingly celebrated literary renaissance centered in North Beach, where a who's who of real and faux "beatniks" congregated. His longtime and continuing interest in poetry and jazz had led him to read publications by the Beats and to visit many nightclubs, so one of the appeals of the summer job was that he might be in contact with cutting-edge writers and musicians.

Don was still teaching part-time at the University of Chicago during the balance of the academic year, and he later admitted that the Aristotelian philosophy of the English Department there ran counter to his, but at least it was a real English Department. Hayakawa also reported that he preferred the diverse enrollment of the evening division, with its "mixed group of people . . . which represented an age range from eighteen to sixty. . . . I can remember an older student horning in on a discussion by saying, 'Well, I worked for the railroad for forty years of my life, and I can tell you you're all wet.'"

Early that year he was named to the board of directors of Consumers Union, symbolic of both his widening reputation and his long-standing populist commitment. The announcement in *Consumer Reports* identified him as "a lecturer at the University of Chicago, and the founder and editor of *ETC.: A Review of General Semantics*. . . . In addition to his work as a lecturer, author, and editor, Dr. Hayakawa has been active in numerous scientific organization, including the American Psychological Association, the American Ethnological Society, the American Anthropological Association, and in consumer cooperatives." That capsule description accurately summarized Don's professional dilemma. In middle age he was so involved with the various strands of general semantics that only an unlikely return to the literary scholarship that had once marked him as a comer was likely to earn him a position in a traditional English Department. His attachment to GS was not merely a convenience; he believed it was "one of the great, liberating disciplines of the twentieth century." As a result, if he was to land another tenured professorship, he would have to find an unusually open-minded English (or perhaps Education) Department. In truth, he had already found such a unit at San Francisco State, and it wanted him. Although many possible problems presented themselves, Don remained both flattered and increasingly tempted by the offer from Shrodes.

Meanwhile, the spring 1953 issue of *ETC.* carried the text of a memorable speech Hayakawa had delivered to the Urban League of St. Louis on Lincoln's Birthday, "The Semantics of Being Negro." His long involvement in the worlds of African American journalism and music, as well as being active in a social circle that included many blacks, gave him a strong sense of what he might and might not know. He opened his talk by admitting, "I personally have led a sufficiently sheltered life so that I have encountered no persecution—and, compared to the Negro population of the United States, little discrimination." His own life as a Japanese in nearly all-white

Canadian towns led him to observe that "an increasing number of young men and women today must take a long chance and train themselves for positions which Negroes have never held before. Hence the basic question facing a young man or woman today in the choice of career is not, 'Is this career open to Negroes?' but 'Is this career one that I care about enough to fight for?' Courageous young men and women, by acting as if there were equal opportunity, will, by terms of the self-fulfilling prophecy, bring about the equality of opportunity that they seek." (Hayakawa was, by the way, one of few prominent male writers of that time who made a point of including references to females when generalizing.) That assessment was a bit sanguine, as the speaker admitted: "The last sentence, I am afraid, sounds inspirational. It is all very well to tell people to be courageous—but . . . preaching is not enough." Educational opportunity and training were also essential, since "not even an FEPC law can compel the hiring of non-engineers for an engineer's job."

By the summer of 1953, with military personnel ubiquitous in the Bay Area due to the Korean conflict, the Hayakawa gang traveled to California for Don's second summer session at SFSC. The family was able to rent the Mill Valley home of Lou and Caroline Wasserman, with whom they would become friendly. Wasserman, a political science professor at State, and his family were traveling that summer. The availability of their large house had prompted Don and Marge to bring to California not only all their children but also both Daisy and Mary.

Abby Wasserman, daughter of the landlords, recalls that the multi-ethnic Hayakawa clan, with their black housekeepers, encountered prejudice "from our redneck neighbor, who complained to my parents." Except for a few domestics, Mill Valley was thought to be lily-white then. The Hayakawas were characteristically unintimidated.

Don was again delighted to be teaching in a college that boasted an active English Department in a city with a lively cultural life and a traditional willingness to consider new ideas. Once again his courses drew enthusiastic crowds, and he began to negotiate seriously with Caroline Shrodes about the possibility of becoming a tenured

228

member of her department. Leaving Chicago would be difficult, but leaving his unsatisfactory teaching situation there would not be. That summer, Marge recalled, she fell in love with Mill Valley—a village built in a series of canyons at the foot of Mount Tamalpias, one of California's most scenic communities—and Don seemed equally enamored with it.

They both enjoyed the greater Bay Area, once more renewing acquaintances with Wally and Mary Stegner, socializing with Joseph Henry Jackson, and enjoying faculty friends like Richard Dettering, Bernice Biggs, and Justine Van Gundy. They also became better acquainted with the families of fellow semantics buffs Doug Kelley, Jim Clark, and Bill Pemberton. Pemberton, who became Don's fishing partner, recalled one day when they were angling in one of the several lakes in the hills above Mill Valley, and Don, whom he described as a "gentle guy," was transfixed by a bobber. When the day ended, Pemberton said, they'd caught a few and Don told him, "You know, I feel as relaxed as I have in long time."

Pemberton laughed and responded, "Of course you do. You've been concentrating on that bobber all day and haven't thought about anything."

"Well," Hayakawa teased, "I'm Japanese so I should catch the most fish."

Another of Don's avocations, jazz, was stimulated by San Francisco's unique music scene; it featured everything from the established style of his old pal Earl "Fatha" Hines to a new version of cool music called "West Coast Jazz," which included young performers like Dave Brubeck, Chico Hamilton, Cal Tjader, and Chet Baker. He also heard young poets on campus and elsewhere reading their verse over a background of muted jazz or less-muted bongo drums. Don didn't like it as well as he did the Dixieland of Turk Murphy and Bob Scobey, but he did like it.

Stanley Diamond remembered attending a Hayakawa evening lecture at Everett Junior High School in the summer of 1953 or 1954: "I was *astonished* because you [Hayakawa] had a house there of, maybe, seven hundred people." Diamond went on to explain:

229

"He was here to demonstrate the difference between New Orleans rhythm and blues and jazz, and what today we would call rock." The popular groups of Vernon Alley and Turk Murphy provided the music.

The Hayakawas traveled enough locally to gain a good sense of the setting. Daisy, the family's other inveterate angler, also remembered that fishing thereabouts was pretty good. She, like her employers, especially appreciated the moderate weather. The sight of afternoon fog, like foam on ale, billowing from the nearby Pacific over a shoulder of Mount Tamalpias, then probing into canyons, never ceased to please all of them.

In the larger world, a cease-fire agreement in Korea was at last signed at Panmunjom on July 27, 1953. As a result, three of the Hayakawas—Don, Marge, and Alan—planned a trip to Japan for August and early September. It would mark the first time that Ichiro and Otoko Hayakawa, as well as Ichiro's aged mother, Misa, would meet their daughter-in-law or any of their American grandchildren. All was not well with the older generation in Japan, however, as a July 29 letter from Don's sister Ruth revealed. Unitas Trading Company Ltd., Ichiro's import-export firm, was not thriving. "In spite of the unfavorable condition of his business," Ruth wrote, "he still has to support his mother, his wife, Grace, Grace's daughter, and the Fumi Hashimoto [his mistress?] I told you about. . . . He is so weary, but feels that he cannot quit working now with all these people depending on him." Ichiro was, moreover, suffering from urinary problems and needed surgery which he felt he had to postpone. Anticipating a visit by Don and his family managed to cheer him.

When Don, Marge, and Alan flew to Japan, Daisy, Mary, Mark, and Wynne returned to Chicago by rail. Mary later wrote to the Hayakawas, "Our trip on the train back was just wonderful. The children were very cute, and everyone wanted to play with them. They were extra nice in the diner, they didn't spill not one bit of food on themselves." Then she added, "*That Wynne* is quite a flirt!" Mary, like Daisy a poor girl from Mississippi, also wrote, "I want to thank you again for the wonderful trip you gave me to California.

Words can't express how much I enjoyed myself! It is a trip that I shall never forget." On their arrival in Chicago, the two women and two children were met by Marge's mother, who eventually took everyone to Taliesin at Spring Green, Wisconsin, when a heat wave struck Chicago.

The international travelers, meanwhile, flew via Honolulu to Tokyo on Pan American Airlines. They stayed at the Frank Lloyd Wright–designed Imperial Hotel and sallied forth to various locales: Osaka, Nagoya, Kyoto. Marge found Kyoto particularly scenic, in large measure because it had not been "bombed at all and has not been going through the hideous reconstruction of the other cities."

Marge was an enthusiastic tourist and an astute observer; her letters home reveal that other than the omnipresent rice fields, she found Japan "a surprisingly uncolorful country," deficient in flowers, and "the houses are mostly dull white stucco if they are not the color of old unpainted wood, and the roofs are either dark-grey thatch or dark-grey tile." On the other hand, "There is always some fascinating human activity going on, everywhere you look," Marge wrote. "Farmers in their big hats, working in the rice fields or carrying buckets of 'night soil' on a yoke. Mothers and middle-sized children carrying babies on their backs, fishermen in loin cloths netting something or other in the shallow gravelly rivers. . . . We had not expected to see so much of the old ways in evidence." Noting that no gratuities were expected by the staff of their hotel but that a service charge was added to the bill, she wrote, "I don't know how much was given but it brought out the entire staff and the elderly woman owner, all giving us presents and bowing us out to our taxi—a gauntlet of some 15 or so people."

She closed that informative letter of September 1 on a more personal note: "We have taken leave of Don's father and Grace for this trip—and the partings were very sad, especially with Mr. Hayakawa. He is certainly is [sic] much less depressed about his life and business than when we arrived here—but it was very hard for him to see Don go away again, I'm sure. And he was obviously very fond of Alan.

He is such a nice person and I'm so glad Alan has had a chance to see his grandfather & grandmother over here."

On September 5, Marge wrote to the family back home that she, Don, and Alan were traveling to Kusakabe, "the home of Grandmother H., and . . . tonight we shall be sleeping on the floor under a big mosquito net tent." The hamlet, "where the Hayakawa family has lived for several hundred years," gave the Americans a taste of rural life. They found the tables turned, because "however much of interest the village is to us, it is nothing compared to the interest we are to the villagers":

> When we arrived and the next morning the neighborhood children gathered outside the house to stare at us. Between 20 and 30 children, tiny ones to high school age with little ones on their backs, lined up outside the glass sliding doors and peeked in at every crack making loud comments which unfortunately I could not understand.
>
> Yesterday we felt like the Pied Piper, on our way to the station about a mile from here, as we attracted a vast parade of village children. . . . Unfortunately Alan is not able to be amused by all this attention and took it hard the first day—reacting in a somewhat wild and show off manner.

Record heat scorched the travelers, but it didn't lessen the joy of reunion. Don was especially delighted by the meeting between his grandmother Hayakawa and Alan, her American great-grandson. Marge described the old lady as "pretty spry for 90. She is a small woman and in addition her back is humped and bent almost double. . . . She sits on cushion by the door and smokes her tiny pipe with a long stem. She sits in a froglike position with her chest on her knees, and when she isn't smoking she constantly revolves a reed flyswatter in her hand and slaps it rhythmically on the floor. She can still read a newspaper but complains about her hearing, which doesn't seem to be too bad."

Don wrote to Wynne and Mark to tell them that their mother, father, and brother would sail home from Yokohama on September 11. The ship, he noted, "seems to be quite a barge. We expect to be in San Francisco about Sept. 23." Marge penned a final note home while awaiting the arrival of the vessel in Yokohama. "Mrs. Hayakawa [Otoko] is playing *go*, or a children's version of it, with Alan," she wrote. "They get along very well, and it will be a very sad leave-taking. We are urging her to come to the U.S. for a visit, and I think even the possibility of such a thing makes the parting seem less final."

The Hayakawas sailed aboard the *Philippine Bear*, a freighter with a deck for passengers that included four staterooms, a lounge, and a dining salon, as well as several pleasant companions. The day before they departed, Ichiro had written to Don and Marge, saying in part, "Goodbye you two and Alan. I shall never forget those days with you in Kansai. When you get back send my love to your other children. . . . Once more Goodbye and Bon Voyage!" Ever practical, he added a postscript: "If you stop at Honolulu and have time to go ashore, please buy and send me a little of Hawaiian macadamia nuts in packages or tins. Glass jar may break." As it turned out, the *Philippine Bear* stopped at Okinawa and Hong Kong but not at Honolulu.

twenty-six

Don remained in close touch with Caroline Shrodes and others at San Francisco State after his second summer session there. He knew that a position at SFSC was his for the taking. "Caroline thought he was a real catch," recalled Professor Dan Knapp. Still, the decision to leave Chicago was by no means easy for the Hayakawa family. They had many dear friends in their several Chicago coteries.

Marge was still serving on the board of the Hyde Park Co-op as well as remaining a prominent reviewer. While Don was not particularly rewarded by his academic responsibilities in the Windy City, his *Defender*, co-op, and general semantics work took him to everything from community group meetings to art museums to nightclubs where the blues and jazz thrived; he shared those interests with other writers, intellectuals, and even big-league ballplayers. Chicago Cubs pitcher Jim Brosnan and Don had become friendly; Brosnan was six foot four, Don five foot six, and they looked like the long and short of it when together at a jazz club or a cocktail lounge, where both liked music, dancing, and a few sociable drinks. In fact, Hayakawa was considered a fine dancer by a later partner, Allene Arthur. He was "a dancing fool," she wrote in a 2008 article, "as loose as a marionette, graceful as a chorus boy. Energetically, he danced with joy, doing twirls and little side kicks. I could barely keep up."

In the early 1950s, when people learned that Hayakawa wasn't a U.S. citizen, many assumed he was a Japanese national; some wanted to know if he was actor Sessue Hayakawa's brother; others wanted to know if he *was* Sessue. Few suspected that he was a Canadian. In fact, he had continued to follow events in the country of his birth by reading periodicals and by communicating with friends and relatives there.

Despite his objections to the McCarran-Walter Immigration Act's mandates in 1952, Don had been increasingly thinking about taking advantage of it to become a naturalized American citizen. He knew it was unlikely that he'd ever again establish a permanent residence in the nation of his birth, but a certain loyalty to the Canada that had shaped him, and perhaps the lingering if slight possibility that he might one day pursue a political career there, held him back. Nevertheless, Don had long since become a fan of the United States. "America is an open society," he wrote, "more open than any other in the world. People of every race, of every color, of every culture are welcomed here to create a life for themselves and their families." In 1953 he had initiated the formal process that would lead to citizenship.

When in 1954 at a ceremony in Chicago he finally did become a naturalized American, the occurrence went virtually unnoticed by all but his closest friends. As he put it, "I ceased to be the one foreigner in my family." That family made no public issue of the change, and only Marge accompanied him to the Federal Building, where he was sworn in. "I remember my mother telling me when I got home from school," says Alan, "and I don't remember anyone else being around at that moment—'Your father became an American Citizen today' and telling me a little bit about naturalization. No celebration."

Don and Marge continued to discuss a move to the San Francisco area. By then all three of their children were enrolled in Chicago schools; the Hayakawas of course remained socially active, and they now owned that stylish apartment building in which they lived, so cutting ties would not be easy. Then Marge suffered a shock that may have prompted her to rethink many things, including whether to leave the city where she was so well established. She learned of Don's infidelity "with one of Marge's best friends and . . . co-worker at *Poetry*," recalls Alan. She likely had earlier inklings of womanizing—since it seems to have been no secret to his friends—but this confirmation stunned her. There was no emotional scene that her son recalls, and Daisy, too, recalls no outburst, since Marge tended to internalize pain. Nevertheless, Alan believes it "added to her emotional retreat from the world. . . . I think after all that she simply resolved never to have feelings again."

During the chill that followed, Don buried himself in work. He also worried about the revelation that a new, more horrible weapon, the H-bomb, had been secretly tested two years before; what kind of world would his children inherit? Spreading the insights of general semantics seemed more necessary than ever. To help accomplish that he edited an anthology, *Language, Meaning, and Maturity*, which was composed of selections that had appeared in ETC. between 1943 and 1953. His foreword compared Korzybski's work with Freud's, summarizing by arguing that the Count perceived "that language, far from being a tool incidental to thought and communication (as is still commonly thought), carries within itself a whole body of assumptions about the world and ourselves—assumptions which go a long way toward shaping and determining the kinds of thoughts we are able to have." The volume's contents illustrated how far from general semantics orthodoxy Hayakawa continued to drift as an editor. He included essays on everything from the language of mysticism to the language of radio commentators.

As reviewer Joshua A. Fishman later summarized, *Language, Meaning, and Maturity* offered "as much substantive and stylistic diversification as anyone could desire," but Fishman was far from sanguine about general semantics or this book. His review in the spring 1956 issue of ETC. likely spoke for much of academia when it challenged the value and uniqueness of the movement. "If general semantics is really a partner . . . in the worldwide intellectual revolution of this century, *what* has *it* contributed and how does *its* contribution compare with those of the other partners? . . . This volume offers no direct answers to these questions, and the indirect answers, it would seem, are far from flattering to general semantics." To Hayakawa's credit, he titled Fishman's review "A 'Loyal-Opposition' View" and published it without a rebuttal.

236

Fishman's skepticism notwithstanding, Don's reputation among semantics buffs remained considerable, but his personal life continued to be troubled. More family problems—these in Japan—delayed the final decision about moving to California. Don heard again from his father, as well as from his sister Ruth, that Ichiro's business was still sinking despite all the old man's hard work. The aging father was the product of a different time, and he was out of step with Japan's post–World War II economy. The following April, Don responded to the situation:

> I have not written for a long time because your last letter sounded very discouraged and unhappy, and I have not known what I could say to be of any help.
>
> Somehow or other, I should like to help. Are there problems of your business such as can be met with further capital? If so, I should be glad to try to make an investment. I can easily send you $500. If necessary, I can dig up more.
>
> Or are your business problems such that they can be solved by your traveling to see your customers, in India or Europe or American or wherever? If so, I could help financially.

Despite help from his sons, Ichiro's postwar business ventures never thrived.

In June 1954 at a Conference on General Semantics held at Washington University in St. Louis, Don drew once more upon his extensive experience in the music world, codifying ideas that had been rumbling around in his head, to write and deliver one of his most entertaining and memorable papers: "Popular Songs vs. the Facts of Life." It would not be published until the next year, but its presentation at the meeting not only stirred the audience but immediately attracted mainstream media attention.

In a full-page-plus article entitled "Word Germs," *Time* magazine of July 12, 1954, referred to Don as "word man Hayakawa" and presented his thesis that the love lyrics in popular songs, "pretty much the product of white songwriters for white audiences, are full of wishful thinking." Don further asserted that pop lyrics led to something Wendell Johnson had called the "IFD disease": "'a triple-threat semantic disorder' of *Idealization* (the making of impossibly ideal demands on life), which leads to *Frustration* (when *Idealization's* demands are not met), which in turn leads to *Demoralization*.'" Hayakawa's recommendation to avoid the infection, the magazine asserted, is "the Negro Blues," since "as a recurrent theme they assert 'the will to live.'"

His actual script dug deeper than *Time's* article revealed. For instance, citing lyrics such as "Nobody wants a baby when a real man can be found / You been a good ol' wagon, daddy, but you done broke down," he observed, "I am often reminded by the words of blues songs of Kenneth Burke's famous description of poetry as 'equipment for living.'. . . [T]he blues are equipment for living humble, laborious, and precarious lives of low social status or no status at all—nevertheless they are valid equipment in the sense they are the opposite of escape literature."

Hayakawa's presentation on song lyrics took on a life of its own. On July 8 he turned "Popular Songs vs. the Facts of Life" into a lecture-recital at San Francisco State and was accompanied by Bob Scobey's Frisco Band as well as singers Claire Austin and Clancy Hayes. At the Folk and Jazz Festival in Lenox, Massachusetts, that year he once more delivered his talk—a little more polished each time—accompanied by the Sammy Price trio, Myra Johnson, and blues legend Jimmy Rushing. While there he also joined old friends Langston Hughes, Mama Yancey, and Eubie Blake at the concurrent Folk and Jazz Institute's annual roundtable. Later he was appointed to the board of directors at the Jazz Institute in New York, and over the next couple of years, with the assistance of Scobey's Band and blues singer Lizzie Miles, Don continued presenting updated versions of his talk about lyrics at venues as diverse as Northwestern University; University of California, Davis; Beloit College; University of Chicago; Purdue University; and San Jose State College.

Future novelist James D. Houston, then a student at San Jose State, attended Hayakawa's "road show." Houston later explained, "I'm a World War II kid, and that was the first time I'd ever seen a person of Japanese descent in a prominent position like that. I'll bet it was the first time most of us in the audience had. Hayakawa was a kind of academic star, smart and witty and he knew how to hold an audience." Another student, Isao Fujimoto, who would become a professor at the University of California, Davis, attended that same jazz event at San Jose State. He recalled, "Hayakawa really knew what he was talking about and that really impressed us. It was counter intuitive because we thought jazz and the blues as a black domain. He carried himself with absolute confidence."

The essay/speech churned up plentiful opposition, and it seems clear that one of Hayakawa's purposes had been to stimulate discussion. As was so often true of his articles, he had presented a stimulating, somewhat maddening thesis with just enough depth to make it impossible to casually dismiss, but not rigorous enough to threaten deeper orthodoxy. Without being shallow, his mind seemed to spread out more than dig deep. He had the creativity of a theorist but not the single-mindedness, and of course he was also a gifted writer. Don could certainly stir things up, and he had in this case once more demonstrated why he was so widely recognized.

By then his wife's emotional wounds had somewhat healed, and Marge decided to move to the Bay Area in the hope of a fresh beginning. At San Francisco State, the fact that a nationally celebrated scholar and writer might soon join the faculty and bring an increasingly prestigious academic journal with him seemed a great coup. Don understood that as a distinguished graduate of a then-undistinguished school, the University of Manitoba, he was a good fit for San Francisco State. From his perspective the clincher was that San Francisco State, with its lively, innovative English Department, genuinely wanted him. "Caroline Shrodes . . . gave me every encouragement," he remembered. Besides, Don had come to feel certain that he and his family were a good fit for the Bay Area, while Marge was ready to depart Chicago with its recent legacy of emotional pain.

twenty-seven

Early in the summer of 1955, S. I. Hayakawa formally accepted a professorship at San Francisco State College. It would be a new start for his career, a dramatic change in social and physical environment for his family, and a fresh start for his marriage. They began house hunting immediately, and Mill Valley, where they had so enjoyed their previous stay, was their preferred location.

Before that adventure, though, Don returned to the University of Denver late that summer to again teach. By then he had many friends in that area, too, so he immediately reconnected not only with Elwood Murray but also with Woody and Jeanne Martin. He lectured at the Las Casitas Consumer Co-op "in the worst Mexican slum," and was appalled that it was being run by a handful of unelected men who did not follow cooperative principles but did as they pleased. Don had been invited there by a new friend, Enrique Hank Lopez, who would soon become the first Mexican American graduate student at Harvard (many years later, he would write a seminal book, *The Harvard Mystique*). He and Don had more than academia in common, since Lopez was about to marry his fiancée, Betty Grant, "whose parents, esp. mother, is all upset about Hank's being Mexican, and is all set to have hysterics on the subject." Prior to his marriage, Lopez—whom Don described as "a thoroughly charming person"—became Hayakawa's summer roommate.

Later, once the move to California was at last under way in the fall, Don learned that his pal Bill Pemberton had heard that a property there owned by a widowed friend of his, Verenice Mills, was about to come on the market. Although the house needed work, it was situ-

ated downslope in wooded Blithedale Canyon, and both Hayakawas
fell in love with the setting.

After arranging the purchase, Don and Marge returned to Chicago
and settled their affairs as best they could. Then they drove back with
Alan to California to meet the vans delivering their belongings, while
Daisy and Mary accompanied the other two children west on the
train. Mary, who had not been a live-in helper in Chicago, eventually returned there, but Daisy stayed with the family in California,
albeit reluctantly. Don and Marge told her "they would love to have
me come and they said, 'You can try it.' So I did because I couldn't
stand to part with my friend Mark. My boy."

Like Don and Marge, Daisy fell in love with the location, although
at first the condition of the house left her with questions. The remod-
eling process, with Wes Peters directing, started immediately, and
when a few walls were knocked out, some uninvited guests didn't
charm Daisy. Raccoons visited nearly every evening. "They busy . . .
get into everything," she remembered. She also admitted that she
later mellowed and fed the critters on the deck.

Despite that minor invasion, the finished residence became a show-
place that would be featured in newspaper and magazine spreads.
Its graceful lines and natural wood siding seemed to fit the location
perfectly. Inside, Wes created a large, bright living room/dining
room/sunroom combination on the main floor illuminated by vast
west-facing windows opening to a deck and the surrounding woods;
also on that level were a master bedroom suite, Mark's bedroom,
Daisy's quarters, and a kitchen that also opened onto the expansive
deck. Alan's and Wynne's rooms were upstairs, while a large library
office, more bedrooms, and storage were below. The Hayakawas'
apartment in Chicago had been roomy, but this house was significantly more commodious.

The California that had become the Hayakawas' home was distinct
from the middle America they had left; it was also distinct from
pre–World War II California. The Golden State was in the process
of becoming the eighth-most-productive "nation" on Earth, as well
as a crucible for artists alienated, in part at least, due to commercial

expansion. World War II veterans had profoundly enriched the state's population. "Young, productive, highly skilled, and eager for success, they gave the state a transfusion of new blood and great energy," write historians Richard Rice, William Bullough, and Richard Orsi. The defense and aerospace industries that the war had spawned became increasingly important, growing until they challenged oil, agribusiness, and entertainment as the state's peacetime economic leaders, and a population boom was one result.

Hayakawa wasn't naive, and while he appreciated the new opportunities for his students to rise in society as he once had, he also understood that those opportunities might amount to little more than enhanced occasions to accumulate wealth and crassness, and thus to cheapen the culture. The generation that was coming of age after World War II when new opportunities were taken for granted could realistically imagine itself pursuing higher education and rising in the society, and perhaps even reshaping it. Young Californians such as Richard Rodriguez and Joan Didion, Mario Savio and Ronald Takaki, Maxine Hong Kingston and Willie Brown would be able to do that in part at least due to public colleges that welcomed them. Many became advocates of civil rights; some in the next decade became leaders in an anti-war movement, and some would insist on environmental sensibility. In the 1950s, the liberal Hayakawas—even though they were not "beatniks" or "hipsters"—shared those sentiments.

The Hayakawa family quickly adjusted to Mill Valley's setting and weather: no one missed Chicago winters. The kids found good schools and new friends, while Daisy located a satisfying church in San Francisco. Marge was soon involved with native-plant and co-op groups, her horticultural interest heightened by the large, terraced yard that surrounded their house; she would soon turn it into a marvel. Her husband found a fencing club for a physical outlet, and added tap dancing in his unorthodox quest for fitness. He also found that his old friend Earl "Fatha" Hines was still playing at Club Hangover in San Francisco, where the professor spent some pleasant evenings.

One afternoon shortly after they moved into the Blithedale Canyon property, Don in grubby clothes was working in the yard when a neighbor he had not met, Lenore "Lee" Awner, walked by. Each said hello, and she commented on how nicely the yard was coming along, so Don—assuming she thought he was the Japanese gardener—offered to introduce her to the new owners. She followed him to the house, where he presented Marge and then announced, "I'm the husband." Lee, who became Marge's closest neighborhood friend, realized she'd been tricked. Don was delighted.

The Hayakawas had actually settled in one of the world's best habitats for their interests and even for their ethnicities. "Mixed" marriages were not as rare in the Bay Area as in the heartland from which they had moved, in part because the West Coast hosted a diverse population with many Asian Americans, major elements of its cultural texture. The situation was by no means perfect, of course, and attorney Gerald Hill recalls that "Hayakawa was blackballed by the Marin Rod and Gun Club." Don survived that affront, and the club would later be embarrassed when reminded of its action.

Don and his old pal Bill Pemberton soon developed an informal musical duo—Bill on bass, Hayakawa on piano—that entertained at parties, of which there were plenty. Pemberton remained, of course, one of Don's principal angling partners; Hayakawa was selective about whom he'd fish with, but two others were Daisy and Mark. The former said, "Mark and his father—it was a very, very close relationship. Mr. Hayakawa would go fishing and he'd take Mark."

At the fall 1955 general faculty meeting at San Francisco State, Don was greeted by many new colleagues eager to meet the noted lecturer and author of the much-admired *Language in Thought and Action*. Humanities professor Joe Axelrod described him then, as "very cordial, very laid back, listening intently to others." His colleague Doug Stout reported that Don was "an exciting presence, but low-key, not overbearing at all, not a prima donna."

Stout and Hayakawa would share an office, and Stout, who specialized in English education and teacher training, saw Don usually only before classes, since the semanticist would return home after sessions to write and edit in his office, while Doug was often away observing student teachers. Nevertheless, he found Hayakawa to be a "cordial and kind" office mate, one who took a special interest in Stout's plans to visit Japan. In fact, Don not only offered suggestions but also arranged for a meeting in Japan between his parents and Stout. "I only met his father because his mother was ill, but Mr. Hayakawa was very nice," Stout remembered.

That first year at State, Don began lobbying for a GS track within the English major, or perhaps even a general semantics major, and for a time at least he was supported by the department chair, Shrodes. Although several other noted semanticists—Eugene Rebstock, Richard Dettering, and Dean Barnlund, most prominently—would be hired and offer related courses, no GS track ever evolved.

How such a rejection affected Hayakawa's attitude toward his fellow professors was not immediately clear, but "he became 'famous' for going to sleep in department meetings," remembers colleague Thurston Womack. Before long, too, Dan Knapp revealed, a pattern would emerge: Don turned much of his undergraduate instruction over to teaching assistants while he worked closely with his graduate seminars. He also moved toward night classes—the pattern he had developed at the University of Chicago. "He didn't seem altogether interested in teaching," recalls Womack, "although I heard from students that he was a good teacher."

Apparently so, for Don's classes immediately became some of the department's most popular. Robert Wanderer enrolled in an evening lecture-discussion attended by more than three hundred. "I was stunned," he admitted. "How was it in two years of college I had never heard about the problems of words and images and reality? Nor about the subject-predicate structure and its effects on our thinking, and other problems stemming from our language." Another student, William C. Roth, also much appreciated the class, but recalled a curiosity. In those days when ashtrays were provided in classrooms, he noted that Hayakawa, a longtime smoker who was trying to limit himself, still "had the interesting habit of cutting his cigarettes in two equal pieces-the first smoked at the 1st class break, the second at the second brake [*sic*]." (In 1961, Hayakawa finally gave up smoking.)

Professorships in the entire California state college system then supposedly emphasized teaching rather than publications, so to some Hayakawa might have seemed to be a poor fit. The truth was, however, that he was only one of many on the faculty whose prestige arose primarily from publications. He soon spent the balance of most days in his large home-office, editing ETC., writing his own latest speech or essay, perhaps researching a promising topic. Although he was admittedly "self-absorbed" when he wrote, his wife described him as "a very easy writer to live with": "He was always very approachable and was never temperamental about interruptions and such things . . . and the children did play around with him. He had a wonderful double-desk with a hole all the way through, and that was a marvelous place for little children to go crawling through. They were around all the time. And he was very patient and not all temperamental about it. And we always talked about what he was writing and thinking about."

To clear his mind he frequently ventured out for walks, and Daisy chuckled when she remembered the time he brought home a batch of wild mushrooms. "I'm not gon' eat those," she told him. "We grew up eating these," he insisted. After consulting a mushroom book, he placed the fungi on a paper to make a "print." When he returned to view the print, Daisy recalled, "he found a pile of worms!"

A sense of the family's style can be gained from Daisy's stories. She remarked, "This is the losin'est house," revealing that someone was always looking for something. She also said she would occasionally say to Don after a minor or mock disagreement, "No one loves me, I'm gon' quit." Alan, who was growing up a bright, sensitive boy, was worried and warned her (in Daisy's words), "Just keep a-sayin' that. He gon' take you seriously." She knew better, but she was touched at the boy's concern.

The Hayakawas continued to enjoy travel, and Don's habit of teaching summer sessions in interesting locales would make that possible; instead of San Francisco, it might now be New York or Connecticut

245

or Hawaii. Usually the family accompanied him. Daisy, who couldn't swim, especially remembered the first of two summers in Hawaii, the only other place to which Don and Marge ever considered moving, according to Alan. Daisy never forgot and barely forgave Alan, who had talked her into trying a surfboard. "He said, 'You can't sink. This is salt water.'" She had no sooner begun paddling the board when "there come a wave. That board went straight up in the air and I went under. But a wave bring me in. Mrs. Hayakawa said if that ever happen again, you draw your legs up and you automatically come up." Daisy said she didn't let it happen again.

If she couldn't swim, Mark certainly could, and she marveled at that. The boy had rejected formal swimming lessons. "He wouldn't do as you tell him . . . he'd do it the way he wanted," reported Daisy. Unlike her, Mark was never afraid of the water, and he trained himself, staying in shallow water until he could actually stroke.

Daisy marveled at Marge's generosity: "For church, I used to take flowers for the table." She was allowed to use "anything in the house, it was all right with her . . . even a silver tray." But within Marge's special domain, the garden, "Don't let me get a pair of scissors and start out in their yard. . . . I done ruined a bush and killed a tree and everything. Whooo-eee!"

Daisy also noted that although "Mr. Hayakawa" didn't attend church, he nevertheless had a great appreciation for Christianity. (He once wrote in an essay, "When Christ taught us to love and not to hate, He was not just teaching morality. He was teaching sanity.") She also noted that Don and Marge would go to church with her when she asked, which was usually when something special was scheduled. Occasionally, "Mr. Hayakawa" was the something special; he spoke at her church many times at her request, and "He was good at the Bible," as well as "Negro history and African art," she added.

Late in most afternoons Don would climb the stairs from his office and join the children, Marge, and Daisy in the kitchen, sitting at the counter and often enjoying a drink, a conversation with his wife, or perhaps romping with the kids. He also took delight in Daisy's rich sense of humor and her southern ways, so he might tease her about fishing or bowling—two of her favorite pursuits—and she gave as well as she took.

"You call that little thing you caught yesterday a fish? That was a minnow," he'd grin.

"Least I caught somethin'! You didn't get nothin'!"

"It looked like bait."

She would wave him off, saying, "Never you mind," then both would laugh.

He could be mischievous. Several colleagues recall that, along with drinks in the kitchen, he treated them to a Japanese "delicacy"; he didn't tell them it was composed of salted tuna guts, and they remember the grin on his face when they took their first bites. Pemberton also recollected that when Don got wind that some members of his small volunteer staff at ETC. were referring to him as "the Pope," he responded, "I look like hell in purple," and enjoyed a good laugh. He was also a playful parent, Alan and Wynne agree. For example, his daughter recalled baths in the large tub of the master bedroom. "We grew up unembarrassed about nudity, so we'd all line up—Mark, me, Alan and Don—sitting in the tub and pretend it was a bobsled going—whoosh—to the left, then—whoosh—to the right. We kids loved it and he did too. Mark was never left out," she added; "he was always in the middle of things."

Alan added that his father "did tell me there was a taboo in some cultures about seeing one's parents naked, especially one's father, and he thought it was silly." Wynne added, "My mother was not comfortable with her own nudity, but I think she was pleased that Don was so open-minded and bodied."

Both Clara Peters and Daisy had by then become second mothers to the children, especially Mark. Contrary to earlier dire predictions by physicians, the retarded boy developed into "a sweet child," Daisy reported, one who delighted his parents with his small triumphs and honest emotions. As his older brother once observed, "Mark may be retarded but he's not stupid," and the younger boy developed into a major cog of the family largely because he was honored in a loving home. "He just liked everybody," said Daisy.

Mark was enrolled in a special school that his parents hoped would allow him to develop his intellectual potential and teach him practical skills. Don and Marge were active in the Marin Association for Retarded Children, whose acronym—MARC—delighted the family, especially the younger son. At home he showed a great affinity for music, so records and a phonograph player were provided for him and he often sang along. His father recalled that one day a group of what used to be called club women visited the house to invite Don to lecture for their group: "They were very well-dressed—hats, gloves, that sort of thing—and we showed them into the living room where everyone sat, drank tea and made small talk. Well, Mark, who of course had the run of the house just as his brother and sister did, walked into the room and I introduced him. He had no inhibitions and was a genuinely loving child, but the ladies didn't look altogether comfortable in his presence. When the first one extended her hand, Mark took it then kissed her on the lips. You should have seen her expression!"

The Bay Area's liberal political bent and intellectual inquisitiveness jibed with Don's own, so he was a popular speaker in the region. Years later, he laughed and admitted that he'd found "new audiences for some old topics, plus some new ones." On September 3, 1955, for instance, he addressed the Mental Health Society of Northern California on "The Fully Functioning Personality"—a topic he had first introduced in 1954 as part of a lecture series for the Chicago chapter of the International Society for General Semantics. His 1955 version showed him to be in good form, citing especially examples from the humanistic psychology of Carl Rogers and Abraham Maslow, as well as from Korzybski. "Most importantly, this sane person that I have been describing in the abstract may suffer from anxiety and fear and doubt and foreboding—because such feelings can arise from non-neurotic sources in this troubled world. . . . But his troubles would be real ones and not self-contrived ones."

Although Don was generally well liked by his new colleagues, rumors that he was guilty of marital infidelity soon led to more than a little speculation among them. Several of those colleagues claimed to be aware of such activity: "Everyone knew that Don was a womanizer," Dan Knapp bluntly asserted. Womack added, "They had an open marriage . . . or Don did, anyway." Pemberton agreed that Don "was quite a womanizer." He also said that he once found himself concurrently acting as therapist to Hayakawa and to one of Hayakawa's lady friends. "She eventually married a musician and Don was heartbroken," he reported.

Publicly, Marge and Don appeared to be a warm and considerate couple when together, and her responses to her husband's asserted philandering were never recorded. She was inherently a private person, not given to public displays of emotion, but her daughter says simply, "Of course those things hurt her." They would continue to bother her, although the couple stayed together. Indeed, her devotion to him seemed if anything to intensify as he slid downhill toward the end of his life. They had shared wonderful memories and sad ones, and others that must have been nearly unbearable.

The year that had begun with S. I. Hayakawa a discontented, part-time teacher in Chicago ended with him a relatively contented and prominent full-time teacher in San Francisco. He enjoyed the attention he received in the Bay Area, and he earned even more acclaim with his continuing output of articles, essays, and speeches, as well as a certain maverick style that made him unpredictable and newsworthy.

twenty-eight

Beginning the second half of his professional life in California, Don Hayakawa remained a popular figure on the national lecture circuit and was considered interesting by at least some of his new colleagues. Manfred Wolf observed, "He was a fencing master, an expert on jazz, and a collector of African art. Seeing him . . . so lithe and uninhibited, I realized that he took pride in being a man of the body as well as the mind. It was fitting that after years in the Midwest he should have come to perform on the brighter, brasher stage of California." Some considered him something of a character, one who would whip out his harmonica or demonstrate tap dancing if invited—and sometimes even if not. Author Dikran Karagueuzian cites a new professor at San Francisco State who said of Don, "He was not like some other professors around here. If you met him in the halls, he would nod smilingly, say hello or something." The noted biographer Jackson Benson, a student at SFSC at that time, recalls Don differently; "He had a reputation among the grad students of being very prickly—approach with caution."

Old Hayakawa associate Vladimir Dupre observed, "Don would have a hard time making an intimate friend. He wouldn't get really close to people because he was pretty full of himself. He didn't like to share the spotlight because he was competitive. Sharing the limelight wasn't comfortable for him." Bill Pemberton had to agree that Don was competitive: "He hated for me to catch more fish than he did." Marge, on the other hand, Dupre added, was "reserved, but warmer and more personable." He also noted that Marge was "more impressive physically, while Don was small in stature, a bantam rooster who liked to strut around."

Hayakawa was by then an unconventional scholar with a strong liberal bias, and the move to California had provided him with time and stimulus to continue his eclectic output. His opinions continued to be sought on a wide range of subjects. For instance, he presented his lecture "How to Attend a Conference" at the opening session of the International Design Conference at Aspen, Colorado, on June 12, 1956. Once more he was in provocative form. Employing a hypothetical discussion of Frank Lloyd Wright's Robey House as an example of what he called "the terminological tangle, in which discussion is stalemated by conflicting definitions of key terms," he explained that this was largely due to relating language to more language rather than to what semanticists called extensional or objective reality. When that happens, said Hayakawa, "it will be just as well if . . . the audience adjourns to the bar, because no further communication is going to take place." The core of his advice is that one must truly listen in order to communicate. That seems obvious, of course, but he phrased it a bit more specifically: "Listening means trying to see the problem the way the speaker sees it—which means not sympathy, which is *feeling for him*, but empathy, which is *experiencing with him*. Listening requires entering actively and imaginatively into the other fellow's situation and trying to understand a frame of reference different from your own. This is not always an easy task."

Hayakawa's writings after the move demonstrated originality and a willingness to take chances in public pronouncements. Don had developed that contrarious style that both livened much of his work and rendered him suspect in some circles because he consistently refused to go along with "default assumptions"—the acceptance of a complex of opinions because some part of them was considered true. For example, he believed that all sides of an issue should be aired, not merely those sanctioned by the orthodoxy presently in vogue, so he opened the pages of *ETC.* to conflicting opinions. To do otherwise, he believed, was to forfeit the right to be heard.

A few critics complained that Hayakawa's interests were "all over the map," but Don had grown to accept that he seemed perpetually willing to explore new topics. In his book about the SFSC strike, Dikran Karagueuzian quotes him: "Here you see a pattern developing which is very much me. . . . I got a Ph.D. in English, the conventional literary scholar. I make my reputation in something else altogether, in semantics. From there on I wander off into modern art, into psychology and anthropology. So that's a characteristic form of my life. Suddenly instead of going more deeply into any one subject, I spread out in new directions altogether." Some colleagues considered him a mere gadfly.

Nevertheless, the California College of Arts and Crafts found reason in 1956 to present him with an honorary Doctor of Fine Arts degree, and in 1959 the University of Montreal awarded him the Claude Bernard Medal for Experimental Medicine and Surgery. A state-certified psychologist, he was also named a Fellow by both the American Association for the Advancement of Science and the American Psychological Association, so he likely wasn't quite the lightweight some of his opponents wished him to be. Nor was he as swept by illusions of infallibility as some wished to think; when Stuart Mayper, later editor of *General Semantics Bulletin*, in early 1960 proposed an article in *ETC.* refuting attacks on general semantics, Don said, "I would write the article myself if I could understand the g.s. theories better," and urged Mayper to undertake the task.

In 1956 Don toured the Midwest with Bob Scobey's Band and singers Clancy Hayes and Lizzie Miles, presenting the latest version of "Popular Songs vs. the Facts of Life." Never shy, he wrote a cordial note to Ralph J. Gleason, the *San Francisco Chronicle*'s music writer (who had earlier in the pages of *Downbeat* slammed Don's presentation), and requested that he mention the tour in his newspaper column. That same year, a local chapter of the International Society for General Semantics began to coalesce around Hayakawa's San Francisco State classes, and it soon commanded much of the fourth floor of the college's Downtown Center. The advanced class that fall brought together such future stalwarts as Bob Wanderer,

George Moore, Hazel Friedman, and Stanley Diamond; Diamond served as the chapter's first president. "When the class ended the group began meeting once a month at the Spaghetti Factory, a local bistro," recalled Wanderer. At Hayakawa's suggestion the group issued a newsletter, *The Map*, edited by Wanderer, who explained, "As interest mounted, other key people joined. . . . The first issue of *the* [*sic*] *Map* was dated November 1957, our big organizational meeting was February 7, 1958, and our first lecture was April 25 with anthropologist Ethel Albert." One of Don's presentations drew an overflow audience of 950. "Those were heady days," Wanderer recalled. "At that time general semantics was on the cutting edge in the San Francisco area, attracting many people seeking a system that was new and exciting and helpful in dealing with life's problems and perplexities (not to mention its applications in the business and educational fields)."

Professor Thurston Womack acknowledged that while "most colleagues thought S.I.H. was a real catch, . . . the 'literature people' in the Language Arts Division of that time were fairly skeptical of General Semantics." A rumor circulated that Hayakawa had been presented with what amounted to a signing bonus, or that he was earning a salary much higher than his colleagues'. With a statewide across-the-board salary scale determined by a board of trustees, it's unlikely that any exceptional amount could have been offered, although the new professor was certainly hired at the highest level permitted. Considerations other than pay had led him to join the faculty at SFSC, and jealousy likely led to some at the school not liking him.

Doug Stout, Hayakawa's SFSC office mate, reported that Don "kept his ambitions to himself, so he would often surprise you when he finally revealed his stand on this or that." Womack also noted that his own wife, Helen, soon became friendly with Marge, since they shared interests in horticulture and liberal politics. Like Don, Womack was an aficionado of jazz, so the couple was more than once invited to the Hayakawas' house to listen to Don's extensive collection of recordings. The host "would sprawl on the floor and beat time" while the music played. "Some of us admired his museum-quality collection of African art," the neighbor added, then chuckled, "some of us were invited to his house . . . on New Year's eve. SI on the stroke of twelve shot off some sort of firearm."

The way Alan Hayakawa told the same story, it wasn't Don who fired the shot but Bill Pemberton. The latter earned Marge's nearly eternal enmity, Alan said, for bringing a loaded shotgun to her home. Pemberton had earlier broken a chipped antique glass that she cherished, so "He wasn't one of Marge's favorites," the son concluded. Pemberton, who said Marge was "a very talented and organized lady," never seemed aware of her pique.

In the spring 1957 issue of ETC., Don published another of those articles that inflamed GS purists and earned him the scorn of some colleagues who accused him of being a popularizer: "Sexual Fantasy and the 1957 Car." American auto builders, he asserted, "have decided that the supplying of means of transportation is but a secondary reason for [the automobile's] existence, and that its primary function is the allaying of men's sexual anxieties." Horsepower, acceleration, and design, he suggested, combined to create huge phallic symbols with fins. "What about horsepower over 160? I believe it can be safely said that every single horsepower above that figure is purely symbolic, and has nothing to do with transportation except to make it more hazardous." The editors of *Car Life* were taken with Don's perverse message and chiding tone and reprinted the article in their November issue.

That article stirred up more letters to Hayakawa than anything since his incendiary "Popular Songs vs. the Facts of Life," achieving his goal of stimulating people to think about the subject. The following year he expanded on the automotive topic in "Why the Edsel Laid an Egg: Motivational Research vs. the Reality Principle," an article originally published in ETC., then later reprinted in both *Advertising Age* and *Madison Avenue*, where it caused considerable controversy. Hayakawa opened the piece by deflecting the complaints of some general semantics mavens: "Among the questions raised by my correspondents is why automobiles are discussed at all in a journal of general semantics. This question is easily answered. As *ETC.*'s cover says, it is 'concerned with the role of language and other symbols in human behavior and human affairs.' The automobile is certainly one of the most important non-linguistic symbols in American culture." Hayakawa went on to suggest that motivational researchers employed by American automakers "seem not to know the difference between the sane and the unsane." As a result they urge the car builders to "abandon their basic social function of providing better, safer, and more efficient means of transportation in favor of entering the business of selling dreams . . . the Phallic Ford, the Edsel Hermaphrodite and the Plymouth with the Rear-End Invitation."[1]

Meanwhile, events were under way that would change the nature of San Francisco State College. In 1957, Glenn S. Dumke was appointed the school's president, and Hayakawa would establish a friendly relationship with him, as did other colleagues. Three years later, on April 27, 1960, under the aegis of the Donahoe Higher Education Act, San Francisco State was joined with other state colleges (including such well-established institutions as Fresno State, San Jose State, and Chico State) to form what would become the multi-campus California State University, the largest institution of its kind in the world. Dumke was appointed to serve as its second chancellor following the resignation of Buell Gallagher.

San Francisco State continued on its innovative way, hiring the best talent it could tempt, which led to more than a few clashes of ambition and ego. With the support of Caroline Shrodes, Don still hoped to at least develop a general semantics track in the freshman composition classes, just as he had so long before at the University of Wisconsin. At a department meeting held in his Mill Valley house, Don was discussing his plans when novelist Mark Harris said, "I do not think we ought to hand the course over to an unscholarly discipline."

---

1. What kind of car was Hayakawa driving when he wrote his articles on automobiles? A 1952 Nash Ambassador, a 1954 Hillman, and a Citroen 1D-19 (acquired in 1959). He also for a time drove a Checker.

According to Manfred Wolf, "Hayakawa looking surprised, said softly, 'Why would you say that?'

"'Because General Semantics is a popularized discipline.'

"'Well, not exactly, you see . . .'

"'I just don't think we should concern ourselves with *unscholarly* approaches,' repeated Harris, pronouncing the word as if he had spent his whole life examining Attic Greek manuscripts." Afterward, "colleagues stood around and talked about the quarrel, while in a corner of his living room Hayakawa played the harmonica, which he always did when he felt blue."

Always active off campus, Hayakawa had joined the Press Club shortly after relocating to the San Francisco area and was among its more active members. Bill Pemberton recalled that at one luncheon meeting the guest speaker was the noted psychotherapist Virginia Satir. Don was seated with her at the head table, and after he rose and introduced Satir to the assembled club he returned to his seat and immediately fell asleep. "When she was through—quite a long presentation—he just opened his eyes," revealed Pemberton. "He always said, 'I'm resting my eyes.' I said to him in all seriousness one time, . . . 'For goodness sake Don, why don't you tell people you have a touch of narcolepsy?' And he just totally denied it."

Off-campus political events were already churning in the Bay Area in the late 1950s, events that would portend a memorable decade to follow. With their "ultra-liberal" bias, the Hayakawas continued to be subjects of interest for hunters of "parlor pinks," especially when Don publicly criticized the rather promiscuous efforts of the House Un-American Activities Committee (HUAC). In 1960, in the shadow of the U-2 fiasco and deteriorating relations with the Soviet Union, the Hayakawas had supported the candidacy of John F. Kennedy, and they were delighted when he won and a Democrat once more inhabited the White House.

The House Un-American Activities Committee held hearings in San Francisco's City Hall on March 18, 1961; activists mounted an unexpectedly large protest to disrupt the meetings, and that in turn led to demonstrators being knocked down the inner steps of City

Hall by the powerful spray from fire hoses, then arrested. Don and Marge were among the many who protested what they called police "overreaction." In fact, Don had been among the most prominent of 165 San Francisco State professors publicly objecting to the local HUAC meetings. Both Hayakawas would later reveal that they were neither shocked nor saddened when the committee's meeting was vigorously protested. It was an opening salvo of the decade when students came to understand that they could, to a degree at least, shape the course of both local and national politics.

About a year and a half later, on October 22, 1962, Kennedy announced to the nation that Soviet missile and bomber bases were being built in Cuba and that he had authorized a blockade to commence on October 24. Suddenly, it seemed to many that the world was on the brink of nuclear war. On the day the blockade was to commence, the *San Francisco Chronicle* published an editorial mildly critical of Kennedy's action, suggesting in part that other measures, such as a face-to-face meeting with Castro, might first be attempted. It also pointed out the parallel between U.S. bases in Turkey and the Soviet presence in Cuba: "We may not like it, but international life is a two-way affair, and as a Dutch statesman remarked yesterday, maybe the Americans who now have the shivers will begin to understand why Russian citizens are so nervous about the close-up U.S. missiles aimed at them." The editorial concluded that until "debate has been heard . . . we find ourselves unprepared to give unqualified endorsement to the step that has been taken."

What might have been a local opinion piece took on new life when it was reprinted as an ad in the *Washington Post* on November 1, 1962, with the note, "This editorial appeared in the *San Francisco Chronicle* on Wednesday, October 24, at the height of the Cuban crisis. Although the severest phase of that crisis is now past, the undersigned Californians believe that the views expressed now more than ever, merit the attention of our national leadership." Among the fifteen signatories were Mortimer Adler, Henry Nash Smith, Jessamyn West, Herbert Gold, and S. I. Hayakawa, who had recently been lauded as an outstanding educator in *Life* magazine.

Also in the early 1960s, Warren Robbins, Don's friend and fellow GS buff, arranged for him to be invited to Germany as a lecturer in the State Department's Cultural Exchange Program. Strolling in Bonn one day, the two men found an antique shop with a rich collection of African art, where Robbins ended up buying thirty-two pieces. Hayakawa, Robbins later said, "was among the principal influences that prompted me to establish what has now become the National Museum of African Art, a branch of the Smithsonian Institution." Don was a founding trustee of that museum.

In 1962, when drama students at San Francisco's George Washington High School were preparing to stage a version of *The Adventures of Huckleberry Finn*, attorney Terry Francois, head of the local chapter of the National Association for the Advancement of Colored People, publicly objected. That stirred longtime NAACP member Don Hayakawa to write an open letter to Francois, saying in part, "You are quoted as saying that you do not know if the play is good or if the characterization of Negroes is good or bad, but that you simply object to the depiction of Negroes as slaves. What are you trying to say? That Negroes never were slaves? That would be as absurd as my trying to deny that the Japanese ever attacked Pearl Harbor." As for the controversial character "Nigger Jim," Hayakawa pointed out, "Jim is shown throughout the story as having great intelligence, strength of character, and perhaps most important, a rich store of native wit—something that the present officers of the local NAACP seem to lack."

The big news among the Hayakawa clan that year also had to do with a performance: Ichiro, then seventy-eight, was cast as a geisha master, Mr. Kaida, in the Shirley MacLaine–Yves Montand–Edward G. Robinson film *My Geisha*. "His principal claim to fame at the moment is that he was 'discovered' by the movies recently," wrote Don to popular *San Francisco Chronicle* columnist Herb Caen. "He has a handsome speaking part."

Hayakawa's name was familiar to readers of Caen's column, which had quoted him on matters as diverse as co-ops and cars. The two men had become, if not pals, at least cordial local celebrities. They shared a tendency to employ a light tone when possible, and in Hayakawa's case it was not always clear in his notes to Caen when he was serious about issues. In the same letter, for instance, he extolled the Anti-Digit Dialing League's efforts to resist all-numeral telephone dialing, quoting the mayor of Rapid City, South Dakota, W. H. "Bill" Raff, who promised that "multitudes of community leaders in Rapids City are eager to join your forward-looking movement." Since all-numeral dialing soon became the norm, Rapid City's "multitudes" were apparently not multitudinous enough.

twenty-nine

One campaign that didn't fail occurred a year later when Don and Marge were involved in the founding of "Friends of Free Radio" to support KPFA-FM in Berkeley as a "progressive" source of information and entertainment. In fact, Don for a time came to be seen as a voice of the "Friends," since he so promoted it and was a well-known figure in the Bay Area. He and Marge also became active in the Berkeley Co-op, which they saw as a logical extension of their work in Chicago, and in the mid-1960s they helped establish a short-lived extension of the co-op in their home county, Marin.

In the early 1960s the family unit had changed a bit when Marge's mother, Clara, moved in with them in Mill Valley. Alan, Mark, and Wynne were delighted to have their grandmother there, and Daisy recalls, "She was such a nice lady, and wonderful with the children." She was also wonderful with her son-in-law, with whom she had developed a warm relationship. Marge, of course, had always been close to her mother, so generational tension was held to a minimum. "Everybody just pitched right in," says Daisy.

In November 1963, when he was interviewed by the *San Francisco Examiner*'s Walter Blum, Don made a statement that would later take on considerable importance: "Prejudice—racial, religious, what have you—is just another form of misinterpretation, of mistaking the stereotype for the man. Think of what a difference it would make, for instance, if we changed the expression 'part-Negro' to 'part-white.' Same idea, only a different word. And if we did that, there'd be a lot fewer Negroes in this world,"

By 1964, the year of Freedom Summer in Mississippi, Bay Area demonstrators were marching to overturn racism and to enlarge civil rights for African Americans. Pickets protesting job discrimination at San Francisco's Auto Row and at the Sheraton Palace Hotel downtown had, according to Hugh Pearson, "opened the door to hundreds of jobs for nonwhites," but "the courts decided to send demonstrators a strong message: causing widespread unrest in the South was fine, but not in the urban area that thought of itself as the nation's most liberal." While Hayakawa agreed with demonstrators' ends, he wasn't always comfortable with their means. He didn't favor ham-handed police tactics either, and cautioned against them, knowing that they did little but fuel activism. Sensing that momentous times were upon us, Don had told more than one group of students at San Francisco State that how the United States resolved its history of racism would in large measure determine its moral compass and value as a nation.

That fall, reportedly pressured by Senator William Knowland, publisher of the often-picketed *Oakland Tribune*, authorities at the University of California moved to prohibit political groups from setting up tables on a twenty-six-foot strip of university property at Telegraph Avenue and Bancroft Street and back onto Sproul Plaza, the campus's center of political activity. The ban guaranteed a confrontation with SLATE,[1] an organization founded six years earlier to support student groups seeking to influence off-campus issues. On October 1, a former graduate student, Jack Weinberg, who was manning a table for the Council for Racial Equality, was arrested, and what has come to be called the free speech movement was under way at U.C. Berkeley.

In December, one of Hayakawa's associates, radical writer Paul Jacobs, addressed what was then called the Hayakawa Colloquium hosted by the San Francisco chapter of the ISGS. He strongly endorsed the students' positions and actions. Twenty-one years later, Bob Wanderer would write, "Some experts in Hayakawaiana contend that SIH's negative reaction to Jacobs' favorable report on the UC

---

1. SLATE is not an acronym. It stood for a slate of candidates at U.C. Berkeley who ran on a shared platform.

Free Speech Movement at the 12-4-64 Colloquium was an important early step in his transformation from 'liberal' to 'conservative.'"

Don, meanwhile, seemed to have abandoned his hope for a general semantics major, or for a less ambitious "General Semantics Institute," or even the GS composition track for which he had lobbied at San Francisco State. Eric Solomon opined that "by 1964 S.I. Hayakawa had fallen on lean academic times. . . . Hayakawa had been ready to out-McLuhan McLuhan, to create a Center for Semantics, to market television-teaching, creating a financial empire for himself and his colleagues. . . . [T]hey refused his gambit." What's certain is that Hayakawa had settled into teaching, but that role seemed to increasingly take a backseat to his writing, editing, and lecturing. As had been true in Chicago, he still preferred night classes, and he continued to be a drawing card for the college.

In those days, when smoking cigarettes during class was common, seminars could be "pretty hazy," recalls ex-student Clark Sturges. Sometimes the content of the class was a bit vague, too. Sturges says "Hayakawa and his teaching assistants fell into a pattern: they'd meet for drinks and dinner at a restaurant in Stonestown before the evening class, then show up late." The actual class sessions, he further recalled, "were poorly organized and unenthusiastic . . . but [Hayakawa's] written comments on papers were brilliant." Also, recalls Sturges, who for a time was one of Don's teaching assistants, the Hayakawas hosted a party for his graduate seminar students each year, and Don "danced with all the pretty young women."

Writer Joseph Cohen, on the other hand, was impressed by Hayakawa's year-long "Problems of Communication" seminar: "Our class procedure, though unstructured by normal standards, had a structure all its own, with variations. We divided the two and a half hour period into three parts. The first hour and a half about 25 of us formed a wide circle to discuss questions as a group. Then we broke into assigned groups of five or six person in each to rehash. The last half hour we reassembled in an effort to tie together the threads of our thinking." Stanley Diamond agreed with Cohen, noting that Hayakawa "not only was a marvelous lecturer, but it was all easily understandable and loaded with examples." Much influenced by the work of his friend Carl Rogers, Don seems to have acted as an effective facilitator—for Cohen and Diamond, at least.

Old habits do indeed sometimes die hard, so Don's personal life didn't run as smoothly as his seminars. Rumor at that time had it, according to Bob Wanderer, that Marge had during that period given her husband an ultimatum with regard to a girlfriend: "She goes or I go." That likely referred to Don's erstwhile paramour at *Poetry* magazine, who had relocated to the Bay Area, perhaps following Hayakawa. "I think Don had an affair with her that was very damaging to Marge and Julie both," Alan Hayakawa said. Apparently that wasn't his only outside interest. Alan's sister, Wynne, recalled, "Near the end of his life, I asked Don if he ever considered leaving Bama for any of his girlfriends. He said 'Marget' was the only one who really got to him."

In a 2001 note, Alan surmised that Don's "Japaneseness . . . showed up in his attitude toward sexuality—he was not burdened by any leftover Puritan moral attitudes—and the high value he placed on public respect and reputation." That S. I. Hayakawa, like his own father, would turn out to be a ladies' man may very well have been closely linked to that same father's absence from so much of his son's life. Although Don seems to have had an abundance of male friends, Alan speculates that his father "was never as comfortable with men as with women (witness the disappearance from his life of all his male peers), and I see him turning to women over and over again for acceptance and reassurance."

As the temper of the time changed, Don developed an interest in the symbolic aspects of the counterculture that was beginning to sweep the Bay Area, beatniks morphing into hippies. He communicated with friendly nemesis Gregory Bateson about the influence of LSD and other drugs, and encountered more than a few students willing to share their own stories of "trips." In 1965 he led a seminar at Esalen, where he again met many folks who were veterans of "inner journeys." The symbolic power of men wearing long hair, of braless young women, of brightly colored costumes, and of acid rock music that could clear earwax fascinated him. He remained open to and curious about the cultural change those things might represent; rumors spread that he had tried LSD, but Adolph Hoffman recalls "meeting him and talking to him, specifically about LSD, asking if he would try it. He said, no, he wouldn't, didn't need anything like that." Walter Truett Anderson reports that Don's Esalen seminars were "always well prepared, always very intellectual, but he was no dusty pedant. He liked to play the piano for songfests in the lodge, and one visitor remembers seeing the future senator lead . . . a snake dance across the lawn."

Due to his unique background, Hayakawa had long been deeply concerned with civil rights and the movement for black equality. He continued to speak and write passionately on the subject, often employing unique insights. In "Reflections on a Visit to Watts," a 1966 essay, he and psychologist Barry Goodfield wrote:

> Basically, Negroes are victims of a caste system which was origi-
> nated in the South after Reconstruction in order to avoid the
> social adjustments made necessary by the abolition of slavery.
> The victory of the south lies in the unconscious absorption by the
> rest of the nation of Southern caste attitudes toward the Negro.
> Nevertheless, caste remains so entirely foreign to American ide-
> ology that articles on the subject in encyclopedias . . . deal with
> the caste system of India—and never mention the situation of
> the American Negro! Hence, the same people who vehemently
> oppose open housing for Negroes (for what are clearly reasons
> of caste separation) are likely to deplore the Indian caste system
> and to espouse vehemently a completely equalitarian philosophy.

He expressed such views at forums as diverse as Pomona College's 1964 Conference on Civil Equality and Daisy Rosebourgh's Baptist church in San Francisco.

Although by then he already considered himself a Californian, he later admitted that he hadn't foreseen the racial trouble brew-ing in the southern part of the state. The black population in Los Angeles had grown from 171,209 in 1950 to 334,916 in 1960 and to an estimated 400,000 in 1968, the overwhelming majority crowded into the city's south-central area due to de facto segregation. While white commentators sanguinely noted that African Americans' per capita income was higher in Los Angeles than in any other black community, they also had to admit it was far below the income level of whites there. When an apparently routine traffic arrest went wrong in south-central, "the Watts district, the area of most intense Negro deprivation and alienation, . . . erupted in an orgy of loot and arson," reported author Theodore H. White. Nearly a week of what the press called "the Watts Riots" followed.

Eventually, the effect of police and National Guard presence, as well as exhaustion, quelled matters in Watts, but large questions remained. While many were wringing their hands and focusing on the chant "Burn, baby, burn," Hayakawa and Goodfield tried to look more deeply at the events and their causes. They concluded that the ubiquity of television sets in the poverty-stricken community, and the kind of shows commonly available, provided ample evidence to residents of Watts of how disadvantaged and exploited they were.

The New Left's use of civil rights arguments to oppose the national administration and the war in Vietnam equally offended Don and Goodfield. In the essay they asserted that the Left's "campaign is admittedly not in behalf of the Negro at all. It is rather an attempt to use the disadvantaged Negro as an instrument with which to embarrass and discredit a national administration which, in civil rights legislation, education, voting rights, and the creation of economic opportunities, has done more for the Negro in three years than *any* previous administration has ever done in a comparable period." They also suggested that "the only hope for minorities, including the Negroes of Watts, lies in the broad center of both great parties — in those whose minds are neither in an imaginary past nor a visionary future, but in the realities of the present."

Hayakawa refused to be drawn into glib explanations for what he saw as a complex, systemic problem: black Americans had not been restored to full human dignity after the Civil War and slavery, and there would be no quick fix for that. Speaking on October 14 at the

265

University of Southern California, near the epicenter of the trouble, he told an audience of GS buffs that communication problems exacerbating other issues could be at least partly blamed for the riots in Watts. "I should like to reject . . . the John Birch Society theory that [the] whole Negro civil rights revolution is a communist plot," he said. "On the contrary, it is the result of a capitalist plot on the part of General Motors, General Electric, and General Foods, aimed at all of us."

Those who opposed Hayakawa's perspective found Pollyannaish his observation that for blacks "there are still barriers to surmount, but these barriers have only the sanction of custom, not of law. America remains an open society—and nowhere is this openness more apparent than in California. To be a Negro in California is a far, far cry from being a black in South Africa." The Compton Council on Human Relations, which had earlier distributed copies of Don's essay "Communication: Interracial and Intercultural," immediately requested copies of "Reflections on a Visit to Watts."

Hayakawa remained an important figure on the national lecture circuit then, and civil rights increasingly became his topic of choice. More than once audiences heard him persuasively assert that the "Negro problem" was actually a "White problem," and that whether or not the United States lived up to the promise of its Constitution would determine its place in world history, a public position he had held since the 1940s. On a practical level, he "called for a number of special public-private measures to assure equality, including initiatives by labor unions and businesses to recruit minorities, the end of segregation in public facilities, and incentive bonuses to attract talented teachers to schools for the underprivileged."

In fact, the lecture grind was beginning to wear on Hayakawa in the mid- to late 1960s. While he remained on the surface a hale fellow who enjoyed good food and drink as well as the company of cordial men and pretty women, he later admitted that he was dragging. Friends advised that he visit the renowned Chinese American physician Colin Dong, who told him, "You've been eating like a white man. It's time to get back to a fish-and-rice-based diet. No more red meat or dairy for you." After embarking on Dr. Dong's regimen his weight quickly dropped, his symptoms disappeared, and he felt energized.

Academically, though, Hayakawa continued to live in that nether world—no longer a literary scholar, not formally trained as a linguist, and renowned for that misunderstood field often mistakenly called simply "semantics." In the popular press he was commonly referred to as a "linguist," but linguistics professor Thurston Womack remembers that Don, "as far as I could tell, was not interested in modern 'scientific linguistics.'" There was a significant difference between "semantics," the study of meaning practiced by linguists, and the much broader field "general semantics" championed by Hayakawa. He was by no means ignorant of linguistics, however, and poet Don Emblen remembered a Hayakawa presentation on the history of the Finno-Ugaric languages in 1962: "I took notes . . . like crazy as he drew a map of Europe (squares, circles, lines) and then arrows all over the place showing how Hungarian and Finnish had come from the same sources about 3000 years ago and how they had split due to migration, wars, and cultural changes."

Some colleagues believed—to cite Dan Knapp—that Don continued to "want his own private property." Several professors recall that Hayakawa gave scant time to faculty affairs and, while not aloof or unfriendly, simply wasn't around much of the time. When present, though, he was something of a maverick. Manfred Wolf recalls that at a time when San Francisco State was being touted as "the most innovative, creative campus in the [State College] system . . . maybe in the whole country," Don "told us in an English Department meeting that we were 'an institution of secondary distinction,'" and "an audible gasp went through the room." He made no friends that day.

As a result of such candor, it's little wonder that some colleagues openly resented his prominence and independence. Others were bemused by him; "He came to meetings when he felt like it . . . which wasn't often," smiled Professor John Dennis. "He was a solid guy, just not part of the gang." Womack said, "Don was our celebrity prof."

By then the Hayakawas were well settled into the Bay Area scene, and Marge's life continued to be busy. Unfortunately, her mother began exhibiting symptoms of dementia mid-decade, so Marge and Daisy were dedicated to helping her. Still Marge remained active in the California Native Plant Society—and eventually edited its journal, *Fremontia*—and the Pacific Horticultural Foundation, where she would become founding editor of its journal, *Pacific Horticulture*. As Wynne Hayakawa later recalled, her mother was "an environmentalist before the word was invented. I think she really discovered the natural world when she came to California—the flowers blooming in February made a very strong impression on her."

The Hayakawas' long-standing interest in co-ops led to a high-profile dustup in 1967 when Marge, a director of the Berkeley Consumers' Cooperative—the nation's largest—opposed the renomination of board members Robert Treuhaft, Robert Arnold, and Maudelle Shirley, who "insisted that the nine-member board take a more aggressive stand on social issues." Although still very much a liberal Democrat, Marge pointed out that one of the founding principles of the co-op movement was neutrality in religion and politics: "We have some people who are quite conservative politically going to the co-op to shop. There are no ideological tests for membership."

Leftist attorney Treuhaft wasn't renominated by the board, so he filed a successful petition to be included on the ballot. Five others with similar philosophies also qualified for the ballot, and that led Don to fire off a letter to the *San Francisco Chronicle*. "The petition candidates," he wrote, "all expressly advocate the co-op's 'taking its proper role in community issues,' specifically protesting the war in Vietnam, boycotting Dow Chemical Co. . . . supporting the Delano Strikers and taking stands on local bond issues." He called this "the new Berkeley mentality," explaining, "It is a kind of dogmatic zealotry about the big problems of the world: Racial prejudice, economic inequality, and war."

Treuhaft and his wife, writer Jessica Mitford, immediately responded with their own, somewhat disingenuous letter in the *Chronicle* asserting that the real issue was the decline of the co-op's business with an attendant drop in patronage refunds. "We didn't deny that we were Left and liberal," Treuhaft later explained, "but we thought that politics would be a good thing in the Co-op, politics of this kind." A record turnout reelected both Treuhaft and Marge Hayakawa to the board, and soon, in sympathy with the United Farm Workers, the co-op was boycotting California table grapes and pursuing other progressive issues. Although Marge described herself as a "middle-of-the-road liberal Democrat," Treuhaft characterized her as "very much status quo, conservative, on the board." The Hayakawas had absorbed a lesson in the leftward drift of Bay Area politics toward what came to be called political correctness.

At the end of 1967, Don was awarded an honorary Doctor of Letters degree by Grinnell College in Iowa. According to columnist Herb Caen, while there Hayakawa also "tangled hotly with the sainted Marshall McLuhan. . . . In fact, Don won a standing ovation when he snapped at McLuhan: 'You thoroughly confuse people by taking ordinary words and shifting their definitions to your own use.'" Don later informed Caen that he had not won a standing ovation.

From Grinnell, the Hayakawas joined Julia Child and her husband, Paul, as dinner guests of Lyndon and Ladybird Johnson at the White House. Caen's report of that part of the trip asserted that Don had asked Child, "Is Texas food the reason our policy is in such bad shape?" That prompted a heated letter to Caen from Hayakawa:

Dear Herb:

If you want to make snide remarks about the White House or the President, go ahead—but don't put them in my mouth. . . .

You erroneously quote me as making a crack about "Texas food" while a guest at the White House. This is a breach of good manners I hope I would not commit anywhere, let alone the White House. Besides, I have nothing against "Texas food." But I have a lot against culture-snobs who never tire of sneering at Texas and Texans.

269

To correct the record, Julia Child (not Childs) and her husband, the retired diplomat Paul Child, who were visiting the White House to prepare a program on state dinners as an arm of diplomacy, spoke highly of White House cuisine. I too found the dinner at the White House excellent, and especially enjoyed the well-chosen California wines. If you Francophiles want to make anything of this, go ahead.

Two days later, Caen corrected the mistake, closing with the words, "Slate clean for now."

[eight]

ON STRIKE!

thirty

S. I. Hayakawa observed with considerable interest the transformation in attitudes that the civil rights struggle and opposition to the continuing war in Vietnam was bringing to society in general and to college campuses in particular. The Democratic Party was becoming polarized, with Hayakawa among those supporting President Lyndon Johnson's policies, while many colleagues at the college not only opposed the war but also found Johnson's civil rights stand tepid.

No one, least of all students dreading the draft, could fail to recognize who was doing the fighting—the dearth of wealthy or well-connected white kids on the front lines made that clear. Issues emanating from racism, privilege, and the war abroad would dominate American life for more than a decade and change the style of behavior on college campuses, where the upheaval and the language of the New Left increasingly offended old leftist Hayakawa. San Francisco State was no exception to college librarian Helene Whitson's generalization, "The academic machinery was creaky and unused to being called to account for its actions." To many students there seemed to be no orderly way to effect major changes.

Hayakawa's future behavior was perhaps foreshadowed when Phil Garlington, an editor of San Francisco State's student newspaper, the *Daily Gater*, wrote a column printed November 21, 1966, making fun of efforts of teachers' unions to organize at SFSC. Garlington asserted, among other things, that "the profession has always attracted the lazy, the unambitious, the timid, the characterless, the dull-witted." He added, "Most students, despite the propaganda, recognize teachers for what they are: petty bores incapable of larger things." The

273

column stirred more than a little faculty passion. Hayakawa's response, though, was to send a personal note to Garlington pointing out a better way to proceed, and likely revealing resentment smoldering beneath his own placid exterior:

> Basically, I agree with you. The idea of unionizing college teachers is to me a bad farce. Also, as you say, there are a lot of lazy, over-verbalized bores in any college faculty, including our own—people unfit for any other work but drinking coffee and chewing the fat with their juniors.
>
> But please don't destroy the effectiveness of your message by your shotgun methods. Such writing merely arouses angry responses while distracting attention from the point you really want to make.
>
> Pinpoint your target. Use a rifle. Aim carefully. Hit *only* the target you want to hit—and not the innocent bystanders. Then you'll have everyone on your side except the guys you are after.
>
> Forgive me for making like a teacher. You write well and with spirit. I would like you to become a hell of a good writer.
>
> Best wishes [signed]

Due to his own sporadic presence on campus, Hayakawa may have missed the growing militancy among both students and faculty that sometimes burst into view, often around the speaker's platform near the college gym. Not only helplessness in the face of the growing American involvement in Vietnam and the military draft prompted student protest, but also general inequality and the realization that just as civil rights was coming to the fore nationally, the population of black students on campus was dropping. In May 1967 a sit-in at the office of president John Summerskill protested the practice of providing students' academic records to the Selective Service. Chancellor Glenn Dumke subsequently affirmed the existing policy, so faculty and students picketed the administration building. Later, military recruiters on campus were rendered ineffective by demonstrators.

Speakers from the Socialist Labor Party, Students for a Democratic Society, and the increasingly militant Black Students Union, as well as various conservative groups, gathered in noontime crowds, and at least once a fight broke out between white "jocks" and black students after a conservative speaker defended the on-campus Air Force ROTC program. When militant African American attorney Donald Warden spoke about racial equality, some conservative students sought unsuccessfully to disrupt his presentation.

Hayakawa, a great admirer of Martin Luther King Jr., remained firmly committed to the elimination of discrimination and the imminent, orderly racial integration of American society; he also came to believe that militants like Stokely Carmichael and H. Rap Brown not only retarded progress but were actually agents of white resistance. "I wonder who's paying them to undo all the good-will Dr. King has created?" he asked. At another point, he applied a simple general semantic principal when he observed, "If we call our college racist, what term do we have left for the government of Rhodesia?"

Through all the controversy, Hayakawa remained a determined assimilationist, and that attitude ill suited him to understand the rise of militant separatism on the San Francisco State campus; large numbers of white students also seemed not to understand the level of frustration and rage simmering among what were coming to be called their "Third World" colleagues. For instance, at the end of the 1967 spring semester the Carnegie Corporation invited San Francisco State to apply for funds to develop programs in black studies. For reasons never entirely clear, Jim Vaszko, editor of the *Daily Gater*, the next semester announced in an editorial that he had written to the Carnegie Corporation urging that it not grant money to the college's "service programs." On November 6, Vaszko, who had also infuriated members of the Black Students Union (BSU) with his published opinions about Muhammad Ali, was beaten by several members of the BSU—including future movie actor Danny Glover—who invaded the newspaper's office and also trashed equipment. Six of the assailants, among them Glover, were arrested.

When the college's Board of Appeals and Review held a closed hearing on the assault, the event was picketed by students supporting the BSU. Nevertheless, the six attackers were suspended from the college. President Summerskill appointed a faculty committee to investigate the cause of the attack, but faculty consensus was that San Francisco State, like nearly every other college in America, reflected tensions within the larger society. There developed, for example, a relationship between the campus BSU and the Black Panther Party, and with that came increasingly bold pronouncements and dramatic confrontations. The very style of the Panthers—the black leather jackets, the berets, the guns—became a statement radicalized students of all colors soon imitated.

Hayakawa thought things were going backwards: "I'm afraid we're leaving white racism so we can endure black racism," he observed, apparently not realizing that San Francisco State had entered a new era. Early in the spring semester of 1968, under the aegis of a history professor on a one-year appointment, John (later, Juan) Martinez, approximately three hundred minority students from nearby high schools and junior colleges visited campus and requested that some admission requirements be waived for the coming fall. Shortly thereafter, Martinez's contract was not renewed, and tension spiked once again, revealing the difference between the views of at least some history department faculty, who saw Martinez as an opportunist seeking to transform a one-year appointment into a tenure-track position, and some students and faculty union members, who considered him the victim of repression. Given that the precedent for student activism was already well established in the Bay Area, rumors of forthcoming rebellion on campus soon circulated.

Later that spring, the noted African American playwright LeRoi Jones was a visiting professor at SFSC, much to the discomfort of the chancellor and trustees of the state college system, who did not hide their pique. Then, in March, the BSU, the Asian American Political Alliance, the Latin American Students Organization, the Philippine American Collegiate Endeavor, the Intercollegiate Chinese for Social Action, the Mexican American Student Confederation, and a group of Native Americans coalesced to form the Third World Liberation Front (TWLF) at San Francisco State. Two months later, on the heels of the assassination of Dr. Martin Luther King Jr. and the high-profile police killing in nearby Oakland of a Black Panther

Party recruit, sixteen-year-old Bobby Hutton, the TWLF staged a sit-in at the office of President Summerskill.

Don Hayakawa clung to values that had marked him as a dangerous liberal for decades, but was less and less in agreement with the actions of the radical left. He began meeting with like-minded professors, calling themselves the "Faculty Renaissance"; drawn from "the more conservative sectors of the campus such as the faculties in business, physical education, and industrial arts, it had a wide sprinkling from other areas as well." The group tried to map a course that would buck the current and lead from confrontation to cooperation. When invited by old friend Thurston Womack to join the American Federation of Teachers, Hayakawa brusquely declined. On May 21, 1968, President Summerskill called in police, and twenty-six students were arrested at an administration building sit-in demanding an end to the Air Force ROTC on SFSC's campus, the admission of four hundred "ghetto students," the hiring of nine more minority faculty members, and the retention of Professor Martinez. As the school year ended in June, the assassination of Robert Kennedy thrust the campus community into despair, leading to a vigil and renewed commitment to "the dream." It had been an academic year characterized by great turmoil at SFSC, but it was only a prologue.

On June 1, 1968, the increasingly eccentric Summerskill, on thin ice with the trustees of the state college system for his accommodationist policy, resigned. He was replaced as college president by a popular professor, Robert Smith. At the beginning of the fall semester that year, Smith announced establishment of a black studies program with Professor Nathan Hare to be its chair.

Before the semester had much advanced, though, a part-time English instructor, who was also minister of education for the Black Panther Party, George Mason Murray—earlier part of the BSU group that had attacked editor Jim Vaszko—caused a brouhaha when he declared at a rally at Fresno State College, "We are slaves and the only way to become free is to kill all the slave masters." Murray also compared the American flag to toilet paper that should be flushed.

Later, back at San Francisco State, he urged that black students "bring guns on campus to defend themselves against racist administrators," and "pointed out the necessity for political assassinations to rid the country of people like [State Superintendent of Public Instruction] Max Rafferty, [Governor] Ronald Reagan, and [college president Robert] Smith himself." Writing six years later, Hayakawa asserted, "George Murray deliberately provoked his own suspension to justify the BSU strike. . . . [T]he BSU had made its strike intentions known (except for the date) weeks before."

The Bay Area was by no means immune to what writer Tom Wolfe labeled "radical chic." In fact, the style of the Black Panthers was increasingly appealing to activist students, professors, and hangers-on of all colors; Hayakawa recognized that the style *was* to some degree the message. On October 9 the Panthers' minister of information—ex-prisoner, neophyte author, and the Peace and Freedom Party's candidate for president of the United States—Eldridge Cleaver, was presented with a lifetime membership in the Associated Students of San Francisco State College, the highest honor that organization could award, for his contribution in race relations. Then, according to *San Francisco Chronicle* reporter Michael Grieg, "in a rambling litany of hate and some eloquence, before more than 2,500 students assembled on the dew-drenched commons . . . Cleaver hurled four- and twelve-letter obscenities at his enemies."

It is emblematic of that polarized time that the same day in Sacramento, assemblyman Ray E. Johnson of Chico urged that the state constitution be amended to give the state legislature direct control of the University of California because that institution's academic senate had overwhelmingly approved a resolution in favor of hiring Cleaver as a guest lecturer. "Our old theory of no political interference at our university has been thrown out the window by the university itself," asserted Johnson.

Many on the faculty at San Francisco State College, including Don Hayakawa, felt as though madness was indeed on the march. The California state colleges' board of trustees demanded that Bob Smith reassign George Murray to a non-teaching position, but Smith refused. Next, Chancellor Dumke ordered him to suspend Murray, and Smith delayed until November 1, when he finally obeyed. Hayakawa described President Smith as "a fine, brave man, but he had one psychological weakness. He didn't like to take orders from anybody."

On November 6, a previously planned "one-day" student strike was initiated by the Third World Liberation Front and the Black Students Union and various supporters. Dissidents issued long lists of demands:

Black Students Union
1. That all black studies courses being taught through various other departments be immediately part of the black studies department and that all instructors in this department receive full-time pay.
2. That Dr. Nathan Hare, chairman of black studies department, receive a full professorship and a comparable salary according to his qualifications.
3. That there will be a department of black studies which will grant a bachelor's degree in black studies; that the black studies department, chairman, faculty, and staff have the sole power to hire faculty and control and determine the destiny of its department.
4. That all unused slots for black students for fall 1968 under special admissions program be filled in spring 1969.
5. That all black students wishing so, be admitted in fall 1969.
6. That twenty full-time teaching positions be allocated to the department of black studies.
7. That Dr. Helen Bedesem be replaced from the position of financial aid officer and that a black person be hired to direct it, that third world people have the power to determine how it will be administered.
8. That no disciplinary action will be administered in any way to students, workers, teachers, or administrators during and after the strike as a consequence of their participation in the strike.
9. That the California state college trustees not be allowed to dissolve any black program on or off San Francisco State College campus.

10. That George Murray maintain his teaching position on campus for the 1968–69 academic year.

Third World Liberation Front

1. That George Murray and any other faculty person chosen by non-white people as their teacher be retained in their position.
2. That a school of ethnic studies for the ethnic groups involved in the third world be set up with students in each particular ethnic organization having the authority and control of hiring and retention of any faculty member, director and administrator, as well as the curriculum in a specific area of study.
3. That fifty faculty positions be appropriated to the school of ethnic studies, twenty of which would be for a black studies program.
4. That in the spring semester, the college fulfill its commitment to the non-white students in admitting those that apply.
5. That in the fall of 1969, all applications of non-white students be accepted.

Such daunting lists of demands guaranteed that no de jure triumph was likely for the strikers, and that even de facto success might not be possible. The "one-day strike" ended up lasting 167 days, and "on the first day of the strike, fast-moving gangs of students and non-students, in a grotesque parody of guerrilla tactics, ran in and out of classes, one of them mine," reported English professor Manfred Wolf. On November 13, Smith called police to quell aggressive strikers, who responded by throwing whatever they could find at the "pigs." Smith finally closed the campus indefinitely.

Despite such actions, at first the protest didn't generate much general support. A flier from "The Resistance" was posted around campus. It asserted, in part, that "the demands were created because 3rd World people felt they were justified in expecting as relevant an education as anyone else." It also asserted that students were "being *trained* by this college for the sole purpose of maintaining the traditional institutions of this country." The flier closed with the following all-caps challenge: "UNLESS YOU'VE BEEN COMPLETELY DEHUMANIZED YOU WON'T BE IN THE CLASSROOM."

Hayakawa noted that the demands were "valuative statements" whose real meaning was something like "we are angry," "we are powerful," and "we won't be dominated any more." Novelist James D. Houston observed that "student protestors couldn't directly attack or change the CIA or the Pentagon or the White House, so they went after the authority figures they could influence, and maybe intimidate, at the universities." Jacob Perea, now dean of the College of Education at State, then a graduate student, explains, "The issue of access for students of color was the main driving force behind the strike."

After the demands were issued, Don Hayakawa sent what would turn out to be an important letter to Chancellor Dumke and to the trustees urging that the administration not give in to what he believed were unreasonable demands and high-handed behavior, suggesting instead a hard line. Meanwhile, for some demonstrators the conflict at San Francisco State became an end in itself, "a kids vs. cops battle," remembers student Bill Johnston. Others described it as a class war: blue-collar cops versus "elite" students and professors. (More accurately, though, it might be characterized as blue-collar cops versus blue-collar students and their allies.)

More students soon joined the BSU and the TWLF, and so did radicals from off-campus who were angry about racism and the general powerlessness of young people in what seemed to be an insensitive society; the most galling cause of discontent remained the war in Vietnam. Writer Paul Auster, a student at Columbia in 1968, recalls, "Being crazy struck me as a perfectly sane response to the hand I had been dealt—the hand that all young men had been dealt in 1968. The instant I graduated from college, I would be drafted to fight in a war I despised to the depths of my being." Scores of idealistic young people like Auster, plus others simply looking for action, began to gather on San Francisco State's campus each day. They encountered among the police many men drawn from the generation that had fought in World War II and the Korean War. In a sense, both sides then embarked on a battle between generations, with neither understanding the values or motivations of the other.

Finding himself caught between the demands of intransigent trustees and uncompromising demonstrators, President Smith resigned less than six months after being appointed. To the surprise of most observers, Hayakawa, the leader of that small anti-strike faculty group, was named acting president. He was on record as opposing the strike, and only twelve days before his appointment he had delivered an emotional pro-Smith, anti-strike speech at a full-faculty meeting. He also had no administrative experience. Stories of how that appointment occurred proliferated, but apparently Dumke recommended Hayakawa, as did some trustees who had worked with him, and showed Governor Ronald Reagan the letter he had earlier received from Don. One version of events, quite possibly apocryphal but much repeated, has it that Reagan said, "Who the hell is this Hayakawa?" After Dumke's explanation, the governor supposedly replied, "If he'll take the job, we'll forgive him for Pearl Harbor."

Hayakawa's selection ignored the traditional practice of allowing a faculty committee to recommend candidates to the chancellor, who in turn forwarded his own ranking of them to the trustees. Don had, in fact, been a member of the ongoing presidential selection committee—which had "agreed to try and find a qualified black president"—and, as such, had agreed not to become a candidate for the presidency without first notifying other members of the group and resigning from it. When later asked by fellow committee member Eric Solomon why he had accepted the position, he reportedly replied, "It was an emergency."

Marge vividly remembered the phone call from Dumke offering Don the acting presidency: "That day the world changed considerably," she said. "Afterwards, he said to me, 'Guess what? . . . They want me to be president of San Francisco State,' and I said, 'Good God, no!'" Her husband said, "I was damn glad to be appointed president. . . . I really felt strongly that someone ought to take charge." Later, Marge would admit, "Through the turmoil, . . . I tried to keep my cool. The thing is, my husband is the one who sustained me. He's very cool and calm . . . and he never lost his sense of humor and goodwill."

Shortly before accepting the appointment, Hayakawa had told friends that he believed a minority of students and faculty was denying education to a majority, and that public education was in jeopardy. This was an enduring theme in his thinking; if he was wrong he was not opportunistic or inconsistent, except that now he had the opportunity to do something about it. According to Robert Smith, Richard Axen, and Devere Pentony, authors of *By Any Means Necessary*, "Nothing illustrates the huge gap in understanding between the trustees and faculty more than the appointment of Hayakawa as San Francisco State's acting president."

Librarian Helene Whitson summarizes: "If the word 'reasonable' can be used to describe President Smith, then 'authoritarian' must be used to describe President Hayakawa. His administration would not accept change through intimidation." The older generation had found in Hayakawa a general who would say "Enough!" Don was determined that the school remain open and operating for the majority of students, those not striking. On November 29, the *Los Angeles Times* editorialized: "For daring to remind the campus population of what a college is all about, Dr. Hayakawa was hit with all of the usual epithets which New Leftists so often use to hide their inability to think or argue straight."

Fortunately for Don, who was by no means an experienced manager, he inherited a seasoned team of administrators: Glenn Smith, Harvey Yorke, and especially Donald Garrity, among others. They would in a real sense control the day-to-day operation of the school after Hayakawa moved to stabilize it. A cooling-off period was imposed following Thanksgiving break. Hayakawa's unconventional approach surfaced immediately when he suggested that along with police, he would invite his friend, the gospel singer Mahalia Jackson, to sing at noontime on the day the campus reopened in the hope that her performance would calm students. The plan wasn't implemented.

Black studies professor Nathan Hare, meanwhile, predicted, "Hayakawa will go out faster than Smith. If he takes the hard line, we'll be ready for him." Roger Alvarado of the TWLF said, "We are not going to let the school open until we get our demands." Neither proved an accurate prognosticator.

The campus reopened on December 2 under a "state of emergency" that officially limited demonstrations. The day before, Hayakawa had seemed to send a mixed message when he had informed economics professor William Stanton, a strike supporter, that he had been denied tenure, but had reinstated George Murray to a non-teaching position. When a sound truck cruising Nineteenth Avenue stopped in front of the college and blasted a message urging students to strike, the acting president walked to the vehicle and asked a man in the cab "if I might use his equipment to explain the new regulations to the students. He slammed the door in my face." Don then "climbed on the back of the truck to speak to the crowd. When I began to do so, the soundtruck operators increased their volume to drown out my voice." He then "told the guys . . . to shut off that damn sound, and they [had] answered me in two words: one a transitive verb and the other a personal pronoun." Hayakawa looked "quickly around me, I noticed the wires leading to the loudspeakers, so I pulled them from their connections."

The event was literally stunning, since previously action had been the domain of demonstrators, hand-wringing the domain of administrators. Journalist Ed Salzman called it "the single event that made Dr. Hayakawa a folk hero." Some strikers began chanting, "Freedom of speech, Dr. Hayakawa! What about freedom of speech?" Others were shouting the familiar "On strike! Shut it down!" Still others, according to writer Kay Boyle, who was a pro-strike professor, "were laughing at the sight and admonishing him: 'Now, remember, no violence, no violence! We can't have anything like that!'"

This last was, of course, at best hypocritical, since many strikers had publicly condoned what they called revolutionary violence. Professor Leo Litwak writes that some strikers "raided classrooms and jostled students and professors and forced classes to end. Bombs went off in the Administration Building, the Creative Arts Building and the Psychology Building; the house of an acting dean was bombed. One professor who opposed the black studies program had the tires of his car slashed. A bomb was found outside his office door." Ex-student Marek Breiger recalls that a baseball player, "not a political person, but white . . . was beaten up because he tried to go to class." The intimidation of both faculty and student opponents was standard fare for strikers. "Up against the wall, motherfucker!" had become a mantra; BSU spokesman Jerry Varnado at one point told the crowd at a strike rally, "We've got to put Hayakawa up against the wall!" Soon strike leaders Varnado, Hari Dillon, John Levin, Tony Miranda, Roger Alvarado, and Murray (again) were suspended by "the fussy little rationalist."

As it turned out, neither side had exclusive rights to hypocrisy, and some faculty found themselves swept up in the excitement of the time. Manfred Wolf recalls that a fellow teacher, "a Harvard Ph.D., something of an elitist," declared, "They're using violence as a means of communicating," and that in view of the "institutional violence" faced by minorities, "their resistance was not violence at all." Wolf replied, "That's right out of Orwell." He also heard another colleague declare, "This is our Vietnam!" In response to Wolf's "Surely not!" the professor said, "How can you fail to note the similarity? . . . The U.S. is a police state, like Argentina." What Wolf did see was "the faddishness, the emotional sweep numbing all skepticism." Other observers saw a looming, likely violent nexus between anti-administration and anti-demonstrator sentiments. The acting president noted those things, but he still believed that some sort of rational discourse was possible. "Hayakawa could never really understand why any intelligent person should take a different view from his," points out Wolf.

On the sound truck, Hayakawa had begun tossing "Loyal to Dr. Hayakawa" scrolls tied with blue ribbons to the crowd, and more than a few were flung back at him, as were cups, coins, and even a few books. Then students were clambering onto the truck bed, but the five-foot, six-inch semanticist stood his ground, and the melee that ensued—pushing, shoving, and a few wild punches—revealed that the strike, like the acting president, was by no means unanimously popular on campus. "Half of them were pro–sound truck and pro-strike, half were pro-Hayakawa," the administrator later claimed, "and I didn't know which was which. There was one who said, 'Don't fight with me, Doctor. I'm your friend.'" The acting president was reportedly hit in the face with a gym bag.

In the midst of this, Boyle—who had once covered Nazi war-crime trials for the *New Yorker* and was "a great emotionalist who rose and fell with deep-sea tides of feeling"—became perhaps the first, but by no means the last, to tumble into hyperbole by suggesting a Holocaust parallel when she shouted "Hayakawa Eichmann!" The acting president's response is in dispute: Boyle claimed that he snapped at her, "Kay Boyle, you're fired!" but Hayakawa said his reply was, "Kay Boyle, you should be ashamed of yourself." Wolf reports that Hayakawa also said, "What a shame a fine writer like you should be at the head of a lynch mob." Perhaps she *should* have been ashamed. As her colleague and fellow striker Irving Halperin noted, "it is unconscionably obtuse to draw any comparison between what is happening on campus and a horrific situation such as the Holocaust; one does not compare hell with a single fire."

After Hayakawa climbed down from the truck, "the crowd began to appear menacing" and college business manager Orrin DeLand set about rescuing the acting president. The menace dissipated, but a demonstrator snatched Hayakawa's tam-o'-shanter and it was passed around the crowd. According to Dikran Karagueuzian, a student editor at the time of these events, "when the helpless administrator failed to get it back, he began to walk away amid general laughter."

As has proven true of so many memories of the strike, everyone seems to recall that their side emerged in some fashion triumphant, but if striking students had indeed laughed, their high spirits would soon be dampened. Hayakawa himself was not sanguine; in a memoir written in 1972, he explained:

> The entire sound truck incident took about four minutes. It might have become just another anecdote, except for the good fortune to have news and television cameras record the event. . . .

Within hours, pictures of my crazy antics were on all of the local television stations, in the afternoon papers and, before nightfall, I was on national television. Within days the story and pictures had travelled most of the world. Suddenly I was a symbol of courageous resistance to student anarchy for millions of people and "hot news" for dozens of editors.

The acting president's action seems in retrospect both bold and effective, fashioned to fly in the face of expectation and to toss the internally contentious strike on its ear. Harvey Yorke, Hayakawa's press aide, aggressively publicized the incident, and urged him to match the militants' publicity machine. As it turned out, he more than accomplished that. Governor Reagan reportedly remarked, "I think we have found our man."

thirty-one

Hayakawa's actions on the sound truck by no means stopped the strike, but they did change the terms of engagement; the *San Francisco Chronicle* of December 3 called it a "bravura performance." Don later explained that he had been determined to end the "reign of terror" that had gripped the campus, but he kept his own actions in perspective; when rumors that he had a black belt in karate began circulating, he later recalled, "I suddenly had an image of absolute ferocious masculinity, none of which I deserved."

Leo Litwak and Herbert Wilner recounted that a Black Students Union spokesman had earlier threatened faculty union leaders: "If you teach anywhere, he said, we'll stop it. We'll come after you. It don't matter where you are. And we'll hold this executive board responsible. We'll come with guns and get you. We'll get machine guns and get all of you. There ain't going to be any teaching!" Student Eric Richardson reported, "Ten black guys would walk into class and announce, 'Class is over' and the first one out the door would be the professor." Journalist Art Lozano elaborates: "In many classrooms strikers made their presence known, walking in front of instructors to write 'STRIKE' on chalkboards. Students who continued to go to school were confronted and called 'racist scabs.'" One result of such raids was that a number of professors began to hold classes off-campus, many in their homes.

Hayakawa didn't hesitate to seek law-enforcement support, and from the view of many strikers, the police and the school's administration were the real instruments of violence. Novelist Gerald Rosen, then an East Coast activist, has written, "In the Sixties an entire generation went crazy, wouldn't listen to reason, turned to violence and almost wrecked our nation. That was the adults."

Of course, another thing that was "almost wrecked" was the illusion that "adults," such as Hayakawa and the cops, were all soft. The acting president explained, "We have a professionally trained body of men, namely the police, . . . if order has to be restored—in an airport, a supermarket, a church, a university—we just call upon professionals to do that job." Hayakawa thus—in the view of strikers—violated the tradition of the campus as sanctuary. He also accurately sensed class tension when he addressed the police officers assembled near campus. "They were all very skeptical of my academic and cultivated voice. . . . I could see that on their faces, so . . . I wound up the speech by saying. . . . [I]f you do find it necessary to make an arrest, keep a friendly smile on your face as you drag the son-of-a-bitch off campus. And the cops just gave a roar of applause at that moment."

Noting the number of non-students among the San Francisco State strikers, Hayakawa again employed his sense of symbols (and of photo ops) prior to the new semester in 1969. He used a brick that had been thrown through his office window to pound in a sign on the edge of campus. It read: "Persons who interfere with the peaceful conduct of San Francisco State College are subject to arrest." Hayakawa's voice later echoed from loudspeakers on the roof of the administration building warning bystanders and curiosity seekers to leave campus and stay away from the police.

"Pigs off campus!" was the response of many strikers. Laureen Chew of the Third World Liberation Front—now Dr. Laureen Chew, an associate dean at San Francisco State—was jailed for twenty days. "Once I got involved, there was no turning back," she says. "I really felt we could challenge this world." One of the "pigs," Dick Yoell, reported that "a lot of (confrontations) were orchestrated by organizations like the SDS [Students for a Democratic Society]. . . . They would start violence in the back of the crowd and the guys in front would get the brunt of it."

Litwak believed that "the general sentiment of students and faculty nonetheless favored a negotiated settlement. The BSU claimed to be unwilling. But it became apparent that the governor was every bit as intransigent." Most professors, as it turned out, were politically at least as opposed to extremist demonstrators as to a reactionary administration and overly aggressive police. Like most students, however, they found themselves caught in the current. Knowing that the general public wasn't apt to understand their motives, they at least had to try to stop the violence from escalating.

On January 6, 1969, the college's local 1928 of the American Federation of Teachers (AFT) set up a formal picket line, demanding lighter teaching loads, automatic sabbatical leaves, other educational reforms, a collective-bargaining agreement for the state college system—economic demands necessary if a strike sanction was to be okayed by the Labor Council—plus removal of police from campus, and agreement to student terms. Approximately three hundred of a faculty of thirteen hundred honored the strike. Non-striker Manfred Wolf later wrote, "I had no doubt that the better people in the [English] Department were out on strike. They were moved by a desire to help, to do good, to support underdogs, and less nobly, to be on the right side of history." He added, "Those of us who were in the middle tended to be quiet. . . . The more extreme views, and the more extreme personalities, held the stage," referring to both Hayakawa and his foes. Of the acting president, he further observed, "Hayakawa was an opportunist but not merely an opportunist. He had fought many battles for minority rights, and he had taken on odd, unpopular causes."

The March 13, 1969, issue of the *New York Review of Books* carried an open letter from English professors Wilner, Boyle, Litwak, and Ray B. West Jr., presenting their perspectives: "We do admit to opportunistic action. We saw the opportunity to avoid mass murder on our campus, and we acted on behalf of that opportunity. We have so far been successful. We saw the opportunity to object effectively to the high-handed appointment of Hayakawa to the Acting Presidency, and we took it. And at this time we remain the only outspoken and organized agency to attack Hayakawa's irresponsible and inflammatory mismanagement of the crisis." Hayakawa's use of police was considered an especially egregious example of "mismanagement of the crisis." About then, too, a poster appeared on campus showing a protester being clobbered by a cop; it was labeled "Haya education."

The mere presence on campus of police was enough to attract significantly more demonstrators, since "the pigs" were cast as the enemy, the force of repression. In a surreal observation, ex-student John Lovejoy remembered that one day, the police tactical squad assembled off campus "dressed in protective head gear with clear plastic facemasks and long billy clubs, marched onto campus singing 'Little Liza Jane,' for some weird reason." Lovejoy also recalled that his wife "had a professor who absolutely refused to hold his classes off campus, and she had to sneak into San Francisco State or fail the course." Meanwhile, Marge Hayakawa sent "sandwiches to the embattled administration and staff when they were surrounded in their offices."

Some faculty and students who did not support the strike, and perhaps who did support the police, acknowledged that they had laid low in order not to be called racists or to invite BSU retaliation. Dr. Joseph White, the dean of undergraduate studies and likely the campus's most prominent African American, was caught in the crossfire. "The students were mad because they didn't feel like I was revolutionary enough," he recalls. "The senior administration was mad because they thought I should settle those kids down. It was intense."

BSU rhetoric escalated after Don's appointment as acting president. Spokesman Jack Alexis reportedly "told blacks that Hayakawa was a reactionary who would do exactly what the governor and the trustees wanted, or at least nothing of which those authorities disapproved." Moreover, according to Dikran Karagueuzian, Alexis also said of the BSU, "From that time on, we became a military group. All we discussed was military strategy. There would be days, after Hayakawa took over, when as many as fifty black students came to campus armed with revolvers just in case the police used their firearms." Don, it seemed, was doing exactly what most of the public wanted, thus exactly what many faculty and apparently all the strikers didn't want. With characteristic candor, Leo Litwak later wrote of the acting president, "He had a brazenness which—if I were on his side of the quarrel—I could view as courage."

On what had come to be called "Bloody Tuesday," December 3, 1968, major figures in the black community—publisher Carleton Goodlett, Assemblyman Willie Brown, Rev. Cecil Williams, and Berkeley city councilman Ron Dellums, among others—had appeared at a rally in support of student demands. In an indictment of both sides, Herbert Wilner described the events of that day this way: "There had been mayhem on campus at noontime. Some students armed themselves with pieces of brick, and one of the thrown objects felled an officer, stretching him on the grass. The police went wild. Charging in squads at knots of students, they whacked away with their clubs. By the time it was over, more arrests had been made, more blood spilled, and more serious injuries inflicted than on any previous day in the past month of confrontation."

English professor George Price was caught in the melee, beaten and maced. As he was thrust into a paddy wagon a policeman said, "How do you like that, you fancy pants professor?" and hit him with a baton. Mark Hurley, the Roman Catholic bishop of Santa Rosa, who chaired a Concerned Citizens Committee during the strike, recalled imploring police captain Don Scott to restrain his forces, many of whom were Catholics.

Those clashes led to one of Hayakawa's more infamous quotations. On "Bloody Tuesday," the acting president had remarked: "It's the most exciting thing since my 10th birthday when I rode a roller coaster for the first time." Later he admitted that "there's good excitement and bad excitement." A few observers suggested that Hayakawa had become a mirror image of the violent strike leaders; they had created what they now faced, and couldn't control him. None had expected the administration to fight back.

These wild events occurred only a little more than a year after the "Summer of Love" had drawn thousands of rootless young people to the city. Many had remained, and by the second month of the strike, events at San Francisco State had become a "happening," attracting increasing numbers of demonstrators who had no formal connection to the college. As events spun increasingly out of control, Jack Alexis reportedly told a crowd at the speaker's platform, "We have to shut down the other state colleges until all our demands are met." By then the striking faculty were becoming a problem for the most radical students and their sympathizers. Recalls Litwak, "The students were never entirely reconciled to our strike. While they were able, with our help, to paralyze the campus, that was only incidental to their objective. . . . The sound and the fury had been indispensable to their strategy, and the faculty picket line stifled that. It removed the action from the center of campus. And we faculty were law-abiding citizens, opposed to violence."

According to English professor Eric Solomon, "My side continued on its way to glorious self-destruction. We made common cause with the students because we feared and hated the increased use of the Police Tactical Squad, and we wanted to forestall what later became a reality at Kent State." By no means did all strikers appreciate that. An online history of the African American Studies Department at San Francisco State now asserts that the AFT only purported to support the student strike. "In fact, they helped kill it."

That seems unlikely, since the AFT strike was sanctioned by the San Francisco Labor Council, which, in turn, kept other union members from crossing the teachers' picket lines. No supplies were delivered by truck, for instance, and foodservice workers among others didn't report for work. Those actions certainly facilitated whatever impulse the state college trustees had to negotiate, although they conceded precious little. The faculty strikers certainly helped reduce the level of violence on campus. Smith, Axen, and Pentony also assert that "most striking faculty were convinced their painful efforts would be wasted unless they helped force administrative negotiations with the BSU and the TWLF." Moreover, as journalist Dick Meister has observed, "The faculty strike was a true landmark," yet paradoxically, the striking faculty were in some ways the big losers; a March 4, 1969, *San Francisco Examiner* editorial was not atypical; their strike, it asserted, "sullied the public image of college professors as professional men and women of high purpose."

At the center of this was S. I. Hayakawa, who had come to San Francisco State as a left-liberal maverick unopposed to change, and who had at one point in the strike actually advised the BSU to ask for more from authorities. As Karagueuzian pointed out, "No administrator in recent memory had dared to tell the blacks openly what to do." Moreover, in private conversations at least, Hayakawa had not opposed the development of ethnic studies programs, but had opposed their independence from normal academic governance. He was, it seemed, as dubious of the motives of strikers as they were of his. Professor Jason Ferreira, who wrote his doctoral dissertation on the SFSC events, reports that strikers "cut electric cords on typewriters, telephones and copy machines in academic offices, while toilets and bathroom sinks were backed up and overflowed into hallways." Their chants of "All power to the people!" actually promoted power only for themselves and their sympathizers. "Everyone else was a 'pig.'"

Eventually the BSU issued three conditions (which strongly resembled added demands) to any negotiations about the "non-negotiable" demands: first, the removal of all "pigs" from the campus and surrounding areas; second, the dropping of all charges and outstanding warrants against the strikers; and third, the reinstatement of all suspended students and teachers, without prejudice. Those "conditions" were not met, but after 167 days and complicated attempts to mediate by many parties, a settlement was achieved, and both sides have been spinning its terms ever since, claiming to have won. The administration agreed to expand the preexisting black studies program, but not to abdicate control over it, and to establish a School (later College) of Ethnic Studies, also subject to normal governance, while students had to give up their demands to control hiring, salaries, curricula, and open admissions. "Elaborate plans were agreed to in the settlement document for the creation of a School of Ethnic Studies, but this had been preordained in November," according to Smith, Axen, and Pentony. The Black Studies Department received not the twenty positions demanded, but 12.3; thirty had been required for Ethnic Studies, but only ten were approved. George Murray and Nathan Hare were not rehired for the 1969–70 school year, but Helen Bedesem—whose firing had been demanded—was retained and eventually promoted to dean of students.

In the short term, the big winner was Hayakawa. Along with civil rights leader Bayard Rustin and Governor W. Averell Harriman, for example, he in 1969 received one of the Awards for Excellence at the New York Council of Churches' Seventh Annual Family of Man awards dinner; a Gallup poll named him the nation's top educator; and at the annual Washington Gridiron Dinner "he received the greatest applause of the night seated between General [William] Westmoreland and Senator Edward Kennedy." He was, moreover, Richard and Pat Nixon's guest in the White House. But the tide of history was on the side of the young (though not exclusively of the strikers); soon they would *be* the Establishment, and many of their best ideas would be implemented while they outgrew many of their worst ones. San Francisco State's student population and curriculum soon became more diverse. "When you say Kent State. I think of anti-war protests. When you say free speech, I think of UC Berkeley. If you say multi-ethnic struggles, it is San Francisco State," asserted Kenneth Monteiro, current dean of the College of Ethnic Studies at SFSU. "This was one of the watershed events, that blast opened the doors. It wasn't that the other struggles weren't important, but this was Normandy." Hari Dillon, a member of the Third World Liberation Front's Central Committee, said in 1988, "What we did at State grew out of the times. It was part of the times and actually sort of catapulted the times further along."

Of course, for black and third world students, the struggle didn't end when the strike was settled. As Smith, Axen, and Pentony observed in 1970, "They proceeded with zest, enlarged ranks, and developed flexible strategies to work within the institution rather than without to achieve their goals of self-determination and a relevant, revolutionary educational program." History, it seems, may be written less by the victors than by the survivors.

In the eyes of others, the loser was the institution itself, or at least its older incarnation. According to English professor Dan Knapp, "State was never the same. Too many friendships had been ruined and too much trust had been destroyed. People stopped socializing. There were no more faculty meetings. Untenured faculty were fired, so all the young people were gone. The whole sense of community was destroyed." Nearly two thousand protestors had been arrested, and more than twenty faculty members had lost their jobs. As late as 2009, English Department chair Beverly Voloshin would observe, "The school still hasn't completely healed."

The strike certainly did contribute to the ease with which several nearby colleges established or expanded ethnic studies programs, since no administration wanted a repeat of the chaos that had marked events at San Francisco State. If the strategy behind such unrealistic student demands as financial autonomy had been to make other goals—like the establishment of an ethnic studies program—appear reasonable, then it certainly *was* effective. According to one of Hayakawa's most eloquent faculty critics, Herbert Wilner, "The students gained nothing they might not have gained without the war. . . . They went to war and lost." Professor Carlos Martinez Jr., on the other hand, in 2008 said, "Jesse Jackson had not yet organized the Rainbow Coalition. What happened at State was the first large-scale multi-cultural effort and set the tone for that kind of rainbow politics."

Many dissidents made a mistake—if they hoped for support of the general public—by adopting the confrontational style of the Black Panther Party. Hayakawa came to believe that at least some of his opponents had rallied behind slogans and buzzwords, exploiting the academy's traditional support of liberal causes while failing to recognize the differences between a Martin Luther King Jr. and a Huey Newton or a Bobby Seale. He also believed that elements of the BSU had deliberately provoked trouble in an attempt to assume control of the nascent ethnic studies program. This clash was, in part, a semantic dilemma, he also suggested; the Aristotelian dichotomy as articulated by Eldridge Cleaver—"You're either the problem or the solution, dig?"—seemed as false in this circumstance as it always had.

Hayakawa eventually earned grudging respect from some—but by no means all—of his faculty foes. Eric Solomon, who acted as a spokesperson for faculty supporting the strike, later admitted, "We opposed him but admired him—against our will—for the skill with which he established himself." Bishop Hurley recalled that Hayakawa became messianic about his role: "He said to me, 'For this was I born, for this I came into the world.'" Then the cleric, who worked closely with both the acting president and the strikers, added, "Sam was tougher than students understood." Some strikers had seemed to believe "soft Asian—tough African," "soft old—tough young" stereotypes—until they dealt with the acting president.

Don needed to be resilient, because his reputation among many colleagues had been destroyed. Pronouncements made in anger during and following the strike also revealed simmering resentment felt by those who found it necessary to denigrate Hayakawa's entire career. Don had so thrust himself into the limelight that ad hominem attacks were inevitable. He was a mere generalist and popularizer, "full of vanities." His earlier liberal and academic accomplishments were forgotten or ignored, or even denied. Intentionally or not, he had begun to move from one political world to another and was destined never to return.

Some colleagues at the time claimed that the acting president was out of touch. Apparently someone was, if opinion polls are to be believed. Litwak and Wilner, both pro-strike professors, acknowledge that "it was a revelation to discover that we were among the bad guys, damned by eighty percent of the public, to whom S. I. Hayakawa appeared—however implausibly to us—as some kind of Messiah." Perhaps the strikers so hated Hayakawa because he embodied the public's disdain for them. Certainly many in the general population had by late 1968 come to believe that college professors and administrators across the nation were irresponsible and gutless, bending to student demand after student demand, only to be presented with more. There was a related aspect of this: the battles at San Francisco

State vicariously pitted one generation against another, students against parents, new values against old ones. As an unnamed radical at Kent State observed, students were "determined to tear the university down and build a better world."

For a time during and after the strike, Don was protected by bodyguards, which usually meant a police escort. Although his Mill Valley house was also for a time patrolled by police, life there remained relatively normal. There had been crank phone calls, of course, and a few neighbors had turned icy, but the general response to his actions was positive. Perhaps because of her independence, Marge absorbed little criticism or even comment upon her husband's actions as she pursued her professional life. Parishioners at Daisy's largely black church seemed tolerant if not entirely supportive of Hayakawa, whom many had come to know over the years. None of Don and Marge's children reported any dramatic encounters as a result of his presidency.

In a postmortem of the strike that appeared in *Liberal Education*, Hayakawa explained his approach this way: "I got a reputation for having taken a hard line, though I only took a hard line in response to an even harder line." He also pointed to an irony of the student disruptions: "These things have not mainly happened where education is most old-fashioned or rigid or repressive. The outbursts have come from places where the atmosphere is most liberal, like Berkeley, Columbia, Harvard, Stanford, Swarthmore. . . . And many of the general public are infuriated that the most highly privileged of young people should be the least grateful for their privileges."

Nearly twenty years later, Jean Hayward, who had been a physician at the sfsc Health Center during the strike, attended a reunion at her alma mater, Ohio Wesleyan. When she was asked about Hayakawa and the strike, "I told them the university had been ruined by him, and that the students had been on the right track." In the course of the evening she encountered a classmate, Mary, who also lived in the Bay Area. She, too, had been fielding questions about the strike, "except that she had said something like, 'He was the savior of the university, just wonderful.' It reminded me why I hadn't liked her."

thirty-two

S. I. Hayakawa emerged from the strike with far greater name recognition and a positive popular image, and thus new possibilities.
"True," agrees striking Professor Dan Knapp, "but for all the wrong
reasons." Nevertheless, Don was touted for public office; he became
one of the nation's most popular public speakers, reportedly donat-
ing between $60,000 and $70,000 earned from lecture fees to SFSC,
plus nearly $300,000 in cash gifts he had received. During and after
the strike he had also received "cartons of fan mail." Stanley Diamond lived in Park Merced adjacent to the campus, and he helped
Hayakawa sort through the notes. He recalls, "I remember going
into Don's office when he was president, and . . . it was *crazy*. There
was correspondence from all over the world, stacked up. . . . There
were thousands and thousands of letters. We brought them here
[Diamond's residence]. We set up a room where we opened them
all and set them in little piles, depending on what was said—pro,
con, strong, weak, that sort of thing."

   In late 1969 a study team headed by William H. Orrick Jr. reported
to the National Commission on the Causes and Prevention of Violence, saying in part, "The deeply rooted problems which underlie
San Francisco State's crisis—and which plague many of the country's
higher education institutions—remain to be solved. Among these
problems are long standing social and economic injustices and ineq-
uities and the reluctance of the so-called establishment to respond
rapidly to change." Many Californians remained angry after the
San Francisco State settlement, and the study team further pointed
out that "the State colleges must . . . respond to the voting public"

if changes were to be financed. The team offered the following advice: "On the part of the administration, patience, firmness, and recognition of curriculum deficiencies will be needed. On the part of student leadership and their faculty supporters, there must be lasting recognition that the language of the gutter, the shock rhetoric, a willingness to 'mount the barricades,' vandalism, and personal assault do not constitute a valid or effective means of getting better education for themselves or their followers."

As it turned out, the very idea of "non-negotiable demands" by students rather than requests or suggestions, or even *demands* that were negotiable, had from the start angered many in the general populace, and many faculty, too, just as they had Hayakawa. Thus, he rode a wave of public support into his presidency. It was well understood that some student ultimatums had been crafted so that they couldn't be met, ostensibly to stimulate more protests or at least a continued examination of the status quo. The assertion that universities were instruments of oppression and discrimination didn't gain traction among most of the population, as public-opinion polls demonstrated.

While Hayakawa gained thousands of fans, many of them not aware of his earlier accomplishments, in the Bay Area, where he had been a prominent and respected intellectual, his reputation endured a sea change among liberals and progressives. Suddenly he was "Reagan's boy," the brutal president who had pandered to conservatives and called in police to break the SFSC strike. Don Hayakawa, it was asserted, had sold out to a know-nothing establishment represented by Reagan, Dumke, and a faceless, unenlightened "silent majority." To Hayakawa himself, however, his challenge was indeed messianic: "I think that in another time I would have been a priest," he said. "Colleges today are very much what the medieval church was—all of that to which the hopes of human salvation are entrusted."

Many of his progressive ex-pals believed he had condoned or even initiated a police riot. His ex-students were of several minds: some supported his actions, some did not, and even more just couldn't decide. Most of his friends at the Berkeley Co-op abandoned him, as did the KPFA-FM group he'd helped found; younger members of the Japanese community disavowed him, too, as did more than a few of his associates in the International Society for General Semantics. Most galling, perhaps, was that several prominent liberals, including powerful politicos John and Philip Burton, people he had previously supported, also attacked him. When Don lectured at Northeastern University in January 1970, a handbill from the Weather Underground identified him as "the noted facist [*sic*] who grooves on watching pigs beat up white demonstrators and shoot black and brown people."

Don had been much occupied with affairs at the college rather than with general semantics, so he received a shock in 1970 when the board of the ISGS announced that Thomas Weiss would replace Hayakawa as editor of *ETC*. Since the journal had been in many ways Don's one-man operation, this was no small matter to him. It was no small matter to the society, either, since Hayakawa had been its public face. Word spread that he had been sacked due to his political stance at San Francisco State, but Muriel Wanderer, widow of board chair Bob Wanderer, denied that. As Hayakawa became increasingly busy on other matters, she explained, "Bob and others on the ISGS board were all troubled by SIH's seeming inability to get *ETC*. out on time—sometimes 3 issues were finalized late—all at once—and they believed they were losing subscribers/memberships as a result." She added, "SIH was a special person to them all, but some probably saw these delays as due to personality . . . or simply a procrastination—though that seems unlikely as *Etc*. [*sic*] was his 'baby.'"

When journalist Ed Salzman wrote, "Academicians say he is the only folk hero to have emerged from American higher education," many of Don's erstwhile colleagues were enraged. Folk hero, indeed! His enemies' version of Hayakawa was that he was a drunk (untrue) and a womanizer (true) who had passed as black in order to avoid internment during World War II (untrue). Don recalled that "when B'nai B'rith honored me as the 'Man of the Year' and the SDS Jewish radical students protested it, they yelled over and over again, 'Where were you during World War II?'"

His name continued to evoked scorn from many in the Bay Area.

Herbert Wilner recalled an unnamed colleague who had "ridiculed semantics, the Hayakawa version, and berated Hayakawa as a popularizer whose huge enrollments in his lecture courses on campus were comprised mainly of middle-aged female enthusiasts of the garden club variety." Rivals began discussing him even more dismissively: he was a mere clown. The apotheosis of this was a booklet, *The Sayings of Chairman S. I. Hayakawa* (later reissued as *Quotations from Chairman S. I. Hayakawa*), edited by Richard Paris and Janet Brown and featuring cartoons by Roberta Christiansen and Victor Fisher. It was published by the San Francisco local of the American Federation of Teachers, which promised that "the money collected from the sale of this book will go toward bail bond, fines, and the legal defense aid, and AFT Local 1928 Strike Fund." If they couldn't beat him, they could at least make fun of him, and Hayakawa's sometimes shocking pronouncements and unexpected behaviors were used to some effect against him.

One rumor about Hayakawa that had at least some basis in truth and that was widely accepted was that as president he had been influenced, perhaps even manipulated, by Chicago insurance mogul C. Clement Stone. According to Kay Boyle, Stone sent Hayakawa "a $100,000 check . . . along with a bushel basket of orchids from Hawaii." Stone was also suspected by some to have dictated most of the terms of the strike settlement. Several ex-colleagues said they'd heard that Stone had hired a publicist to improve Hayakawa's image—something confirmed by the *San Francisco Chronicle*—but most of them estimated Stone's donation as closer to $10,000. "Clem" Stone was indeed an old Chicago friend of Don's and a benefactor. An examination of their correspondence reveals no abdication of purpose by Hayakawa, himself a man of strong opinions, but he and Stone shared many values. It might be more accurate to say that Stone reinforced Don's existing beliefs but did not shape them. For example, few conservatives, including Stone, agreed when before a congressional committee, Don "urged more flexibility in curriculum choices between different departments to fit students' over-all needs."

In fact, at that point, shortly after the strike, Hayakawa still clung to most of his liberal positions. Despite having been demonized by

302

the Black Panthers as well as by Black Students Union spokespersons and other leaders in the black community, Hayakawa emerged from the strike convinced that "black radicals want a better America. And they may use revolutionary methods at moments, but they are willing to give them up as soon as it's clear that the administration is willing to do something to improve the quality of their education and their opportunities within the system." He remained unambiguously opposed to most white radicals, saying, "Generally, the black students are fighting for a place in society. . . . White activists, such as the Students for a Democratic Society, are fighting to destroy the society, although they have nothing better to propose as a substitute to improve America."

Testifying before the House Committee on Campus Unrest on February 3, 1969, Don had employed a compelling analogy:

> If we were dealing with hunger instead of education, you can imagine what would happen if we had a walled city in which the citizens had all the food they needed while outside there were hordes of starving people. We could not open the gates just a little to admit handfuls of the starving and expect the rest to remain patient outside. . . .
>
> We would have to be prepared to open the gates wide and to admit everyone, or be prepared for a riot. That is the situation now with higher education.
>
> We have opened the doors just a little with special programs that serve hundreds while thousands are clamoring for education. I believe that we should open the gates fully, even at enormous expense, to provide educational opportunities at every level . . . for our minority and poor populations. We should mobilize the best brains available, just as we did when the nation attacked the problems of modern science, to solve an educational crisis that means as much to our national welfare as our efforts in outer space.

To those supporters and opponents who had come to identify the "new" Hayakawa with little more than prompt, severe, and seemingly insensitive action, that was a surprisingly thoughtful analogy

303

and suggestion. Don's confidants, however, understood that he had never opposed black aspirations, only the violent and uncompromising style in which they had been cloaked by San Francisco State's strikers. Like most of California's elected officials then, he was the product of an earlier, more decorous time. So were many faculty, and it had been tough for them to stand between the police and what Kay Boyle described as "our long-haired, tattered, chanting army."

The acting president's strong response during the strike, though, had left more than a few old colleagues baffled and angry. "You know," Knapp says, "Don Hayakawa seemed in many ways like a very admirable guy. The strike seemed to bring out the worst in him. After the strike, though," he adds, "Hayakawa was in a position to really savage his opponents, but he didn't take mean revenge." Hayakawa's aide Gene Prat agreed: "Don didn't hold grudges. He didn't purge. He wanted to bring order to the campus, not destroy the organization."

Asked if he thought that Hayakawa's own rationale—that he simply wanted to keep a public institution open for the public—might explain his actions, Thurston Womack nodded: "It might, in part. But the thing took on a life of its own." Anthropologist Jim Hirabayashi—who, during the strike, had carried signs reading "We Orientals may all look alike, but we don't think alike" and "Tojo is alive and well and lives in Marin County"—said that he believed that Hayakawa "didn't really believe in a community of scholars." Eventually, Hirabayashi became director of the ethnic studies program, and he reports, "I didn't see Hayakawa very much. He just didn't want more trouble."

During the strike and its immediate aftermath, Hayakawa's responses to stress were active and somewhat unpredictable. Michael Garrity recounts, "One day at about fifteen minutes to five, 'Don' Hayakawa called the VP's and the school deans to his office. He then proceeded to show the Dean's [sic] his new tapshoes and did a couple of steps for the assembled academicians." Aides recalled him occasionally doing more than a couple of spontaneous tap moves in his office during that period. Prat says, "If he got bored in a meeting, he'd put the [tap] board on the floor and dance a bit, or get up and water his plants (his office was like a jungle)." It was rumored during that period that he played his harmonica as he drove to and from work.

When Don was invited to address students at the University of Colorado in 1969, supporters of Students for a Democratic Society threw everything from folding chairs to bottles at him. By then used to student protests, he was unflustered and reportedly said, "To hell with you. I'm not going to get off this platform. I'm going to talk." When the dissidents began chanting rhythmically, he showed his disdain by doing equally rhythmic tap steps on stage.

One of the stranger episodes occurred when Professor Daniel Peck and *Los Angeles Times* education writer John Dreyfuss found themselves with appointments to see Hayakawa scheduled at the same time, so both were invited in and given drinks. In the midst of a less-than-clear interview,

> the new president raised himself to the edge of his desk. After briefly dangling his unshod feet in the air, he jumped back onto the floor and curled his toes into the plush carpet. Offering his guests another drink, he said pensively, "You know, one thing bad about this job is that I don't get enough exercise." He explained that he had a crick in his neck and that turning somersaults helped it. After taking a quick gulp, the new president began to do jumps. While the amazed reporter tried to continue the interview, Hayakawa went to a corner of the room opposite him, got down on his haunches, and turned a somersault, landing in the middle of the room.

Hayakawa continued his fencing, too, practicing regularly at the Pannonia Athletic Club. One of his partners there was Elvira J. Orly, a university student who would later become a member of the national fencing team and who would, later still, serve on Hayakawa's staff. She recalled, "Don had been fencing longer than I had and beat me all the time. Then as I fenced more, I got better and eventually I got to the point where I could beat him, and he kids that that's when he quit."

Although still a registered Democrat, Hayakawa remained a favorite target of those who had supported the student strike and the radical movements of the 1960s in general and who felt betrayed by his actions at the college; ironically, he felt betrayed by them, too. Eric Solomon asserts, "The stories of his presidency are a tissue of anti-climaxes. He drank a lot and dozed a lot." Many old colleagues recounted with something like glee the recurrent tales of Don napping in meetings, and it was rumored that he suffered from narcolepsy. Others remain baffled at the new president's behavior: "He ruined the college, then just went on about his business," says Knapp.

To the general public he seemed neither drowsy nor the one who had ruined a college. Hayakawa was the man who had saved San Francisco State. As a result, more and more accolades and speaking opportunities—the latter bringing higher and higher honoraria—became available to him. He was suddenly a far more prominent figure nationally, much celebrated in the media. A *New York Times* article published on August 17, 1969, speculated whether Don—by then president rather than acting president of SFSC—would run for the U.S. Senate seat held by George Murphy. "Last May the California Poll . . . showed that Dr. Hayakawa had a phenomenal 89 per cent name recognition." Asked about his political ambitions, Hayakawa responded, "The way I feel about it now, as I become increasingly absorbed in the operation of the college, is that the possibility of my running for the Senate or any other office, recedes. But I have not closed the door on the possibility."

Hayakawa could read polls, and he knew that the state's voting public held a high opinion of him, so he began a low-key search into the possibilities of a try at elected office. He was being mentioned as a candidate for the post of state superintendent of public instruction, and the California Poll showed him with a two-to-one margin over any opponent—but that wasn't his goal. He was looking at Congress, but he received scant encouragement from his family—especially Marge—which was already beleaguered by his celebrity. Recalled Daisy, "That phone, it never stopped ringin'." Friends he consulted gave him mixed messages when he mentioned a possible political run.

Marge urged him to return to his scholarly and literary pursuits. In 1968 his *Funk and Wagnalls Modern Guide to Synonyms and Related Words* had been released to excellent reviews. The following year, with coeditor William Dresser, he published *Dimensions of Meaning*, an anthology that included Don's essays "General Semantics and the Cold War Mentality" and "Semantics and Sexuality." Again, reviews were uniformly positive.

By then the college had settled back into some form of orderly activity, and it soon became clear that Don was not an administrator; the minutiae of the job bored him. His administrative style was, essentially, hands-off until his aides had thoroughly researched an issue. He also embellished that reputation for snoozing during long meetings. One of his supporters observed, "He did turn the tide; he did have the guts. . . . But since then, the institution has had to learn to live without a president." Hayakawa himself said that he was a different kind of president, one "whose role is public relations, interpreting the university to the general public, sort of charismatic. . . . [T]hanks to television, I was able to exercise this latter role." Journalist Noel Greenwood wrote that "most theories are that Hayakawa behaved the way he did because he never wanted the presidency as such. . . . His was a singular mission . . . and once relative peace was restored, Hayakawa was frankly bored with the job."

Another SFSC professor explained, "The chore of running the campus fell most heavily on two vice presidents, Glenn P. Smith and Donald L. Garrity. . . . They deserve an awful lot of credit for keeping the institution afloat." Garrity "chaired the Council of Academic Deans and more or less ran the academic program all during this period," recalled James Hirabayashi. "Garrity was the academic continuity," Dan Knapp agreed, "and Glenn Smith was a major factor, too."

In the meantime, in a broadside the Faculty Grievance and Disciplinary Action panel, a pro-union group, found the president guilty of not respecting the presidential selection process and of playing a "destructive, intemperate, and abusive role in the famous sound-truck incident." Further, it admonished him to "apologize to the owners of the truck and reimburse them for damages he caused." The same broadside also asserted that "the S. I. Hayakawa who is California's man of the hour is the creation of a highly paid public relations expert."

Garrity, Glenn Smith, Earle Jones, and others ran San Francisco State, while Hayakawa became a columnist for the *San Francisco Examiner* and the *Register and Tribune* syndicate. As in his *Chicago Defender* days, he wrote on a range of topics and, over time, revealed less and less empathy with the liberal positions he had once embraced. On August 1, 1970, for instance, his column titled "The Sansei and the Black Panthers" in the *Examiner* pulled few punches. After noting that "it is almost axiomatic that Americans, especially when young, derive an important part of their culture from the American Negro," he then argued that many "white radicals around Berkeley and UCLA. . . . are simply playing Black Panther, with their scowling looks, clenched fists salute, hair in a fuzzy mop, the Afro print shirts." Sansei students, he asserted, "are so fully assimilated into white culture that they do exactly what white youths of the same social class do—they also play Black Panther." Hayakawa went on to allege that "what infuriates the radical sansei most of all is his parents who, despite the raw injustice of the wartime relocation, lived through it patiently, fought with honor for their country in World War II, and came home to study and work hard and prosper—so that their children could go to college. It humiliates the sansei to think that their parents submitted to the relocation instead of, as they imagine the Black Panthers would have done, shooting it out with authorities."

Marge's family endured its own unexpected notoriety in 1970 when Olgivanna Wright, the widow of Frank Lloyd Wright and mother of Marge's late sister-in-law, Svetlana Peters, became convinced that Josef Stalin's daughter, Svetlana Alliluyeva, was the embodiment of her own dead girl—or so she claimed; Olgivanna was noted for being more than a little manipulative. A disciple of the Russian mystic

Georgi Gurdjieff, she implored Marge's brother, Wes Peters, who had taken an immediate liking to Svetlana Alliluyeva, to marry her. The latter also thought it was a good idea, and the couple married only three weeks after Svetlana has arrived at Taliesin West in Arizona on an extended visit.[1]

1. Roger Friedland and Harold Zellman report in *The Fellowship: The Untold Story of Frank Lloyd Wright and the Taliesin Fellowship*: "At the ceremony, which received intense publicity, Olgivanna introduced her [Svetlana Alliluyeva] as 'my daughter, Svetlana.' The apprentices showered her with jewelry. 'Now I can say again, "Svetlana and Wes!"'" Olgivanna exulted. . . . Svetlana was even expected to call Olgivanna 'Mother'—just as some others did" (568). The marriage, which produced one child, Olga, in 1971, lasted only twenty-two months before Mrs. Peters left her husband, citing the restrictive life at Taliesin West as a major problem. Wes disagreed, defending the communal living and denying the existence of any limitations on personal freedom.

nine

THE SENATE

thirty-three

No matter what his foes thought of him, Hayakawa continued to accumulate accolades—an honorary Doctor of Humane Letters from Pepperdine University and honorary Doctor of Laws from both the Citadel and Johnson and Wales College in the early 1970s. He was also named a Fellow by the American Sociological Association and by the Royal Society of Arts. All the while his columns were appearing in newspapers nationally and he published pieces in popular magazines such as *McCall's, Reader's Digest*, and the *Saturday Evening Post*. He also remained among the nation's most popular public speakers, so he was on the road a great deal. "Even when he was in town," reported Noel Greenwood, "his closest associates found him hard to reach or, when he was reached, hard to pry a decision from."

During the early 1970s, too, Hayakawa was invited to join the Bohemian Club, the illustrious (or notorious) organization of movers and shakers that had once been the realm of artists and authors. Associating with business and political heavyweights appealed to Don, and he much enjoyed the summer retreat at Bohemian Grove on the Russian River north of San Francisco, taking pals like Clem Stone with him. That membership reinforced the image of him as a member of the Establishment and made him few friends in academia, but the accoutrements of success seemed to mean much to him then.

Also in the early 1970s, accompanied by his son Alan, S. I. Hayakawa visited Japan to celebrate his father's eighty-sixth birthday. He sat at the old man's feet, saying, "I have been very successful. I have written a book that has sold hundreds of thousands of copies and has been translated into several foreign languages. I have lectured all over the world. I am now president of my college."

In the quiet of the room, time seemed to stop; then, as Alan later recalled, "I think I just heard my dad thinking: 'Is it enough?' Grandfather didn't answer."

Sammy Hayakawa, the boy who had struggled to please his ambitious Japanese father, had never left the man, S. I. Hayakawa. He was driven to excel, and excel he did, smashing stereotypes and both enraging and delighting people in the process. Some old friends feared he had destroyed himself along the way, but many others wondered at all he had accomplished.

In April 1972, Hayakawa announced that he would retire from the presidency at San Francisco State the following October. That revelation set off a wave of coverage that revealed his continuing popularity. An editorial in the *Monterey Peninsula Herald*, for example, asserted, "His contribution to the school has been tremendous. By refusing to give in to the idiot demands of student and faculty radicals, by doing the right and obvious things at the right and obvious times, he saved his institution's reputation, and restored it to good academic standing." *San Francisco Examiner* columnist Guy Wright pointed out that "Hayakawa took charge and brought order out of chaos. A great many people have never forgiven him. . . . Most of the students of that day have departed, but their successors have inherited the conditioned reflex of Hayakawa-baiting. And the bitterness in the faculty is like a cyst."

At Hayakawa's retirement press conference at San Francisco's Press Club, however, ex-student-striker Charles Jackson interrupted and demanded, "Ask him about the blacklist. What about the blacklist?" Jackson, who was suing Hayakawa and other university officials, "alleged the use of a list of those arrested in the 1968–69 strike to deny employment" at the college. One faculty member told reporter Carl Irving that Hayakawa "was totally disengaged from anything central to the college."

Well, not totally disengaged, it seems, since he not only promoted day-care centers, birth control at the health center, and environ-

314

mental sciences, but also inarguably brought wider awareness of the institution and raised funds for San Francisco State. He was willing to challenge authorities when necessary, such as when the governor and his allies sought to cut the college's funding. Saying he was unhappy with Reagan's budget, Hayakawa explained, "He's under enormous pressures from his constituency and I'm under enormous contrary pressures from mine. We've never agreed on everything. After all, he's a conservative Republican and I'm a liberal Democrat." In fact, Don was by then feeling abandoned by the party he had for so long supported. Liberal Democrats, many of them old friends, were attacking him for having resisted student and faculty demands, and for having condoned police violence.

Hayakawa's interest in politics then remained more active than his family knew. He had talked to aide Gene Prat about running for office, mentioning governor and senator. Prat asked, "What do you want to accomplish?" After a moment Hayakawa responded, "To be a statesman," and both of them knew the U.S. Senate was where he might accomplish that.

Prat also remembered one "statesmanlike" incident when, at a Press Club luncheon, Hayakawa passed a list to be signed and his gold pen around the table. When the list reappeared sans pen, he quietly ordered, "Dr. Prat, lock the door! Who's got my pen?" The instrument was soon returned, amid laughter, by the embarrassed journalist who had forgotten to pass it on.

In 1973, Don contacted attorney Harry V. Lehman, expressing an interest in running against Democratic senator Alan Cranston in 1974. Lehman, an experienced operative, suggested he instead consider the Sixth Congressional District seat of Republican William Mailliard, believed to be vulnerable due to redistricting and rumored to be considering retirement. Lehman further suggested that Don might wait and face Senator John Tunney in two years. "Tunney is a turkey, and not too bright besides. While you're a long shot against Cranston, I feel you'd have a very good chance against Tunney."

Despite Marge's entreaties that he not enter politics—but with the encouragement of most of his Faculty Renaissance colleagues,

315

Don pursued his goal of serving in the Senate. Adviser Sandy Weiner had warned him that he couldn't beat the incumbent Alan Cranston in the Democratic primary, but probably could win in the broader-based general election. In 1973, Hayakawa switched parties so that he could run in the next year's Republican senatorial primary. His actions caught some old pals by surprise, since he had so long been an active liberal. Even a few Republicans, who welcomed his candidacy, wondered what had catalyzed his action. It seemed an opportunistic sea change.

As soon as his name was mentioned, Don became a public favorite—but not for long. His late switch of parties did not meet the statutory requirements for candidacy. Hayakawa protested and appealed, but the state supreme court ruled against him and, as pollster Mervin Field noted, "eliminated the toughest potential challenger to incumbent Sen. Alan Cranston." Field added, "The colorful Japanese-American college professor had a clear lead among Republican candidates." Making the best of the situation, Hayakawa and his advisers studied California politics while biding their time for another shot at the Senate. "Needless to say, he was a quick study," said Prat.

Don and Marge became grandparents for the first time on September 18, 1973, when Alan's wife, Cynthia, gave birth to a little girl they named Lilith. Everyone from Daisy to Mark to Wynne joined in the celebration, and friends, some of whom had already been grandparents for two or more decades, well understood how thrilled the Hayakawas were, offering them congratulations, advice, and more than a little teasing.

By mid-decade, Don Hayakawa was keeping his name and ideas before the public with weekly newspaper columns that were syndicated nationally. As a result of contact with and urging from people like Dr. Clifford Uyeda and journalist Phil Jordan, Don looked into the case of Iva Toguri d'Aquino, the American woman who had been scapegoated as the infamous "Tokyo Rose." Mrs. d'Aquino had served six and a half years in prison and paid a $10,000 fine for treason in the early 1950s. Don wrote three columns—"The Woman Who Was

Not 'Tokyo Rose'" (March 20–21, 1976), "A Pardon for Iva Toguri d'Aquino" (March 27–28, 1976) and "'Giri'—A Sense of Personal Honor" (April 3–4, 1976)—arguing for her innocence and insisting on a full pardon for her.

After dealing with the death of his father in 1975, Hayakawa turned his attention to building a machine to defeat incumbent senator John Tunney in 1976. He engaged the issue-advocacy advertising agency run by Dick Woodward and Jack McDowell to spearhead a low-budget campaign. Don also reluctantly changed his public nickname to the more easily remembered "Sam" and altered his public appearance, too, friends have reported, with more and darker hair. He also turned his tam-o'-shanter into a trademark as he assembled a staff that included friends Elvira Orly and Gene Prat. At one point, the candidate traveled from small town to small town amid the state's rural reaches in an RV, often plucking a ukelele while an aid drove, and he gave stump speeches in places where voters were unaccustomed to attention from candidates. Don knew those were apt to be folks who had supported his stand against student radicals, and he wanted them to vote. Prat recalls, "He loved to mix with people in cafes, bars, even streetcars."

Before he could face Tunney, though, Don almost shot himself out of the water. *Farewell to Manzanar*, James D. and Jeanne Wakatsuki Houston's classic recounting of the World War II internment, had been produced as an award-winning film for television in 1976 by John Korty. In an essay review carried by *TV Guide*, Hayakawa repeated his by then well known opinion that "whatever the heartbreaks and losses created by the wartime relocation, there were unforeseen benefits." He explained, "Through the adventure of relocation, almost all Nisei and many Issei were thrown out of their ghettoized Japantown existence into the mainstream of American life. . . . They learned to be at home in their own country." His use of the word "adventure" especially grated many, and Jeanne Wakatsuki Houston commented simply, "Easy for him to say. He wasn't interned." In Canadian writer Greg Robinson's view, though, "Hayakawa was genuinely sympathetic to Nisei victimization by official prejudice (disdaining euphemisms, he spoke of Japanese Americans having been 'herded into concentration camps'). However, his powerful faith in assimilation and resistance to ethnic particularism led to clashes." Even Hayakawa's use of the term "relocation" caused him problems. It was viewed at best as a euphemism.

Don was in any case fortunate not to have been seeking the Democratic Party's nomination, but he still had to wrest the Republican nomination from former U.S. congressman Alphonzo Bell and two former lieutenant governors of California, John L. Harmer and Robert Finch. The latter, also a former secretary of health, education, and welfare during the first Nixon administration, was the clear favorite of the Republican Party machine. Finch had actually received more votes as a candidate for lieutenant governor than had governor-elect Ronald Reagan in the 1966 race, and he was beneficiary of not only the party's apparatus but the GOP's considerable checkbook.

Anything but a business-as-usual year, 1976 was one of those anti-politician seasons that sweep California voters from time to time, and Finch had his hands full. On the other hand, "Sam" Hayakawa played up maverick and outsider images, the non-pol' who would shake things up in Washington. Elvira Orly recalled, "Our campaign was not geared toward focusing on Finch. It was a positive campaign to promote Hayakawa, and the name recognition."

Name recognition was key, as the future senator himself pointed out: "What made me a pretty good candidate for senator is that I had really dramatic confrontations with radical students at San Francisco State . . . mixed up with sufficient dramatic confrontations in front of television cameras. I didn't plan it that way, but that's the way it worked out." If few voters had read *Language in Thought and Action*, a great many had read headlines about Hayakawa's battle with campus radicals; ironically, the radicals thus considerably helped to elect him.

Journalist Bill Stall noted that despite Hayakawa's talk about removing "the shackles of overtaxation and overregulation," the center of his campaign remained "that eight-year-old image of the peppery little professor taking on the student dissidents." A photo of Don pulling out the speaker wires on the sound truck at San Francisco State graced his campaign brochure, and his trademark tam-o'-shanter was ubiquitous. Stall also reported that Hayakawa defined the difference between Republicans and Democrats by talking about the plight of a drowning man who is fifty feet offshore: "The Republicans are the people who throw him 25 feet of rope and expect him to swim the rest of the way because it would be good for his character. . . . And the Democrats are the people who throw him 100 feet of rope and walk away to do another good deed."

Daisy's response when she learned that Hayakawa was planning to run for political office was direct: "All I said was 'Oh pooh. You're not a politician; you're an educator!' That was it." Asked by Julie Shearer in 1992 if she thought education was a higher calling than politics, Daisy responded, "Yes, I still do. Politics is all right, but it can't beat education."

With a campaign that cost less than $400,000 but was energized by volunteers working out of neighborhood headquarters in private homes, Don rode a groundswell of resentment against politics-as-usual. He opposed big spending, opposed access to agricultural-union organizers, opposed commuter "diamond" freeway lanes, and argued that we should keep the Panama Canal. As journalist Tom Goff noted, "He is telling Republican voters the things they want to hear."

Finch attacked Hayakawa's lack of political experience and his advanced age, but Don's responses were often off-the-wall—almost non sequiturs—and difficult for Finch to rebut: "Before World War II in Japan they killed off all the older politicians. All that were left were the damned fools who attacked Pearl Harbor. I think that this country needs elder statesmen too."

Hayakawa defeated Finch, Bell, and Harmer, plus others, by a plurality of eleven points. The election's result stunned GOP leaders. Observed *Time* magazine: "He will be 70 next month, has no previous political experience, raised far less money than his main rival, could not afford television commercials, has a rambling speaking style, and sometimes seems so becalmed that he is said to wink by opening one eye," but S. I. Hayakawa won the Republican Senate nomination in California.

The Democratic race featured its own unconventional political newcomer, a kind of mirror opposite of Hayakawa. Leftist political activist Tom Hayden—husband of actress Jane Fonda, a former spokesman for Students for a Democratic Society, and a defendant at the Chicago Seven conspiracy trial—opposed incumbent John Tunney. Hayden sensed that it was time to move into the mainstream, so his challenge to Tunney, who was backed by the party's hierarchy, slowly transformed from a laugher into something close to a contest. Hayden's poll numbers crept up steadily and began to rise above 40 percent as the two candidates publicly savaged one another. The underdog ran negative TV ads and claimed that Tunney was dating teenagers, calling the recently divorced senator "a Chappaquiddick waiting to happen." Since Tunney had roomed with Teddy Kennedy at Harvard, no one missed the insinuation. Tunney countered by assailing "peacenik" Hayden's days as a revolutionary and pointing out that Fonda's leftist fund-raising clout and Hollywood connections were providing her husband with a half-million dollars of campaign funds, plus well-known spokespersons.

When the votes were finally counted, Hayden had won only 36.7 percent, but the winner appeared vulnerable. California political journalist Ed Salzman observed, "The only surprises of the June 8 primary—John Tunney's relatively weak showing and S. I. Hayakawa's surprising strength—suggest that Hayakawa's biggest asset in the upcoming race for the United States Senate will be his opponent." As the incumbent, Tunney was the early favorite in the general election, and even Hayden endorsed him as the lesser of two evils.

Time characterized the race that followed as pitting "tony, tall and suave young Democrat v. saucy, short and blunt old Republican. Young Democrat with twelve years' experience in elective office; old Republican with none." It was, of course, about far more than that, and matched candidates of more substance than that presentation might suggest. Tunney, for instance, had sponsored thirty-eight Senate bills that became law, more than any other freshman elected in 1970. He had defied the Nixon administration by opposing the war in Vietnam and by his amendment to cut off secret American aid for the war in Angola, both of which should have endeared him to the left.

But this turned out to be an election much about image, and many voters—including many Democrats—considered Tunney a "fake Kennedy." He had entered the Senate after beating one tap dancer, George Murphy, and was about to confront a second, less adept tapper in Hayakawa. But Hayakawa was more a fighter than a hoofer, as Tunney soon realized. As Don's colleague Stanley Diamond once observed of him, "When things get a little bit tough, he's a very gutsy guy." Hayakawa's campaign spots were mild, although they emphasized the incumbent's poor attendance record and hinted that he was a playboy. Before long, the campaign's "Sayonara Tunney" buttons became collector's items. In general, though, Hayakawa ignored his opponent, saying, "I want to stand on my own merits. Let others talk about his character. I go out and meet the people. What more is there?" He did refer to the inconsistent Tunney as "Senator Flip-Flop."

One development, though, troubled some of Don's ex-students and colleagues who otherwise supported him. They later admitted they'd sensed a change in Hayakawa's style during the campaign. His language seemed to have dropped a register, becoming more vernacular: less rich vocabulary, more profanity, fewer factual details, even less complexity of syntax, hinting at less complexity of ideas. Always a man of great curiosity, prodigious memory, and eclectic knowledge, he now claimed to know or care little about many issues—as if that were somehow a virtue—and evidenced an edge of insouciance. They feared he was "dumbing down" in a quest for votes.

For instance, when *Time* asked about a ballot proposition seeking to legalize greyhound racing, Hayakawa responded, "I don't give a good goddamn about greyhounds. I can't think of anything that interests me less." He reportedly told another audience, "U.S. Senators don't know everything. For every damn Senator, there are

57 subjects they don't know a damn thing about." It hardly seemed an auspicious endorsement for the group he so sought to join, but little about Don's campaign seemed normal, least of all the candidate himself.

Although he led the polls by a comfortable margin as the election neared, Hayakawa almost torpedoed his own campaign when, in a televised debate, he urged that American troops be sent to southern Africa to prevent bloodshed there. Pressed by reporters, he added, "I would encourage insurrection in Hungary, or Poland, or Latvia, or Lithuania, or Estonia, or Tibet for that matter—those poor crushed nations that have been under communist tyranny all these years." He had been leading Tunney in polls by as much as 12 percent on the day of the debate, but by the end of the following week Tunney had built an 11 percent margin. Hayakawa's campaign managers, Woodward and McDowell, advised the candidate to stop ad-libbing foreign policy. Hayakawa stopped and he began to close the gap. But even up to the Sunday and Monday before the election, Hayakawa was still trailing by 2 percent. The Tunney camp was confident.

As Hayakawa might have told them, the map is not the territory, and when the actual votes were counted, "Sam" won the election with 50.18 percent (3,748,973) of the vote to the incumbent's 46.89 percent (3,502,862). Word was that the incumbent had genuinely expected to win, and that he was stunned. *Time*'s election postmortem started this way: "In a major victory that reflected voter frustration with ordinary politics and ordinary politicians, Republican S. I. Hayakawa ousted Democrat John Tunney from his U.S. Senate seat. . . . On TV, Tunney, despite his reputation as a swinging, divorced playboy, seemed uptight, while Hayakawa displayed a jaunty—and politically effective—cool." Ever the off-the-wall speaker, Hayakawa reportedly told CBS that the win was helped by anti–Washington feeling and that the "election probably confirms California's penchant for offbeat politics."

His opponents at San Francisco State continued to be both chagrined and fascinated by Hayakawa's rise. "Hayakawa has the greatest gift that can be granted a public figure," observed Eric Solomon:

"simply the sheer luck of the natural opportunist: the ability and timing and skill to be the right person in the proper place at the exact moment." Whatever the cause, Don Hayakawa found himself embarking on a new career. Orly and Prat, in the meantime, began the tedious task of assembling a Washington staff for the new senator. They wanted to have at least some key staff in place by the new year.

In the December 29, 1976, issue of *The Map*, published by the San Francisco chapter of the International Society for General Semantics, editor Bob Wanderer mused,

> Semanticists like to think that their discipline deals only with reality, but semanticists too sometimes dream, the impossible dream. We were amused 20 years ago when s.i. HAYAKAWA mentioned his Walter Mitty dream—to move to Hawaii, to run for senator when it became a state, & possibly to be elected, with the large Japanese-American population there. If that sounded like an impossible dream, how about this one: election to the senate from the most populous state, defeating a popular incumbent, as a new Republican in a year with a nationwide Democratic sweep. Fantastic, Don (or Sam, if you prefer).

thirty-four

S. I. Hayakawa enrolled in a program for freshman congressmen offered at Harvard University, admitting, "I've never held public office before. I'm starting absolutely raw, a real rookie." His administrative director, Elvira Orly, remembered that while the senator-elect was working in one of the seminars, university staffers mentioned they were much impressed that he was taking notes in Japanese. Orly told them, "No, no, he was taking notes in shorthand!" His high school secretarial training was still paying off.

Don much enjoyed the society of his fellow newcomers at the seminar, but he found many of the sessions boring, so almost immediately a characteristic that journalists would enjoy exposing throughout his term was on display: "during seminars he was caught napping." Hayakawa excused himself by explaining, "I must admit that I may have dozed through some of the sessions, but I haven't had a good rest since the campaign." Johnny Carson soon picked up the theme, and a decision made by members of Hayakawa's staff in 1977 would come back to haunt them. Carson, whose *Tonight Show* dominated late-night television, began joking about Don—*What would S. I. Hayakawa's personalized auto license plate be? zzzzzz*—but he also offered the new senator the opportunity to appear on the show. Without consulting Don, his staff decided, as Elvira Orly later explained to Hayakawa, "that as a U.S. Senator, . . . it would not be appropriate for you to be going on 'The Tonight Show' as a guest."

That may have been the single most telling error his inexperienced advisers made. Given Hayakawa's own sharp wit and pleasant demeanor—Eric Solomon, hardly an ally, once described him as "wistful, charming, full of stories"—it seems likely that he would have more than held his own with Carson, but apparently one refusal was all he—or his staff—got. Soon Diana McClellan, who wrote a column for the *Washington Post*, joined the "Sam-the-snoozer" brigade, as did the *San Francisco Chronicle*'s Herb Caen, then Art Buchwald and others, and the moniker "sleeping Sam" would haunt Hayakawa. He served as the butt of sleeping joke after sleeping joke throughout his tenure in Congress. Journalist Cathleen Decker later called the assignment of that nickname a "politically ruinous event."

It didn't take Hayakawa long to both fascinate and alienate at least some members of the Capitol Hill press corps. A January 5, 1977, article in the *Los Angeles Times* described "a news conference in which Hayakawa, with diminishing patience, gave guarded answers to increasingly sharp questions." Asked about his snoozing at the Harvard seminar, he responded, "I have a low threshold of boredom." Finally, "As the new senator hurried off down the corridor, a pursuing reporter asked him what his chief goals here would be. 'Avoiding the media,' Hayakawa said under his breath as he pushed toward an elevator," an odd oath for one who had been the media's darling.

Even before being formally sworn in as a senator, Hayakawa had taken advantage of his popularity in the Republican Party to meet with President Gerald Ford to discuss the "Tokyo Rose" case, requesting on the basis of overwhelming evidence of Iva Toguri d'Aquino's innocence that the president issue her a full pardon. The president, who never quite got Don's name right, calling him "Hayakama" and "Hiawatha," promised to look into the matter, and on January 19, 1977, he issued d'Aquino a pardon.

The next day, in seven-degree weather, Don left President Jimmy Carter's inauguration, telling fellow senator Joseph Biden, "My feet are cold." That walkout may have contributed to one of the zanier political stories of the year. A letter ostensibly from Hayakawa, but full of misspellings, marginal grammar, and non sequiturs, was delivered to many southern California voters. It began, "A constituent of mine—Gen. James Jackson . . . has proven that James Carter is a Communist who won the presidential election by extortion and murder. Shortly after his nomination for President, the general publicly stated Jimmy Carter is a Communist who intends to bankrupt this country and turn it over to the Russians." Since no one could find "the general," even Hayakawa's political foes laughed at the suggestion that California's junior senator was responsible, and his press secretary, Patricia Agnew, explained, "The only thing we can figure out is that somebody got hold of a robo (automatic) pen and did some cutting and pasting." It remains one of the more bizarre episodes involving a new legislator.

Don had been innocent of the General James Jackson controversy, but he committed a major gaffe when he skipped the black-tie dinner sponsored by the Washington Press Club that gave "legislators a coveted opportunity to make a dazzling first impression." Since he had been one of the scheduled speakers, his absence offended not only the pundits but some of his new colleagues. "He was bushed," an aide explained. By 1977, Hayakawa had been a professional lone wolf for so long that he seemed not to understand or much appreciate how to be part of a team, even one as prestigious as the U.S. Senate. Journalist Marlene Cimons observed, "It isn't so much that Hayakawa is bruising protocol as, at age 70, he begins a new career. He is just ignoring it, behaving in the same unorthodox way he did during the campaign." The sometimes charming eccentricity of his campaign ill served him once he was elected.

Still, most of his new colleagues were inclined to give the newcomer from California the benefit of the doubt. That spring he would tell *New York Times* writer Linda Charlton, "I find Senators an awful lot more interesting people than professors." When asked whom he particularly found intriguing, he named Republicans Howard Baker Jr., Jacob Javits, and Strom Thurmond and Democrats Herman Talmadge and Edmund Muskie. He also described himself as a "Republican unpredictable" and quoted Chinese philosopher Lao-Tzu: "You should govern a great nation as you fry a small fish—with little stirring about."

326

Hayakawa had shown his emotions when he stood before his Senate colleagues and said, "I cannot believe that I, the son of Japanese immigrants, am standing here addressing you on the floor of the United States Senate." Representative Peter Kostmayer, a Democrat from Pennsylvania, reported, "I was really prepared to dislike him, but I found him a rather engaging fellow, very friendly." Hayakawa's first legislative project was a joint effort with Democrat Alan Cranston, the Majority Whip, to add $70 million to a bill that had passed the Senate in 1976 but had not made it out of the House. The two solons also joined forces to create a bipartisan California Judicial Selection Commission to survey potential candidates for California's four U.S. attorney positions and future judgeships.

They differed almost immediately, though, on a bill sponsored by Cranston that would substantially expand Redwood National Park in northern California. Throughout 1977, the two exchanged barbs as Hayakawa took the side of logging communities and companies. "I want to stress the callousness of people who don't seem to care about economic disaster," he said. He also claimed that his opponents had an "anticorporate view" and called the bill "an excuse for excessive land grab by the federal government." Such conservative buzzwords cast a doubt on his sincerity, especially in the light of worker-protection provisions in the bill. Cranston, meanwhile, pointed out that the great trees were a finite resource; of the two million acres of redwoods Euro-American settlers had found in the early nineteenth century, only 270,000 remained. He also observed that families in Humboldt and Del Norte Counties didn't have special claim to the trees, saying, "Redwoods are not just a California resource but a national heritage." When early in 1978 Hayakawa lost the battle—the Senate vote was 74–20—he acknowledged it had been the roughest fight of his brief political career.

Don's early cooperative efforts with Cranston gave hope to many of the new senator's liberal friends that he would adopt moderate positions, and for a time Senate watchers didn't seem to know what to make of Hayakawa. One of his fellow neophytes at the Harvard

seminar told journalist Cimons, "First let me say that he is probably one of the brightest people I've ever met. . . . Having said that,
however, one has to modify that view, considering his age and his
problems with memory." Don, according to that legislator, was "too
open, too frank."

At the end of 1977, as Hayakawa became more and more a favorite source of quotes and quips for reporters, his old student, Bob
Wanderer began including in each issue of *The Map* "Hayakawaiana
for Hayakawawatchers," and it quickly became a favorite section of
news, rumor, and occasionally humor. One item, for example: "An
article in the SF Chronicle 3-21-78 suggests that expansion of the
redwood park (which he unsuccessfully fought) presents problems
of dredging & erosion. Don visited the park & 'didn't fall asleep
once.'"

Some mainstream journalists began to emphasize the more bizarre
elements of Hayakawa's behavior, everything from his sometimes foppish attire to various of his edgy pronouncements, while downplaying
any substantial contributions. Elvira Orly recalled one incident:

> There was a piece of legislation that the senator had co-sponsored
> and helped introduce. During the committee markup, the legisla-
> tion was severely altered, so much so that it was no longer along
> the philosophical lines that he had originally urged. So when the
> legislation moved forward, he was no longer in support.
>
> I remember the *Los Angeles Times* headline: "Hayakawa Votes
> Against Bill He Co-Sponsored." Now, this is the type of story that
> is very frustrating, because this reporter never looked at the issue
> and what had occurred. . . . They wrote it as if he didn't know
> what he was doing. The senator knew *exactly* what he was doing.
> That's why he voted against it.

Other journalists and commentators, however, realizing that Don
was too old to worry about building senatorial seniority, were less
shocked at what he said and less apt to distort it for entertainment
value.

Hayakawa's voting record during his first six months in office was distinctly partisan; *Congressional Quarterly* revealed that he supported the Republican Party's position 85 percent of the time and conservative positions 90 percent of the time. "He supported the party more loyally than such stalwarts as Barry Goldwater of Arizona, Robert J. Dole of Kansas and [Strom] Thurmond of South Carolina," reported Ellen Hume in the *Los Angeles Times*. The new solon also aligned himself with Goldwater, Paul Laxalt, and Lowell Weicker, along with a few others, to vote against a new, tighter code of congressional ethics, a vote that his side lost 9–86. His liberal and moderate friends in California were astonished at how far to the right he seemed to have moved, but he did occasionally cross up opponents and supporters alike, such as when he endorsed the Panama Canal treaties. Despite having the eighth-worst attendance record for Senate votes, Hayakawa was found by an April 1977 California Poll to be the state's most popular politician.

In January 1978 the Hayakawas flew to Japan, where they visited Don's mother and his sister Grace Emi. This stay was different from any previous one because, as a United States senator, he was invited to pay a courtesy call on Prime Minister Takeo Fukuda, a proud event indeed for his ninety-three-year-old mother, and no small matter to her son. While in Japan, Hayakawa also met with leaders of industry and agriculture, urging them to open themselves to a more equitable trade balance. He later explained part of the problem: "In the eyes of the world, Japan is a big, powerful industrial nation. (But) their own image of themselves as a poor little nation is the psychological reason for so much protectionism."

Hayakawa's Senate committee assignments were the subject of an article he published in *Harper's* that same month. "I was put on the Human Resources Committee, which makes a lot of sense because Human Resources includes Education." He was also assigned to the Agriculture Committee, which also made sense, since California — far and away the nation's leading farm state — "had not been represented on the Agriculture committee for something like thirty years." His most problematic assignment was to the Budget Committee, "because

I have the greatest difficulty balancing my own checkbook and my wife handles our investments." To his tongue-in-cheek astonishment, "The numbers you work with on this committee turned out to be very simple. You are always dealing with hundreds of millions—or billions. Therefore, when we say 1.0, that means $1 billion. Then we have .1; that means $100 million—and that's the smallest figure we ever deal with in the Budget Committee. . . . It's all simple addition. *You don't even have to know how to subtract.*"

The article's jocular tone changed, and Don asserted a frequent conservative complaint that "with the prevailing political philosophy of rewarding the unsuccessful and punishing the creators of our national abundance, there is no guarantee that we shall continue to be people of plenty." Some old allies were shocked less at the expression of a conservative cliché than at the article's absolutist tone, and that led to rebukes two months later in the magazine's "Letters" section. Vaughn Kendrick, for instance, pointed out that "The beneficiaries of our system are not 'the unsuccessful,' but rather the well-off fortunates. Striving for justice in this area is a mandatory function of any representative government."

As "fortunates" themselves, the Hayakawas were able to buy a large older house on Capitol Hill, which they then had refurbished. They immediately learned, though, that Mark, who was accustomed to the surroundings and routine at Mill Valley, could not adjust readily—if at all—to being relocated. Soon he and Marge returned home, where Daisy remained. Marge continued her own busy professional life there, visiting Don in Washington periodically. He missed her, his only editor and best friend, more than most knew. Says Gene Prat, "Rumors to the contrary notwithstanding, Don was pretty lonely after they left."

Don remained a curiosity on the Washington scene; a 1978 *People* magazine article by Leroy Aarons described him as "a man who dared stand up to the anarchy that seemed to be engulfing the nation," and added, "this peculiar little old man who commutes to work in a 1970 Plymouth and takes scuba diving lessons . . . makes the disco circuit in Washington on occasion, boogying with attractive partners (he is visibly appreciative of feminine charm). He takes tap dancing lessons from an old-time black hoofer called Mr. Rhythm." The senator explained, "It's terrific exercise. And it gives me an excuse to listen to all my old jazz records."

In March 1978, Don learned that a Field Poll showed his public approval rating had dropped from 32 to 25 percent, while the percentage of those who thought he was doing a poor job had increased from 7 to 21 percent. As usual, he surprised reporters with his comment, "I didn't deserve the high rating I had at the beginning. . . . but I'm not trying to be popular so much as I'm trying to be right." That same month, a *San Francisco Chronicle* article described him speaking on the Senate floor wearing "plaid slacks, green jacket, blue shirt & a bright red tie"; one supporter reportedly remarked, "How could you take him seriously in that getup?"

Later he endorsed the infamous Jarvis-Gann Proposition 13 on the California ballot, which would place a cap on property taxes and require a two-thirds vote of the legislature to pass fee increases, saying it would be a shock and lead to fiscal common sense. He also introduced Proposition 13's irascible spokesman, Howard Jarvis, in Washington as "my fellow ornery Californian." When the proposition passed in June, it was hailed by many as the first shot in a national taxpayers' rebellion. Later, columnist Jack Anderson revealed that Jarvis had in 1976 organized a "flim-flam known as the Friends for Hayakawa Committee" and collected $57,454, "none of which was used in SIH's campaign."

Herb Caen's *San Francisco Chronicle* column on August 11, 1978, reported that a female living across the street from Don in Washington DC, "says he tap dances in his underwear in front of an open window before retiring." He was also spotted dancing at a charity soiree sponsored by the *Washington Star* where, it was reported in *The Map*, the senator "remained wide awake throughout the waltzes, fox trots & the Blue Tango." Fortunately, Don was able to meet frequently with old pal Warren Robbins in Washington. Robbins recalled, "Often, Hayakawa lectured (always without honorarium) in programs I was conducting on inter-racial communication[,] so strongly did he believe in the need for better understanding between black and white Americans."

While Don certainly didn't mind being something of a celebrity, the novelty of living in Washington soon wore off. He missed his family and was much missed by them. Alan and Wynne were involved in their adult lives, but Mark, in particular, yearned for his dad, and Don could hear that in his voice when they spoke over the telephone. He could also sense that from his son's undisguised joy when his father returned to Mill Valley for visits.

Throughout his first two seasons in the Senate, Don's name appeared frequently in California newspapers: he was defending the use of saccharin; endorsing the commutation of Patricia Hearst's prison sentence; suggesting a $1.50-an-hour "subminimal" wage for fourteen- and fifteen-year-olds; authoring a bill that would force cities to allow taxi drivers to ply their trade without limitations. He also continued to make statements that bordered on the outrageous, such as "The redwood is a crop, just like cabbages," or saying that his next career would be "Playing a piano in a whorehouse," or his much repeated campaign dictum on the Panama Canal, "We should keep it—we stole it fair and square."[1] No one knew quite what to expect from him next.

In another surprise, he voted for federal funds to support abortions for poor women. Why? "That's none of the government's business. It's up to the woman, the father and the doctor." That vote led some to call him a libertarian. Later in the year, in another manifestation of his libertarian impulse, he opposed controversial California Propositions 5 and 6. The former—known as the Clean Indoor Air Act—would have required separate smoking and non-smoking areas in workplaces and public facilities; the latter, also called the Briggs Initiative, would have prohibited gays and lesbians from working in public schools. Don did support Anita Bryant's successful campaign to repeal an anti-discrimination ordinance in Florida, though he defended the privacy rights of consenting adults.

1. Two decades later, Hayakawa told Julie Shearer, "Well, 'we stole it fair and square' [laughs] was a wisecrack. It wasn't intended to be a policy statement, but it was taken by some people—sort of literal-minded people—as a policy statement."

The Panama Canal Treaty melodrama cast Hayakawa into higher relief, since his votes—two roll calls were taken—were crucial. President Jimmy Carter proposed a treaty that would cede control of the canal to Panama by 2000, believing that the image and influence of the United States in Latin America would thereby be much improved. Don extracted a price for his support; first of all, he insisted that three conditions be met: "The transfer of operational and administrative procedures would have to be a gradually evolving process; the new treaty should not place an undue burden on U.S and world commerce. The Senate should not be expected to simply rubber-stamp a *fait accompli*, and, most important, we had to retain control of the canal's military defense in perpetuity." The conditions were met, yet just prior to the vote, Hayakawa announced that he had become "indecisive."

After finally casting "Aye" votes on both rolls, though, he admitted that his indecision had been "a political tactic to gain influence in the oval office." He had called President Carter at 5 p.m. the day before the vote to ask for monthly meetings at the White House to discuss foreign policy. The president not only agreed to the meetings, Hayakawa said, but he told him he had been reading Hayakawa's book *Language in Thought and Action*.

Senate Minority Leader Howard Baker Jr., a proponent of the treaty, had also "dangled" a seat on the prestigious Senate Foreign Relations Committee before Hayakawa to influence him just prior to the vote. In December, Don formally applied for a position on that committee, saying in part that while he was no expert, one of his qualifications was "I am neither white nor black and sometimes can win the confidence of both."

A result of Don's high-profile activities and pronouncements was that at the time he received more letters a week than any senator other than Ted Kennedy. After the canal vote, he received more criticism than he had expected from his newfound conservative allies who remembered his campaign declarations. Liberals, meanwhile, gave him little credit for his votes, and his independence seemed to be confused with inconsistency. Don remained untroubled; "I knew that I had done the right thing for my country," he explained.

No sooner had the dust from the Panama Canal battle settled than another high-profile and familiar issue involving California's junior senator arose. In July 1978, delegates to the national Japanese American Citizens League convention in Salt Lake City endorsed a plan to ask Congress to approve $25,000 reparations for each person incarcerated in internment camps during World War II (or for their surviving heirs). Hayakawa publicly disagreed. Then he riled up academics when he "told the Novato, California, Chamber of Commerce that he favors the 'business elite' of people 'who know what it's like to meet a payroll' over the 'knowledge elite' . . . whose 'fundamental failure is their thought that they know better than the people how the people should live.'" That stale opinion helped convince more opponents that he was slipping into simplistic anti-intellectualism.

In one reminder of his earlier life, Don did take the time early in his Senate tenure to work with San Francisco State colleagues Arthur Berger and Arthur Chandler to revise *Language in Thought and Action* and to reissue it in a fourth edition. He also assembled a collection of his previously published essays, *Through the Communication Barrier*, for Harper and Row. His most prestigious and satisfying publication, though, came when the editors of *Poetry* magazine issued *The Poetry Anthology, 1912–1977* and included a 1934 poem "To One Elect" by S. Ichiye Hayakawa, reminding him of a different time and a different set of ambitions. It may also have reminded him of what might have been.

thirty-five

Despite his social life in Washington and his busy office schedule, Don was growing increasingly lonesome. He had established a routine of flying home to California once or twice a month, but the journeys were taxing. Departing Washington on Friday evenings and flying back on Sundays gave him little more than a day with his family in Mill Valley—if demands of the local Republican party didn't encroach on that time. For a man of his age, it was little wonder that he often returned exhausted.

By 1979, Don's congressional activities were dominated by his deepening interest in foreign affairs. In January he was one of six Republican senators who flew to Moscow to meet with Premier Leonid Brezhnev and discuss the Strategic Arms Limitation Treaty (SALT II). The Carter administration's recognition of China, estranged from the USSR at that time, added tension to the meeting.

Less than two weeks later, in one of his seemingly ubiquitous op-ed pieces, Don revealed that some of his experiences in Russia had been eye-opening. Members of the senate delegation had been, he wrote, "ready to listen, to argue and perhaps to find some common ground on which we could agree. In the Senate, as in America generally, that kind of communication is commonplace. In the Soviet Union, we soon discovered, it's unheard of. . . . The Soviets . . . didn't vary at all." The trip, which also included meetings with Soviet dissident Andrei Sakharov and the commander of NATO, General Alexander Haig, proved to be a valuable introduction to the world of international realpolitik.

At the California Republican Convention in February, as a new member of the Senate Foreign Relations Committee, Hayakawa's keynote speech discussed the conflict between China and Vietnam and the possibility of Russian intervention on the side of the Vietnamese. He criticized President Carter's pragmatic establishment of diplomatic relations with China, too, saying, "We are behaving like a second- or third-rate nation." He also added some of those strange pronouncements—likely intended to be humorous—that delighted his opponents. As the minority party, the GOP, he suggested, should search for prospective candidates among "housewives who are over 35 and aren't needed at home anymore," and noted that "eloquent and social-minded preachers" and "thoughtful professors" might be worthy candidates. In the context of the talk, those seemed to be non sequiturs.

Hayakawa then crossed up critics and supporters alike by joining Senator George McGovern in suggesting that a team of "private American citizens" be sent to observe elections in Rhodesia, although some African delegates to the United Nations protested the possibility. As it turned out, Africa would eventually become his major foreign policy area of interest. Later, on a visit there, he tried to effect a compromise in Rhodesia by calling a meeting of warring sides at his hotel. Gene Prat recalls, "Both sides sat there fully armed and glared at one another."

A couple of months after the meeting in Rhodesia, though, the once-noted orator again ignited protests with a misstatement. In the midst of a fuel crisis, he remarked that gas prices should be allowed to rise beyond the means of the poor. When his staff urged that he issue a clarification, he did, but saying essentially the same thing: "The genuinely poor don't need gasoline because most of them can't afford to own a car. . . . They are a very small part of the gasoline problem in California." His office was swamped with irate callers, and political writer William Endicott would later observe, "That seemed to be the beginning of the end." When the tempest didn't quickly blow over, Hayakawa refused to back down. "The price of bread, of beef and pork, of bacon and hamburger, tomatoes and lettuce goes up, up, up steadily. What happens as a result? There is no uproar in the media. But once I said let the price of gasoline go up, there are screams of rage and horror, and accusations I am indifferent to the lot of the poor," he said.

Pressured at a news conference, he once again stood by his remarks, then added, "I am not a politician. I am not trained that way. I'm just crazy, that's all. I mean I just say things spontaneously—if I say I'm crazy I mean simply that I'm not accustomed to exercising political caution when I open my mouth."

Matters of transportation then gripped Hayakawa: he introduced to an existing bill an amendment to repeal the federal speed limit of fifty-five miles per hour and return control to the states, then another to establish an Office of Ridesharing, both of which were quashed. Next he proposed an amendment to abolish the National Highway Traffic Administration, then he co-sponsored a resolution limiting members of Congress to twelve years in office. He also cast one of only four negative votes against a bill providing federal funds for the care of pregnant teenagers, explaining: "By assuming financial responsibility for unwed mothers, we subtly condone the lack of responsibility on the part of young people, their parents, their churches, their communities."

A familiar shoal lay ahead. When it appeared that the $25,000 reparation figure for Japanese Americans would not gain sufficient congressional support, the Japanese American Citizens League asked that a neutral commission be established that could determine how to indemnify economic losses incurred due to the World War II internment. Debbie Nakatomi, spokesperson for the JACL, reported that the group's leaders had been unable to get an appointment with Senator Hayakawa to discuss the matter. As a result, a thousand Japanese Americans took out an advertisement in the *Washington Post* that assailed Hayakawa and his stated position.

They didn't have long to wait for a response. That same week, Don published an op-ed piece in the *Los Angeles Times* titled "Reparations for Japanese-Americans? No!" The essay contained little new, but he went on the offensive. "The demand by the Japanese-American

Citizens League for 'redress,' reminds me uncomfortably of a fashionable minority-group game that was all the rage in the 1960s. First, you claim to be a victim of racial injustices; that makes Whitey feel guilty—and he loves to feel guilty. Then you make him pay and pay. It has been a very profitable hustle."

Most letters to the editor that followed attacked Hayakawa's stand. His claim that the internment was for the protection of Japanese Americans, for example, led Ann Bourman to write, "If Japanese-Americans were threatened by mob action, then they should have been offered protection not horse stalls at Santa Anita, not bleak prisons in the desert, not barbed wire or loss of property or breaking up of families." That clash of opinions would resonate in varying degrees throughout the remainder of Hayakawa's political career.

The senator's bad stretch didn't end there. A few days later, at a White House meeting to discuss the gas crisis in California, he slept at least part of the time when President Carter and Governor Jerry Brown discussed how to end the state's fuel shortage. Hayakawa also acknowledged that he had neglected to take his Dexedrine, commonly prescribed for narcolepsy, a disorder his staff insisted he didn't have. Art Buchwald then opened his June 3 nationally syndicated column this way, "When it was revealed that California's Sen. S. I. Hayakawa fell asleep during a White House meeting on his state's oil crisis a few weeks ago, a lot of people were shocked. I think Hayakawa did the right thing. There is nothing that can put anyone to sleep faster than people talking about the gasoline shortage." Questions of Don's health, age, and ability to serve, once whispered, became more common among his constituents and colleagues alike, although he was lively enough to continue playing in congressional softball games.

The senator had certainly been feisty at the end of May at UCLA, where an estimated thousand-plus students greeted him with boos, catcalls, and a chant: "Fee, fie, foe, fum, Hayakawa is a bum!" Don responded, "This is the type of student outrage that got me elected to the Senate. . . . If they keep this up, I'll be president." He added, "It sounds like the good old days." Journalist Richard Bergholz reported that Don badgered students "with taunts about their conduct and

intelligence. . . . [A]fter an almost incoherent statement and question from the audience, Hayakawa said 'I wonder about the level of
English and rhetoric that is taught at this university.'"

His prepared speech at UCLA had, in fact, been a thoughtful exposition of a plan he and Mexican ambassador Hugo Margain had
developed to allow Mexicans to work in the United States. The
ambassador and the senator proposed that migrant laborers post a
$250 bond, then be allowed in to work in the United States, and for
the bond to be reclaimable (with interest) in no more than six months.
Quite sensibly, Hayakawa added that as long as a vast difference in
pay exists between the woven economies of the United States and
Mexico, "they're going to stream in, legally or illegally." He would
go on to host several semi-formal conferences with immigration
authorities in an effort to resolve issues of mutual concern.

Shortly after the UCLA event, Steven V. Roberts of the *New York
Times* identified Hayakawa as a member of an informal but powerful
group of conservative Republican senators known as "the Steering
Committee." That cohort, which met for lunch each Wednesday and
occasionally hosted prominent guests like Phyllis Schlafly and Tom
Wolfe, included Utah's Jake Garn, South Carolina's Jesse Helms, and
Nevada's Paul Laxalt among its sixteen members; they were joined
in "a new effort to promote conservative principles," according to
an anonymous staff member. Ironically, one of its explicit goals had
been to block the Panama Canal treaties for which Hayakawa had
voted.

Don's work on the Foreign Relations Committee dominated his
interest throughout 1979. He continued to be, for instance, actively
involved in the SALT II talks, and he asked the committee to consider
four amendments it had previously rejected dealing largely with
military parity. In a public session, "he saw a 'foreboding parallel'
between the present debate and the failure in 1919 to ratify the
Treaty of Versailles." Although SALT II was finally sent (despite
Hayakawa's negative vote) to the full Senate in early November for
consideration, it was never ratified.

At about the same time, though, he joined ultra-liberal Jane Fonda,

339

among others, to support Operation California's efforts to send medical supplies and food to Laotian, Cambodian, and Vietnamese refugees caught in the latest flare-up of war in Indochina. As seems to have become the rule, his actions gained him little or no liberal support but cost him conservative backing. By the end of November, a *Los Angeles Times* poll showed him with an unfavorable rating of 68 percent and a favorable rating of only 29 percent. Asked if he thought his position required him to vote the way a majority of his constituents wanted, he responded, "Perhaps it's part of an earnest politician's job to create enlightenment where it doesn't exist and where no other politician touches the issue." Then he added, "I don't give a damn about the *Los Angeles Times* or the Field polls or anything else."

He had by then established solid personal relationships with a number of colleagues, and in the private dining room for senators he loved the luxury of thoughtful luncheon discussion with colleagues from both parties. In that setting, without the pressure of microphones or cameras, senators actually got to know one another. Hayakawa especially hit it off with Jesse Helms. "He took me to North Carolina with him once," Don recalled, "and in a halfhearted way, I wanted to test him—so I took a black girl out from my staff to North Carolina. . . . He treated her just royally. He'd say, this is Senator Hayakawa's staff member, Miss So-and-so. . . . She really was very black, and very shy, and very nice. Wherever we went, he . . . treated her with the utmost courtesy and Southern courtliness. Of all the people in the Senate that I could like so very, very much was Jesse Helms, although I disagreed with him so often. He was considerably to the right of Genghis Khan [laughter] but a wonderful fellow."

For a time, Don's sister Ruth lived with him in the Washington house, and his sister-in-law Svetlana Alliluyeva Peters was an occasional houseguest. Gene Prat also recalls that Don would have his driver take him to nightclubs occasionally, "and both of them had a hell of a good time." The maverick Democrat Daniel Patrick Moynihan, who lived up the street from Hayakawa, was another special pal. They met with some frequency at one house or the other for drinks and conversation that varied from hilarious anecdotes to mock-heated debates. As Prat recalls, "Ideas really flew when those two got together."

On November 4, 1979, a mob of Iranian students overran the U.S. Embassy in Teheran and took more than sixty Americans hostage. President Carter tried to pry the hostages loose with economic sanctions and diplomacy, but by March of the next year the American public—stirred by nearly constant media coverage, by yellow ribbons, by calls for armed intervention—was growing frustrated with the administration's efforts and putting more and more pressure on Congress. Alan Cranston responded by calling for cutting all diplomatic relations with Iran and suggesting that Iranian diplomats in Washington be interned or deported and that a total trade embargo be imposed on Iran.

Hayakawa went a step farther when he said, "After what's happened, we have every right to declare a state of belligerency and round up all non-citizen Iranians and put them in relocation centers." That stimulated a smattering of support from the far right, but it eroded his credibility among mainstream Republicans. Carol Hallett, the GOP leader of California's assembly, said such suggestions were "basically disgraceful." Karl Kobuyuki, national director of the JACL, called it "a ridiculous proposal," and Republican leader William Campbell of the California Senate was even more blunt: "I don't think we have to get down in that same kind of pigsty," he said. Hayakawa defended his suggestion, saying, "Pro-Khomeini Iranians are spitting in our faces, & we call it rain." His staff reported that 84 percent of his mail favored his stand, and Don's ex-student Bob Wanderer wrote in *The Map*:

> The line "nobody supports him but the people" seems not far off. On the Iranian matter as well as on some others, the press & "experts" speak of his "unpopular stand" & a few people whose buttons are pushed denounce him, yet he draws overwhelming support by mail & by phone. As one longtime Washington observer

341

said, "When he does get a negative reaction from the public, it is usually because he has spoken bluntly & without the usual fluff politicians mask bad news with. And the price of non-political straight talk is a bad press."

Early in 1980 Hayakawa praised President Carter's proposal to reinstate draft registration and added that women should register too, but not serve in combat. He next added that it would be "a very nice thing" if the handicapped were given the opportunity to serve. What followed was another of those pronouncement that his critics loved to pounce on: "For gosh sakes, a handicapped person with only one leg can become a tail gunner."

A domestic issue finally diverted attention from Hayakawa's "relocation" and "tail gunner" proposals. Trouble was brewing on the California coast in the summer of 1980, and it would soon pit Don against not only Alan Cranston but also the legendary photographer Ansel Adams. Adams, as spokesman for environmental groups, asked Congress to create a Big Sur Coast National Scenic Area. "Surely," he commented, "no more beautiful and spiritually uplifting coastline exists on this earth." At the behest of the Wilderness Society, Cranston then introduced a bill that would place more than a thousand square miles of California's coastal land under the supervision of the U.S. Forest Service, and Congressman Leon Panetta introduced a less sweeping, but similar, bill to the House of Representatives.

Calling the region "a crazy place," Hayakawa sided with the locals, who overwhelmingly opposed federal control of any kind. The residents "have a culture not quite comparable to any scenic or vacation area in the country," he explained. "The people . . . are hippies [who] have rejected conventional life-styles. . . . They believe they should be left alone by the federal government." The normally liberal-to-radical residents of the coast found themselves grateful to have a conservative advocate in Don. Adams disagreed. "The Cranston Bill is excellent," he wrote to fellow environmentalist Edgar Wayburn. "Senator H. is *impossible*—and an embarrassment."

"Now I admire Ansel Adams—he's a superb photographer—but I

342

think he's been looking through his viewfinder a little too long," Don responded in a letter to the *Los Angeles Times*. He then attacked that newspaper's endorsement of a federal takeover, saying in part: "You make the Big Sur controversy sound like a balanced battle, with half the residents supporting government control and half opposing it. In reality, very few residents of Big Sur want federal intervention." Local resident Joan Steffy wrote, "It is particularly ironic to find the liberal and passionately environmental Big Sur community *opposing* the Sierra Club and Wilderness Society, yet having Big Sur's rights protected by Sen. S. I. Hayakawa. The circle comes around!"

New York Times writer Robert Lindsey offered this perspective: "In many ways the dispute appears to represent a collision between two political attitudes—the environmental ethic of the 1960s, with its emphasis on preserving natural beauty, and the more antigovernment tide of conservatism." The Cranston Bill did not pass, and Bob Wanderer in *The Map* summarized:

> Blocking federalization of Big Sur, "my great legislative victory to cap 1980," came about when SIH spotted a legislative trick. His colleague Senator Cranston called up on the senate floor a noncontroversial "Yolo-Zamora (water district) bill, as amended," & asked that reading of it be dispensed with. A suspicious SIH objected; it turned out that the "innocuous" bill had acquired a "rider" to federalize Big Sur. SIH threatened a filibuster, & Cranston withdrew the amendment. Later, Cranston reportedly told SIH, "You were too tough."

Gene Prat said simply, "Don Hayakawa saved Big Sur."

If so, he reaped scant rewards in the press, and although he was named Environmentalist of the Year by the Friends of the Big Sur Coast, his poll numbers remained low and he continued to be a favorite target of humorists such as Art Buchwald, who told an audience at UC Irvine, "Jerry Brown and Hayakawa have helped California live up to its national image of being crazy." Washington columnist Jack Anderson called Don "the most visibly lazy member of the Senate, one who proposes nothing, though blessed with a superior intellect." Don had by then become a favorite target of Bay Area journalists like Abe Mellinkoff and Charles McCabe; the inept Hayakawa they portrayed wasn't someone old friends or foes recognized—although the latter certainly hoped it was true—so a certain disconnect developed. Later that year Don was named the nation's least effective senator by *Washingtonian Magazine*, and the liberal National Committee for an Effective Congress selected him as a target for 1982.

The year's most satisfying event for the senator was his ninety-six-year-old mother's visit to Washington. Senator Howard Baker hosted a reception for her graced by sixty solons. She also attended a Senate session and heard her son deliver a speech, then was welcomed to the Oval Office. President Carter was photographed with the demure mother and her beaming son. "I had many disagreements with President Carter," Don later said, "but he was always a gentleman. That visit was my mother's greatest thrill on the trip." That she found herself in the heart of a nation that had once denied her entry wasn't lost on Mrs. Hayakawa. The Japanese ambassador later hosted a farewell party for "this beautiful little lady," and the senator and his sister Ruth "danced up such a storm that everybody stopped and watched." Mrs. Hayakawa's final visit to the United States was memorable indeed.

thirty-six

During the presidential election year of 1980, the Republican platform committee meeting in Detroit went on record as opposing both legalized abortion and the Equal Rights Amendment. Hayakawa then shocked his GOP associates and liberal opponents alike when he sent presidential nominee Ronald Reagan a telegram urging that he pick a female vice-presidential running mate, suggesting specifically Ambassador Anne Armstrong or Senator Nancy Landon Kassebaum. "A lot of women are damned mad" about the party's abortion and ERA stands, he asserted. "These are both first-rate people, . . . and the choice of either of them would do much to unify the party."

Reagan did not select a female running mate, but he did change the balance of power in Washington with a one-sided victory over incumbent Jimmy Carter in November. A worsening economy and the Iranian hostage crisis gave the California governor all the ammunition he needed, and his victory suddenly placed Hayakawa in the majority party. This time Don did attend the inauguration, delighted that a small-government conservative from California would now sit in the Oval Office.

On January 20, 1981, twenty minutes after Reagan's inauguration, the Iran hostages were released. Almost as quickly, Don disbanded the nine-member California Judicial Selection Commission that he and Alan Cranston had earlier organized, saying he would appoint his own nonpartisan group. *Los Angeles Times* writers Paul Houston and Kenneth Reich suggested there might have been more to it than a mere assertion of power. "In California political circles, Hayakawa's move to put his own stamp on judicial and U.S. attorney appointments is viewed in part as a step to assert his political power at a time when many active Republicans are tending to write off his chances to be reelected to the Senate." Among journalists and some colleagues, the question of whether Hayakawa would or should run for reelection was being openly discussed. Unlike experienced politicians, Don had spent little time raising funds during his Senate years, and that was enough to convince some journalists and other observers that he had no intention of contesting another election. The senator himself insisted that he would indeed stand for reelection and that he would kick off his fund-raising with an event at Big Sur, where he remained something of a hero.

Following a rather muddled Hayakawa press conference in February 1981, Representative Paul McCloskey, who planned to oppose Hayakawa in the Republican primary, said it underscored Don's "essential fuzziness . . . the fuzziness of old age," although when the senator "is awake and alert he can say things better than any one in the country." Alan Hayakawa, by then an experienced journalist who had joined his father's team on the assumption that the senator would seek reelection, wasn't encouraged by what he found when he surveyed the Washington office crew. "The Senate staff seemed to be organized around getting Don to 'look like a senator,' 'talk like a senator,' 'act like a senator'" based on their separate mental images of the ninety-nine role models around him, he later recalled. "I don't think there was anyone there who encouraged him to figure out what it was that he alone could do, and concentrate on that."

Whatever problems existed in the office, Don plowed forward, still charting a course not always easy to follow. After John Hinckley Jr.'s attempted assassination of President Reagan on March 30, Hayakawa said, "I pray the shooting of President Reagan will be the last reminder we need before moving to effective gun control," surprising many liberals. He shocked them again by opposing oil drilling off the northern California coast, and when he co-sponsored a bill to rename the Department of Commerce's building for Herbert Hoover. When complaints about his snoozing arose once more, he said, "At some hearings people testifying take 40 minutes to say what could be said in 7, so I doze," leading political columnist Earl Waters to observe about Don's naps: "Far from being evidence of aging, they demonstrate an ability many people envy; ask any reporter who's had to sit through hours of dull legislative sessions."

More important to the senator was that he secured three subcommittee chairmanships in the new, Republican-dominated Senate. His voting record generally remained conservative, and those who didn't understand the dimensions of California's agriculture smirked when he pointed with pride toward his efforts to increase foreign import quotas on fruits and nuts grown in the Golden State. His longtime interest in farming and Mexican laborers in the United States led him to formally frame the ideas he'd first presented two years before, now called the Guest Worker Act of 1981, seeking to establish a five-year temporary visa program that would allow participants to work in this country after posting a bond.

In his new capacity as chair of the East Asian and Pacific Affairs subcommittee, he visited Laos and suggested that Laotians provide an accounting of U.S. soldiers missing in action there in exchange for the United States dealing with unexploded bombs on prime Laotian farmland. In a related occurrence, he was presented the first-ever award given by the National League of Families of American Prisoners and Missing in Southeast Asia for his efforts to obtain information on POWs and MIAS.

Meanwhile, Hayakawa and his friend Moynihan bet a case of wine from their respective states over the outcome of the 1981 New York Yankee–Los Angeles Dodgers World Series. When the Dodgers won the series 4–2, a reporter asked Hayakawa if he was implying a parity of quality by wagering straight up. "Courtesy compels me to say yes," he replied, and Moynihan interjected, "You don't have to choke on it!"

Despite his activity, many ambitious politicians sensed vulnerability, so the list of his potential rivals continued growing to include talk-show host Maureen Reagan, banker Arthur Shingleton, and Representatives Barry Goldwater Jr., Robert K. Dornan, John Rousselot, and Paul McCloskey. A California Poll in February indicated that

347

"two out of three Republican voters opposed Senator Hayakawa." Asked why he was determined to run in the face of so much opposition from his own party, Hayakawa said, "I'm a member of the majority party [now] and I'm really euphoric about the opportunities to be of greater service." McCloskey probably spoke for most of Hayakawa's rivals when he explained, "Let me be blunt about it. If he runs again, he will lose to any strong Democratic candidate. This happened in California a few years back when an elderly Republican named George Murphy ran one time too often and lost the seat to John Tunney."

In private, Hayakawa was less sanguine about his chances for reelection. He was receiving little encouragement from Republican Party officials, his family wanted him home, and he had drifted away from two of his closest Senate friends, Moynihan and Ted Stevens. Also, on a personal level, his principal aide, Elvira Orly, had married and left his team in 1980. On top of that, the novelty of living like a bachelor in Washington had long since worn off; he was tired and discouraged by all the journalistic sniping he continued to endure.

His son Alan remembers "wondering what Don could possibly do or say to persuade voters to support him for another term." Then in April 1981 Alan was shown a draft of what came to be called the English Language Amendment. "This is it," he thought. "It's everything he'd need. It's exciting, original, dangerous, possibly demagogic, red meat for the right, fodder for the press and a fundraising goldmine. Too bad it's two or three years too late." On the twenty-seventh of that month, Senator Hayakawa introduced a constitutional amendment to make English the official language of the United States. Representative Dornan quickly submitted a version of the same amendment to the House. Don's proposal died without a hearing, and Dornan's did no better, but Alan Hayakawa had been prescient to assume it would be an issue that would slowly create a groundswell.

Don Hayakawa, meanwhile, explained in an October *New York Times* op-ed piece, "At one time, most immigrants' first task was to learn English." The original concept of bilingual education, he wrote, had been "the use of the immigrant's native language as a transitory tool that will accelerate the process of learning English." What had developed, however, was a situation in which "young immigrants are having their entire curriculum taught to them in their native language," which retards learning America's de facto national tongue. To forestall rebuttals, he added, "The amendment would not scrap all bilingual programs, nor would it prohibit foreign-language requirements in schools or colleges. I strongly believe in learning more than one language, and feel our tendency toward monolingualism has put us at a disadvantage in the international business community." Asked later how he had come up with the "Official English" idea, Don responded, "It has something to do with my being Canadian. Canada has two official languages. . . . I kept thinking, 'We have enough Hispanics in this country to put on the pressure to declare Spanish the second official language of the state of Arizona or wherever.'"

Despite the "Official English" hubbub, which kept his name in the news when it was vigorously attacked by some educators and ethnic advocates, pressure from the party was increasing on Don to either energize his reelection campaign or drop out of the coming race. One story, perhaps apocryphal, was that Hayakawa told Edmund "Pat" Brown at a Bohemian Club gathering that he couldn't understand why people who had supported him in 1976 were abandoning him. Brown reportedly replied that those people had used him to defeat a perfectly good senator but now had no further use for him.

Don's war chest was nearly empty—only about $200,000 remained —with few donations coming in. Richard Bergholz reported, "Last summer a small group of GOP contributors, many of whom had been his staunchest supporters, met privately with Hayakawa . . . and told him he would have to build up his political standing—particularly in the polls—or they would walk away from him and line up for someone else." As if that weren't pressure enough, a liberal group, the Progressive Political Action Committee, targeted him for a negative advertising campaign that featured a caricature of him as a do-nothing senator and pointing out that only one of the forty-three bills he proposed had passed. Orly later insisted, "There were a lot of things that he worked on, that he was instrumental in getting passed, which didn't bear his name." He was soon targeted by the right as well as the left when he and Connecticut's Lowell Weicker became the only two Republican senators singled out for defeat by the anti-abortion Life Amendment Political Action Committee.

On January 24, 1982, the *New York Times* carried an article headlined "Hayakawa Resists Idea of Dropping Out of Race." One week later, another headline read "Hayakawa Abandons Race for a Second Term in Senate." Before informing anyone officially of his decision, he had met with his son. Alan recollects, "He and I had a long talk, in the little kitchen of the Washington house, in which he laid out for me the reasons why seeking reelection wasn't a good idea. All the reasons were familiar to me, but as I listened, I realized he was in a sense asking for my agreement, almost my permission, not to run. . . . Of course, I told him, I supported his decision, and I was touched that he even asked me."

Senator Hayakawa informed Howard Baker and Paul Laxalt of his decision; later he personally told President Reagan at the White House. He formally announced his intention to the semiannual California state GOP convention in Monterey, adding, "I make this choice without urging or pressure from anyone." There was little else for him to say.

Hayakawa did get in a final lick or two before stepping away from the fray. In his speech before the Monterey convention, he said, "The difficulties of campaigning while continuing to do one's legislative work are well illustrated by Congressman McCloskey's voting record of 57% and Barry Goldwater, Jr.'s record of 58% during the past year. . . . Having decided to run for the Senate, they made a deliberate choice of campaigning rather than earning a high voting average. My own voting record was 93% — and I am not boasting when I say this. I made the choice to stay with my legislative duties in preference to campaigning." Journalists had their own views and were not reluctant to offer them. Kenneth Reich pointed out that when Don "finally made up his mind, without too many staff consultations, not to stand for reelection, it was more out of personal feeling than political calculation."

Hayakawa's decision seemed to bring special joy to his enemies in the Bay Area, where anger still festered over his role at San Francisco State. Friends confided that in his mid-seventies Don, who despised fund-raising, seemed worn out by the stress of his position. What they didn't know is that he was having trouble controlling his blood pressure as well as suffering from lethargy and shortness of breath that one physician feared might be caused by a serious pulmonary problem. X-rays were inconclusive, and he was advised to monitor his condition closely.

Likely the more leisurely world of academia had ill prepared him for the stress of the Senate. "You're not given time to ponder big issues," he told political writer William Endicott. "I felt incredibly frustrated many times because here I was voting on this very important issue and I had to take my staff's word for it that this is the right way to vote because they'd read the literature and I hadn't." Reich pointed out that while the senator had been debating another run for office, he had seemed aged and almost enfeebled. Once the decision had been made, "He suddenly seemed younger, not older, than his age."

Rumor had it that a presidential appointment was Hayakawa's for the asking if he didn't run, but a staff member said the senator did not want an ambassadorship or a job in the administration. He preferred to return home following his term to resume his career as a writer and lecturer. Several years later, Don said that the principal reason he retired was that "Marge couldn't move with me to Washington, and I didn't feel comfortable being away from home for most of another six years."

Hayakawa's absence from the senatorial field, in the meantime, opened it to all comers, and finally thirteen, mostly minor, candidates vied for the GOP nomination (the Democrats had eleven, including Don's pal Bill Pemberton). San Diego mayor Pete Wilson eventually won the Republican primary and would face California's governor, Jerry Brown, for the Senate seat in November.

Don, meanwhile, offended his conservative colleagues when he opposed requiring that parents be notified when teenagers receive prescription contraceptives from clinics funded under Title X of the Public Health Services Act of 1970. Ideally, teenagers should of course be able to confide in their parents, he pointed out in a May 3, 1982, letter to the *New York Times,* but that simply isn't everyone's reality. He concluded the missive, "The increase in teen-age sexuality is a reality. Notifying parents will not curb this increase, but education might. Both parents and children need help—not a confrontation initiated and enforced by government regulations."

Using what was left of his bully pulpit, Don continued lobbying for formally declaring English the national language. He "held colleagues and a congressional hearing audience in rapt attention" in April when he explained that he had learned English the same way most children learn language, by "total immersion. . . . My first language must have been Japanese, . . . [but] as soon as I went out on the street and played . . . I learned English." As long as bilingual education involved total immersion in English, he was not opposed to it, but when it was used as a way to avoid using English in school he was much in opposition.

Don's frequent use of an analogy between Quebec and the United States soon came under attack. "There is no comparability whatever between what is happening in the U.S. and Quebec," asserted McGill University professor Calvin Veltman. In Quebec, French is the language of business, education, government, and entertainment, while in the United States, English fills those roles. "With mass communication and mass culture—the McDonald's, the Dunkin' Donuts and all that—the immigrants assimilate pretty quickly. For Chicanos in urban America, the long-term survival potential for their native language is really not very high." David G. Savage, *Los Angeles Times* education writer, reported: "By the third generation, almost all Latino immigrants are predominantly English speakers, even though they have learned Spanish at home." He added, "The latest data say that Latino immigrants are switching to English at about the same rate as the German, Italian and Polish immigrants who came before them."

Hayakawa had far more to say on the issue, but he would say it later. And say it. And say it. As he had often insisted that the internment of Japanese Americans had produced at least some positive results, he continued to insist on linguistic nationalism. That, of course, became fodder for vituperation as well as humor.

The San Francisco State strike was the topic when that college's newspaper, *The Phoenix*, interviewed the lame duck Hayakawa. Asked, "Isn't it odd that you—a semanticist and communicator . . . repressed free speech?" Don responded, "I was trying to maintain free speech, the opposite. It was radical students who were stopping free speech by saying 'if you teach your class, we'll beat the shit out of you.' That was suppression of free speech, of anything except their point of view." The years seemed not to have mellowed him on that subject.

Hayakawa was soon engaged in what seemed to be a paradoxical conflict, given his expressed bias for states' rights. The Reagan administration in July advocated California's right to create more rigorous environmental rules than the federal government's, but the senator said he was "distressed" that "the states have been placing excessive and burdensome requirements on chemical companies to register pesticide products." He remained distressed, because the existing rules were extended.

In September 1982 the Senate passed a sweeping revision of immigration law. Its sponsor, Alan Simpson of Wyoming, agreed to an amendment offered by Don which declared that "the sense of the Congress that the English language is the official language of the United States." Don also floated a proposal to nudge the "voluntarily unemployed" off welfare and food stamp rolls, arguing that able-bodied people could live as well or better on welfare than by working at a minimum-wage job, but injecting a note of compassion when he added, "Once they fall into this dependency, they are sentenced to lives with no futures." Critics called his proposal cruel and ill-timed. Don responded by citing a survey in Baltimore showing that 89 percent of those jobless six months or more thought they could get a job if they looked for one.

Conservatives as well as liberals felt Hayakawa's sting. When Don's old friend Jesse Helms drafted a rider severely restricting abortion rights to a bill raising the national debt ceiling, a battle ensued. Opponents, including Hayakawa, staged a filibuster against the rider; when Helms's supporters failed for a third time to invoke cloture, Don moved to table the Helms amendment, a move that effectively killed the possibility of new restrictions when it passed. He remained adamant that abortion not be restricted for poor women as long as affluent women suffered no similar limitation.

Meanwhile, in the November race to which the White House assigned high priority, Pete Wilson defeated Jerry Brown to win the Senate seat vacated by S. I. Hayakawa. But by no means did Don shut down shop in advance of his January retirement. He directed his staff to send out questionnaires on the possibility of developing an organization to promote English as a national language, promising to remain active in such a group in order "to prevent racists from capturing the issue for their own use."

When Don finally left office, an editorial in the *San Francisco Chronicle* included an unexpectedly positive note summarizing his tenure, saying he "has never been your conventional, run-of-the-mill legislator. His healthy disregard for the established political verities has been refreshing, as has his provocative turn of mind." More predictably, *Taxpayers Watchdog* called Don "a free spirit, unmortgaged to outside interests" who "had reached the Senate without the kingmakers & resented their maneuvers to get him out." Many years later, columnist David Brooks observed, "Being a senator is a craft"; it is a craft at which people like Edward Kennedy and Robert Dole excelled, but one that S. I. Hayakawa never quite mastered.

While not exactly saying good riddance, Alan Cranston had a different view, explaining that he'd had little success "in getting Senator Hayakawa's cooperation on California issues" such as suggesting parcels to be designated wilderness areas. "As a result of our failure to reach agreement," he said, "it may now be too late to save several areas that otherwise might have been protected and preserved."

ten

U.S. ENGLISH

thirty-seven

After Hayakawa was replaced by Pete Wilson, some members of Don's staff blamed his relations with the press for the lack of support he'd suffered, but were shocked when the ex-senator—ever the general semanticist—said, "I had no complaints about the press." He elaborated: "There's no blanket characterization. Some were hostile. Some were very, very friendly. Some were objective; some were not." Don seems to have too late come to understand that shooting from the lip was rarely a good idea in Washington; he had usually remembered that only after having shot. "I blurt things out which newspapers take advantage of to caricature me," he admitted. "But damn it, I'm the kind of guy that blurts things out as they come to me. And that's been very damaging."

Don's departure from the Washington scene was accomplished with far less fanfare than his entry six years earlier. He did not attend Pete Wilson's swearing-in ceremony, although he had been invited. Remarked Otto Bos, Wilson's press secretary (and a San Francisco State graduate), "Maybe it just slipped his mind." The stereotype of the bumbling senator apparently lingered among some in his own party. The busywork of shutting down the Washington house, saying good-bye to staff and pals, and formally signing off as a senator occupied him for a time.

Don returned home to the delight of his family and Daisy, and he began organizing his senatorial papers so that they could be sent to the Hoover Institute at Stanford University. There was talk of writing an autobiography or at least a memoir on the Senate years, as well as another revision of *Language in Thought and Action*. Everything and nothing loomed ahead.

In 1983 Otoko Isono Hayakawa, Don's ninety-eight-year-old mother, died, but that year the family also added its first grandson, Nathaniel Hayakawa, son of Alan. The baby's father had returned to his job with the *Portland Oregonian*, where he served as art and architectural critic. Alan's sister, Wynne, was by then building a reputation in the art community. Mark continued living at home and working at a facility for developmentally disabled adults in Marin, and Daisy "ruled the roost," according to Wynne. Marge had pursued her professional life in her husband's absence. She continued to serve as president of the California Horticultural Society and editor of its journal.

Daisy revealed another aspect of the family's life during that period when she revealed to interviewer Julie Shearer that while "Mr. Hayakawa" was a senator, "My niece, Julie Pope, came out here and she stayed three years right here in this house. . . . He said to her, 'Now if you go back to school, I will give you a job in my office.' So she worked at his senatorial office in San Francisco every day after school. . . . He put that girl through school." She added, "Julie would get up in the morning, and Mrs. Hayakawa would give her some breakfast. . . . Mrs. Hayakawa was very, very wonderful."

Ironically, several old chums who had vehemently disagreed with some of Don's political stands in the Senate remained close to Marge, a fact that bemused her husband. In many cases, social rapprochement ensued after he had returned to Mill Valley. As for Washington, he acknowledged, "I miss my friends there, but I don't miss the tension, the rapid pace." Old pals noted that he'd lost a step or two during his years in the nation's capital, not surprising given the pace of life there and his advanced age. The former senator comfortably slid into fishing excursions with Mark or Daisy or Bill Pemberton, but he was not quite through with government service.

In 1983, Don accepted an appointment as special adviser on Southeast Asian and Pacific Basin matters to Secretary of State George Shultz. "He will continue his work with Laos on the missing-in-action matter, with Japan on trade, with the Philippines on improved relations, & other such issues," reported *The Map*. In that capacity he would later in the year represent the secretary of state and lead a delegation to the Pacific Economic Cooperation Conference in Bali. He also visited Laos in May seeking more information on MIAs. In September he headed a delegation from the Filipino-American Chamber of Commerce in San Francisco on a trade mission in Manila, and represented the State Department at the Pacific Mayors' Conference in November. Able to focus his attention largely on foreign affairs, Hayakawa made a genuine contribution.

His retirement was becoming active, especially since that year he co-founded, with Dr. John Tanton, "U.S. English," a citizens group "dedicated to preserving the unifying role of the English language in the United States." He began serving as honorary chair and de facto spokesperson for the group, which assembled a blue-chip advisory board that included Alistair Cooke, Walter Cronkite, Saul Bellow, Norman Cousins, Gore Vidal, Norman Podhoretz, and Arnold Schwarzenegger. Both *U.S. News and World Report* and *Newsweek* carried articles discussing the movement, which opponents continued to suggest was racist, anti-immigrant, and unnecessary, while Hayakawa and his allies said it was exactly the opposite because speaking English was the admission ticket into the culture of the United States. They wanted to aid newcomers to America.

Throughout his life Don Hayakawa remained deeply and idealistically committed to the notion that the United States was a nation of immigrants. He would fulsomely explain his position in a 1987 article in *English Journal* titled "Why the English Language Amendment? An Autobiographical Statement." "Within the lifetime of people reading this," he wrote, "new names, strange names will take their place in business and industry, in show business and sports, in government or the military: names from Vietnam and India and Cambodia, from Ethiopia and Indonesia, from Paraguay and Iraq. . . . People have long ago ceased asking where Deukmejian and Hayakawa came from. . . . English is the key to participation in the opportunities and self-realization that American life has to offer." Unfortunately,

Don's association with the controversial and somewhat shadowy Dr. Tanton—called by some a visionary, by others a bigot—clouded his efforts for the group—clouded but didn't stop them. Hayakawa now began repeating variations of his arguments for the public endorsement of English while denying any anti-immigrant intent: "People can continue to play mah-jong in Chinese and crap games in Serbo-Croatian, but the official language should be English," he asserted.

As a delegate to the GOP convention in Dallas in 1984, Don talked with other delegates about a national English Language Amendment or a state-by-state adoption of English as the official language. In the California election that year, Proposition 38, an advisory measure Don sponsored which urged that ballots be printed only in English, raised hackles. Arnoldo S. Torres, director of the League of United Latin American Citizens, wrote, "This is a backhanded attempt to further ostracize Hispanics and other language minorities from fully participating in society in the same way that Jim Crow law ostracized blacks." Journalist Smith Hempstone disagreed, writing, "There is nothing chauvinistic in asserting the primacy of the English language." Apparently voters agreed, since the proposition passed with 71 percent of the vote. While it became habitual for Bay Area reporters and columnists to dismiss or belittle the ex-senator ("S. I. Hayakawa has never known when to shut up," asserted the *San Francisco Chronicle*), the people at U.S. English found him to be their most powerful representative and their most recognizable public face. Even liberal columnist William Raspberry would write, "Hayakawa, who was wrong on any number of important issues when he was in the Senate, is right on this one."

Don's health became an issue in 1985 when the left side of his face drooped and it was feared that he'd suffered a stroke. As it turned out, he was diagnosed with Bell's palsy, which partially paralyzed his face. Fortunately, a specialist was able to clear the neural blockage, but it was a reminder to family and friends alike that he was nearing eighty.

The past returned to haunt Hayakawa that year when a lawsuit that had been creeping through the courts since 1969 was finally settled in favor of students who had been arrested during the strike at San Francisco State and who sought to have their disciplinary records purged. The Ninth U.S. Circuit Court of Appeals ordered that a monitor be appointed to make certain that college officials did what they were required to do. Hayakawa was unimpressed and unrepentant.

About then, too, some critics began pointing out that, with U.S. English, Hayakawa might be fighting battles in a phantom war, since a 1985 Rand Corporation study reported that 90 percent of U.S.-born Mexican Americans were proficient in English and that more than half of their children were monolingual in English. Nevertheless, by 1986 Hayakawa and his U.S. English mates were pushing for what became California's Proposition 63 to declare English the official language of the state, leading Irvin Lai, president of the Chinese American Citizen Alliance, to wonder about the motive: "Why now do we have to affirm ourselves that English is the primary language? What is behind it?"

Hayakawa's response was consistent with his earlier statements. "People ask me why I am devoting my retirement to the cause of safeguarding and protecting the English language in California," he wrote in a *Los Angeles Times* op-ed piece. "The answer lies in the fact that a common language between people is the critical element that enables us to resolve differences, cooperate with each other, understand and respect other points of view and work toward realizing our individual social, cultural and economic goals."

Privately, he also said that the forces marshaled against Proposition 63 were supported by what had become "the bilingual-education industry" and some Latino idealists hoping to obtain control of the Southwest. Most Californians, as it turned out, supported Hayakawa's stand, and—despite the opposition of Governor George Deukmejian, whose parents were Armenian immigrants—Proposition 63 passed in 1986 with a whopping 73 percent of the vote. Norman Cousins then resigned from the board of U.S. English, criticizing the "negative symbolic significance" of Proposition 63 and warning that "it could lead to discrimination against language minorities."

During that period, Don hired Jeanne Griffiths as an office assistant. In her pre-employment interview she revealed misgivings about U.S. English, and Don replied, "Do you think I'm going to fire you if you disagree with me?" He didn't. Griffiths also revealed that Hayakawa had grown teary when Mark was upset by a storm that knocked out power to the Hayakawa house. "He doesn't understand and I don't know what to do for him," the father said. Jeanne suggested, "Come, Mark, let's play the piano," and they played "Twinkle, Twinkle, Little Star," which "seemed to calm him a little bit."

Don could have used some calming in 1987 after a lung biopsy revealed that he—a former pack-a-day smoker who had quit cold turkey at age fifty-six—was suffering from pulmonary fibrosis; that meant the air sacs in his lungs were gradually filling with fibrotic tissue, causing the irreversible loss of the ability to transfer oxygen into the bloodstream. With no curative treatment available, he began to use supplemental oxygen at night and during exercise, though not in public.

Also in 1987, he was awarded the National Americanism Medal by the Daughters of the American Revolution. About then, too, one of his ex-students informed Don that he was using *Language in Thought and Action* as the textbook for a composition class at a nearby university, and Hayakawa responded, "Would you like me to drop in for a visit?" A couple of weeks later, the ex-senator and his wife sat in a small classroom at Sonoma State University while he answered the questions of sixteen freshmen who were by no means familiar with his accomplishments. "How did you get to be a writer?" asked one, and Hayakawa replied, "It started in a class just like this one." Then—speaking softly as always—he explained how practice made, in his case, not perfect but pretty darned good. When he returned to his car following the session, Hayakawa immediately sat on the edge of the front seat and inserted nasal tubes, turned the valve on an oxygen bottle, and breathed deeply, saying something about recharging his batteries.

Don was delighted the following year when Linda Chavez, the much admired former director of public liaison for the Reagan administration as well as staff director of the U.S. Commission on Civil Rights, accepted an appointment as the executive director of U.S. English. Unfortunately, in 1988 a private memorandum by John Tanton was leaked to the press. Hayakawa's associate, who was also the head of the Federation for American Immigration Reform (FAIR), an organization Don did not support and from which he had distanced himself, managed to denigrate Hispanics ("low educability") and Catholics (they'll "pitch out the separation of church and state"). Chavez immediately resigned and Walter Cronkite soon left the group's advisory board, pressuring Tanton to quit. Hayakawa then informed all directors that U.S. English and FAIR could not in any way be united, including joint board membership. Tanton, meanwhile, started another organization he called ProEnglish.

The *New York Times* that year editorialized against imposing an official language, even though it agreed with U.S. English that "English is, and should be, America's language." That led Don to fire off a letter to the editor in which he pointed to a practical absurdity: "Private citizens in Colorado, who were collecting petition signatures for a ballot initiative to make English the official state language, were told by a Federal judge that they had violated the law by not printing their petitions in Spanish."

Voters in Arizona, Colorado, and Florida—three states with Hispanic names—passed "Official English" amendments to their state constitutions in 1988. At approximately the same time, the Ninth U.S. Circuit Court of Appeals overruled California's English-only workplace rules and declared Proposition 63 to be primarily symbolic. Alan Hayakawa had certainly been correct when he'd sensed that Official English was a powerful if controversial issue.

The years continued to soften Hayakawa's memory of the World War II internment camps, and in 1988 he sent a letter to White House Chief of Staff Howard Baker in which he asserted his belief that, while uncomfortable and unjust, the relocation was in no way punitive and had actually led to some positive results, such as the breakdown of self-segregation. His apparent inability to empathize with the outrage festering within the Japanese American community led some old admirers to question Don's direction. Pulitzer Prize–winning poet Gwendolyn Brooks, who had once won a Chicago poetry contest judged by Hayakawa and who had long been one of his admirers, sadly observed: "S. I. Hayakawa was a great liberal in those [Chicago] days. The way he's narrowed is a lesson. I hope that I'll be able to keep seeing 'the light' and marching in accordance with it. You can't stop growing."

Her use of the word "narrowed" resonated with some of Don's old friends, who had noted that the mind that had once reached out for new ideas and created a unique synthesis now seemed increasingly focused on U.S. English and little else. They did not know that those health problems were limiting Hayakawa's strength and even his concentration. A visit to Dr. Dong by Don in April revealed high cholesterol, high triglycerides, high glucose, and very high lipids, so Hayakawa's diet was again shuffled to exclude sugar, red meats, eggs, fats, and chicken and to include lobster, crab, kidney, liver, and safflower oil. A year later his tests had returned to a normal range, but shortly thereafter he experienced a transient ischemic attack and later noticed episodes of memory loss and even some occasional problems with cognition; soon he began employing bottled oxygen more frequently and more generously.

By then he had voluntarily given up his driver's license, so Gene Prat took him to a party in Napa. "He livened right up, had a couple 'pops,' and he disconnected himself from the oxygen and began dancing. One of his first partners said, 'Senator, I voted for you.' Don responded, 'Would you do it again?'" Her answer wasn't recorded. Between dances, Hayakawa rested and used the bottled oxygen; then he'd find another partner. "He had a hell of a good time," Prat recalled.

On October 8, 1988, the past made the news again when, according to the *San Francisco Chronicle*, "a bunch of old radicals from the 1968 student and faculty strike held a reunion at the scene of their battles with police and school president S. I. Hayakawa 20 years ago." Hari Dillon, a Black Students Union spokesman during the strike, said, "The members of the Third World Liberation Front did not fight in vain." Actor Danny Glover added, "We didn't give up and you can't either." James Garrett said, "It's important to remember that institutional racism is still very much a reality in this country." Hayakawa offered no comment, but a contemporary student named Shawn Sulhi remarked, "I'm interested in more current issues. That stuff's over and done with. Let's protest the parking situation on campus. Now that's a real problem."

While the fray over Official English occupied him, associates and family continued to observe that Don was less and less lively. Only his family and physicians understood the gravity of his ongoing breathing problem. "You could tell the energy just wasn't there," said Bill Pemberton, "but I just figured he's in his eighties, so what can you expect?" Don was spending little time writing and made few public appearances; he had become more a name than a presence at U.S. English. Daisy later recalled the noted author, professor, college president, and senator "coming into the kitchen every night before he really took ill. He would always wipe the pots and pans."

Jeanne Griffiths, his office assistant, observed the memory lapses but pointed out that "his personality didn't change. . . . He didn't become short-tempered with you because you'd say something and he couldn't remember. He would sit there and I would simply refresh his memory. I'd give him a copy of a letter, for example. He would read it, and he would say, 'Now refresh my memory. What brought this about?' And after we discussed it for a few minutes, then it would dawn—everything would come back."

Don's once-brisk walk had turned into a shuffle when he and Marge attended a 1990 reading and book-signing at the Depot bookstore in Mill Valley. When the event ended, he rose and began pulling his oxygen caddy toward the door when two old English Department colleagues and Mill Valley neighbors, Thurston Womack and John Dennis—both of whom had been AFT strikers at San Francisco State, and neither of whom had spoken to Hayakawa since—approached and said hello. Womack and Dennis had to tell Don who they were, then both shook his hand and embraced Marge. That led to an invitation to the Hayakawas' house for a drink, which they accepted.

365

Once there, the conversation was carried mostly by Marge and the two old friends, while Don sat nearby in his favorite chair, but Womack was startled when Hayakawa looked up and asked, "Who are you, again?" Womack, who'd once been a special pal, told him, then Don said, "Thurston, do you know I wasted six years of my life in the United States Senate?"

thirty-eight

By 1990, S. I. Hayakawa had climbed onto the medical treadmill so many senior citizens endure: visit the doctor for this, then that goes wrong. Take care of that, then hospitalization for another thing. His blood pressure wouldn't stay under control, causing considerable worry about a stroke, and his breathing grew worse. He and Marge talked about the unpleasant options—what to do if he *could* be revived but with no chance that he might function as a husband, a father, a friend; what to do if he *couldn't* be revived. Both Marge and Daisy became visibly more protective of him.

As Don weakened, Bill Pemberton visited him during one of the ex-senator's hospital stays, and he recalled Hayakawa saying to him, "It's true. I have narcolepsy." Hayakawa did not reveal why he had tried to keep that a secret. Once Don was out of the hospital, though, Pemberton took him and his oxygen bottle fishing at a private pond in nearby Sonoma County. For some reason, Hayakawa was using a nine-foot fly rod equipped with a spin reel, and wasn't having much luck. "I think he was really sliding away at that time, but I was determined that he'd get a good-sized bass," Pemberton remembered. "And, lo and behold, he got about a 2-pound bass." The two old pals had been fishing partners for more than forty years, and that was their final trip together. In February 1992 a heavy cold morphed into bronchitis; Don's doctor feared it would progress to pneumonia, given Hayakawa's weakened immune system and damaged lungs. At Marin General Hospital, a tracheotomy was performed that was painful, so Don pulled out the tube, and a nostril-feed for his oxygen was substituted. Not long thereafter, a nurse recalled seeing him reading a newspaper in bed. The next time she walked by his room, he was unconscious, having suffered a major stroke. S. I. Hayakawa died without regaining consciousness at 1 a.m. on February 27. He was eighty-five years old.

Hayakawa's role as a strikebreaker and as a senator dominated newspaper obituaries. Many of the public comments he received were predictably laudatory. Ronald Reagan said, "He was invaluable during some very difficult times—a courageous man of integrity and principle. Nancy and I are saddened by the death of our dear friend." Pete Wilson called him "a great California iconoclast," and added that "certain images from S. I. Hayakawa's life will be burned into our memories forever." Alan Cranston admitted, "Sam and I agreed on practically nothing. Still I respected him as a feisty but sincere battler for his beliefs."

More telling, perhaps, was the observation of David Tulanian, who had been a congressional page. "In the Senate," he wrote in a March 9, 1992, letter to the *Los Angeles Times*, "I watched the senator vote his conscience and convictions. While most other politicians would take the opinion polls into great consideration before voting, Hayakawa would have none of it. And while most politicians seemed mainly preoccupied with raising funds for the next election, Hayakawa would not bow to the moneyed Californian Republican kingmakers. He was quite rare." Writing in the "rival" *General Semantics Bulletin*, Robert P. Pula, director emeritus of the IGS, asserted that Hayakawa "clearly achieved a major infusion of aspects of general-semantics into not only American but world culture." He added, "As with most people who manage to accomplish much, he was not without a sense of self-worth—wedded to a fully developed sense of humor."

On the other hand, old nemesis Eric Solomon of San Francisco State's faculty union said, "He had 15 minutes of glory, he put S.F. State on the map, and he was able to use that fame to get himself elected to the Senate." Then he added, "I can't think of a leadership contribution that he made as far as the institution is concerned." Cressey Nakagawa, national president of the Japanese American Citizens League, observed, "You can't say he was well-liked." If he had been white, she added, "people would have called him a racist." Cultural historian Daryl Maeda summarized in 2002: "To the end of his career Hayakawa retained his commitment to resolving the claims of vying interest groups within a shared democratic system, while ignoring issues of unequal access to the system."

A memorial service was held on March 3, 1992, at the Showcase Theater at the Marin Civic Center. It featured Dixieland jazz by the San Francisco All-Stars, gospel singing from Daisy's church, as well as eulogies and recollections by a number of distinguished guests. Warren Robbins remembered the joke-loving Don once having said to him, "We are both doing God's work. You in your way, and I in His." Robbins also refuted the assertion of some of Hayakawa's enemies that he was shallow, saying he "was a translator. He translated important ideas for our education into language comprehensible in simplicity. He did this in books, in lectures, and in conversation. That was his genius." Minerva Dunn, niece of Jimmy and Mama Yancey, summarized, "Hayakawa loved jazz music and jazz musicians. He was a humanitarian. Race, creed, color made no difference to him."

The most moving remarks were delivered by Wynne and Alan Hayakawa. The daughter concluded, "My father was an affectionate and nonjudgmental parent and . . . he was a lot of fun." Alan noted that "Don was very much committed to the idea of a university as a place where men and women can freely pursue ideas, wherever their study might lead them. . . . In the student strike Don saw a withdrawal of cooperation that no communication skills could overcome. . . . Although he was committed to cooperation over confrontation, he did not believe that confrontation was always to be avoided at all costs. I hold that as a valuable lesson." Don's family scattered his ashes off one of his favorite fishing spots, Point Bonita on the Marin Headlands.

As he had been a man of many careers and accomplishments, he had been a man of many names—Samuel, Sammy, Sam, Hak, Don, Doc, S. Ichiye, Samuel I., S. I.—likely in quest of an identity. He was certainly a man of seemingly conflicting personae: usually gentle and persuasive, he had more than once shown the tough core of a

369

kid often on his own in a society in which he was a highly visible minority. Hayakawa's college friend Ed Mayer assessed him this way: "I think Don viewed much of life as a game. . . . [H]e would love to be best whatever field he played in."

Personal recognition did not necessarily translate into personal fulfillment for him, though; there remained in his life an edge of uncertainty, the shadow perhaps of familial and national and racial realities. He was clearly a man driven to succeed, and never entirely satisfied by his professional situation. With a mind that tended to reach out rather than in, he didn't fit the academic model of his time; he was in fact a masterful synthesizer. In choosing an offbeat academic specialty, he had gambled and lost; general semantics has never been fully accepted within the academy. As years passed, Don was increasingly invited to lecture not on general semantics but about song lyrics or African art or even automobiles; fewer and fewer wanted him to explicitly explore GS, although it influenced nearly everything he wrote and much of what he said.

A tradition of demeaning Hayakawa has arisen among those who felt betrayed by him. Their triumph is that as he grew enfeebled, then died, they convinced many who had scant or no contact with the actual man that he belonged in the same embarrassing category as various buffoons and poltroons. For such enemies, the word has become the thing: "Hayakawa" conjures images—the snoozing senator, the tyrannical president, the silly tap dancer, and so forth—that are only marginally reflective of the complex life led by Don Hayakawa. He has even been presented as a "Mr. Malaprop," despite being among the more quoted Americans of his time and a winner of Toastmasters International's coveted Golden Gavel in 1973.

Hayakawa himself did not dwell on those things, although he well understood the power such misinformation might accumulate. He was also pragmatic enough to understand that his legacy had been severely damaged by his political foray. Asked by *Los Angeles Times* reporter Cathleen Decker in 1984 how he would like to be remembered as a senator, Don replied, "As the person who, in one measure after another, got nowhere because he was before his time." How did he think he'd actually be remembered? He responded, "Sleeping, I guess."

But when Hayakawa is judged by the actual sum of his various accomplishments, a dramatically different picture emerges. He was a gifted but flawed man, one who refused to capitulate to racism or to elitism, to radicalism or to convention, and the sweep of his story is remarkable. He came a long, long way from that Canadian Japanese ghetto to the United States Congress. That he was not an outstanding senator in old age doesn't diminish the scope of his lifetime achievements. Despite their profound political differences, the ultra-liberal Bill Pemberton said of Don, "He was never a bad guy to me. He'd been a liberal democrat, maybe a socialist, but he switched. So what?"

Don Hayakawa believed he was a representative—imperfect but genuine—of his heritage, his time, and his place. "I always thought that, being a Nisei myself, whatever happened to me was a Nisei experience. . . . Nisei are not all alike. . . . We all contribute a portion of the definition of what it is to have belonged to our generation." Then he added with characteristic eloquence, "America, too is a generalization made up of a vast number of individual experiences. The 'melting pot' today is much maligned, but I think it is not understood. It is not so much the acceptance of conformity; it is rather that each American, knowing that the amalgam from the melting pot will be a little bit different because it had included him and his difference, can feel that the American future remains exciting, unpredictable—and something to dazzle the world."

bibliographic essay

The most valuable repository of material by and about S. I. Hayakawa was the family archive controlled by his surviving children, Alan and Wynne Hayakawa. S. I. Hayakawa's personal papers were made available to me by the family without any request that I avoid sensitive or controversial issues, for which I am most grateful. Many of the clippings and photocopies found in the Hayakawa Archive did not contain dates and/or page numbers.

Hayakawa's papers may be found at the Hoover Institute at Stanford University, while the J. Paul Leonard Library at San Francisco State University houses a collection dealing with that institution's student strike of 1968–69. The Jean and Charles Schulz Information Center at Sonoma State University provided us with online archives of the *New York Times*, the *Los Angeles Times*, and *Time* magazine, plus microfilm of the *San Francisco Chronicle* and various other newspapers and periodicals, so it proved to be another exceptional source of Hayakawa material. The recollections of old friends and enemies provided one more trove of material. Don seems to have been nothing if not memorable.

Despite its title, the Freedom of Information Act didn't free any information for this project. My requests were stonewalled. How fifty-to-seventy-year-old records about long-dead subjects could jeopardize national security, or anything else, was never explained in my exchange of letters with the Department of Justice. More likely this is a case of petty officials making arbitrary and not very thoughtful decisions.

General Sources

Julie Gordon Shearer's interviews with the aging Hayakawas in 1989 were invaluable. Published as *S. I. Hayakawa and Margedant Peters Hayakawa: From Semantics to the U.S. Senate, Etc., Etc.*, the finished project also included conversations with associates and friends of the Hayakawas—Stanley Diamond,

Elvira Orly, Jeanne Griffiths, and Daisy Rosebourgh—along with various reprints. Equally valuable was the constant and cordial help provided by Wynne and Alan Hayakawa, and the equally cordial help from Hayakawa's longtime friends Daisy Rosebourgh and Betty Kobayashi Issenman.

Among the many other people who provided observations, insights, or other help as I researched this book were the following:

CONVERSATIONS

Steve Arkin, Joe Axelrod, Ernest Callenbach, John Dennis, Vladimir Dupre, Isao Fujimoto, Masako Gray, Barbara Hayakawa, Grace Emi Hayakawa, Gerald Hill, James Hirabayashi, James D. Houston, Jeanne Wakatsuki Houston, Mark Hurley, Joe Kessel, Dan Knapp, Joseph Medeiros, Steve Mendoza, William Pemberton, Gene Prat, Ronald Schiff, Caroline Shrodes, Doug Stout, Beverly Voloshin, Bob Wanderer, Muriel Wanderer, Manfred Wolf, Thurston Womack, and Liz Young.

LETTERS AND E-MAILS

Virginia K. Anderson, Robert Arnold, Jackson Benson, Glen Bethel, Mike Boll, Lynn Bonfield, Marek Breiger, Alex Brill, Dorothy Lockard Bristol, Francisco-Javier Campos, Bob Collins, Kent Crockett, William Davoren, David Dibble, Ken Eidnes, Louis Fischl, Louis Forsdale, Michael Garrity, Jan Gauthier, Ida Geary, Jerry Gibbons, James Gollata, Pete Green, Robert Guenther, Alan Hayakawa, Grace Emi Hayakawa, Wynne Hayakawa, Jean Hayward, James Hirabayashi, Adolph N. Hoffman, Alice Q. Howard, Betty Kobayashi Issenman, Howard Jarmy, Stewart Johnson, Paul D. Johnston, Jeremy Klein, Chris Knox, Terumi Kuwada, Germaine LaBerge, Maurice Louret, Thea Lowry, David D. Malcolm, Ed Mayer, Felix and Evelyn McGill, Edwin Meyer, Albert L. Miner, Beverly Mooney, Bill Mossman, David Null, Jerry Partain, Ira Pilgrim, Jack Pitt, Bruce Reeves, Eva Revie, Jill Rosenshield, William C. Roth, Donald Schuster, Kay Schwartz, F. J. Shasky, Bill Sirvatka, Charles Stade, Mary P. Stegner, Susan Stevens, David Elliot Stovel, Clark Sturges, George Swift, John Takeuchi, Robert Thacker, William R. Vizzard, Abby Wasserman, Art Weber, Barbara Welch, Helene Whitson, Thurston Womack, Mary Wortham, and Helen Yoshida.

Lists such as these are inevitably, if unintentionally, incomplete. I apologize to anyone I have neglected to mention.

NOTES
Readers who would like to access page-by-page annotations for this book
can find them online at http://www.geraldhaslam.com/hayakawa-notes.htm.

THE EARLY YEARS (CHAPTERS 1–3)
Interviews with family sources such as Grace Emi Hayakawa and her daughter, Masako Gray, as well as letters from S. I. Hayakawa's father, Ichiro,
much enriched these perspectives. The other principal resources for the
early Canadian years were letters and e-mails from Betty Kobayashi Issenman, the Shearer interviews, Ken Adachi's *The Enemy That Never Was: A
History of the Japanese Canadians*, and S. I. Hayakawa's "A Japanese-American
Goes to Japan."

YOUNG MANHOOD (CHAPTERS 4–5)
The Shearer interviews continued to be important in these chapters, but
notes from Betty Kobayashi Issenman were also vital. S. I. Hayakawa's relationship with "the McGill Group" has been noted in print (see his "Dawn in
Canada"), and his own poetry—published and unpublished—demonstrated
growing maturity. After matriculating to the University of Wisconsin in
Madison, he began associations that led to observations from future well-
known authors such as Wallace Stegner, Ken Purdy, and Maurice Zolotow
(see Zolotow's "The Self-Creation of Don Hayakawa").

ROMANCE (CHAPTERS 6–12)
Fittingly, these chapters are dominated not only by Shearer's interviews
but by the diary entries and letters of Margedant Peters Hayakawa and
the poetry of S. I. Hayakawa, which in both content and "feel" trace the
growing intimacy of the couple. I found few notes or letters from him.
Various Wisconsin acquaintances added humanizing insights in their correspondence with me, including Ed Mayer, Stuart Johnson, and Eva Revie.
Notes from Marge's brother, William Wesley Peters, to Hayakawa reveal
a playful, bantering relationship, while the letters from Marge's mother,
Clara, show a softening of her opposition to Don. Various articles by
S. I. Hayakawa in periodicals such as *The Rocking Horse* ("Harriet Monroe
as Critic"), *Dalhousie Review* ("The Japanese-Canadian: An Experiment
in Citizenship"), *Harper's* ("Japanese Sensibility"), and *Asia* ("A Japanese-
American Goes to Japan") demonstrate not only his steadily improving

writing but his intellectual growth. Adachi's *The Enemy That Never Was* continued to offer the most important Canadian perspectives, and Zolotow's University of Wisconsin Oral History tape added valuable information to these chapters. Some later publications, such as S. I. Hayakawa's "My Father, Ichiro Hayakawa, 1884–1976," are also revealing of these early years in the lives of Don and Marge.

GENERAL SEMANTICS (CHAPTERS 13–15)

A reading of Stuart Chase's *The Tyranny of Words* helps explain S. I. Hayakawa's fascination with the work of Alfred Korzybski during the propaganda-ridden late 1930s. Less helpful, because it is far more difficult to read, but important is Korzybski's *Science and Sanity*. The best source, of course, is Hayakawa's own writing. I have drawn upon the opinions and writings of a variety of advocates and enemies of general semantics, including some memorable individuals—Martin Gardner, Vocha Fiske, Charles Stade, Anatol Rapoport, Alan Walker Read, and Charlotte Schuchardt Read. The reviews of Hayakawa's *Language in Action* in periodicals such as *Saturday Review of Literature*, the *Nation*, the *New Yorker*, and *Books* reveal the great initial impact of the book. The high hopes then inspired by general semantics are reflected in Hayakawa's "The Meaning of Semantics" and "General Semantics and Propaganda," as well as in *Time* magazine's "General Semantics." W. Benton Harrison examines Korzybski in "Some Personal Memories of Alfred Korzybski and His Times." Paralleling that, however, were looming war clouds, as revealed in the works of Adachi (*The Enemy That Never Was*) and Ronald Takaki (*Strangers from a Different Shore*).

WORLD WAR II (CHAPTERS 16–19)

At virtually the same time that Book-of-the-Month Club released of *Language in Action*, Japan bombed Pearl Harbor. The internment of Japanese Americans and Japanese Canadians, discussed by writers such as Ronald Takaki (*Strangers from a Different Shore*), Adachi (*The Enemy That Never Was*), C. K. Doreski ("'Kin in Some Way'"), Deborah Mieko Burns and Karen Kanemoto ("Securing Our Legacy: Understanding Japanese American Resettlement in the Midwest"), and Jeanne Wakatsuki Houston and James D. Houston (*Farewell to Manzanar*), became a recurrent, controversial theme in Hayakawa's life. Greg Robinson's "The Complex Life of S. I. Hayakawa" reveals the Hayakawas' efforts to help resettle Japanese Americans. Also, Don's columns in the *Chicago Defender* suggest an the increasingly eclectic direction of his interests: jazz, art, co-ops. Jerry Large examines the importance of the *Defender* in a *Seattle Times* article ("A Plea to Remember *Defender*"). Many of Hayakawa's "Second Thoughts" columns in the *Defender* are cited, and his conversations with Shearer about his wartime activities are important. Letters to and from Don (especially to and from Marge) suggest his emotional state then, as do his varied publications. Letters between various family members were used to personalize events. Early articles Don chose to publish in *ETC.* are revealing of his thinking then.

THE POSTWAR YEARS (CHAPTERS 20–23)

Correspondence, especially letters to and from his father, Ichiro, dominate the immediate postwar period. S. I. Hayakawa's first letter to his father in Japan, however, contained, if not a defense, then an explanation of the wartime internment of Japanese Americans; it seemed a non sequitur in that context. Hayakawa's growing involvement in Chicago's jazz scene is revealed in his various publications (e.g., "Reflections on the History of Jazz" and "Landmarks of Chicago Jazz and Other Hot-Music Items"). He continued to branch out in his topics ("The Revision of Vision: A Note on the Semantics of Modern Art"), but in the postwar morass he was much concerned about his parents' homeland (see "What to Do with Japan" and "Democracy in Japan?"). Conversations with Vladimir Dupre and Daisy Rosebourgh, both of whom then worked in the Hayakawa household, add much personal perspective. S. I. Hayakawa's "Our Son Mark," published in 1969, presented an intimate glimpse into the family of a child with a disability in the late 1940s and early 1950s.

SAN FRANCISCO STATE (CHAPTERS 24–29)

Interviews and conversations dominated material for this section, and Don's letters to Marge reveal his growing infatuation with San Francisco (and its with him) and with the college. Carl Nolte's "Boomers, Beats, and Baseball" presented a picture of "The City" at midcentury. Arthur Chandler's *The Biography of San Francisco State University* tells the story of the school that was luring S. I. Hayakawa from Chicago. Conversations with various faculty—Dan Knapp, John Dennis, and Caroline Shrodes, among others—filled in the story of Hayakawa's early experiences at State. His fishing buddy, William Pemberton, added some anecdotal insights, as did James D. Houston and Isao Fujimoto. Erstwhile acquaintances recalled the freshly resettled Hayakawas: Gerald Hill, Joe Axelrod, and Hayakawa's officemate at San Francisco State, Doug Stout, all provided excellent interviews, and Robert Wanderer wrote about those days ("Robert Wanderer on General Semantics Then and Now" and "ISGS Adventures in San Francisco"). Daisy Rosebourgh's increasing centrality to family life made her later interviews especially valuable. Hayakawa was in his prime, and his own writing was reflective of his unfettered interests: "The Fully Functioning Personality," "Popular Songs vs. The Facts of Life," "Communication: Interracial and Intercultural," and (with Barry Goodfield) "Reflections on a Visit to Watts." Two essays by Manfred Wolf also proved invaluable in writing about this period: "Years of Promise and Strife in the English Department" and "Hope and Unease, Reason and Clamor at San Francisco State." Alan and Wynne Hayakawa provided anecdotal descriptions of Don as a loving father. Thurston Womack's recollections of that time at San Francisco State and as a neighbor of the Hayakawa family were also especially valuable.

ON STRIKE! (CHAPTERS 30–32)

Several general sources, such as Robert Smith, Richard Axen, and Devere Pentony's *By Any Means Necessary: The Revolutionary Struggle at San Francisco State*, Dikran Karagueuzian's *Blow It Up!*, Irving Halperin's "Picket Lines and Books: The Student-Faculty Strike," Leo Litwak and Herbert Wilner's *College Days in Earthquake Country*, Kay Boyle's *The Long Walk at San Francisco State*, and Manfred Wolf's "Years of Promise and Strife in the English Department: San Francisco State, 1962–1970," as well as contemporary newspaper reports and S. I. Hayakawa's recollections, provided the backbone of this section. Providing perspective were interviews with James Hirabayashi, Marek Breiger, Bishop Mark Hurley, Gene Prat, Thurston Womack, Dan Knapp, Doug Stout, and John Dennis, among others. There were also several useful retrospective publications, such as Tanya Schevitz's "S.F. State to Mark 40th Anniversary of Strike," Dick Meister's "SF State Strike: Marking the 40th Anniversary of the Student and Faculty Strike," Eric Solomon's "Mr. Hayakawa Goes to Washington," and Amy Alexander's "Student Rebels' Reunion." A sense of the depth of opposition to S. I. Hayakawa then was found in items such as Richard Paris and Janet Brown's *The Sayings of Chairman Hayakawa* and in *Permanent President* (a broadside), both issued by the American Federation of Teachers.

THE SENATE (CHAPTERS 33–36)

Contemporary newspaper accounts were the major sources for this section. Guy Wright's "Underappreciated Man" in the *San Francisco Examiner*, "Hayakawa's Farewell" in the *Monterey Peninsula Herald*, and Carl Irving's "The Eventful Career of a Many-sided Man," also in the *Examiner*, celebrated Hayakawa's retirement from the presidency of San Francisco State. His flirtations with, then commitment to, political office were also thoroughly covered: Bill Stall's "Hayakawa Puts the Accent on Action in GOP Senate Campaign" in the *Los Angeles Times*, "The Fresh-Faced Elder" in *Time*, Martin Tomchin's "Congressional Freshmen Return to School" in the *New York Times*, and so on. One particularly useful source was Bob Wanderer's "Hayakawaiana for Hayakawa Watchers" feature in each issue of *The Map*, the publication of the San Francisco chapter of the International Society for General Semantics. During these years, Hayakawa became a much-watched senator who did not avoid controversy. He was also seen as something of a character, covered by major political reporters such as Steven Roberts, Richard Bergholz, Ellen Hume, and even Art Buchwald, and Johnny Carson frequently mentioned him on the *Tonight* show. All of those, and many others, were cited in these chapters, as were Hayakawa's own op-ed pieces and letters to various editors: "Paid by the Government to Do Nothing" in the *New York Times*, "Reparations for Japanese Americans? No!" in the *Los Angeles Times*, "English by Law" in the *New York Times*, and so forth. Conversations with Daisy Rosebourgh again provided a sense of the Hayakawas' home life during his Washington years.

U.S. ENGLISH (CHAPTERS 37–38)

Newspaper articles by Cathleen Decker ("Hayakawa Puts Sour Senate Experience Behind, Pursues New Interests") and William Endicott ("Hayakawa Slips Out of Capitol without Fanfare") marked the end of the senator's political adventure. As the title of Hayakawa's article "English by Law" indicates, establishing English as America's official national language was the last great crusade of his life. Don wrote many articles on behalf of the cause—for instance, "Why the English Language Amendment?" in *English Journal* and "A Common Language, So All Can Pursue Common Goals" in the *Los Angeles Times*—and acted as spokesman for U.S. English. In 1988 the newspaper coverage for the twentieth anniversary of the San Francisco State strike seemed inaccurate to him. William Pemberton's recollections of Hayakawa during these years were of great value. Don's death in 1992 led to a range of obituaries; they were by no means consistent. The postmortem observations of Minerva Dunn, David Tulanian, and William Pemberton, contrasted with those of Eric Solomon, Daryl Maeda, and Cressey Nakagawa, seem to well summarize and perhaps shadow Hayakawa's controversial public life.

selected bibliography

Aarons, Leroy. "Samuel Ichiye Hayakawa Is a 72-year-old Freshman Senator of Many Hats—and Parts." *People Magazine*, October 2, 1978.

Abbot, Louise. "S. I. Hayakawa: Semanticist Turned Politician." *McGill News*, Spring 1977, 38–40.

Adachi, Ken. *The Enemy That Never Was: A History of the Japanese Canadians*. Toronto: McClelland and Stewart, 1976.

African American Department History. San Francisco State University. www.sfsu.edu/~ethnicst/afrs.

"The AFT Strike—Costly Failure." *San Francisco Examiner*, March 4, 1969, 34.

Alexander, Amy. "Student Rebels' Reunion." *San Francisco Examiner*, October 8, 1988.

Alinder, Mary Street, and Andrea Gray Stillman, eds. *Ansel Adams: Letters and Images, 1916–1984*. Boston: Bullfinch Press, 1990.

Anderson, Walter Truett. *The Upstart Spring*. Bloomington IN: iUniverse, 2004.

"Ansel Adams Bids U.S. Protect Coast's Big Sur." *New York Times*, May 27 1980, 59.

"Anti-Carter 'Hayakawa' Letter Probed." *Los Angeles Times*, February 19, 1977, B1.

Arthur, Allene. "Hitting the Dance Floor with the Stars." *The Desert Sun*, March 17, 2008.

Atlas, James. *Delmore Schwartz: The Life of an American Poet*. New York: Farrar, Strauss and Giroux, 1977.

Auster, Paul. "The Accidental Rebel." *New York Times*, April 23, 2008.

Averill. John H. "Few Support Bid for U.S. Role at Big Sur." *Los Angeles Times*, April 25, 1980, B3.

———. "Seat on Foreign Relations Unit Dangled before Hayakawa." *Los Angeles Times*, April 20, 1978, 25.

———. "What, Me Worry? Hayakawa Says." *Los Angeles Times*, November 30, 1979, B16.

Beattie, Guila F. "Hayakawa Censured Again." *ETC.: A Review of General Semantics* 5, no. 4 (1948): 286–287.

Beattie, Munro. *Literary History of Canada*. Toronto: University of Toronto Press, 1976.

Benson, Jackson. *Wallace Stegner: His Life and Work*. East Rutherford NJ: Penguin Books, 1996.

Bergholz, Richard. "'Appalled' at Asia Hostilities, Hayakawa Says." *Los Angeles Times*, February 18, 1979. A3.

———. "Hayakawa Acts to Aid Tuna Fleet." *Los Angeles Times*, January 22, 1977, A30.

———. "Hayakawa Drops Out of Senate Reelection Race." *Los Angeles Times*, January 31, 1982, A1.

———. "Hayakawa Gas Remark Brings Howls of Rage." *Los Angeles Times*, May 18, 1979, B3.

———. "Hayakawa Greeted by Boos, Catcalls at UCLA." *Los Angeles Times*, May 31, 1979, B3.

Bergholz, Richard, and Robert Fairbanks. "Hayakawa Wrestles with Tax Issues." *Los Angeles Times*, February 10, 1981, B3.

Blum, Walter. "Hayakawa: 'I Am A Complex Person.'" *The California Weekly People [San Francisco Examiner]*, November 24, 1963, 2–3, 7.

Bois, J. Samuel. "The Alfred Korzybski I Know." In "Alfred Korzybski Remembered by His Students." www.ThisisNotThat.com.

———. *Breeds of Men*. New York: Harper & Row, Publishers, 1969.

Bourman, Ann. Letter to the Editor. *Los Angeles Times*, May 23, 1979, C5.

Boyle, Kay, *The Long Walk at San Francisco State*. New York: Grove Press, 1970.

Brooks, David. *The News Hour with Jim Lehrer* [commentary]. PBS Television, August 26, 2009.

Brudnoy, David. "Hayakawa at Northeastern." *National Review*, February 24, 1970, 202.

Buchwald, Art. "Sleepy Time at the White House." *Los Angeles Times*, June 3, 1979, D3.

Buckley, William F. "Making It with the BSU: San Francisco State College." *National Review*, June 17, 1969, 610.

Bunzel, John H. "An Arrogant Minority Victimized the College." *Look*, May 27, 1969. 62, 70, 72.

Burns, Deborah Mieko, and Karen Kanemoto. "Securing Our Legacy: Understanding Japanese American Resettlement in the Midwest." *Annotation* 30, no. 2 (2002): 1–5.

Caplan, Usher. *Like One That Dreamed: A Portrait of A. M. Klein*. Toronto: McGraw-Hill Ryerson Limited, 1982.

Caudill, William. "Japanese American Personality and Acculturation." *Genetic Psychology Monographs* 45 (1952): 3–102.

Caudill, William, and George De Vos. "Achievement, Culture and Personality: The Case of the Japanese Americans." *American Anthropologist* 58, no. 6 (1956): 1102–26.

Chan, Sucheng. *Asian Americans: An Interpretive History*. Boston: Twayne, 1991.

Chandler, Arthur. *The Biography of San Francisco State University*. San Francisco: Lexikos Press, 1986.

Charlton, Linda. "Hayakawa Finds Senate Friends More Interesting Than Ph.D.'s." *New York Times*, April 27, 1977, 18.

Chase, Stuart. *The Tyranny of Words*. New York: Harcourt, Brace, 1938.

"The Choice at San Francisco State." *Los Angeles Times*, November 29, 1968, A6.

Cimons, Marlene. "Senator Sam: 'Free Spirit' in Washington." *Los Angeles Times*, February 7, 1977, A1, A4–5.

"Cleaver Comes Out Swinging Again." *San Francisco Examiner*, October 10, 1968, 9.

Cohen, Joseph. "Dr. Hayakawa's Many Faces." *CTA Journal*, January 1964, 27–28.

Collens, Lewis. "State of the University: The Scarlet Triangle." September 25, 2001, 1–5. www.iit.edu.

Condon, John C. *A Bibliography of General Semantics*. San Francisco: International Society for General Semantics, n.d.

Crane, Maurice A. "Lines Composed Quite a Few Miles from Tin Pan Alley." *ETC.: A Review of General Semantics* 13, no. 1 (1955): 66–69.

Cronon, E. David, and John W. Jenkins. *The University of Wisconsin: A History (volume 3: Politics, Depression, and War, 1925–1945*. Madison: University of Wisconsin Press, 1994.

Crossman, Richard, ed. *The God That Failed*. New York: Harper & Bros., 1949.

Daniels, Roger. *Asian America: Chinese and Japanese in the United States Since 1850.* Seattle: University of Washington Press, 1988.

Decker, Cathleen. "Hayakawa Puts Sour Senate Experience Behind, Pursues New Interests." *Los Angeles Times*, February 1, 1984, C1.

de Lorimier, Kristi. "Student Leaders Reflect on Past SF State Struggles." *Golden Gater*, October 4, 1988, 4.

De Santis, Christopher, ed. *Langston Hughes and the "Chicago Defender": Essays on Race, Politics, and Culture, 1942–62.* Urbana: University of Illinois Press, 1995.

Doreski, C. K. "'Kin in Some Way' — *The Chicago Defender* Reads the Japanese Internment, 1942–1945." In *The Black Press: New Literary and Historical Essays*, ed. Todd Vogel, 161–87. New Brunswick NJ: Rutgers University Press, 2001.

Drake, St. Clair, and Horace Cayton. *Black Metropolis.* New York: Harcourt, Brace, 1945.

Draper, Jamie B., and Martha Jiminez. "A Chronology of the Official English Movement." *Official English? No!* www.usc.edu/dept/education/.../OfficialEnglishDraperJiminezpdf.

Editorial Board. "An Interview with S. I. Hayakawa President of San Francisco State College." *Amerasia Journal*, June 1971, 19–23.

Endicott, William. "Hayakawa Calls for Woman on Ticket." *Los Angeles Times*, July 12, 1980, A20.

——. "Hayakawa Defends His Vote Attendance Record." *Los Angeles Times*, January 18, 1978, A3, 29.

——. "Hayakawa Slips Out of Capital without Fanfare." *Los Angeles Times* January, 19, 1983, B1, 21.

"English Spoken Here, but Unofficially." *New York Times*, October 29, 1988, 28.

Field, Mervin D. "Hayakawa Ban Aids Cranston, Poll Shows." *Los Angeles Times*, March 1, 1974, Section One, 1.

Fishman, Joshua A. "A 'Loyal-Opposition' View." *ETC.: A Review of General Semantics* 13, no. 3 (1956): 225–31.

Fiske, Vocha. "Sanity Faire, Part I: A Profile of Alfred in America, Being a Casual Account of How I Know a Man Called Korzybski, Also Some Things about His Work Called General Semantics." Unpublished memoir in Haslam Archive.

Flug, Michael. "Chicago Renaissance." Chicago Public Library Digital Collection. www.chipublib.org/digital/digital.html.

Foley, Thomas J. "Hayakawa Testifies in House on Perils of Campus Unrest." *Los Angeles Times*, February 4, 1969, A4.

Fortune, Thomas. "The Politics Were Fast and Funny." *Los Angeles Times*, May 3, 1980, A5.

Fox, Roy E. "A Conversation with the Hayakawas." *ETC.: A Review of General Semantics* 48, no. 3 (1991): 243–50.

Freedberg, Louis. "Ex-Senator Hayakawa Dies at 85." *San Francisco Chronicle*, February 28, 1992, A1, A4.

French, Warren G. "Behind the Popular Front." *ETC.: A Review of General Semantics* 13, no. 2 (1955–56): 127–28.

"The Fresh-Faced Elder." *Time*, June 21, 1976.

Friedland, Roger, and Harold Zellman. *The Fellowship: The Untold Story of Frank Lloyd Wright and the Taliesin Fellowship*. New York: Regan Books, 2006.

"From an Irish Pat to a Dixie Lee." *Time*, November 15, 1976.

Gayles, Gloria Wade, ed. *Conversations with Gwendolyn Brooks*. Columbia: University of Missouri Press, 2003.

Gardner, Martin. "General Semantics, Etc." In *Fads and Fallacies in the Name of Science*, 246–54. New York: New American Library, 1986.

Gartner, Michael. "Legal Counsel Dick Schmidt Has Represented ASNE—and the First Amendment—since 1968." *American Society of Newspaper Editors*, August 24, 1998.

"General Semantics." *Time*, November 21, 1938, 34–35.

Gladstone, Kate. "Words, Words, Words." *Heinlein Society Web Page*. www.heinleinsociety.com.

Gleason, Ralph J. "Dr. Hayakawa, the Semanticist, Has the Word on American Jazz." *This World [San Francisco Chronicle]*, August 24, 1952, 24.

Goff, Tom. "Hayakawa: Soft Sell Pays Off." *Los Angeles Times*, May 5, 1976, A3.

Green, Blake. "Hayakawa Is Still Politicking: The Ex-Senator's Pet Target Now Is Bilingual Education." *San Francisco Chronicle*, April 16, 1984, 19, 21.

Greenwood, Noel. "Hayakawa, S.F. State's Folk Hero, Ends Remarkable Era." *Los Angeles Times*, October 30, 1972, A3, A20–26.

Grieg, Michael. "Defiant Cleaver at S.F. State." *San Francisco Chronicle*, October 10, 1968.

Groden, Michael, Martin Krerisworth, and Imre Szeman. *The Johns*

Hopkins Guide to Literary Theory and Criticism. Baltimore: Johns Hopkins University Press, 1997.

Guluan, Marie Pauline. "Remembering the 1968 Strike: SF State's Revolution." *Golden Gate X Press*, November 5, 2008. www.xpress.sfsu.edu.

Halperin, Irving. "Picket Lines and Books: The Student-Faculty Strike." *Magazine*, Spring 1999, 155–62.

Harrison, W. Benton. "Some Personal Memories of Alfred Korzybski and His Times." *ETC.: A Review of General Semantics* 34, no. 4 (1977): 405–9.

Hayakawa, Alan. Eulogy presented March 3, 1992, at Marin County Civic Center. Printed in *ETC.: A Review of General Semantics* 50, no. 2 (1993): 131–35.

Hayakawa, Ichiro. Interview. "The Elder Hayakawa: 'My son was a very good boy. . . .'" *Phoenix*, March 11, 1971.

Hayakawa, S. I. "The Aims and Tasks of General Semantics: Implications of the Time-Binding Theory." *ETC.: A Review of General Semantics* 8, no. 3 (1951): 243–53.

———. "Anti-Semitism: A Study in Mistaken Map-Territory Relationship." *ETC.: A Review of General Semantics* 6, no. 3 (1949): 197–203.

———. "'Aye' . . . I Knew That I Had Done the Right Thing." *Los Angeles Times*, March 30, 1978, D7.

———. "The Boston Poet Laureate: Oliver Wendell Holmes." *Studies in English Literature* 16, no. 4 (1934): 572–92.

———. "Can We No Longer Talk to Each Other?" Interview. *Pacific Sun*, June 7, 1968, 12–13.

———. "A Common Language, So All Can Pursue Common Goals." *Los Angeles Times*, October 29, 1986, B5.

———. "Communication: Interracial and Intercultural." *ETC.: A Review of General Semantic* 20, no. 4 (1963): 395–410.

———. "Danger in Being Rigid-minded." *Science Digest*, September 1950, 45–46.

———. "Dawn in Canada." *Sewanee Review*, April–June 1934, 248–50.

———. "Democracy in Japan?" Unpublished manuscript, n.d. Hayakawa Archive.

———. "English by Law." *New York Times*, October 1, 1981, A35.

———. "'Farewell to Manzanar': An Unorthodox View of the World War II Internment of Japanese-Americans." *TV Guide*, March 6, 1976, 13–16.

———. "From Science-fiction to Fiction-science." *ETC.: A Review of General Semantics* 8, no. 4 (1951): 280–93.

———. "The Fully Functioning Personality." In *Symbol, Status, and Personality*, 51–69. New York: Harcourt Brace Jovanovich, 1963.

———. "General Semantics and Propaganda." *Public Opinion Quarterly* 3, no. 2 (1939): 197–208.

———. "Happy Mother's Day to a Great Lady." *Hokubei Mainichi*, May 15, 1980, 1.

———. "Harriet Monroe as Critic." *The Rocking Horse* 1, no. 2 (1933): 20–24.

———. "A Hayakawa Sampler." *ETC.: A Review of General Semantics* 48, no. 3 (1991): 251–55.

———. "Holmes's Lowell Institute Lectures." *American Literature* 8, no. 3 (November 1936): 281–90.

———. "How Can SALT II Be That Good for Both Russia and America?" *Los Angeles Times*, January 23, 1979, C5.

———. "How Right Is the Dictionary?" *Science Digest*, March 1950, 44–47.

———. "How Words Change Our Lives." *Saturday Evening Post*, December 27, 1958, 75–88.

———. "The Incident of the Sound-Truck." Manuscript [unpublished?] in Hayakawa Archive, n.d.

———. "A Japanese-American Goes to Japan." *Asia*, April 1937, 269–72.

———. "The Japanese-Canadian: An Experiment in Citizenship." *Dalhousie Review*, April 1936, 17–22.

———. "Japanese Sensibility." *Harper's*, December 1936, 98–103.

———. "Landmarks of Chicago Jazz and Other Hot-Music Items." *Chicago Sun Book Week*, April 28, 1946, 8.

———. *Language in Action*. New York: Harcourt, Brace, 1941.

———. *Language in Thought and Action*. 4th ed. New York: Harcourt Brace Jovanovich, 1978.

———. Letter to M. Kendig. *ETC.: A Review of General Semantics* 8, no. 1 (1950): 72.

———. Letter to the Editor. *Los Angeles Times*, June 13, 1980, A13.

———. Letter to the Editor. *New York Times*, May 3, 1982, A18.

———. Letter to the Editor. *New York Times*, November 18, 1988, A4.

———. "A Linguistic Approach to Poetry." *Poetry* 60 (May 1942): 86–94.

———. "Manual for Verbalists." *ETC.: A Review of General Semantics* 4, no. 2 (1947): 134–36.

------. "A Matter of Linguistics." *New Republic*, January 8, 1940, 43.

------. "The Meaning of Semantics." *New Republic*, August 2, 1939, 354–57.

------. "Modern Art and 20th Century Man." *Transformation: Arts, Communication, Environment: A World Review* 1 (1950): 2–5.

------. "Mr. Eliot's Auto Da Fe." *Sewanee Review* 44, no. 3 (1934): 365–71.

------. "Mr. Hayakawa Goes to Washington." *Harper's*, January 1978, 39–43.

------. "My Father, Ichiro Hayakawa, 1884–1976." *Hokubei Mainichi*, January 24, 1976, 1.

------. "My Japanese Father and I." *Asia*, May 1937, 331–33.

------. "Our Son Mark." *McCall's*, December 1969, 79, 156, 160.

------. "Paid by the Government to Do Nothing." *New York Times*, September 8, 1982, A26.

------. "Poem for Courage." *New Frontier*, September 1936.

------. "Poetry and Advertising." *Advertising Age*, February 11, 1946, 204–12.

------. "Popular Songs vs. The Facts of Life." ETC.: *A Review of General Semantics* 12, no. 2 (1955): 83–95.

------. "Problems of Language." *New Republic*, November 15, 1939, 117.

------. "Protest, Pigs and Power Politics." *Liberal Education* 56, no. 1 (1970): 17–21.

------. "Recognizing Stereotypes as Substitutes for Thought." *English Journal* 38 (March 1949): 155–56.

------. "Recommendations of the Commission on Wartime Internment and Relocation of Citizens." Senate Bill 2116, 8/16/84 and 8/29/84, p. 35.

------. "Reflections on the History of Jazz." *Illinois Tech Engineer* 10, no. 4 (1945): 13–18, 50, 54, 56, 58.

------. "Reparations for Japanese Americans? No!" *Los Angeles Times*, May 11, 1979, E7.

------. "Reply by Hayakawa." ETC.: *A Review of General Semantics* 5, no. 2 (1948): 148–50.

------. "Report of the Retiring President, International Society for General Semantics: 1949–1950." ETC.: *A Review of General Semantics* 8, no. 1 (1950): 72–74.

———. "The Revision of Vision: A Note on the Semantics of Modern Art." *ETC.: A Review of General Semantics* 4, no. 4 (1947): 258–67.

———. "The Sansei and the Black Panthers." *San Francisco Examiner*, August 1, 1970.

———. "Second Thoughts" [columns]. *Chicago Defender*, December 12, 1942, January 16, 1943, February 6, 1943, February 13, 1943, March 27, 1943, April 3, 1943, April 17, 1943, July 3, 1943, August 10, 1943, all p. 15.

———. "Second Thoughts." *Chicago Defender*, n.d., 15.

———. "Semantics and Modern Art." *Thinkers' Digest* 38, no. 3 (1949): 41–44.

———. "Semantics, General Semantics." *ETC.: A Review of General Semantics* 4, no. 3 (1947): 161–70.

———. "Semanticist S. I. Hayakawa Looks at Poetry and Advertising." *Advertising Age*, February 11, 1946, 55.

———. "The Semantics of Being Negro." *ETC.: A Review of General Semantics* 10, no. 3 (1953): 163–75.

———. *Symbol, Status, and Personality*. New York: Harcourt Brace Jovanovich, 1963.

———. *Through the Communication Barrier: On Speaking, Listening, and Understanding*. Ed. Arthur Chandler. New York: Harper & Row, 1979.

———. "To One Elect." *Poetry* 44, no. 6 (September 1934): 319.

———. Untitled, unpublished manuscript of a memoir dated 1972. Hayakawa Archive.

———, ed. *The Use and Misuse of Language*. New York: Fawcett World Library, 1962.

———. "What to Do with Japan?" Unpublished manuscript, n.d. Hayakawa Archive.

———. "Why the Edsel Laid an Egg." In *The Use and Misuse of Language*, ed. Hayakawa, 169–74. New York: Fawcett World Library, 1962.

———. "Why the English Language Amendment? An Autobiographical Statement." *English Journal* 76, no. 8 (1987): 14–16.

Hayakawa, S. I., and Barry Goodfield, "Reflections on a Visit to Watts." *ETC.: A Review of General Semantics* 23, no. 3 (1966): 295–326.

Hayakawa, S. I., and Philip Persky. "Bibliography of the Writings of Alfred Korzybski." *ETC.: A Review of General Semantics* 8, no. 1 (1950): 165–69.

"Hayakawa, S(amuel) I(chiye)." *Current Biography*, 193–97. Bronx NY: H. W. Wilson, 1977.

"Hayakawa Formally Asks for Foreign Relations Seat." *Los Angeles Times*, December 17, 1978, 11.

"Hayakawa Sees 1-legged Tail Gunners." *Los Angeles Times*, February 28, 1980, A2.

"Hayakawa's Farewell." *Monterey Peninsula Herald*, April 20, 1973, 24.

"Hayakawa's Mark." *Los Angeles Herald Examiner*, November 11, 1972, B-6.

Haynes, Winifred. "The Gulf Stream." *The Rocking Horse* 1, no. 3 (1934): 16.

Heath, S. Burton. "Japs Get No Coddling at Detention Camp; Some Say Loyalty to U.S. Has Been Killed." *Evansville Press*, n.d., 8. Hayakawa Archive.

Hempston, Smith. "English Is Our Language, but Amendment Is Wrong." *Los Angeles Times*, July 10, 1984, C5.

The History of Japanese Canadians in Manitoba. Winnipeg: Manitoba Japanese Canadian Citizens' Association, 1996.

Hoekstra, Dave. "Brosnan's Books Cover All the Bases." *Chicago Sun-Times*, August 8, 2004.

Holley, Joe. "Warren M. Robbins, Founder of the Museum of African Art, Dies at 85." *Los Angeles Times*, December 8, 2008.

Houston, Jeanne Wakatsuki, and James D. Houston. *Farewell to Manzanar: A True Story of Japanese American Experience during and after the World War II Internment*. Boston: Houghton-Mifflin, 1973.

Houston, Paul, and Kenneth Reich. "Hayakawa Disbands Judicial Commission." *Los Angeles Times*, January 17, 1981, B1.

Hovey, Graham. "2 Senators Propose Check on Rhodesia." *Los Angeles Times*, March 1, 1979, A1.

Hume, Ellen. "Hayakawa Napped at White House Gas Talks." *Los Angeles Times*, May 25, 1979, SD1.

———. "Hayakawa Unconcerned Over 7-point Slide in Poll." *Los Angeles Times*, March 21, 1978, B3, 23.

———. "Prof. Hayakawa Still a Student in the Senate." *Los Angeles Times*, September 18, 1977, A1, A11–A12.

———. "Senate OKS 48,000-Acre Redwoods Park Expansion." *Los Angeles Times*, February 1, 1978, B1, 23.

———. "Tardy Hayakawa Prolongs Suspense." *Los Angeles Times*, April 19, 1978, A30.

———. "1,000 Japanese-Americans Hit Hayakawa in Newspaper Ad." *Los Angeles Times*, May 10, 1979, D4.

Hutchinson, Emery. "Beat Me, Professor, Eight to the Bar." Unidentified newspaper clipping in Hayakawa Archive.

Inada, Lawson Fusao, ed. *Only What We Could Carry*. Berkeley: Heyday Books, 2000.

"An Interview with S. I. Hayakawa, President of San Francisco State College." University of California at Los Angeles Asian American Studies [*Newsletter*], n.d., 19–23. Hayakawa Archive.

Irving, Carl. "The Eventful Career of a Many-sided Man." *San Francisco Examiner*, October 13, 1972.

Janssen, Guthrie E. "Hayakawa's Article Censured." ETC.: *A Review of General Semantics* 5, no. 1 (1947): 70–75.

"Japanese Is English Prof for U.W. Here." *Waupaca County Post*, November 11, 1937.

Johnson, Michael, with Edward Wilkinson. "The History of San Francisco State University: Celebrating 100 Years of Opportunity, 1899–1999." SFSU *Public Affairs Press Release*, March 10, 1999.

Jones, Jack. "Hayakawa Pushes Alien Worker Plan, Dismisses Boos, Jeers He Got at UCLA." *Los Angeles Times*, June 1, 1979, A5.

Kandell, Jonathan. "Vaunted Vancouver." *Smithsonian* 35, no. 1 (2004): 84–92.

Karagueuzian, Dikran. *Blow It Up! The Black Student Revolt at San Francisco State and the Emergence of Dr. Hayakawa*. Boston: Gambit, 1971.

Kargon, Robert H., and Scott G. Knowles. "Knowledge for Use: Science, Higher Learning, and America's New Industrial Heartland, 1880–1915." *Annals of Science* 59 (2002): 11.

Kato, Hidetoshi. "The Idealization of Places." ETC.: *A Review of General Semantics* 13, no. 2 (1955–56): 136–37.

Kaye, Elizabeth. "Hayakawa at IIT." Source unknown. Photocopy in Hayakawa Archive.

Kendrick, Vaughn. Letter to the Editor. *Harper's*, March 1978, 6.

Kennedy, Leo. "The Future of Canadian Literature." *Canadian Mercury* nos. 5–6, n.d., 100. Hayakawa Archive.

Kerby, Phil. "Ominous Developments at Big Sur." *Los Angeles Times*, May 1, 1980, D1.

"Key Battle for Public Health." *Los Angeles Times*, July 16, 1982, D6.

Kikumura, Akemi. *Through Harsh Winters: The Life of a Japanese Immigrant Woman*. Novato CA: Chandler & Sharp, 1981.

Kikumura, Akemi, and H. H. L. Kitano. "Interracial Marriage: A Picture of the Japanese Americans." *Journal of Social Psychology* 63 (1973): 215–20.

King, Wayne. "Hayakawa Resists Idea of Dropping Out of Race." *New York Times*, January 24, 1982, 24.

Kitagawa, Disuke. *Issei and Nisei: The Internment Years*. New York: Seabury Press, 1967.

Kitano, H. H. L. *Japanese Americans: The Evolution of a Subculture*. Englewood Cliffs NJ: Prentice-Hall, 1976.

Kone, Joe. "Recalling Times Past at Press Conference." *Phoenix*, October 19, 1972, 1.

Lafromboise, T., H. L. K. Coleman, and J. Gerton. "Psychological Impact of Biculturalism: Evidence and Theory." *Psychological Bulletin* 114 (1993): 395–412.

Large, Jerry. "A Plea to Remember *Defender*." *Seattle Times*, April 28, 2006.

Larsen, David. "Uproar over Gas Remark by Hayakawa." *Los Angeles Times*, May 20, 1979, SD1.

"Learned English by 'Total Immersion'—Hayakawa." *Los Angeles Times*, April 23, 1982, A1.

Lee, Lee C., and Nolan W. S. Zane, eds. *Handbook of Asian American Psychology*. Thousand Oaks CA: Sage, 1998.

Legal Discrimination and Disenfranchisement in Canada, Some Facts to Remember . . . Montreal: Center for Research—Action in Race Relations, n.d. Hayakawa Archive.

Lembke, Daryl E. "Routine Berkeley Co-op Election Turns Political." *Los Angeles Times*, January 15, 1967, B5.

Leslie, Charles. "Revising 'The Revision of Vision.'" *ETC.: A Review of General Semantics* 5, no. 2 (1948): 146–47.

Lewis, Steven. "Alfred Korzybski Biography." *Korzybski's General Semantics: Applying Science-Mathematical Methods and Discoveries to Daily Living*. www.kcmetro.cc.mo.us/pennvalley/biology/lewis/akbio.htm.

Lindsey, Robert. "Environmentalists and Coastal Residents Split on a Plan for U.S. Controls at Big Sur." *New York Times*, June 23, 1980, A14.

Litwak, Leo. "We Needed a Revolution." *Look*, May 27, 1969, 62, 65–66.

Litwak, Leo, and Herbert Wilner. *College Days in Earthquake Country*. New York: Random House, 1971.

Lovejoy, John. "Whatever Happened to Those College Days?" *Antioch Ledger*, September 2, 1986.

MacArthur, Henry C. "U.C. May Lose Autonomy Because of Cleaver Resolution." *San Rafael Independent-Journal*, October 10, 1968.

Maeda, Daryl. "S. I. Hayakawa: Asian American Radicalism and the Dilemma of American Liberalism." In *The Human Tradition in California*, ed. Clark Davis and David Igler, 193–207. Wilmington DE: Scholarly Resources, 2002.

Matherne, Bobby. "Review of *Science and Sanity*." *Southern Cross Review* no. 26, n.p. www.southerncrossreview.com.

Mayper, Stuart A. "Hayakawa as an Editor." *General Semantics Bulletin* no. 57 (1993): 27–30.

McCrimmon, James M. "Easier on the Teacher." *ETC.: A Review of General Semantics* 7, no. 2 (1950): 145–48.

Meister, Dick. "SF State Faculty Strike: Marking the 40th Anniversary of the Student and Faculty Strike." October 26, 2008. www.indybay.org.

Michener, James. *Kent State: What Happened and Why*. New York: Random House, 1971.

Miki, Roy. *Redress—Inside the Japanese Canadian Call for Justice*. Vancouver BC: Raincoast Books, 2005.

Miller, Peg. "Grandson of Wright Offers His Memories." *La Crosse Tribune*, December 4, 2003.

Mohr, Charles. "Arms Pact Survives an Amendment." *New York Times*, November 7, 1979, A8.

Morely, Patricia. *As Though Life Mattered: Leo Kennedy's Story*. Montreal: McGill-Queen's University Press, 1994.

Morrison, A. S. "Literature in Manitoba." *Manitoba Historical Society Transactions*, Series 3, no. 9, 1952–53.

Morton, Desmond. *A Short History of Canada*. 3rd rev. ed. Toronto: McClelland & Stewart, 1997.

"Move to Make English Official Language Assailed as Divisive." *Los Angeles Times*, April 23, 1986, D6.

"Mrs. Hayakawa Says Goodbye to Yesteryear's Peace, Quiet." *Los Angeles Times*, November 22, 1969, Part 4, 5.

Mura, David. *Turning Japanese: Memoirs of a Sansei*. New York: Double-day, 1991.

Nance, Molly. "Writing Their Own History." *Diverse Online*, October 30, 2008. www.diverseeducation.com.

"New Member of cu's Board." *Consumer Reports*, February 1953, 57.

Nell, Edward. "The Editor Interviews S. I. Hayakawa, Who warns All Writers of Verbal Quagmires." *Quill and Scroll*, April–May 1949, 7–8, 22.

Ng, Franklin, ed. *Asians in America: The Peoples of East, Southeast, and South Asia in American Life and Culture*. New York: Garland, 1998.

"Nisei Semanticist Declares Refusal to Compromise Led to Riots in Watts." *Nichi Bei Times*, October 20, 1966, 1.

Nishimura, Mark. "Friends Gather to Pay Tribute to Hayakawa." *Hokubei Mainichi*, March 7, 1992.

Nolte, Carl. "Boomers, Beats, and Baseball—The Generation That Came Home from World War II, Rolled Up Their Sleeves, Changed the Country, and Reinvented California. Part Five: Postwar." *San Francisco Chronicle*, May 16, 1999.

Norris, Ken. "The Beginnings of Canadian Modernism." www.canadian poetry.ca/cpjm/vol11/norris.htm.

Northrup, F. S. C. *Man, Nature and God: A Quest for Life's Meaning* New York: Pocket Books, 1963.

Northwestern University Radio Department, *The Reviewing Stand* [radio transcript], wgn Mutual Radio, January 13, 1946, 1–12.

Norton, Terry. "In Era When Protest Exploded, Fuse Was Lit at Berkeley and S.F. State." March 1, 1998. www.sfgate.com.

O'Brien, David J., and Stephen S. Fugita. *The Japanese American Experience*. Bloomington: Indiana University Press, 1991.

Okimoto, Daniel I. *American in Disguise*. New York: Walker/Weatherhill, 1971.

Orrick, William H., et al. *Shut It Down! A College in Crisis*. Washington dc: National Commission on the Causes and Prevention of Violence, 1969.

Paris, Richard, and Janet Brown, eds. *The Sayings of Chairman S. I. Hayakawa*. Cartoons by Roberta Christiansen and Victor Fisher. San Francisco: American Federation of Teachers, Local 1928, 1969.

Pearson, Hugh. *The Shadow of the Panther: Huey Newton and the Price of Black Power*. Reading ma: Addison-Wesley, 1995.

Peck, Anne Merriman. *The Pageant of Canadian History*. Toronto: Long-
  mans, Green, 1943.
"People." *Time*, December 27, 1976.
Permanent President. Broadside issued by San Francisco State College
  Federation of Teachers, Local 1352, n.d.
"Poem for Courage." *New Frontier*, n.d., n.p. Hayakawa Archive.
Pula, Robert. "In Memoriam[,] Samuel Ichiye Hayakawa[,] 1906–1992."
  General Semantics Bulletin no. 57 (1993).
Pyrcz, Heather. "Social Injustices and Disorder—A. M. Klein, Dorothy
  Livesay, F. R. Scott, Leo Kennedy, Dawn Fraser." *A Digital History
  of Canadian Literature*. www.youngpoets.ca/ezine/?q=digital_history
  _of...poetry. Internet publication: League of Canadian Poets, 2001.
Rabinovitch, Arthur. "Who's Running McGill: Another University . . .
  Same Problems." *McGill News*, January 1969, 24.
Rapoport, Anatol. "Alfred Korzybski, July 5, 1879–March 1, 1950:
  Biographical Summary." *ETC.: A Review of General Semantics* 7, no.
  4 (1950): 163–65.
Rapoport, Anatol, with Leo Hamalian. *Semantics*. New York: Thomas Y.
  Crowell. 1975.
Rawls, James J., Walton Bean. *California: An Interpretative History*. 6th
  ed. San Francisco: McGraw-Hill, 1993.
Read, Allen Walker. "Changing Attitudes toward Korzybski's General
  Semantics." *General Semantics Bulletin* 51 (1984): 11–25.
Read, Charlotte Schuchardt. "A Brief History of General Semantics,
  1950–2000." Institute for General Semantics. www.time-binding
  .org.
———. "The International Society for General Semantics: A Brief His-
  tory (1938–1988)." Institute for General Semantics. www.time
  -binding.org.
———. Letter to the Editor. *ETC.: A Review of General Semantics* 49, no.
  1 (1992): 74–75.
Reich, Kenneth. "The Human Factor: An Important Force in Politics."
  Los Angeles Times, February 14, 1982, D3.
Rice, Richard B., William A. Bullough, and Richard J. Orsi. *The Elusive
  Eden: A New History of California*. San Francisco: McGraw-Hill,
  1996.
Roberts, Steven V. "'New Right' Causes Pressed in Senate." *New York
  Times*, June 26, 1979, A13.

———. "Senate Kills Plan to Curb Abortion by a Vote of 47–46." *New York Times*, September 16, 1982, A3.

Robinson, Greg. *By Order of the President: FDR and the Internment of Japanese Americans.* Cambridge: Harvard University Press, 2001.

———. "The Complex Life of S. I. Hayakawa." Part 1. *Nichi Bei Times*, February 7, 2008. www.nichibeitimes.com.

———. "The Complex Life of S. I. Hayakawa." Part 2. *Nichi Bei Times*, February 14, 2008. www.nichibeitimes.com.

Rosen, Gerald. *Cold Eye, Warm Heart.* San Francisco: Calm Unity Press, 2009.

"Sad State of Affairs." *This World*, December 8, 1968, 5–6.

Salzman, Ed. "Hayakawa's Hidden Power." *New West*, July 5, 1978, 15, 17.

"San Francisco State Bans 'Outsiders.'" *New York Times*, January 5, 1969, 57.

San Francisco State Legal Defense Committee. *Insanity in the Courts.* San Francisco: Black Sheep Press, n.d. [1969?].

Savage, David C. "Latinos Are Making the Switch to English." *Los Angeles Times*, May 24, 1982, B1, 20.

Schevitz, Tanya. "S.F. State to Mark 40th Anniversary of Strike." *San Francisco Chronicle*, October 26, 2008.

Schuchardt, Charlotte. *The Technique of Semantic Relaxation.* Chicago: Institute of General Semantics, 1943.

"Semantics in San Francisco." *Time*, December 6, 1968, 83.

Senator Hayakawa Reports to California [newsletter]. Washington DC, Fall/Winter 1981.

Shannon, Don. "Sen. Hayakawa Dots the Eyes." *Los Angeles Times*, January 5, 1977, 1.

Shearer, Julie Gordon, interviewer. *S. I. Hayakawa and Margedant Peters Hayakawa: From Semantics to the U.S. Senate, Etc., Etc.* Berkeley: Regional Oral History Office, The Bancroft Library, University of California, 1994.

Shimizu, Hide Hyodo. "Faces of Redress: Hide Shimizu." *Nikkei Voice*, April 1992, 11.

Shuman, R. S. "Further Revision." *ETC.: A Review of General Semantics* 5, no. 2 (1948): 147.

"S. I. Hayakawa Set an Example." *San Jose News*, October 18, 1972.

Skelton, Nancy. "Hayakawa Denies Saying Ronald Reagan 'Too Old.'" *Los Angeles Times*, July 4, 1979, A6.

———. "Hayakawa Is Called 'Fuzzy.'" *Los Angeles Times*, February 11, 1981, A21.

Smith, A. J. M. "Contemporary Poetry." *McGill Fortnightly Review*, December 15, 1926.

Snapp, Martin. "'Newsroom' the Peak of Wax's Legacy." *Contra Costa Times*. www.contracostatimes.com.

Smith, Robert, Richard Axen, and Devere Pentony. *By Any Means Necessary: The Revolutionary Struggle at San Francisco State*. San Francisco: Jossey-Bass, 1970.

Snyder, Bill. "Former Professor Evolved from Semanticist to Senator." *Oakland Tribune*, February 28, 1992.

Solomon, Eric. "Mr. Hayakawa Goes to Washington." *Mother Jones* 2, no. 2 (1977): 27–29.

Stall, Bill. "Hayakawa Puts the Accent on Action in GOP Senate Campaign." *Los Angeles Times*, April 2, 1976, B5.

Stammer, Larry. "Intern Iranians, Hayakawa Urges." *Los Angeles Times*, March 12, 1980, B1.

———. "Juggled Polls to Aid Hayakawa, Campaign Managers Admit." *Los Angeles Times*, November 12, 1976, B3.

Steffy, Joan. Letter to the Editor. *Los Angeles Times*, April 6, 1980, E4.

Stegner, Wallace. *Crossing to Safety*. New York: Penguin Books, 1987.

Stevens, Peter. *The McGill Movement*. Toronto: Ryerson, 1969.

Stockdale, Steve, ed. "Alfred Korzybski Remembered by His Students." www.ThisIsNotThat.com.

———. "The Institute and the Society: A Self-Reflexive Assessment of Two Organizations, One Discipline." *ETC.: A Review of General Semantics* 60, no. 3 (2003): 271–80.

"Strike Advances Ethnic Studies." *Golden Gater*, October 4, 1988, 3.

Sue, Stanley, and Harry H. L. Kitano, eds. "Asian Americans: A Success Story?" Special issue, *Journal of Social Issues* 29, no. 2 (1973).

Sue, Stanley, and Nathaniel Wagner. *Asian-Americans: Psychological Perspectives*. Palo Alto: Science & Behavior Books, 1973.

Swan, Gary E. "Old Radicals Remember S.F. State's '68 Strike." *San Francisco Chronicle*, October 8, 1988.

Takaki, Ronald, *A Different Mirror: A History of Multicultural America*. Boston: Little, Brown, 1993.

———, ed. *From Different Shores: Perspectives on Race and Ethnicity in America*. New York: Oxford University Press, 1987.

———. *Strangers from a Different Shore: A History of Asian Americans*. New York: Penguin Books, 1989.

Takichi, Amy, Eddie Wong, Franklin Odo, with Buck Wong, eds. *Roots: An Asian American Reader*. Los Angeles: UCLA Asian American Studies Center, 1971.

Thomas, Wright. "S. I. Hayakawa." *Book-of-the-Month-Club News*, November 1941.

Tolchin, Martin. "Congressional Freshmen Return to School." *New York Times*, December 18, 1976, 8.

Treuhaft, Robert. "The Left Wing Faction on the Co-op Board of Directors." *Calisphere*. www.calisphere.univerityofcalifornia.edu.

Tulanian, David. Letter to the Editor. *Los Angeles Times*, March 9, 1992, B4.

Turner, Wallace. "Campus on Coast Remains Closed." *New York Times*, November 28, 1968, 37.

———. "Coast Speculates on Senate Rivals." *New York Times*, August 17, 1969, 67.

———. "Consumers' Co-op in Berkeley Shaken by an Election Battle." *New York Times*, January 16, 1967, 41.

———. "Hayakawa Abandons Race for a Second Term." *New York Times*, January 31, 1982, 24.

———. "Hayakawa May Face Tough Senate Race." *New York Times*, February 12, 1981, A18.

Wanderer, Robert. "Hayakawaiana for Hayakawawatchers" [monthly serial miscellany]. *The Map*, 1977–85.

———. "ISGS Adventures in San Francisco." *ETC.: A Review of General Semantics* 54, no. 2 (1997): 202–9.

———. "Robert Wanderer on GS Then and Now." *ETC.: A Review of General Semantics* 56, no. 4 (1999): 468–72.

White, Theodore H. "A Call for New Thinking About Race Relations in the Big City." *Los Angeles Times*, August 22, 1965, G1–2.

Whitney, Craig R. "Brezhnev Looking to Arms Pact Soon." *Los Angeles Times*, January 11, 1979, A5.

Whitson, Helene. "Introductory Essay." *The San Francisco State College Strike Collection*. www.library.sfsu.edu.

"Why Did It Break at State?" *San Francisco Examiner*, n.d., n.p. Hayakawa Archive.

Wilner, Herbert, Kay Boyle, Leo Litwak, and Ray B. West. "Open Letter." *New York Review of Books*, March 13, 1969.

Wilson, Thomas D. "General Semantics." *Information Research Weblog*, posted January 29, 2003.

Wolf, Manfred. "Hope and Unease, Reason and Clamor at San Francisco State: 1956–1967." *Magazine*, Fall 1996, 11–29.

———. "Years of Promise and Strife in the English Department: San Francisco State, 1962–1970." *Magazine*, Spring 2001, 125–41.

"Word Germs." *Time*, July 12, 1954, 75–76.

"Word Power in Action." *Time*, December 13, 1968, 52.

Wolseley, Roland Edgar. *The Black Press, U.S.A.* 2nd ed. Ames: Iowa State University Press, 1990.

Wright, Guy. "Underappreciated Man." *San Francisco Examiner*, October 25, 1972.

Yoshida, Helen. Untitled eulogy delivered at memorial service for S. I. Hayakawa, March 3, 1992, at San Rafael, California.

Zolotow, Maurice. "The Self-Creation of Don Hayakawa." *New West*, October 11, 1976, 74–81.

———. University of Wisconsin Oral History Project. Madison: University of Wisconsin. Interview no. 369, 1983.

index

S. I. Hayakawa is referred to as SIH in this index.

American Sociological Association, 313

Anderson, Jack, 331, 343–44

Anderson, Walter Truett, 264

Annals of Science (Kargon and Knowels), 120

anti-Asian bigotry, 15, 69–70, 126, 127–31; in California, 6, 128, 216; in Canada, 5, 8–11, 34–35, 72–73, 124, 127; and Frederick Peters, 53–54, 65–66; and interracial marriage, 54, 63, 96, 178, 228, 243; and relocation and internment, 129–30, 139–43, 168–69, 177, 317–18, 334, 337–38, 363–64; and voting rights, 9, 72–73, 79–80, 163, 195; and "yellow-peril" threat, 6, 69, 130. *See also* racism

Anti-Digit Dialing League, 259

Anti-Japanese League, 70

anti-Semitism, 54, 65, 84, 115–16, 154, 162; and *Defender* article, 146–47. *See also* racism

Arden Club, 47–48, 49, 52, 56, 91

Arden House, 48–49, 58, 59–60; Marge Peters's residence at, 54–55, 64; SIH's lectures at, 44, 47. *See also* University of Wisconsin at Madison

Armour Institute of Technology. *See* Illinois Institute of Technology

Armstrong, Anne, 345

Armstrong, Louis, 145, 179, 181

Arnold, Robert, 268

Arthur, Allene, 234

"Asian problem." *See* anti-Asian bigotry

Asiatic Exclusion League, 10

assimilation, 73, 108, 143, 275, 318

Atlas, James, 59–60

Augusta (Marge Peters's aunt), 46, 92

Auster, Paul, 281

Austin, Claire, 238

Austin, Ed, 84

Austin, Wil, 181–82

Awner, Lenore ("Lee"), 243

Axelrod, Joe, 98, 194, 243

Axen, Richard: *By Any Means Necessary*, 283, 293, 294, 295

Bachelard, Gaston, 135

Badger, John Robert, 145

Baker, Chet, 229

Baker, Howard, Jr., 326, 333, 344, 350, 363

Balfanz, Marie, 224

Banno, Edward, 79

Barnlund, Dean, 244

Bateson, Gregory, 263

Beattie, Guila F., 189

Beatty, Talley, 145

Bedesem, Helen, 279, 295

Beecher, John, 221

Bell, Alphonzo, 318, 319

Bellow, Saul, 149, 359

Benson, Jackson, 118, 119, 250

Benton, Thomas Hart, 190

Berger, Arthur, 334

Bergholz, Richard, 338–39, 349

Berkeley Consumers' Cooperative (Berkeley Co-op), 260, 268–69, 300. *See also* cooperatives

Bethune, Mary McLeod, 145

Furuyama, Charles ("Chuck"),
141, 142, 182
Furuyama, George, 141, 177
Furuyama, Helen. *See* Yoshida,
Helen Furuyama
Furuyama, Satoe Hayakawa
("Mary"), 6, 141–42, 195–96
Furuyama, William ("Bill"), 141,
142

Gallager, Buell, 255
Gardner, Martin, 111–12
Gardner, Sid, 20–21
Garlington, Phil, 273–74
Garn, Jake, 339
Garrett, James, 365
Garrison, W. E., 124
Garrity, Donald, 283, 307, 308
Garrity, Michael, 304
general semantics, 196, 227, 236,
254–55, 262; and Alfred Korzybski's death, 204–5; Alfred
Korzybski's theories of, 98–99,
105–6, 108, 109–10, 112, 114–
15, 165, 211; and art, 189; and
"Chicago Criticism," 133–34;
and conferences, 109, 126, 135,
237; criticisms of, 111–12, 115–
16; and "cultism," 111–12; and
dualisms, 167n1; and listening,
251; and loaded terms, 115–16;
and music, 237–38; and "neuro-
semantic relaxation," 109; popularity of, 134–35, 253; popularization of, by SIH, 109, 111,
113, 115–17, 124–27, 134–35,
165, 178–79, 189–90, 212; and
propaganda, 108, 109, 116–17;

proponents of, 101, 109–10; re-
spectability of, as field, 158, 253,
267, 370; and "rules," 114–15;
at San Francisco State College,
244, 255–56; and Stuart Chase,
98–99, 106, 115, 135; as taught
by SIH, 100–101, 109–11, 114–
15, 117–18, 164–65; television
programs about, 208; tenets of,
105, 110–11, 115, 167, 211; and
"time-binding," 105, 211; value
of, 154. *See also* ETC.: *A Review
of General Semantics*; *General
Semantics Bulletin*; Institute of
General Semantics (IGS); Inter-
national Society for General
Semantics (ISGS); *Language in
Action* (Hayakawa)
"General Semantics and Propa-
ganda" (Hayakawa), 109, 116–17
General Semantics Bulletin, 160,
201, 205, 252, 368
Gide, André, 134
Gillespie, Dizzy, 145, 159
Gleason, Ralph J., 218, 252
Glickberg, Charles, 159
Glover, Danny, 275, 365
Goff, Tom, 319
Gold, Herbert, 257
Goldwater, Barry, 329
Goldwater, Barry, Jr., 347, 350
Gollata, James, 87–88
Goluska, Mitchell, 144
Goodfield, Barry, 264, 265
Goodlett, Carleton, 292
Gosling, Harry, 14, 22
Gosling & Hayakawa, Ltd., 14,
17, 22

Gotoh, Mr., 9
Gray, Masako, 7, 10, 14
"Great White Hope." *See* Mayer, Ed
Greenwood, Noel, 307, 313
Gregory, Horace, 58
Grieg, Michael, 278
Griffiths, Jeanne, 362, 365
Guerard, Albert, 124
Guest Worker Act of 1981, 347
Gurdjieff, Georgi, 308–9

Hahn, Hans, 112
Haig, Alexander, 335
Hall, Edmond, 179
Hallett, Carol, 341
Halperin, Irving, 286
Hamilton, Chico, 229
Hare, Nathan, 277, 279, 283–84, 295
Harmer, John L., 318, 319
"Harriet Monroe as Critic" (Hayakawa), 57
Harris, Mark, 221, 255–56
Harrison, W. Benton, 109, 111
Hartman, Lee F., 83
Hayakawa, Alan Romer, 7, 27, 169, 247–48, 369; birth of, 182–83; childhood of, 183, 193, 195, 199, 208–9, 223, 260; children of, 316, 358; on Daisy Rosebourgh, 245; Japan visits of, 230–33, 313–14; on Marge Hayakawa, 209, 236, 254; on Otoko Isono Hayakawa, 15; on SIH's American citizenship, 235; on SIH's childhood, 16, 18, 23; on SIH's education, 28;

on SIH's Japanese identity, 17, 263; on SIH's musical skills, 29; on SIH's political career, 346, 348, 350
Hayakawa, Carol Wynne. *See* Hayakawa, Wynne
Hayakawa, Cynthia (Mrs. Alan Hayakawa), 316
Hayakawa, Fred Jun, 12, 180, 181, 186, 188, 191; bilingualism of, 37; and Harry Kobayashi, 30, 34; identity of, as Canadian, 27–28; and support of SIH, 84, 85
Hayakawa, Grace Emi, 14, 19, 27, 329; birth of, 17; on Japanese identity, 10, 16; in postwar Japan, 176, 177, 231
Hayakawa, Grandmother (mother of Ichiro Hayakawa), 12, 74–75, 76, 232
Hayakawa, Ichiro, 72, 143, 168, 169; business ventures of, 8, 28; and Canadian citizenship, 191; death of, 317; grocery stores of, 12, 13, 14; and Harry Kobayashi, 30; health of, 230; and immigration to Canada, 5–6, 8; imports businesses of, 14, 17, 27, 30, 74, 96, 187–88, 203, 230, 237; infidelity of, 27, 28; letters of, to SIH, 168–69, 175–77, 180–81, 183, 186, 187–88, 191–92, 203, 233; and marriage to Otoko Isono, 7–8; military service of, 6; in *My Geisha*, 258; in postwar Japan, 175–77, 180–81, 186, 187, 191–92, 203; and religion, 16; visits to, by

Hayakawa, S. I. ("Don"), 206, 237–38, 323, 331; and Arden Club, 44, 47–49, 56, 60; and art, 99–100, 132, 152–53, 189, 258; awards and honors won by, 38, 252, 269, 295, 313, 347, 362, 370; birth of, 5, 8, 10; and book reviewing, 83, 131, 160, 165, 181, 188, 210, 211–12; and Canadian politics, 79–80; and charity work, 151–52, 260, 339–40; childhood of, 12–13, 14, 15–16, 18; and citizenship, American, 235; and citizenship, Canadian, 31, 71, 234–35; and civil rights, 260–61, 264–66, 273, 275, 303–4; competitive nature of, 250; conservative opinions of, 262, 300, 316, 319, 329, 330, 339, 352, 353–54; and conspiracy theories, xii, 275; and the Consumers Union, 227; conversational style of, 208–9; and cooking, 55, 193; and cooperatives, 88, 122, 143, 144, 157, 190, 240, 260, 268–69; dating Marge Peters, 47–50, 54, 55, 61–62, 63, 64, 81–82, 90–91; death of, 368; Department of Justice files on, 206n1, 373; desire of, for children, 158; and discrimination, 15, 16, 21–22, 23, 31, 70–71, 85, 86, 129, 140, 227–28, 243, 275; dissertation of, 66; and domestic help, 178, 185–86, 192–93; and drama productions, 60; dressing style of, 1, 14, 35, 39, 43, 64, 65, 133,

286, 319; as editor of *ETC.: A Review of General Semantics*, xi, 156, 159–60, 178, 188, 189–90, 199, 205, 211–12, 236, 245, 254, 301; elementary education of, 12–13, 16, 17–18; and environmental issues, xiii, 327, 342–43, 354; on father's literary tastes, 6; and fencing, 35, 242, 305; and fishing, 215, 229, 243, 358, 367; and the Furuyama family, 141–43; and grandchildren, 316, 358; on grandfather (Dr. Itono), 7; health of, 266–67, 351, 360, 362, 364, 365, 367–68; in high school, 18–20, 22; at Hofstra College, 199–200; honorary degrees of, 252, 269, 313; humor of, 57, 67, 79, 124, 161–62, 193–94, 247; and Hyde Park apartment (Chicago), 171, 178; identity of, as American, 76, 122, 128, 235; identity of, as Canadian, 13, 17, 27–28, 65, 78–79, 139, 235; identity of, as Japanese, 16–17, 18, 70–71, 75–76; at Illinois Institute of Technology, 120–21, 127–28, 131–32, 133, 144, 148–49, 161, 178, 188; infidelities of, 223–24, 235–36, 249, 263; and Institute of Design, 152–53; at Institute of General Semantics, 106–10, 160; and International Society for General Semantics, 200–201, 205–6, 210–11, 225; Japan visits of, 12, 71–77, 230–33, 313–14, 329; and jazz, xi–xii,

Senate. *See* U.S. Senate

"Sestina Written in Dejection"
(Hayakawa), 56

"Sexual Fantasy and the 1957 Car"
(Hayakawa), 254

Shapiro, Charlotte, 60

Shapiro, Evalyn, 202

Shapiro, Karl, 201–2

Shearer, Julie Gordon, 16, 20, 29,
31, 38, 100, 319, 332n1, 358

Shingleton, Arthur, 347

Shirley, Maudelle, 268

Shitara sisters, 167–68

Shrodes, Caroline, 217, 220, 244,
255; and hiring of SIH, 226,
227, 228–29, 234, 239

The Shrouding (Kennedy), 35

Shultz, George, 358–59

Shuman, R. S., 189

Simpson, Alan, 353

Simpson, Claude, 118

Sirvatka, Bill, 148–49

SLATE, 261, 261n1

Slim, Memphis, 150

Smith, A. J. M., 31, 32, 58, 165

Smith, Glenn, 283, 307, 308

Smith, Harrison, 179–80

Smith, Henry Nash, 257

Smith, Hugh Lee, 145

Smith, Jim, 218

Smith, Robert ("Bob"), 277,
278–79, 280, 282; *By Any Means
Necessary*, 283, 293, 294, 295

Smith, Wendell, 145

Society for General Semantics. *See*
International Society for General Semantics (ISGS)

Soldiers' Vote Bill, 163

Solomon, Eric, 293, 297, 324–25,
368; on SIH's career path, 262,
282, 306, 322–23

Sonoma State College, xi, 362

Soper, Oro ("Tut"), 179

sound-truck incident (during
strike), 1–2, 284, 285–87. *See
also* San Francisco State College,
student strike at

Stade, Charles, 108–9, 111, 160

Stalin, Josef, 45, 308

Stall, Bill, 318–19

Stanton, William, 284

"Steering Committee," 339

Steffy, Joan, 343

Stegner, Mary, 118, 218, 229

Stegner, Wallace, xii, 118, 218,
229; *Crossing to Safety*, 38, 119–
20; *Remembering Laughter*, 119

Stevens, Peter, 31

Stevens, Ted, 348

Stevens, Wallace, 58

Stewart, George, 126, 218

Stillwell, Joseph, 140

St. John's High School, 18–20, 22

Stockdale, Steve, 200, 201

Stone, C. Clement ("Clem"), 302,
313

Stout, Doug, 243–44, 253

Strategic Arms Limitation Treaty
(SALT II), 335, 339

strike, student. *See* San Francisco
State College, student strike at

"Structural Differential," 110–11,
115. *See also* general semantics

Student Nonviolent Coordinating
Committee, xii

OTHER WORKS OF NONFICTION BY GERALD HASLAM

Workin' Man Blues: Country Music in California (2000)
The Great Central Valley: California's Heartland (1993)
Coming of Age in California (1990)
The Other California: The Great Central Valley in Life and Letters (1990)
Voices of a Place: Social and Literary Essays from the Other California (1987)
The Language of the Oil Fields (1972)